THE HISTORY OF
THE ENGLISH NOVEL

THE HISTORY OF
THE ENGLISH NOVEL

By Ernest A. Baker, D. Lit., M.A.

THE HISTORY
OF THE
ENGLISH NOVEL

By Ernest A. Baker, D. Lit., M.A.

Volume IX

The Day before Yesterday

New York

BARNES & NOBLE, INC.

First published 1936
Reprinted 1966 by special arrangement with
H. F. & G. WITHERBY, LTD.
326 High Holborn, London, W. C. 1

Printed in the United States of America

27415

PREFACE

IT was intended to finish this volume with two chapters on Conrad and the Scottish group of novelists, from George Macdonald and Mrs Oliphant to "Ian Maclaren," Crockett, and Barrie, so as to begin the tenth and final one with Butler's *Erewhon Revisited* and *The Way of all Flesh*, which had so much effect upon the novelists and playwrights of "Yesterday." These two chapters have had, however, to stand over, and the volume breaks off with Stevenson and the Stevensonians. The final one will deal also with Arnold Bennett, Galsworthy, Kipling, and their contemporaries, and probably end with Katherine Mansfield and D. H. Lawrence.

Many of the works from which quotations have been made are still in copyright, and grateful acknowledgments are due to the publishers and to the executors or other representatives of the authors quoted for the prompt and liberal way they have accorded permission. In particular I would mention Messrs Methuen & Co., Ltd. (works of Oscar Wilde, etc.), Messrs Macmillan & Co., Ltd. (Thomas Hardy, Walter Pater, Henry James, etc.), William Heinemann, Ltd. (George Moore), Messrs Constable & Co. (George Gissing), Ernest Benn, Ltd. ("Mark Rutherford"), Mr A. D. Peters (Maurice Hewlett), Messrs J. B. Pinker & Son (Henry James), Messrs Chatto & Windus (Stevenson, etc.), Messrs Parker, Garrett & Co. (Oscar Wilde), and also to Sir Sydney Cockerell and Mrs Hardy (Thomas Hardy), Mr C. D. Medley, executor for George Moore, Mr A. C. Gissing, for George Gissing, and the Incorporated Society of Authors, Playwrights, and Composers (represented by Mr E. J. Mullett) and Mr Lloyd Osbourne for the works of Stevenson. I must also mention my indebtedness to Mr Morley Roberts and Mr Frank Swinnerton for their kind answers to inquiries about Gissing, and

to Mr C. D. Medley for his remarks on the chapter dealing
with George Moore, which he looked through.   I have drawn
incidentally on many other authors and critics, and if this is
not properly acknowledged in the footnotes I trust they will
pardon any oversight.   Lastly, I have again to thank Dr Edith
C. Batho, of University College, London, for her great kindness
in revising the proofs.

E. A. B.

CONTENTS

THE DAY BEFORE YESTERDAY

CHAPTER I

THOMAS HARDY

MEREDITH's younger contemporary, who after *Far from the Madding Crowd* (1874) was widely acclaimed as his rival for the primacy in English fiction, differed from his senior in many ways, some of them fundamental. They were opposites in character and temper, in outlook and philosophy, and largely in their technical methods, so much so that their novels are often like the products of different arts. To a youthful devotee when these were coming out, loyalty to one seemed incompatible with the least obeisance to the other.[1] But such differences are not uncommon between men of genius, and it was with general approval and according to general expectations that Hardy succeeded Meredith as president of the Society of Authors and then in the Order of Merit. Hardy was on friendly terms with Meredith, who had given him the counsel of experience and persuaded him to withdraw his first attempt at a novel. But apparently he did not like Meredithian fiction, though he paid due tribute to a wit that stripped shams stark naked.[2] He was an uncertain critic either of others or of himself, witness the ups and downs in the quality of his output, evidently to him quite imperceptible. He could read Henry James with appreciation of an art extremely unlike his own, but was unable to perceive the dross in the good metal of

Hardy and Meredith

---

[1] The literary Derby seems to be a national institution—Richardson and Fielding, Dickens and Thackeray, Tennyson and Browning, Meredith and Hardy, Bennett and Wells, running neck and neck.

[2] Comparing James and Meredith in his journal, he said, "Meredith has some poetry, and yet I can look at James when I cannot look at Meredith" (*Later Years,* 169). "Some poetry" is good! But he also wrote:

> He was of those whose wit can shake
> And ridicule to the very core
> The counterfeits that time will break.

Maeterlinck, only deploring the optimistic sophistry of the *Apology for Nature*.[1]

The difference between him and Meredith goes so deep that it is like the break between two literary epochs, one reacting against its predecessor. Hardy was one of those who think life by no means a boon,[2] even when contemplated as he contemplated it, with all its redeeming interests and lofty renunciations in full view. This, in spite of such prayers for a tolerant attitude as his song in a minor key:

> Let me enjoy the earth no less
> Because the all-enacting Might
> That fashioned forth its loveliness
> Had other aims than my delight.

"Happiness," he said, "is an occasional episode in a general drama of pain." The tragedy might enthrall an unconcerned spectator, it could only torment the individual involved in it. Nor was he one that deemed the cult of a fine personality an enterprise worth the exorbitant cost. He laboured, he said, for "the soul's betterment," but only as some alleviation of unavoidable suffering. The life of everyone except his thick-skinned rustics is a state of damnation. Had he been born three centuries earlier, the young man with his craving to write poetry and his constitutional melancholy would have found an outlet for feeling and imagination in such plays as those of Webster, Tourneur, and Ford, who revelled in gloom and terror. At a later date, in default of theatre or prose fiction, he might have outdone Young's *Night Thoughts*, or vied with Leopardi and his own contemporary Laforgue in the poetry of despair and revolt. Though, when the geniality of his spirit towards his fellow-men was not quenched by the haunting spectacle of the general misery, Hardy could find relief in the humours of his rustics, even such intermittent comedy was usually the handmaid of tragedy. Living when he did, he had ready to his hand in the contemporary novel a medium offering the same opportunities as the stage, and even more as a means

[1] *Later Years*, 96–98.
[2] His poems reiterate that, if in the novels he may be said not to speak *in propria persona*.

of rendering life in its fullness.[1] He had begun, like Meredith, by writing poetry, though his verse, whether early or late, was kept from the public eye till all or most of his novels had appeared, and had been accepted, some as failures, some great, but all avouching original genius and profundity of feeling, and all, like Meredith's, saturated with poetry. In the light of his total achievement, Hardy is seen to be a genuine poet, of the reflective and gnomic sort, with a vision of man and the universe as intense and as distinctive as any literary or plastic artist ever unfolded, but a vision utterly different and at odds with Meredith's. The latter had made fiction an adequate mode of setting forth his philosophy of the individual in reaction to the world. Personal development was his chosen theme: his novels are histories of men and women in the act of living and achieving themselves or coming to grief; they show the inner side of this effort, this victory or failure, and the interest lies accordingly in a long range of highly organized and highly self-conscious individuals. Not so with Hardy. He is a critic of life, not of personal character; not an observer of men in society, but of human conditions in the more philosophic sense—an observer who has already made his mind up. The struggle for a tolerable existence, for some equilibrium in the prevailing discord, rather than for any lofty, self-abnegating yet self-affirmative goal, the latent antagonisms and intestine strife of the sexes, and all the other obstacles besetting the human path: these are his dramatic subject. His chief character is Man, and the play Existence. To intellectual and spiritual questions he pays small heed, except as subordinate interests, supernumerary problems embittering the universal anguish. Thus his novels give his natural history of man, and especially woman, who is even more at the mercy of life than her comrade in the fight, too often her corrival. The two novelists may be compared and contrasted, but hardly in terms of each other. Meredith's novels, also, are love-stories. He, however, does not present love as a sexual combat, but rather as a leading episode in the drama of life, the most critical passage in the making, testing,

---

[1] Hardy's novels might perhaps be summed up as a grafting of late Elizabethan drama on prose fiction.

and ennobling of men and women.[1] Hardy's conception of life was essentially tragic: the conflict is one in which there is but the remotest chance of escape, so heavily are the scales weighted by man's impercipience, his inability to coerce his own insubordinate nature, and the checks and snares plentifully sown in his path by some occult malice. Meredith's view could never have been adequately propounded except in the novel: Hardy's might well have gone into drama, as it did when he had the leisure and the ripeness to deal with the world-theme of humanity pitted against destiny in *The Dynasts*. No more signal contrast is imaginable than Meredith's cheerful courage in surveying man's failings and the catastrophes which they entail. He could frame tragedies as stern as those which Hardy perceived everywhere and was always reproducing; but even in his tragic moments he was as alive as ever to the absurdities which gladden the spirit of comedy. In truth, his tragedies had the same genesis as his comedies, both alike being exhibitions of folly and error, bringing down, in the one case ridicule, in the other complete disaster, on his egoists, sentimentalists, or inconsequent blunderers. In this respect he contrasted with his elder George Eliot, as much as with his junior Hardy. They were not more intrinsically serious in their handling of life's problems; but he would not maintain their unrelaxing pose of gravity, and he was incapable of falling into the black mood of despondency which Hardy kept up to the end. Whatever solutions Hardy revolved one after another he eventually gave up the question in despair, unless the faint hope voiced by the Pities at the end of *The Dynasts* is to be regarded as his own in good earnest.[2]

The impact of science on both

Hardy was nineteen, Meredith thirty-one, when *The Origin of Species* appeared, and there was a vital difference in the manner and extent of their acceptance of Darwin's teaching, and of the wider implications of it set forth in the ensuing years

[1] "The chief object in life," says Weyburn, in *Lord Ormont and his Aminta*, "if happiness be the aim, and the growing better than we are, is to teach men and women how to be one; for, if they're not, then each is a morsel for the other to prey on" (chap. xxiv., "Lovers mated").

[2] He said after the great war, so Mrs Hardy reports, "he would probably not have ended *The Dynasts* as he did end it if he could have foreseen what was going to happen within a few years" (*Later Years*, 165).

by Spencer, Huxley, Lecky, John Morley, Leslie Stephen, and other disciples. Evolution itself they both recognized as the rational explanation of the development of life. Hardy without hesitation accepted the whole theory, including that of natural selection as the causative agency. Meredith's firm belief in intuition, spontaneity, free will, on the other hand, was proof against such a mechanical hypothesis. Holding that science has only a limited range, that reason and logic cannot explain all the facts, Meredith, warmly as he welcomed the advance of science, never let himself become obsessed, like Hardy, with the idea of the inexorable working of natural laws: he would have repudiated any contention that mind and conduct were equally at the mercy of such a system of causation, a notion that would cancel individuality. He had rejected *Erewhon*, and probably knew next to nothing of Samuel Butler's later works correcting Darwin.[1] But such intuitions as that of unconscious memory, of a vital impulse, a creative energy, urging the living creature forward, and of an insight solving difficulties as they arise and evolving finer organs to cope with new emergencies, such intuitions as were presently to be coordinated into a philosophy of creative evolution by Bergson, were in thorough accord with Meredith's faith in an intelligence transcending the logical reason, and in a power within man and not outside and beyond him, such as Hardy's supreme will controlling all things, sentient as well as insentient. It might almost be said that Meredith was a Bergsonian before Bergson [2]; for, though he was no systematic thinker and probably never read the French philosopher, his loosely formulated yet coherent

[1] See Volume VIII. 275, 285, and 290. Meredith admitted that Butler's works repelled him (S. M. Ellis, 207).
[2] It is noticeable that the most illuminating short study of Meredith, the chapter in *Messages*, by Ramon Fernandez, is by a thoroughgoing Bergsonian, who shows that Meredith relied on that very *intuition psychologique* which Bergson so brilliantly analysed. Of course, it might be urged that Shakespeare employed the same faculty, or Tolstoy, of whom Havelock Ellis remarks, "It seemed to him that he realized that God is life, and that to live is to know God." Bergson discovered nothing that was not in mind already; he merely showed how the greatest minds have worked. Meredith perceived the value of this mode of grasping and possessing truth, and was wise enough to trust to it. Hardy did read Bergson, and, as might have been expected, saw in his work merely a breach with rationalism (*Later Years*, 167–168). Mme Cazamian says of George Eliot (i. 236), "On peut dire en un sens qu'elle annonce le Bergsonisme."

philosophy of life is a practical deduction from the phenomena as he scrutinized them in operation, forming a sort of independent footnote to Bergson. He watched creative evolution going on, and wrote down what he saw. For Hardy, on the contrary, science merely confirmed a view of existence which was, it would seem, congenial to his native frame of mind, to which, at all events, his experience of living had wedded him.

Effect on literature of the new science All the time that Hardy was writing his novels, literature in general was deeply affected by the questions and the poignant anxieties raised by the recent revelations of science. Darwin and his followers were publishing book after book, carrying the new views into every domain of thought.[1] The poets were inevitably caught in the turmoil of ideas, and the novelists likewise. Hardy read the scientists, he also read the poets. Like Meredith, he wanted to be a poet himself; and, if he could have had his own way and not been obliged to earn a living, he would have written poetry rather than novels, as Meredith confessed that he too would have done.[2] Swinburne was the one who moved him most. *Atalanta in Calydon* (1865), the first series of *Poems and Ballads* (1866), and *Songs before Sunrise* (1871), with their bitterness, their defiance, their revolt against human limitations and celestial injustice, struck a responsive chord in Hardy's soul.

All we are against thee, against thee, O God most high!

---

[1] The reader may like to be reminded of the dates of a few books which are historical landmarks: Darwin's *Origin of Species* (1859), *The Descent of Man* (1871), *The Effects of Cross and Self Fertilization* (1876); Herbert Spencer's *First Principles* (1862), *Principles of Biology* (1864), *The Study of Sociology* (1872–1873), *Data of Ethics* (1879); Huxley's *Man's Place in Nature* (1863), *The Classification of Animals* (1869), *Lay Sermons* (1870); Lecky's *History of Rationalism* (1865), *History of European Morals* (1869); John Tyndall's *Heat as a Mode of Motion* (1863), *The Imagination in Science* (1870); Wallace's *Malay Archipelago* (1869), *Contributions to the Theory of Natural Selection* (1870), *Darwinism* (1889); Morley's *Voltaire* (1871), *Rousseau* (1873), *On Compromise* (1874), *Diderot and the Encyclopædists* (1878); Tylor's *Early History of Mankind* (1865), *Primitive Culture* (1871); Matthew Arnold's *Culture and Anarchy* (1869), *St Paul and Protestantism* (1870), *Literature and Dogma* (1873), *God and the Bible* (1875); Bagehot's *Physics and Politics* (1873); G. H. Lewes's *Problems of Life and Mind* (1873–1879); Max Müller's *Chips from a German Workshop* (1868–1875), *Introduction to the Science of Religion* (1873), *Origin and Growth of Religions* (1878); Leslie Stephen's *Essays on Free Thinking and Plain Speaking* (1873), *English Thought in the Eighteenth Century* (1876), *The Science of Ethics* (1882); Stanley Jevons' *Principles of Science* (1874). The date of *Essays and Reviews* (1860) and of the Colenso case (1862) should also be borne in mind.

[2] Volume VIII. 302.

They played on the same keynote as FitzGerald's translation of *Omar Khayyám* (1859), another of his bedside books, from which he had the famous eighty-first quatrain read to him when he was dying. Swinburne he was always quoting. "Save his own soul he hath no star" is a motto to the second part of *Jude the Obscure*. "I read him as he came out," Hardy said at Swinburne's death, and was gratified by knowing him personally some years before that event. It is significant that one of his poems, "Hap," lamenting Nature's indifference to man, a thought very like some of Swinburne's, was written as early as 1866.

> If but some vengeful god would call to me
> From up the sky, and laugh: "Thou suffering thing,
> Know that thy sorrow is my ecstasy
> That thy love's loss is my hate's profiting."

But it is no divinity persecuting man, only "crass Casualty" and "dicing Time":

> These purblind Doomsters had as readily thrown
> Blisses about my pilgrimage as pain.

James Thomson was writing now, and in *The City of Dreadful Night* (1874), out of suicidal despair, visioned the gloom of a universe in which there is nothing real but man's hopelessness. He imagined a world on scientific lines, which ultimately grows conscious in the human mind.

> Glory to Man in the highest! for Man is the master of things.

Thus he had sung in the "Hymn of Man," in 1871. Out of the same stark materialism, John Davidson,[1] a generation later, evoked the worship of a perfected humanity. God and the gods are man's mistake, which must be cancelled. In *The Testament of John Davidson* (1908), which is his *Prometheus Unbound*, he depicts a universe of matter and force, in which

---

[1] A disillusioned man who attacks worn-out faiths "whilst himself falling a prey to the clap-trap philosophy of the scientific materialists" (R. A. Scott-James: *Modernism and Romance*, 208). But Thomson and Henley's challenge of the unknown and Davidson's materialism may be charitably regarded as partly the results of acute suffering acting upon souls of different strength and temper, and less atheism than discontent with out-of-date creeds and revulsion from new forms of dogmatism.

there is no consciousness, no intelligence, no free will, anywhere, except in man. Man has created the gods in his own image, Jupiter, Apollo, Pluto, Jehovah, Thor; and when he renounces them, and determines to live by the facts of existence, they fade away and cease.

Men are the Universe
Aware at last.

John Davidson, the new Prometheus, is an impatient and unpardoning titan, who slays Apollo, Aïdoneus, and all the other mythic gods, in single combat: they fall nerveless and thinner than impalpable mind-stuff before his conquering sword of knowledge. But it is all illusion: Hell itself, in which he finds himself, is only a fantasy, an aberration of the human mind, which, like sciatica or diabetes at the word of the "Christian scientist," presently vanishes. Davidson was not a Leopardi, and his sublime skirts the ridiculous rather precariously. Leopardi had long preceded both Swinburne and Hardy; the latter read him in a French translation. Other contemporaries had something of his dignity, if not his force; for instance, Lord de Tabley, in poems indignantly challenging divine justice. W. E. Henley's stoicism and defiance of whatever gods there be, Stevenson's brave indifference to the "unparalleled disaster of death" and cheerful exhortations to live daringly, the mystical quest for something higher than deity which was the outcome for Richard Jefferies of a yearning for intenser communion with an illimitable cosmos of thought: these were some of the ways in which the poets faced the new issues. Francis Thompson took refuge in a different mysticism.[1] The self-styled "Decadent" poets and prose-writers of the latter part of the century, the *fin-de-siècle*, in their blend of defiance, of a resolve to get the most out of life whilst they had it, and their pure æstheticism, gave another response. Some

[1] Thompson (1859–1907), a Roman Catholic, became a vagabond on the face of the earth. He was completely indifferent to temporal things, but his faith in the spiritual was as absolute and as concrete as Blake's. His poetry, lovely as it can be at its best, is as lugubrious as the most pessimistic of the pessimists of the Decadence. Such ghoulish melancholy, such morbid horror of all the delights of the flesh, seem a standing witness to the truth and soundness of Meredith's philosophy of blood, brain, and spirit.

still living took part in the same debate, and their utterances
are now historical documents on the period under discussion.

It was plain in the work of Dickens and Thackeray and their *Fiction*
contemporaries that the novel was becoming an organ of moral *an organ*
and social criticism, a thoughtful survey of life, fully alive to *of*
the questions agitating the public conscience, and to others *criticism*
also, and judging them by standards of valuation which might *and philo-*
still be open to challenge.[1] Mrs Gaskell had been heart-struck *sophic*
by the atrocious results of unrestrained individualism, and *thought*
exposed errors, frauds, and injustices in the contrasting light
of her humane picturing of character and personal relations.
Less militant, for her feelings had not been so lacerated by
experiences at close quarters, George Eliot was an analyst of
the mind, like Browning; she applied scientific codes to
character and conduct, but by sympathy and imagination now
and then rose superior to the determinist conclusions of abstract
philosophy. Meredith in his first regular novel satirized the
delusions of a rigorous determinism applied to the education
and even to the mating of a healthy young man. He was
keenly aware of the limits beyond which scientific reasoning
ventured to dogmatize at its peril: what could it possibly have
to say of individual character and the creative energies of
personality? Survival of the fittest was to him the result of
imaginative effort and instinctive intelligence, not of a haphazard weeding-out of imperfections. Life at its highest was
self-conscious, a pursuit of ends apprehended in the steady
advance. Yet now Hardy, believing as seriously as Meredith
that fiction must embrace philosophy, but oppressed by his
tragic view of existence, sees wherever he looks "crass Casualty"
thwarting man's best endeavours, and what the scientist
described as natural selection eliminating with blind indifference
both the fit and the unfit to survive. Gissing was soon to
follow with even more repellent and unvarnished pictures of
the baseness and squalor that outraged his scholarly, sensitive
soul; but with no theory, no criticism, and no more hope than
Hardy. Butler's saner version of the evolutionary doctrine
was then expounded in a series of controversial volumes and

[1] Volume VIII. 164–166.

subsequently in his *Way of all Flesh*, which combined the clarity of fiction with the force of autobiography; it furnished the basis for the creed of social reform to be set forth in novel, play, and pamphlet by Messrs Bernard Shaw and H. G. Wells.

Polemical uses of fiction Inevitably, such a popular, adaptable, and persuasive thing as the novel was requisitioned for all sorts of purposes, some hardly legitimate. Novels are written that are mere diagnoses of prevailing conditions, usually with a definite bias: these are sociology rather than fiction. Much oftener they are used in the service of new creeds and new crazes, and their satirical resources to denounce everything that the writers detest. In some of the shapes it has taken, fiction as an applied art has a specious air of respectability; the aim, at any rate, is meritorious, nothing less than to enlighten and educate those who will not or cannot undertake a serious course of reading for themselves. Thus, Mrs Humphry Ward was in her inoffensive way a forerunner of Lytton Strachey, with her complacent and by no means ironical studies of well-known historical figures and of religious, political, and social problems, some historical, some still agitating the general mind. The evil was when fiction fell into the hands of the exploiters, when such empirics as Marie Corelli and Hall Caine were accepted by multitudes of trustful readers as endowed with preternatural insight, and poured forth their tirades, more pamphlet than novel and more transcendental fustian than either, in the fond belief that they were riddling and destroying Mammon and Antichrist. At a time of such mental and moral bewilderment, when age-old convictions had been uprooted, and all who thought at all were anxiously seeking for some firm truth on which to rebuild, unable to resign themselves to the everlasting Nay, the most scrupulous novelist often could not help taking sides in the world-wide controversy, and many, without meaning or even knowing it, wrote propagandist fiction. The confidence with which a man at such a time submits his personal view of life may be quite enough to give his work a polemical turn. Even the Neo-Romantics of the eighteen–eighties, although much of their æstheticism was a putting of the cart before the horse and their philosophy of decadence purely negative, violated their

own æsthetic rules in the best of their fiction, and out of their
scorn for what was false and hypocritical wrote what was too
honest and sincere to be literally true.

From the first, Hardy's novels embodied a definitely critical *Similar*
attitude towards the world he was depicting. The one that *tendencies*
Meredith advised him to suppress, *The Poor Man and the Lady,* *in*
seems to have been objectionable as a crude socialistic satire on *Hardy's*
the squirearchy. In the melodramatic *Desperate Remedies* and *novels*
in *Under the Greenwood Tree*, and the novels which immediately
followed, he wrote what from this point of view might be
considered straightforward and inoffensive fiction, not putting
life's little ironies too much in the foreground, though such
titles as "Under the Greenwood Tree," "A Pair of Blue Eyes,"
and "Far from the Madding Crowd" may be suspected of
raillery when the books have been read, and anyone looking
below the surface must have fathomed that it was all a sceptic's
presentment of the irony of existence.[1] But for a while Hardy
kept his bitterest reflections for his verse,[2] and it was not till
The Return of the Native that he began to fire off those gibes
at "the grimness of the general human situation," at "life as a
thing to be put up with," at "the quandary" in which man is
placed by "the defects of natural laws," and at Fate's transparent devices to get the better of helpless man. So far he had
kept to the straight path of his greatest predecessors in realism.[3]
But now his novels tend to be burdened with a thesis, an
argument to be pushed to a foregone conclusion, a case to be
established, tempting him to overweight the evidence and
multiply the coincidences and the glaring examples of alleged
malice, for which he had shown a weakness even in *Desperate
Remedies*. A fine tragedy, *The Mayor of Casterbridge*, suffers
from this tampering with the probabilities. *Tess of the*

[1] Hardy was not a thoroughgoing ironist, though his favourite text was the irony
of things, and his clear vision of the general injustice rendered him sardonic rather
than resigned. It was fate and circumstance that were ironical, and he greets them
with a maledictory protest.

[2] Most of his early poetical work was destroyed; but some survives, and probably
the pith of many vanished pieces went into some of those now extant (see *Early
Life*, 71).

[3] Thus, Fielding is himself impassive, perfectly neutral; but can any intelligent
reader fail for a moment to be aware of his moral values?

d'Urbervilles reads like a determined attempt to prove the supremacy of Ahriman, and his controversial animus in *Jude the Obscure* made him pile up the agony to a degree that excites horror and defeats the aims of tragedy, if those had been his sole intention. This manœuvring of the hostile forces was too much in the style of the minor novelist with a message, and seriously disfigured Hardy's later novels.[1]

Hardy's boyhood and start in life

Hardy was born in a tiny Dorsetshire hamlet, like that which is the chief scene of *The Woodlanders*; he was the eldest child of a copyholder of the same class as the leading characters in that novel. His father, a general contractor and builder, sent the boy first to the village school, and then to one in Dorchester, where Latin was an extra. Tom was backward in health, but a precocious lad, observant beyond his years. Music, dancing, the services in church, the performances of the village choir and their personal oddities, made an impression on him that he never forgot. His education on the whole was superior to that of most boys in his circumstances; but the real scholarship which he ultimately attained was the result of his own efforts. He read the Latin and the French classics to enjoy them; and after he was articled to a profession he got an older friend to coach him in Greek, and was disappointed that the need to earn a salary prevented his going on with the study of Sophocles and Æschylus, the two poets who were to have most effect upon his work in literature. The profession decided upon was architecture. The youth became a pupil in an architect's office in Dorchester, and had some experience of the restoration of country churches then going on, before he went to London and became an assistant to Arthur Blomfield. Hardy was five or six years in London, working at his profession, seeing life, and strenuously reading and thinking. He was nursing literary aspirations too, and eventually one of the factors settling the debate in his mind between architecture and authorship was the dread that his eyes might not stand the strain of fine architectural drawing. He had fallen in love, and wanted to marry;

---

[1] M. Firmin Roz puts very neatly Hardy's partiality for the fatal action of chance (97–98): "Le hasard a sa part dans la fatalité; mais il n'y entre pas seul et surtout il n'y entre pas toujours à point nommé. M. Hardy le rend infaillible. Il en fait un magicien astucieux, moins que cela, un féroce escamoteur."

he must make sure of an income somehow. For a year or two
he kept both doors open, and was actually in print some time
before he resigned his post. He had written *The Poor Man
and the Lady* at Dorchester, and when it was condemned he
seems to have taken Meredith's advice too literally, and put
too much plot into *Desperate Remedies*.[1] This was published
in 1871, partly at his own expense. But he realized that it
was a misdirected effort, and in his next novel, *Under the
Greenwood Tree* (1872), he chose a subject and treated it in a
manner both of which his revered friend, the poet Barnes,
would have approved. It was well received, though it did not
yet assure an income. *A Pair of Blue Eyes* (1873), which
appeared just after he had thrown up his assistantship, was still
more successful; and then with *Far from the Madding Crowd*
(1874), which at Leslie Stephen's invitation he wrote for the
Cornhill Magazine, he became a popular novelist, and the
novelist of Wessex, for it was here that he gave the realm he
was annexing that ancient name. He had begun late, though
he had been developing for years, and he had now discovered
his proper range.

There was a moment when Hardy, wanting to write poetry *Free*
and half prepared by his attainments in the classics, thought of *thought*
entering the Church.[2] But the views which he had come to
hold were a barrier he could not honestly set aside. He loved
the Church, though he was severe on its shortcomings; he was
far from being of an irreligious turn of mind. His schooling
in the Bible and his tenderness towards the church service have
left innumerable traces in his work. He was always borrowing
ideas, figures of speech, expressive phrases, as well as the
immortal sayings, from holy writ, and put them with inimitable
force and felicity in the mouth of his rustic sages. He knew
the Prayer Book equally well, and could draw upon it and upon
Anglican tenets just as aptly in his ironical allusions to "Nature's
holy plan" or in his examples of scrupulous obedience to the
letter and disregard for the spirit of the Gospel. He was as
terrible as Swinburne in his power of turning pious sentiments
into maledictions, and almost as good in the similar application

[1] *Early Life*, 83.　　　　　[2] *Ibid.*, 66.

of utterances from ancient Greek poetry. Such a realist as Maupassant could ignore the unseen. The scientist could regard such a myth with a sceptical smile. Hardy could not clear his mind of a theistic conception of the governance of the world, however much he assented to the protests of science that the universe was a system of unconscious and unpurposive mechanism, of blind force and immutable law engaged solely in keeping it going. Inveterate habits of mind compelled him to hypostatize his forces of nature, to deify his Immanent Will. He perceived a predominance of evil, and he had to personify the inimical thing, by a sort of pathetic fallacy or an inversion of his theological preconceptions. *Tess of the d'Urbervilles* is almost a reading of the Bible backwards, so full is it of biblical similes and allusions, above all, of curses. "Where was Tess's guardian angel?" he sardonically inquires, when she falls a prey to the obscene Alec d'Urberville, "where was the providence of her simple faith? Perhaps, like that other god of whom the ironical Tishbite spoke, he was talking, or he was pursuing, or he was in a journey, or he was sleeping and not to be awaked." Or take the recital of biblical comminations put in the mouth of the dying Jude:

Let the day perish wherein I was born, and the night in which it was said, There is a man child conceived.

Let that day be darkness; let not God regard it from above, neither let the light shine upon it. Lo, let that night be solitary, let no joyful voice come therein.

It was not that he was merely turning the tables on devout upholders of an exploded theology: this theology was too deeply ingrained in him: he could only retort upon it, and hurl out reproaches instead of thanksgiving for all that heaven had granted mortality.[1]

According to all accounts of Hardy's early life, his was an extremely sensitive temperament, rather given to melancholy, easily moved to tears, fond of solitude,[2] though by no means

[1] "On 'nature's holy plan' and on 'trailing clouds of glory' Hardy pours out his scorn. Nature is beautiful, yes, but she is the hapless instrument of blind law, and, as such, he is as much convinced of her non-morality as Huxley was" (Grimsditch, 49).

[2] One of his memories of childhood was of once lying in the sun, "thinking how

inaccessible to good-fellowship, and enjoying a good laugh as *Hardy's*
much as anyone, especially if the joke was of a profane or *innate*
sardonic character.[1] All his life he had a weakness for gruesome *predilec-*
incidents, grim legends, creepy stories, accounts of spells, omens, *tion for*
ghosts, murders, suicides, and the like. He was always jotting *tragedy*
down such things in his diary, and would visit the scene to find
out all he could about some sinister event and enjoy its full
flavour.[2] He never seems to have missed a funeral, at least of
anyone distinguished or of his own kin, and is full of reminiscences of those melancholy festivals. This hankering after the

useless he was. . . . Reflecting on his experiences of the world so far as he had got,
he came to the conclusion that he did not wish to grow up" (*Early Life*, 19). A
ploughed vale in Berkshire, called the Valley of Brown Melancholy, made him feel,
"Though I am alive with the living I can only see the dead here, and am scarcely
conscious of the happy children at play" (*Later Years*, 13). The text "Ye shall weep
and mourn, and the world shall rejoice," seemed to him "eternally true." "The
widened view of nowadays perceives that the world weeps and mourns all round"
(*Early Life*, 214).

[1] He liked such tales as that of the wedding, at the end of which the bridegroom
and bridesmaid found themselves man and wife, and the bride and best man the
witnesses; of the curate who met a charming widow, and calling on her a day or two
later was told, "Why, Sir, you buried her this morning!" It was during an epidemic
of cholera. Then there is the ghastly one told by the sexton, who was about to bury
another widow, and found the coffin of her deceased husband turned over in the grave.
Either the next anecdote, of the man who saw the dark figure with a cloven foot
and a little later disappeared one night of lightning and thunder; or the preceding
one of the sick man who told the clergyman that the chapter from the Bible did him
"almost as much good as a glass of gin-and-water," is a welcome antidote to this.

[2] Hardy went with Colonel T. W. Higginson "to hunt up the spot of the execution
of the Duke of Buckingham, whose spirit is said to haunt King's House still" (*Later
Years*, 72). He accompanied H. Lucy to the scene of the Phœnix Park murders, and
was shown the rooms in which the bodies of Lord F. Cavendish and Mr Burke were
placed, "and told some gruesome details of the discovery of a roll of bloody clothes
under the sofa after the entry of the succeeding Secretary. The room had not been
cleaned since the murders" (*Later Years*, 19). Hardy does not betray any sign that
the job was uncongenial when as assistant to Blomfield he had to supervise the
removal of the bodies from old St Pancras churchyard to make room for the railway.
Blomfield had been horrified by rumours of "mysterious full bags of something that
rattled, and cartage to bone-mills. . . . 'I believe these people are all ground up!'
said Blomfield grimly." One coffin fell apart and revealed a skeleton and two skulls;
and Hardy records how Blomfield when they met years after began the conversation
with "Do you remember how we found the man with two heads at St Pancras?"
(*Early Life*, 58–59). It is only fair, however, to quote the very different impression of
Hardy's character formed by Mr A. Compton-Rickett, who knew him for more than
a quarter-of-a-century, and says in *Portraits and Personalities* (1937): "My ultimate
impression of his personality is diametrically opposed to the popular view. Spoken of
so frequently as a melancholy man, who took a drab and pessimistic view of life, I have
often thought how strangely different this is from the bright and jolly companion
whom I knew. . . . He was a quiet little man with sardonic eyebrows and twinkling
eyes. Watch him tucked away in a corner of a rural inn, laughing heartily over some
rustic tradition and telling in his turn a story of tragic or comic import."

gloomy, the ghoulish, and mysterious helps to account for what has been called the "fetishism" in Hardy's view of nature and man. To him there was no such thing as inanimate nature.[1] He could never banish his deep-rooted sense of the supernatural, or reduce himself to the calm indifference of a Huxley or a Leslie Stephen. By accepting the scientific attitude he rationalized his acute apprehension of mankind's tragic plight; but it was only with his intellect that he accepted it, something deeper was always in conflict with the rationalization. He never found full satisfaction in the materialistic philosophy to which he resigned himself. It was not merely that he had repudiated one orthodoxy to capitulate to another, that other by no means more stable, if so be that rationalism ignores faculties of the mind as valid as pure reason, if pure reason be only one half of human intelligence. It was not merely that his mind staggered and oscillated from one theory of causation to another, from seeing man in the grip of hostile forces to the acceptance of pure chance as the arbiter; and then from a view approximating to the idea of character as fate to the conception of an immanent will pervading and controlling all things, but unconscious of any purpose. He had a grudge against the universe which he could not throw off, a feeling of resentment at injustices and wanton cruelty which must have some object on which to wreak itself. The problem of evil was a monstrous and harassing conundrum. Assuredly, some power that hated good must be in the saddle, thwarting every endeavour of man to circumvent his fate. The absurdity of a trust in Providence drove him to the opposite belief. Events were too plainly ironical, they must have been contrived. Hence the mishaps and coincidences, hence the inverted plots in his novels, everything happening awry, coincidences invariably turning out unlucky: a stroke of good fortune never occurs but it is instantly reversed in a stroke of savage derision. All this was his reading of the facts of average life, and symbolical of the infernal malice which ruled the world—"the ingenious machinery contrived

---

[1] It is Dr Hedgcock who remarks this (pp. 358–359). The fancy which endues inanimate objects with life, in Dickens, Charles Lamb, Shakespeare, etc., is a different sort of animism. More akin to Hardy's is the dark, myth-making fancy of Synge and other Irish writers.

by the gods for reducing human possibilities to a minimum."[1]
There is no response possible but despair and passive revolt.
The theory of evolution that he has accepted brings him at last
to the outcry, "Man shall cease," instead of Meredith's vision
of radiant and more perfect races.[2]   For science is the villain
of the plot, in Hardy's philosophy, and in more than half of his
novels.   But it was a mythopœic instinct going beyond science
that conjured up his Immortals, the Spirit of the Years, the
Immanent Will,

> The purposive, unmotived, dominant Thing.

This is no mere personification of natural causes.   Hardy has
succumbed to a sort of Manichæism in which mankind is the
only discernible force on the side of goodness.   His God is not
a Christian.   The good in man is confronted by evil which
seems to be omnipotent.   Like that other determinist,
Meredith's Sir Austin Feverel, overwhelmed by the general
malevolence of things, Hardy sees the devil.[3]

---

[1] *Mayor of Casterbridge*, xliv.

[2] It is perhaps unfair to quote Meredith's censure of the impatient individual who
fancies himself the special victim of fortune, and thinks that everybody else has all the
luck: "The reproaching of Providence by a man of full growth, comes to some
extent from his meanness, and chiefly from his pride.   He remembers that the old
Gods selected heroes whom to persecute, and it is his compensation for material
losses to conceive himself a distinguished mark for the Powers of air" (*Sandra Belloni*).
Hardy does not envisage such narrow selfishness; his vision embraces the world.   Life
itself is a failure, and he can only bear it like a Stoic:

> Let me enjoy the earth no less
> Because the all-embracing Might
> That fashioned forth its loveliness
> Had other aims than my delight.
> > *Time's Laughing-Stocks.*

A finer wisdom, at any rate, than that of the young man who girds at

> A senseless school, where we must give
> Our lives that we may learn to live!
> A dolt is he who memorizes
> Lessons that leave no time for prizes.
> > *Ibid.*

[3] "A Manichæan tendency, from which the sententious eulogist of nature had been
struggling for years (and which was partly at the bottom of the System), now began to
cloud and usurp dominion of his mind.   As he sat alone in the forlorn dead-hush of
his library, he saw the devil" (*The Ordeal of Richard Feverel*, xxxiii.—"Nursing the
Devil").   Elsewhere Meredith wrote:

> Count Nature devilish, and accept for doom
> The chasm between our passions and our wits.

Hardy's phil- osophy   It was Hardy's own fault if people would insist on discussing his philosophy. He pleaded that he was not a philosopher, which was true[1] ; yet he was continually talking about this philosophy of his and explaining it, and not merely explaining it away either. It consisted of the general conclusions to which he had been driven by his reading of the scientists and their expositors and annotators. It was unfortunate that he kept shifting his ground, and that the metaphysics underlying *A Pair of Blue Eyes* do not tally with those of *The Return of the Native*, or these with *Tess* and *Jude*: Hardy was always seeking a better theory to substantiate his tragic view of things, and at any rate each novel maintains consistency from beginning to end. Hardy was a confused thinker: his greatness was in his having embodied a profundity of meaning in his characters and their histories, to have made the drama in which they play their own parts a symbol of humanity at war with the universe. He had every right to give his own imaginative sense of reality. Truth to life in fiction is only a minimum; realism is only a method, a means of showing things in the pattern into which they fall when reflected in the writer's consciousness.[2]   But, whilst the meaning which there was for Hardy should clearly emerge, the drama should at the same time be a transparent likeness of the existence with which all are familiar. Yet, as already observed, a story by Thomas Hardy continually betrays that he has a case to state, an indictment to argue; there is an obvious overplus of mischance leading to a solution, or insoluble enigma, obviously ready-made; in fact, the problem is usually set out in such terms that the tragic conclusion is inescapable.

[1] When he goes out of his way to attempt formal philosophizing, as when on more than one occasion he explains that "the world is only a psychological phenomenon," he talks neither philosophy nor common sense, though he is trying in his own way to state a doctrine of Schopenhauer. George Eliot would have known better than to indulge in such irresponsible sallies, which are irrelevant and oddly at variance with the general proposition that we are but toys in the grasp of some outer reality. Hardy declared that he had not read Schopenhauer at the time of writing *Tess*, and Gosse confirmed the statement. But Schopenhauer was in the air at that period, and as Dr de Ridder-Barzin says, "Après tout, peut-être ne sont ce que des échos d'une lecture métaphysique qui avait frappé Hardy, pendant un certain temps à ce moment de sa vie, et puis, qui se sera évanouie, sans laisser de trace" (166). See also p. 164, where Dr de Ridder-Barzin shows Hardy as *philosophe sans l'admettre*.

[2] "On écrit de telles choses pour transmettre aux autres la théorie de l'univers qu'on porte en soi" (Renan, Préface à *Souvenirs d'enfance et de jeunesse*).

To make these surreptitious aims more glaring, and his tinker-
ing with the circumstances more suspicious, he interjects his
indignant outbursts and denunciations: it is as if a playwright
walked upon the stage and began talking fiercely about the
ulterior meanings of the play. Tragic as are such novels as
The Mayor of Casterbridge, *Tess*, and *Jude*, they all have
in them something that exceeds the scope of tragedy: they
are an arraignment and an accusation; in other words,
they embody an emotive exposition of Thomas Hardy's
philosophy.

The popular novelists of the day when Hardy was recom- *His*
mended to write something more to the taste of ordinary *early*
readers were the veteran Charles Reade and Wilkie Collins, and *novels*
the latter's crude but far from unsuccessful followers, Miss
Braddon and Mrs Henry Wood. Collins had made a great hit
with *The Dead Secret* (1857), *The Woman in White* (1860), and,
only the other day, *The Moonstone* (1868), in all of which the
mechanics of plot were developed in elaborate mystifications,
solved by a well-laid surprise, characterization being subordinate. Hardy modelled his new attempt [1] upon *The Woman in
White*, and did it so ably that his publisher, Tinsley, who had
been rather scurvy in the matter of terms, had to admit afterwards, "'Twas a blood-curdling story!" Hardy showed often
enough later on that he had a natural bent for the exceptional,
the bizarre, both in situation and in strange and intricate
concatenations of events—people married to the wrong partners,
fantastic scenes in the most unlikely surroundings, and sensational incidents skirting the incredible.[2] The plot could be
matched by some of his *Life's Little Ironies* or such of the tales
in *A Group of Noble Dames* as "Barbara of the House of Grebe"
or "The Marchioness of Stonehenge," not to mention plenty
of instances in the novels. For Hardy believed in the extraordinary as the right subject for fiction. Among his notes for
an article never written he jotted down:

[1] *Desperate Remedies.*
[2] "A curious concern for the fantastic, the grotesque, the quaint, marks Mr Hardy
strongly: were he a mediæval builder, his cathedrals would display the richest
gargoyles in Christendom" (Lionel Johnson: *Post Liminium, essays and critical
papers*, 148).

The real, if unavowed, purpose of fiction is to give pleasure by gratifying the love of the uncommon in human experience, mental or corporeal.

Lifelikeness is essential, to make the reader believe in the personages set before him; but care must be taken to preserve the uncommonness, without which there would be no interest.

The uncommonness must be in the events, not in the characters; and the writer's art lies in shaping that uncommonness while disguising its unlikelihood, if it be unlikely.[1]

This curious doctrine, so candidly avowed, accounts for many seemingly freakish departures from normality in what still purports to be realism.[2] Thus, a deliberate choice of the odd and abnormal for its own sake must be taken into account, along with an addiction to ghost stories and the like, nourished by his zest for Wessex superstitions, which might bring forth surprising issue in conjunction with his belief in an invisible overriding Fate.

"Far from the Madding Crowd" and "A Pair of Blue Eyes" Hardy really discovered "Wessex" in that light and charming picture of rustic life, *Under the Greenwood Tree* (1872), though he did not at once recognize it as the promised land. This brief novel contains just one touch of the irony which was to be the theme of all the rest: Fancy Day, engaged to marry Dick Dewy, is momentarily tempted by the glamour of social superiority into accepting the young vicar; and, when he advises her to confess the act of weakness to Dick, she keeps it for ever secret. Observe Hardy's benevolent cynicism in the nutting episode: "Fancy," he said, "why we be so happy is because there is such full confidence between us." Vicar Maybold perceives that Fancy is "less an angel than a woman." Irony, however, is the burden of *A Pair of Blue Eyes* (1873) from start to finish. *Under the Greenwood Tree* was subtitled "a Rural Painting of the Dutch School," and keeps within that

[1] *Later Years*, 193–194. In an article, "The Science of Fiction" (*Life and Letters*), he speaks of "the need for the exercise of the Dædalian faculty for selection and cunning manipulation."
[2] See a formidable catalogue of old-fashioned melodramatic devices which are basic features, not only in the short stories, but in the main thread of nearly every novel he wrote (Beach, 19).

definition, not trying for any effects beyond the average. In this next novel, however, there is no lack of improbability in the story, though the characters are as ordinary as Hardy's rule demanded. In *A Pair of Blue Eyes* the proprietor of these fascinating orbs is a country girl, a village clergyman's daughter, who has had an innocent escapade with a young fellow, now gone to India as an architect's assistant.[1] Before leaving England, Stephen told the whole story to his friend Knight, an older man whom he venerated as his intellectual and moral guide; but he has never let out his sweetheart's name. Knight happens, however, to be a connexion of Elfride's family—it is a coincidence of quite another colour that he also happens to be the reviewer who cut up Elfride's innocent novel. He comes down to Endelstow, and falls in love with her himself. Stephen is on his way back from India, where he has secured big commissions and is making money, when accident throws Elfride into Knight's arms. She has not the courage to make a clean breast of her previous affair, and her peculiar charm for Knight is that she has had no previous affairs. Hence when it all comes out the consequences are serious: this second engagement is broken off. But the grand stroke of irony is yet to fall. Knight and Stephen meet, and find that they are rivals. Yet Elfride has done nothing wrong; she has only been timid and inexperienced. Both men have a revulsion of feeling, and, unknown to the other, each hurries off to Cornwall to claim her as his bride. There are a number of funereal omens in the previous course of events, but the final taunt outdoes them all in cynical humour. The lovers travel down by the same train; they catch sight of each other, and at length ride in the same carriage. On the train there is a dark, mysterious van, about which they speculate. The van contains the mortal remains of Elfride, who has been broken-hearted over each of them in turn but has married neither, and is now the dead wife of another man. The chain of events leading to this climax is hardly sound. If

---

[1] The story is full of recollections of Hardy's experiences of church restoration in Cornwall in 1870. Stephen and his father were sketched from men he knew; Knight is the character most like himself (*Early Life*, 96–97). There had been four or five architects in *Desperate Remedies*. He still had to rely a good deal on actual reminiscence.

it is credible that Elfride would have kept silence in spite of every encouragement to unburden herself of such a peccadillo, it is hard to believe that in her desperation she would have written to her greatest enemy imploring silence, in a letter that would almost certainly be used against her. Stephen's successful concealment of his homely parentage when he visits his native place, as a stranger come to inspect the church professionally, is a trifle compared with so many far-fetched coincidences, which envenom the tragic circumstance and bring affairs to the deadliest point. Stephen and Elfride making love on her earlier admirer's grave, the knell greeting Stephen when he comes back to the village, the family meeting in the sepulchral chamber, the ill-timed discovery of the lost earrings on which such a tale of previous love-making hung, and the fall of the tower just as Elfride had told Knight that he was her strong tower and hope against the enemy, all bring to mind the taste for ghoulishness noted in Thomas Hardy.[1]

"Far from the Madding Crowd" *Far from the Madding Crowd* (1874) breathes irony in its very title. It is the tragi-comedy of rural life, pathos mingling with its opposite and settling at last into a measure of chastened happiness for the principal characters, with the main stress, however, on the furious passions, thwarted purposes, and shattering griefs which are the reality behind the idyllic calm of the pastoral scene. The pictorial method of narration which was to prove so apt at conveying Hardy's sense that the particular drama envisaged was part of the general human drama, nay, of the drama in which are implicated all things that breathe, and that all this is part of the mighty drama of the universe, is now fully developed. The natural scenery is no mere setting, but an integral element, human activity being thus shown in the grip of vaster forces, a life within a greater life, part of the infinite.[2] Hence, when in a brief first chapter

---

[1] The famous episode of Knight's duel with the Cliff without a Name, and his rescue by Elfride from "Nature's treacherous attempt to put an end to him," magnificent as it is in imaginative reach, will not stand criticism from one familiar with such situations, the quality of holds, the margin of safety, etc. It is a pity Hardy went into so much detail!

[2] It would be worth while comparing Hardy's pictorial method with De Quincey's, *e.g.* "The Spanish Military Nun," "On Murder, considered as one of the Fine Arts," or "The English Mail-Coach—The Glory of Motion," "The Vision of Sudden Death,"

he has introduced, in the same pictorial fashion, the one steadfast character in his group of passionate, unruly, capricious children of the soil, Farmer Oak, and then the giddy Bathsheba Everdene, still a prey to "woman's prescriptive infirmity," yet plastic enough to make in the end a sortable mate for Oak— after all this he devotes the best part of a second chapter to one of his great pictorial evocations of the face of nature, intimating that the stage is not limited to this little corner of Wessex but is boundless, that in these localized passions and conflicts man is to be seen fighting with destiny, and that the rustic protagonists are no humbler or less worthy of regard than the heroes and monarchs of more grandiose tragedy.

The poetry of motion is a phrase much in use, and to enjoy the epic form of that gratification it is necessary to stand on a hill at a small hour of the night, and having first expanded with a sense of difference from the mass of civilized mankind, who are dreamwrapt and disregardful of all such proceedings at this time, long and quietly watch your stately progress through the stars. After such a nocturnal reconnoitre it is hard to get back to earth, and to believe that the consciousness of such majestic speeding is derived from a tiny human frame.

Even Oak, who is without æsthetic sensibilities and regards the sky appreciatively as a useful instrument, is for a moment impressed "with the speaking loneliness of the scene, or rather with the complete abstraction from all its compass of the sights and sounds of man."

Human shapes, interferences, troubles, and joys were all as if they were not, and there seemed to be on the shaded hemisphere of the globe no sentient being save himself; he could fancy them all gone round to the sunny side.

Hardy's characters are rarely if ever moved, as he is moved, by the beauty of the environment in which he situates them;

"Dream-Fugue." George Moore said that the pictorial method is "what differentiates the literature of the nineteenth century from that of all preceding centuries," it is the effort "on the part of the pen to compete with the brush." Balzac, he says, was the inventor of the method, "and the most dexterous exponent; but hardly a single great writer in France and England has refrained from the new method of expression" (*Impressions and Opinions*—"Balzac").

he sometimes rebukes the more philistine and unresponsive for their crass insensibility. But he shows them unconsciously influenced; that, indeed, is the insistent theme in *The Return of the Native*, and in many chapters of *Tess of the d'Urbervilles*.

Some melo-drama

In the present case, Hardy's straining after the uncommon brings in some melodrama. This appears in the character and the doings of Sergeant Troy, that disturber of the peace, and in Farmer Boldwood, whose personal tragedy is dragged in to clear the air, dissipate illusions, and prepare the harmonious union of Oak and Bathsheba. The tragic catharsis is turned to the benefit of others. Boldwood is the traditional calm, self-disciplined nature stung to infatuation by a woman's capricious blandishments; Troy the rake in a military tunic, selfish and cynical, though not quite unfeeling, a trifle histrionic, and irresistibly debonair. Troy is an emissary of the general malevolence. When Bathsheba gives in to his easy flatteries, "the careless sergeant smiled within himself, and probably the devil smiled from a loop-hole in Tophet, for the moment was the turning-point of a career"; and when, long supposed drowned, he returns to confound Boldwood's chance of happiness on the very point of fulfilment, he appears as "the impersonator of Heaven's persistent irony towards him, who had once before broken in upon his bliss, scourged him, and snatched his delight away." "Troy began to laugh a mechanical laugh: Boldwood recognized him now." Apart from the complications hingeing upon Troy and Boldwood, Hardy relies on what has now become his regular fatalistic machinery. Oak's sanguine expectations are brought to nothing by "malicious hazard"; his flock of two hundred ewes rush through a gap into a chalk-pit, and the savings of a frugal life are dispersed at a blow. He is ruined, but he shows his manhood by the one sentence he utters: "Thank God I am not married: what would *she* have done in the poverty now coming upon me!" A string of further accidents, the fire among the ricks, the storm that nearly destroys Bathsheba's harvest, and the poisoning of the sheep in the clover-field, are fatalistic only in their cumulation, and not more decisive in their consequences than the valentine which in a childish freak she sends to Boldwood. One little mishap often to be utilized in other stories, Fanny Robin's mistake between All Saints' and All Souls', and Sergeant Troy's indefinite postponement of their wedding, falls into this category; whilst the sarcastic comment of the gargoyle, pouring torrents of water on Fanny's grave and washing away the flowers planted by her penitent lover, is another of those ghoulish incidents which Hardy relished. Fanny's story is the common one of a village girl's seduction by a soldier; but Hardy raises it to a dignity superior to the commonplace trials of her mistress Bathsheba. The pathos of the long night when Fanny crawled half-dying to the Casterbridge workhouse is curiously ennobled by the intervention of the dog, that mysterious creature who seemed "the ideal embodiment of canine greatness" and to personify the solemnity of night. Throwing half her weight on the animal she struggled on to the workhouse gate, where she is found by the watchman in the morning and lifted in by two women.

"How did she get here?" said one of the women.

"The Lord knows," said the other.

"There is a dog outside," murmured the overcome traveller. "Where is he gone? He helped me."

"I stoned him away," said the man.

Hardy is rarely cynical, if that is the word for the bitter indignation in his reticence here.[1] Fanny has her revenge when Bathsheba settles the question whether there are two of them by unscrewing the coffin and finding herself face to face with the dead girl and her babe. She is surprised by her husband, and asks sarcastically if this is someone he knows.

This is what Troy did. He sank upon his knees with an indefinable union of remorse and reverence upon his face, and, bending over Fanny Robin, gently kissed her, as one would kiss an infant asleep to avoid awakening it.

It is more than Bathsheba can bear. "The revulsion from

---

[1] Hardy's tenderness towards dumb animals comes out often in this novel; for instance, in the little incident of the toad which Oak found "humbly travelling across the path," one of many portents of the mighty rain about to fall and put Bathsheba's corn in jeopardy. "Oak took it up, thinking it might be better to kill the creature to save it from pain; but finding it uninjured, he placed it among the grass."

her indignant mood a little earlier, when she had meditated upon compromised honour, forestallment, eclipse in maternity by another, was violent and entire. All that was forgotten in the simple and still strong attachment of wife to husband."

"Don't—don't kiss them! Oh, Frank, I can't bear it, I can't! I love you better than she did: kiss me too, Frank— kiss me! *You will, Frank, kiss me too!*"

Bathsheba is made of ingredients that are not usually held good enough for heroines: Hardy analyses her sometimes so candidly that the effect is almost satirical. Anyhow, she is thoroughly alive, and she is an epitome of her sex. It is also safe to say at the end that she will now make Gabriel happy, which she might have failed to do had he won her earlier.

"The Return of the Native" *The Return of the Native* (1878) is a confutation of free will. Man is represented as the helpless plaything of invisible powers, ruthless and indifferent, whose checks and caprices fall lightest on such as are too passive and bovine to struggle against them or exert the slightest will of their own. These are as happy as man or beast may be, on such an earth as this. Here, on the other hand, is the history of two or three people who are conscious of the dilemma in which Nature has put them, trying fitfully to play their own parts in the life to which they have been condemned; and a sorry drama it is. Every exertion of individual will ends in futility. The pictorial opening of the novel is famous. It introduces the chief character; for in Hardy's stories, Nature, the Earth, Existence, is always a personage, and that chief personage is embodied this time in Egdon Heath, the dark, immemorial environment whose influences control obscurely the lives and destinies of those who dwell contentedly amid its gorsy wildernesses or feel themselves cruelly out of their element there. Egdon Heath symbolizes the whole cosmic order, in which man is but an insignificant particle. And it seems to be alive, to be impassively aware of what these men and these women are doing and suffering.

The place became full of a watchful intentness now; for when other things sank brooding to sleep the heath appeared to awake and listen. Every night its Titanic form seemed to await something; but it had waited thus, unmoved, during so many centuries, through the crises of so many things, that it could only be imagined to await one last crisis—the final overthrow.

Having depicted this eternal, brooding presence with the brush of a seer, Hardy introduces his human characters, in the same pictorial way; they are visualized as objects in the landscape till they make themselves known as animate beings. So Hardy's pen works: to tell what happens and how, he depicts the look and gesture of the doer. And his scenery is not scenery in the ordinary sense, not decoration in purple patches, not mere background, but an integral part of the drama. All is made visible, the landscape and the life going on upon it. And there is no shock in the passage from description to narrative. His pictures of external nature expound the same philosophy, and are of a piece with the story; they have precisely the same meaning. The first character to appear is, not the Native, but another of those who are out of gear with the existing order. "Eustacia Vye was the raw material of a divinity." "She had the passions and instincts which make a model goddess, that is, those which make not quite a model woman." Shallow, sensuous, high-strung, a typical "decadent," she is keenly aware, so far as she herself is concerned, that she is a victim of the perverse dispensation of things. Circumstances have put her in the wrong place; juxtaposition with the heath is the bane of her existence, and by that token everything is wrong. "How I have tried and tried to be a splendid woman, and how destiny has been against me! I do not deserve my lot!" she cries, in a frenzy of bitter revolt. "O the cruelty of putting me into this ill-conceived world! I was capable of much; but I have been injured and blasted and crushed by things beyond my control!" "O how hard it is of Heaven to devise such tortures for me, who have done no harm to Heaven at all!" The heath calls up images of all that contrasts with it—"sunny afternoons on an esplanade, with military bands, officers and gallants around, stood like gilded letters upon the dark tablet of surrounding Egdon."

An environment which would have made a contented woman

Types of dis- illusion- ment

a poet, a suffering woman a devotee, a pious woman a psalmist, even a giddy woman thoughtful, made a rebellious woman saturnine.

She is a Shelleyan creation, in her quarrel with the stern realities and her joy in "what seems"; she yearns for a palace of delight, she would quaff all the moment can give, lest the cup should be snatched from her lips. "Pleasure not known beforehand is half-wasted; to anticipate it is to double it"; and again, "You are sad—never mind what it is—let us only look at what seems." [1]   The morbid Eustacia when she comes on the scene is entangled in a clandestine affair with the local innkeeper Wildeve, a chip of the same sensual block as Troy. Like that other scamp, Wildeve takes advantage of a slip of inadvertency to evade marriage with the simple Thomasin, towards whom he feels indifferent.[2]   From an intrigue that is growing wearisome Eustacia is suddenly roused by the news that Clym Yeobright is coming back to his native place.   He is from Paris, and in her eyes is at once decked with all the glamour of that famed metropolis of pleasure.   But, though Clym also turns out to be one of the disillusioned, his pessimism is of a very different origin from Eustacia's.   It is the hollowness of modern life seen in its most glittering aspects in Paris that has revolted him, and sent him back home with some vague idea of cleansing himself by renewed contact with nature, and of

---

[1] Shelley is often quoted by Hardy.   *The Woodlanders* is full of him.   Fitzpiers rhapsodizes over Grace:

> She moved upon this earth a shape of brightness, etc.
>
> .   .   .   .   .
>
> Towards the load-star of my one desire
> I flitted, like a dizzy moth, etc.

Adonais is quoted also, and Marty South's lament for Giles Winterborne might have been inspired by Demogorgon's epilogue in *Prometheus Unbound*—

> To suffer woes which Hope thinks infinite.

Far from the Madding Crowd, Ethelberta, and other novels have striking quotations, and there are numerous parallels of sentiment, thought, and even expression, which testify to something more than mere congruity of mind.   It may sound fanciful to suggest any parallel between *Jude the Obscure* and *Laon and Cythna*, but some parallel there is, as well as coincidence of view in the indictment of social restrictions, including the marriage laws, the present exclusiveness of universities, etc.

[2] Already besides Troy and Fanny's mishap, there had been the accidental hitch through which Stephen and Elfride were never married, in *A Pair of Blue Eyes*. More will occur in the novels that follow.

evolving some plan of activity worth a man's energies. Clym has in him the makings of an Edward Carpenter, but is as ineffectual as a Richard Jefferies. If he cannot write, he will preach; and his scheme at present is to open a country school, and teach something akin to Rousseau's gospel of nature and simplicity as the antidote to artificial diseases. "All things considered, I can be a trifle less useless here than anywhere else." For his is less a social philosophy than a counsel of despair. It does not appeal to Eustacia.

Take all the varying hates felt by Eustacia Vye towards the heath, and translate them into loves, and you have the heart of Clym. He gazed upon the wide prospect as he walked, and was glad.

Egdon Heath is in his blood; but his nostalgia is as morbid as Eustacia's melancholia, and it cannot turn the sentimental idealist into a man. Though he fancies himself strong and determined, he suffers from paralysis of the will.

They are strangers to each other as yet. Eustacia makes *A* Clym's acquaintance by one of those fantastic devices for which *tragedy* Hardy had a weakness. She dresses herself up as a man, and *of opposite* goes with a party of mummers to the Yeobrights' house to *attitudes* reconnoitre the newcomer. They fall in love; and, although Clym's plan is the last thing in the world Eustacia would ever approve, she feels sure that, once married, she will easily induce him to abandon such a quixotic scheme and take her to Paris. Obviously, any such marriage is foredoomed. The pair are out of sympathy with each other; and, unless one or the other gives way, they will drift further and further apart. This is indeed what happens.

But the growing rift between the wife and husband is not enough for Hardy; he accelerates the pace of events, and embitters the inevitable disaster with a series of accidents most of which would have had the odds against them in average life. That Clym's eyesight should fail, forcing him to give up his educational project, and leaving him with no resource but to earn his living as a labouring man, may be no violation of probability. But the confluence of untoward incidents that usher in the catastrophe is as glaringly the result of deliberate intention as are the cruder coincidences. From one point of view it is fate showing the cloven hoof, from the other it is the author giving events an illicit push. Clym has broken with the mother whom he adores, for she sees through Eustacia and suspects her of still being on improper terms with Wildeve.

But the poor old lady would be glad to break down the estrangement. She sends her son and her daughter Thomasin, now married to Wildeve, fifty pounds apiece, their shares of a legacy. Wildeve encounters the messenger, and wins the money from him at dicing. Sequel, the picturesque scene in which Thomasin's humble adorer, Diggory Venn the reddleman, suddenly appears and challenges Wildeve to another bout, in which chance or destiny lets him win back the whole sum, after they are reduced to casting the dice by the light of glowworms. Even this discomfiture of Wildeve, however, makes matters worse, for Diggory sends all the hundred pounds to Thomasin.

It had not been comprehended by the reddleman that at half-way through the performance the game was continued with the money of another person; and it was an error which afterwards helped to cause more misfortune than treble the loss in money value could have done.

This unfortunate occurrence is followed by the still more unfortunate chance that Wildeve calls on Eustacia and her husband the very afternoon when old Mrs Yeobright has determined to come and make up the misunderstanding with the young couple. He found Clym asleep, and was practically alone with his old flame. Mrs Yeobright knocks: she has seen a woman's face at the window, and she knows that Clym is at home. Eustacia leaves it to her husband to open the door, whilst she is getting rid of Wildeve. Mrs Yeobright waits, and there is no response. She believes her son and his wife have shut her out. Wounded to the soul and worn out with her long walk, she sits down on the heath, and drowsing on a bed of shepherd's thyme is stung by an adder. Clym finds her dying, and learns the truth, and rather more than the truth, from a little boy who has walked with her part of the way, and tells his mother: "That woman asleep there walked along with me to-day; and she said I was to say that I had seed her, and she was a broken-hearted woman and cast off by her son." There is a terrible scene between Clym and his wife, ending in a rupture. Eustacia returns to her old home with her grandfather. Wildeve meanwhile has received a handsome legacy. He entreats her to fly with him; and she, still half hoping her husband will come back to her, gives a conditional assent. Clym has indeed written a letter admitting that he was too severe and asking her to return. But, alas! another chapter of petty accidents intervenes; the letter never reaches her. Eustacia gives the agreed signal, and in a night of drenching rain sets out to join Wildeve. She falls in the dark into the weir-pool. Wildeve hearing the splash plunges in to save her, and both are carried under.

This summary of a well-known story was required to bring out the peculiar nature of Hardy's method in a work so representative of his peculiar genius. Put thus baldly, it all seems a tissue of contrivances for checkmating any possibility of a happy issue for these two beings, symbols of humanity in the hands of some power against which it is vain to contend. This is not a tale of love winning its way in spite of obstacles, or of seduction and its consequences, or of exciting hazards and escapes; it is not one of those stories which the reader follows with eager suspense wondering what will happen next. Hardy's conclusions, as already noted, are implied in the preliminary situation. He states the problem, but the resultant is inevitable; whatever may be the fortuitous course taken by events, they will come to the same thing in the end. Clym and Eustacia's union was foredoomed to woe; if one thing had not gone wrong another would. Each of his greater novels is Thomas Hardy's picture of the general human situation. This is summed up here in the inflexible opposition of inner or of outer circumstances to the desires of two people who would fain be free agents, but can only struggle blindly and convulsively in the net of destiny in which they are caught. Whether the hostile influences are external to man, and even to be termed supernatural, is for the philosophic reader to

Symbolism in scenery, characters, incidents

interpret, who may pronounce them to be simply the composite result of man's weaknesses and accumulated blunders and the recalcitrance of brute matter.   Whatever it be, Hardy shows this arbiter in final control.   Fate, or providence, or circumstance, has put Eustacia, his tragic heroine, in the wrong place; Clym fails to deliver her.   Nothing they can do will liberate them or provide a happy and worthy existence.   Hence their history consists of painful stresses rather than of actions, tensions between them and their environment, tensions between each other.   The scenery is obviously symbolical of the predicament in which humanity finds itself.   But the incidents, also, especially those which seem like the interferences of an overriding fate, are equally symbolical, and necessary to Hardy's statement of the case.   Though there is much talk about the general predicament of mankind, there is otherwise little evidence to substantiate it.   The reader may assent wholeheartedly to the sentiment that times are not fair, and that Egdon Heath is a far more appropriate setting for the human drama to-day than any Vale of Tempe could be.

The time seems near, if it has not actually arrived, when the chastened sublimity of a moor, a sea, or a mountain will be all of nature that is absolutely in keeping with the moods of the more thinking among mankind.

The reader may indeed feel sure that a marriage such as Clym and Eustacia's, nay, such ignorance of the realities and such flimsy aspirations as Eustacia's, spell disaster.   But the graphic symbolism by which the unseen powers, whatever they be, are shown fitfully interfering, or engaged in a steady and inexorable process of causation, is as necessary to Hardy's picture as was Flaubert's relentless analysis of mind and motive applied to Madame Bovary, a parallel but essentially different case from Eustacia Vye's.   Hardy's epilogue to the tragedy is the paragraph on Clym's "wrinkled mind" in the aftertime.

He did sometimes think he had been ill-used by fortune, so far as to say that to be born is a palpable dilemma, and that instead of men aiming to advance in life with glory they should calculate how to retreat out of it without shame.   But that he and his had been sarcastically and pitilessly handled in having such irons thrust into their souls he did not maintain long. It is usually so, except with the sternest of men. Human beings, in their generous endeavour to construct a hypothesis that shall not degrade a First Cause, have always hesitated to conceive a dominant power of lower morality than their own; and, even while they sit down and weep by the waters of Babylon, invent excuses for the oppression which prompts their tears.

Between his more solid and serious novels, Hardy used to let his brain lie fallow, or gave it a little recreation. Between *Far from the Madding Crowd* and *The Return of the Native* he wrote what in a later classification he termed one of his "Novels of Ingenuity," *The Hand of Ethelberta: a comedy in chapters* (1876); then came a pair of his "Romances and Fantasies," *The Trumpet Major* (1879) and *Two on a Tower* (1882), with another ingenuity, *A Laodicean* (1881), before he braced himself to the sterner task of *The Mayor of Casterbridge* (1886). Hardy put *A Pair of Blue Eyes* and his last novel but one, *The Well-Beloved*, among the romances and fantasies, and *Desperate Remedies* among the novels of ingenuity. Ethelberta is his Becky Sharp. She is an adventuress of humble origin who makes her way into society, fights down the social prejudices which she, like her author, abhors, and saves herself in the nick of time from losing every material prize by marrying a rich old sensualist. Hardy "took no interest in manners, but in the substance of life only"[1]; society bored him, and the novel of manners he disdained. Hence he did not shine when he deserted Wessex for those West End drawing-rooms that he was glad to know nothing about. A better study of a woman also obliged to rely upon herself is Paula Power, in *A Laodicean, or the Castle of the De Stanceys*, which is a novel of love, rivalry, and underhand intrigue, almost as ingenious as *Desperate Remedies*. *The Trumpet Major*, which preceded this, is that rare thing among Hardy's novels, one which is all good nature and happiness, though, oddly enough, the time pictured is that of the Napoleonic terror, and a French landing is momently

Novels of Ingenuity" and Romances

---

[1] *Early Life*, 137. He used even to take notes of "his experiences of social life, though doing it had always been a drudgery to him" (*Later Years*, 66).

apprehended somewhere on the south coast, where the scene is laid.   Hardy was already amassing the immense and minute knowledge of this period which he was to put to such excellent account in *The Dynasts*.   He evidently knows all about George the Third's visit to his favourite watering-place, Weymouth, at a date when camps, marches, and great reviews, going on in the background, throw the peace and quietude into higher relief.   His sailor lover is a jovial creation; and the brother who stands aside and lets him win the girl they both love is sensitively drawn, even if the magnanimity be a little forced. The bullying, swaggering Festus Derryman is good farce, and his miserly uncle, though near the border-line, good comedy.

"Two on a Tower"   *Two on a Tower: a romance*, might well have been placed with the novels of ingenuity, though the object of the plot is not sensation, but to put the characters in positions with regard to each other as extraordinary as they are ironical.   The tower figuring in the title is where a young astronomer watches the stars, and where a lady of higher degree, who hopes and believes that her brutal husband is dead, makes love to him, much her junior.   Hardy sees these two as infinitely small against the stellar universe; but he does not fall into the astronomical fallacy of confusing scales of incommensurable magnitudes, for the tiny human pair, he hints, are of the more spiritual importance.[1]   How they marry, only to learn that she was not yet a widow at the time, and how when free she lets him go before she knows that she is to have a child by him, and is left with no resource but to accept another suitor, a bishop, who speedily discovers why she listened to his addresses: these are but the leading incidents in a story awkwardly designed to show human creatures the sport of untoward and unforeseeable circumstances —fatalism working openly and unashamed.   Hardy palpably overreached himself this time with his elaborate plotting and laying the blame on his mock-providence; but he made some

[1] It is the terrors of the sky that thrill and fascinate St Cleeve, and sometimes give him nightmares: "if . . . you are restless and anxious about the future, study astronomy at once.   Your troubles will be reduced amazingly.   But your study will reduce them in a singular way, by reducing the importance of everything.   So that the science is still terrible, even as a panacea.   It is quite impossible to think at all adequately of the sky—of what the sky substantially is, without feeling it as a juxtaposed nightmare" (c. iv.).

amends by conceiving such an heroic and devoted love as Viviette's for Swithin, a fickle person and quite unworthy of such greatness of soul. He treated a perilous theme with such disregard of cherished reticences in sexual matters then, dragging in a bishop too, that there was an immediate outcry; a scandal which the unorthodoxy of his general views on the universe failed to provoke was to be aggravated by more and more offences, till they culminated in *Tess of the d'Urbervilles* and *Jude the Obscure*.[1]

In his next novel, Hardy tried to dispense with the crude fatalistic machinery of *Two on a Tower*, external events persistently interfering with human intentions, and to imagine a man bringing sorrow and disaster on himself through his own defects of character. *The Mayor of Casterbridge* (1886) reverts in some measure to the causative structure of George Eliot's novels, which were expositions of determinism, her characters bearing their destinies within them in the master-tendencies of their appetites and wills. The conflict is transferred to the inner arena, and the adversary is now ancient habits, rooted impulses, uneradicated vices. In the upshot, Henchard is reduced to impotence: the destiny within him triumphs, and he is humbled to the dust. It is not so much that free will is an illusion, autonomy of the self a figment, as that every free act is turned to derision, through the effects of bygone failures, and of fresh misfortunes that no foresight or effort can avert. For the habit of detecting malice behind every accident was too strong for Hardy to keep within the limits proposed, and *The Mayor of Casterbridge* is as bitter an exposure of "the machinery contrived by the gods" for stultifying mortal activities as any of the preceding novels.[2] It is clear, however,

Fatalism transferred from without to within

---

[1] The writer can remember, however, how, long before *Tess* and *Jude*, worthy and intelligent people were apprehensive of the results on susceptible readers of this denial of Providence, and were upset by Hardy's free-thinking and heterodox scale of values. It is easy to fancy that Meredith was thinking of Hardy in *One of our Conquerors* (1891), where he keeps asking, Is Nature our appetites? Take, *e.g.*, the following: Nataly's "intellect and her reverence clashed. They clash to the end of time if we persist in regarding the Spirit of Life as a remote externe, who plays the human figures to bring about this or that issue, instead of being inside us, within us, our breath, if we will; marking on us where at each step we sink to the animal, mount to the divine, we and ours who follow, offspring of body or mind" (xvi.).

[2] "A partir de 1887" (actually 1886) "le mécanisme extérieur qui régnait dans les romans de Hardy laisse au déterminisme intérieur une place de plus en plus grande;

that he thought he had succeeded in presenting a man whose egotism and obstinacy are the sole agents of his ruin. But, apart from these extraneous interventions, the odds are piled up beforehand. Henchard is not a fair specimen of normal, albeit unregenerate man. He is the deliberate embodiment of a vice or overwhelming propensity, combined with fatuous self-confidence, such as Æschylus made the sure instrument of tragedy. Hardy's fatalism, in short, is simply transferred from outside to inside. Whereas he was wont to weight the dice against his characters in their external circumstances, this time he weights the individual himself. Henchard is one who can never master an insubordinate temperament. He has striking abilities, many virtues, he is generous and soft-hearted; but the ungovernable devil in him keeps breaking out, and, though he knows his own failings, no one better, secures the upper hand in the direst emergencies. This is no study of gradual moral corruption, like Flaubert's of Madame Bovary or George Eliot's of Lydgate. It is the pursuit of a man's original sin to the bitter end, like *Jude the Obscure*, where, however, there is more attention to the inner life; here the psychology is rudimentary.

Super-erogatory mis-chances Those chief characters of Hardy's which symbolize the human situation are obviously of conceptual origin. His philosophy precedes and determines his fiction; he is the contrary to Meredith, who builds up a philosophy in his novels as he goes. Whatever residue of spontaneity Hardy allows them, it is the barest leavening. These characters are the terms in which the case is to be argued; and, since the conclusion is manifestly predetermined, the argument is never conducted quite fairly. In the present instance, the argument is further sophisticated: the devil inhabiting Henchard is aided and abetted at every turn by that other devil, now a rather dilapidated bogy, the perversity of material circumstance. Things are always against him, always lying in wait to trip him up. His evil self cannot succeed single-handed in ruining Henchard; the well-worn

les forces morales s'affirmant avec une puissance croissante; le facteur psychologique regagne son importance; dans *Jude le déshérité*, il détermine rigoureusement les événements. On verra d'ailleurs à mesure que cet élément prend toute son ampleur, comment lui aussi est dévié par le parti-pris pessimiste de l'auteur" (Cazamian, i. 413).

coincidences and other paraphernalia have to be produced from the same old drawer. What Elizabeth-Jane, the daughter who so distressingly proves not to be his, calls "the persistence of the unforeseen" begins early, and comes to an end only with his life. The sale of Henchard's wife in a fit of drunken savagery may be accepted as the wild act such a man might commit, before he saw the ruin impending and changed his courses. That happened long ago. When the drama opens, it is forgotten history, which he never dreams will come to light with fatal effects upon his fortunes, now that he is at the pinnacle of glory as the richest citizen and the mayor of Casterbridge. But it does come out, and combines with other events in the most sinister concatenation. The very day that Farfrae, soon to be Henchard's friend and partner and later his rival in both business and love, arrives for the first time in Casterbridge, it is he who notices Elizabeth-Jane serving as a waiting-maid in a public-house, an incident which has to be lived down when she is presented to local society as the mayor's stepdaughter. She has just arrived at Casterbridge with her mother, the woman sold eighteen years ago, before Henchard gave up drinking and became respectable. The mayor now marries his deserted wife, and everything goes smoothly until she leaves him a widower. On her deathbed she gives him a letter, not to be opened till the day Elizabeth-Jane marries. But Henchard, left alone in the world, cannot refrain from confessing his old escapade and telling the young woman that she is his daughter, and not Newson's, the man whom her mother married when he had cast her off. She is surprised, but not wounded in her feelings, and agrees to take his name. The very hour of his elation at having his child really and truly restored to him, Henchard unseals the packet, and discovers that Elizabeth-Jane is Newson's daughter after all, his own having died in babyhood. Crushing is the irony when the girl next morning comes to embrace him, and promises to be more to him than a wife could have been. As time goes on, he cannot help treating her coolly, and at length she cannot bear his indifference, and goes to live as companion with a lady recently arrived in Casterbridge. That lady is no other than Lucetta, Henchard's

quondam mistress, who has come into money, and hopes
Henchard will now marry her. And why not? But things
are too perverse. Farfrae and Lucetta fall in love, at the very
moment when Lucetta's fortune would have saved Henchard
from bankruptcy. By a stroke of savage irony, it is decreed that
Henchard should one day rescue a young woman from a
dangerous bull. The young woman proves to be Lucetta.
Will she as a slight recompense come with him to his chief
creditor, and say they are about to be married? This is the
one thing Lucetta cannot do: she became Farfrae's wife that
morning.

There are other blows and other mishaps, letters going astray
and falling into the most malicious hands. More than this, far
more, Henchard's paternal, more than a lover's love for
Elizabeth-Jane is crossed and torn and tortured by doubts and
fears and the unexpected return of Newson. His one remaining
earthly bond is strained and almost broken. No wonder he
determines to wash his hands of life "from his perceptions of
its contrarious inconsistencies." It is a great and simple tragedy
complicated with hackneyed and unnecessary corroborations.
The pity is that it cannot be disengaged from these excrescences,
and that the pathos of Henchard's end and the simple goodness
of Elizabeth-Jane cannot stand alone in their beauty and
modest grandeur. As Herman Melville said, "Disaster,
heroically encountered, is man's happy ending"; Henchard at
all events dies a hero.[1]

"The   There are only a few touches of rural charm in the austere
Wood-   grandeur of *The Mayor of Casterbridge*; but *The Woodlanders*
landers"   (1887), which immediately followed, is full of it. The setting
in the Hintock woods is as idyllic as that of the Mellstock
hamlets in *Under the Greenwood Tree*; and the tragic portion,

---

[1] In what is still one of the best studies of the novelist, *Thomas Hardy, penseur et
artiste*, by F. A. Hedgcock (1910), it is contended that Hardy turned over a new leaf
with *The Mayor of Casterbridge*, entirely abandoning the plot-machinery that seemed
to be set in action by powers outside man. "Il serait difficile de formuler un pareil
reproche au sujet du roman que nous venons d'analyser," c.a.d. *The Mayor of Casterbridge*. "Là, on ne remarque pas de ces curieuses combinaisons d'évènements qui,
dans les œuvres antérieures, accablaient les personnages," etc. One is sorry to disagree
with such a critic as Dr Hedgcock; but even his own analysis demonstrates sufficiently
that the curious combinations are as rampant as ever.

the story of Giles Winterborne and Marty South, which through the exigencies of a romantic plot is relegated to a subordinate place that it does not deserve, is as beautifully and profoundly wedded to the natural surroundings as was that of Clym Yeobright and Eustacia Vye. The woodlands are much more than mere background; they are the very stage of life, and have the same vital part in the drama as Egdon Heath in *The Return of the Native*. The lives and the environment respond to each other as the mind to the body. Here again, by dint of his pictorial method of telling the story, Hardy's people seem to emerge as items in the landscape; like the birds, the sylvan beasts, and the trees, they gradually become distinct, but they remain Nature's children, with an insight born in them into Nature's life.

The casual glimpses which the ordinary population bestowed upon that wondrous world of sap and leaves called the Hintock woods had been with these two, Giles and Marty, a clear gaze. They had been possessed of its finer mysteries as of commonplace knowledge; had been able to read its hieroglyphs as ordinary writing; to them the sights and sounds of night, winter, wind, storm, amid those dense boughs, which had to Grace a touch of the uncanny, and even of the supernatural, were simple occurrences, whose origin, continuance, and laws they foreknew. They had planted together, and together they had felled; together they had, with the run of the years, mentally collected those remoter signs and symbols which seen in few were of runic obscurity, but all together made an alphabet. From the light lashing of the twigs upon their faces when brushing through them in the dark, they could pronounce upon the species of the tree whence they stretched; from the quality of the wind's murmur through a bough, they could in like manner name its sort afar off. They knew by a glance at a trunk if its heart were sound, or tainted with incipient decay; and by the state of its upper twigs the stratum that had been reached by its roots. The artifices of the seasons were seen by them from the conjuror's own point of view, and not from that of the spectator." [1]

Marty said of Giles after he was gone, "He could speak in a

[1] Chap. xliv.

tongue that nobody else knew—not even my father, though he
came nearest knowing—the tongue of the trees and fruits and
flowers themselves." These two peasants are Hardy's noblest
impersonations of moral endurance and pure unselfishness. All
that the rest of the story has to do with them is to tell how they
were separated for ever, this pair, born such perfect mates for
each other. The rest of it is a commonplace love-tale, good
enough to eke out a three-volume novel, but fiction of a totally
different order from the solemn idyll of Marty's unrequited
love. There are three grades of characters in Hardy's novels:
first, those who are protagonists of the whole human drama;
then, the people in contact with them or who have some part
in their affairs; these are cogs in the machinery and of small
interest in themselves; and lastly, the rustic bystanders, who
provide comic relief, but also fulfill a much more important
function. Their services in making the machinery run smoothly
and perspicuously are invaluable, and they also help to bring
out not only the immediate but also the ulterior significance
of all that is taking place. In a sense, they represent Hardy
himself.[1] They are quiet but deeply interested observers who
see more of what is going on than the gentlefolks are aware, and
they are continually dropping shrewd comments. Diggory
Venn, in *The Return of the Native*, is a conspicuous example.
Thomasin's tutelary genius turns himself into a regular spy and
detective, watching over her affairs. He knows all that is
happening, before and behind the scenes, and through him the
reader obtains a perfect understanding of the most complicated
and mysterious occurrences. The protagonists are usually of
a superior class to the peasants. In *The Woodlanders* they are
peasants themselves, but protagonists of what is ostensibly the
underplot. Ostensibly, the foremost place is allotted to Grace
Melbury and the local medical man, Fitzpiers, who cuts out
poor Giles, marries Grace, and still carries on his affair with
Mrs Charmond. Grace is the hinge on which everything
pivots; but she is of trifling interest in herself. Fitzpiers is

---

[1] This view is confirmed by the analogy of *The Dynasts*. There the Pities and the
Ironies are counterparts of the rustic chorus, intermediaries of the author, and interpreters of the cosmic drama to the spectator, *i.e.* to man.

the ordinary sensual amorist, and Mrs Charmond simply the frail, sentimental lady who falls a victim, or the reverse, to the man of such a stamp. Hardy evidently thought he had produced a study of some psychological value in Grace—"this impressionable creature, who combined modern nerves with primitive feelings, and was doomed by such co-existence to be numbered among the distressed, and to take her scourgings to their exquisite extremity." But she is almost a nullity, and interests no one except as the girl that happened to fascinate Giles, who watches over her even more steadily and unflinchingly than Diggory Venn over Thomasin, and, unlike the reddleman and Farmer Oak, does not get his reward. It might be pleaded that *The Woodlanders*, subplot and all, is a drama of character and nemesis. Such grief as all of them come to is due to their yielding the reins of life to their passions or their weakness. Grace is timid and vain, Fitzpiers unprincipled, Giles shortsighted and obstinate, in spite of his primitive greatness and chivalry. Mr Melbury, Grace's father, has his faults, and Mrs Charmond many. But all this is of minor import measured against the intrinsic grandeur of Giles Winterborne's selfimmolation and Marty's grief.

"If ever I forget your name let me forget home and heaven!
. . . But no, no, my love, I never can forget 'ee; for you was a good man, and did good things!"

The pitiable anticlimax by which Grace, for whom Giles Winterborne died, is after all handed over to Fitzpiers, may most charitably be put down to the imperative demand, in the days of serials and three-volume novels, for so-called poetic justice, the regular euphemism for "a happy ending." [1]

---

[1] *Far from the Madding Crowd, The Hand of Ethelberta, Two on a Tower, A Laodicean,* and even *The Return of the Native,* suffered more or less from this handicap. Most of Hardy's novels appeared first in magazines, and he had to adapt them to editorial anxieties for the tender feelings of readers. His general practice was to restore excised passages when the book appeared in volume-form. But he had to earn his living, he had to be read; and allowance must be made for the limitations and the sentimental tastes to which he had to bow. The general effect upon fiction of that day of the circulating library and the requirement that a novel should fill three volumes of a regulation length, and be more or less written to a formula, would make a chapter in itself. It was a similar convention that gave the Royal Academy so many huge canvases that were fondly supposed to be works of art.

CHAPTER II

HARDY'S LATER WORK

His short   AFTER *The Mayor of Casterbridge* chance plays a diminishing
stories   part in Hardy's novels.   There is only one instance of any
moment in *The Woodlanders* of those malign conjunctions
which seemed to him typical of the way the world goes.   The
person on whose life Giles Winterborne's leasehold has depended
dies before that lovelorn young man takes steps to secure a
renewal; and, as he has just chanced to offend Mrs Charmond
who could have extended the holding for his lifetime, Giles
loses his houses, with the result that he loses Grace Melbury.
A brace or two of similar mishaps have fatal consequences in
Tess of the d'Urbervilles.   But such things now occur chiefly
in his short stories, many of which were written long before
they appeared in *Wessex Tales* (1888), *A Group of Noble Dames*
(1891), *Life's Little Ironies* (1894), and the round dozen headed
A Changed Man (1913).   These far-fetched contingencies pass
muster in a tale, where as a rule they arrive singly, and are
among those remarkable things which may reasonably be
considered as making a tale worth telling.   A tale is an account
of something noteworthy that came to pass, and verisimilitude
in the characters and other details is one of the principal means
of convincing the reader that it did come to pass.   But, if
singly, they come again and again in different tales.   Clym's
sentiment that "Life is a thing to put up with" is the continual
burden of *Wessex Tales* and the *Ironies*; and the anecdotes of
long ago told by the antiquaries in *A Group of Noble Dames*
seem to attest that it has always been the same.   But there is
no escaping the reflection that a painter of the human scene
who thinks the existing dispensation fundamentally unjust,
and that it is his business to display it in its true colours, should

52

be careful to show that the wrongs are the result of general and
invariable causes; whereas Hardy's catastrophes are strangely
fortuitous, and, worse still, seem due to the capricious snares
of some treacherous foe.[1] However much he believed in the
exceptional as the richest source of interest in fiction, the place
for it was not just where verisimilitude is most strictly a virtue.
Surely, if the world were as consistently evil as he makes out,
there would be no need for this continual straining of the laws
of wont and probability. Though nearly all centre in the idea
of life's irony, the stories are fairly miscellaneous. Many are
expanded anecdotes or traditional tales, or the sort of good
story picked up somewhere as worth treasuring, when recast in
a shapely form. A number are nothing else than abridged
novels, unless they are perfunctory sketches for novels that
were never written. Not many could be set beside the masterpieces of this particular craft. Compared with Hawthorne,
Maupassant, Chekhov, Kipling, and a dozen others, Hardy
shows himself artless and halting: he often ought to have done
better, put in more point, strengthened his effects. Only a
few reach anything like the level of his best novels. *A Group
of Noble Dames* is the least heterogeneous, though *Life's Little
Ironies* seeks consistently to distil the essence of his philosophy
of life in a series of disillusioning sequels to fair beginnings,
with the antidote studiously appended in a bunch of stories
uproariously comic.

There is nothing finer in *Wessex Tales* or the subsequent "*Wessex
gatherings* than "The Three Strangers," a compact little drama *Tales*"
which at Barrie's suggestion he adapted for the theatre in a
one-act play, *The Three Wayfarers*. The escaped sheep-
stealer, followed not long after by the hangman, actually on his

<hr>

[1] The first half of a valuable study, *Le Pessimisme de Thomas Hardy*, by Louise
de Ridder-Barzin (1932), largely consists of an account, often tabulated in long notes,
of such mischievous coincidences, down to *The Mayor of Casterbridge* (pp. 10-11).
Dr Ridder-Barzin confirms the view already stated that this novel is as flagrant an
example of such fatalism as the preceding novels, *pace* Dr Hedgcock. Hardy saw, not
simply blind hazard, but cruelty and derision in these interventions of some occult
power (p. 26). The changes in his philosophy are traced; but it is impossible to agree
that "Hap," "ce poème de jeunesse, . . . nous montre que, sur ce point essentiel, la
pensée de Hardy n'a point varié et qu'il est demeuré fidèle au sentiment qui se précisait
en lui aux environs de ses vingt-cinq ans." "Hap" is definitely blind chance (see
above, p. 17), and not the determinism of his final phase of thought.

way to string him up next morning, who come in out of the weather to the christening-party merry-making round the fire in a shepherd's cottage on the Wessex downs; and finally the condemned man's brother, on his way to bid him a last farewell, who opens the door and is thunderstruck to see these unlikely partners hobnobbing over a flagon of mead; make a grotesque scene such as Franz Hals would have gloried in putting on canvas. Never did Hardy's pictorial method stand him in better stead. The grotesque is followed by the gruesome. The ghastliness of the stigma, in "The Withered Arm," imprinted in nightmare on a wife's arm by the poor seduced woman whom she has supplanted, and cured by the miraculous touch of a hanged man's warm flesh, is heightened by horrors of Hardy's own devising.[1] The hanged man is the unhappy son of her own husband and the woman whom he deserted, and she learns the dreadful truth when the three face each other over the corpse. "Fellow-Townsmen" and "Interlopers at the Knap" are undeveloped novelettes, and would have made good "Ironies," as the gist of the former may illustrate. Mr Barnet marries a wife whom he speedily detests, having taken "no" for an answer too precipitately from the woman whom he really loves. The moment he becomes a widower, he offers himself to his old love. He is half-an-hour too late: she has just accepted the old friend to whom he had recommended her for the care of his children.

The events that had, as it were, dashed themselves together into one half-hour of this day showed that curious refinement of cruelty in their arrangement which often proceeds from the bosom of the whimsical god at other times known as blind Circumstance.

Nor is this the end. After wandering about the globe for several years, Barnet comes back to find her a widow. They are elderly people now, yet he asks her to marry him. She refuses, and again he takes "no" for an answer, and returns to his hotel. But on second thoughts she drops him an affectionate

---

[1] The magic stigma and the cure by contact with a hanged man's neck are relics of the same old superstitions current in Wessex that Hardy drew upon in *The Return of the Native*, *Tess of the d'Urbervilles*, and many other places.

line, and hopes he will pay her another visit.   Alas! Barnet has
departed; she never sees him again.   The last piece of the set
is the mirthful tale of a smuggling parish in days long gone by,
"The Distracted Preacher."

Comic relief is far to seek in *A Group of Noble Dames*, in which *" A*
the story usually turns upon itself at a certain point, and the *Group of*
feelings and motives of the various parties towards each other *Noble*
flow in exactly the contrary direction: this is the tragic irony. *Dames"*
and
"The first Countess of Wessex," to escape a husband thrust *" Life's*
upon her by her father, goes so far in her desperation as to infect *Little*
herself with smallpox.   But the man she has chosen to run off *Ironies"*
with is a craven who shrinks from her embrace, whilst Reynard
proves himself a hero.   He is not afraid to kiss the lips that
kissed the plague-stricken villager.   She is blithe to go back to
her husband.   Ghoulishness rises to a climax in "Barbara of
the House of Grebe."   Barbara worshipped her handsome first
husband, till he was hideously disfigured by an accident, and
from an Antinous became a monster.   She hates her second
husband, who cures her aversion, however, by painting the
marble statue of her first love in all the horrors of his deformity
and setting it by her bed.   "The Marchioness of Stonehenge"
goes to the extreme of tortuous plot-work.   The earl's daughter
loves her father's steward and weds him in secret.[1]   One night
he suddenly drops dead in her chamber.   She has the body
smuggled to a graveyard; and then the high-born lady discovers
that she is with child.   How she persuades a cottage girl to
confess to a love-affair, and pass as the dead man's widow and
mother of his child, produces one of those situations that
Hardy loved.   He no doubt also enjoyed his postscript, in
which the grown-up son is offered the choice between the
mother who bore him and the mother who loved and brought
him up.   Just such another tragic reversal of the situation
forms the pith of "The Lady Mottisfont"; in short, all alike
are grim and sardonic.   As to the characters, they are drawn
in the shallow lines suited to the anecdote; and the general
style is curiously simple and plain, smacking of the antiquarian
field-club, Hardy having kept to the illusion of an impromptu

[1] See Beach (14), on Hardy's addiction to secret marriages.

batch of tales that had stuck in the memory. In *Life's Little Ironies*, all the pathetic stories—that is, the ironies—are grouped together, and the funny ones are put under the separate head of "A few Crusted Characters"—a good instance of Hardy's habit of engrossing his mind with one sentiment at a time. The ironies are of one pattern: human hopes and efforts turned to derision by the unexpected sequel, though not here, as a rule, by anything attributable to external malice. The irony is bitter enough, however, in such a tale as "For Conscience Sake." A man tries to make reparation to the woman whom he betrayed many years ago; but by marrying her he frustrates his and her daughter's impending marriage. Aching from his wife's reproaches, he sees no remedy but to disappear. "A Tragedy of Two Ambitions" gives a foretaste of *Jude the Obscure*. The sons of a village tradesman, who has consumed their little inheritance in drink, make their way nevertheless, more successfully than Jude, one to be a clergyman, the other headmaster of a school. The ne'er-do-well father comes on the scene, and public shame stares them in the face, at the moment when their sister is about to marry a wealthy squire. The old scapegrace tumbles into a mill-leet, and they do not lift a finger to save him. They have escaped disgrace; but at what a price! They ruminate over it together:

"To have *endured* the cross, *despising* the shame—there lay greatness! But now I often feel that I should like to put an end to trouble here in this self-same spot."
"I have thought of it myself," said Joshua.
"Perhaps we shall, some day," said his brother.
"Perhaps," said Joshua, moodily.

Hardy relates in his memoirs that James Bushrod of Broadmayne saw the two deserters shot in 1801 who are the subject of "The Melancholy Hussar of the German Legion," and that real names are given in the story.[1] Hardy's tale certainly looks like one improvised to give pathos to the bare facts, which it does by imagining a young girl half in love with one of the two soldiers, and failing him at the last moment,

[1] *Early Life*, 153.

when he and his comrade were to take her in a boat over to France. "To Please his Wife" is a highly artificial tragedy. A mariner's wife, nettled at the prosperous marriage of a former rival, encourages her husband and sons to go on a risky cruise which might make their fortune; and they never return. Much superior, though the situation is as bizarre as Hardy could have prayed for, is "On the Western Circuit." The wife of a dull and unresponsive merchant in Melchester (Salisbury) finds that her pretty maidservant is in love with a young lawyer on circuit. The girl is entirely illiterate, and the mistress writes her love-letters—first for the girl and then for herself.

She was now clearly realizing that she had become possessed to the bottom of her soul with the image of a man to whom she was hardly so much as a name. From the first he had attracted her by his looks and voice; by his tender touch; and, with these as generators, the writing of letter after letter and the reading of their soft answers had insensibly developed on her side an emotion which fanned his; till there had resulted a magnetic reciprocity between the correspondents, notwithstanding that one of them wrote in a character not her own. That he had been able to seduce another woman in two days was his crowning though unrecognized fascination for her as the she-animal.

It is these wonderful love-letters that determine Raye to marry the girl. The secret inevitably comes out. Not little Anna, but Edith and he, are "lovers—devoted lovers—by correspondence."

"It is no use blinking that. Legally I have married her—God help us both!—in soul and spirit I have married you, and no other woman in the world!"

"What are you doing, dear Charles?" Anna asks him, as they sit at opposite windows in the railway carriage on their wedding journey. "Reading over all those sweet letters to me signed 'Anna,'" he replied, with dreary resignation. Two of the "colloquial sketches" entitled "Some Crusted Characters" are first-rate: "Andrey Satchel and the Parson and Clerk" and "Absentmindedness in a Parish Choir." Both are as broad as they are short; but the choir and the violins, all much the worse for liquor, playing "The Devil among the Tailors" instead of the evening hymn, bears off the palm. "Tony Kytes, the Archdeceiver," is a pretty comic fancy.   It was clever of Hardy to get the three amorous maids, unbeknown to each other, into the light-o'-love's cart, and keep back the counterstroke and showing up till they all tumble out together.   But the end would have been more pungent if Milly also had said "No" to the arch-deceiver.

Hardy's character-drawing here and in the novels

As a story-teller, Hardy had one invaluable gift: he could swiftly, in a few trenchant strokes, silhouette a character, and convey the illusion that it had been made known at full length. Such are the vivid figures of the hangman in "The Three Strangers," the farmer in "The Withered Arm," proud of his young wife and savage at the mysterious blemish that has marred her beauty, or the patient milkwoman whom he seduced, and who without meaning to has her terrible revenge.   They seem to be striking individuals; and in fact they have all the individuality required.   For a story is not a novel, and elaborate drawing of character would be out of place and contrary to the specific needs and nature of a story.   As already said, a story is the account of an action or adventure or some moving experience that is supposed to have happened.   "Story" is short for "history." [1]   Its subject is not a person or set of persons, but an event.   Often it is difficult to put a given work in the right category.   Many tales and stories are simply miniature novels, or abortive novels, or bits of novel, as if brevity made all the difference.   But novels and stories are not different merely on the score of length; there are novels which are only stories long drawn out, as there are stories which are simply novels gone wrong.   Both novels and stories may indeed be written with similar ends in view, but the ends will be attained by different means; the point of view, the lay-out, the very technique will be different.   Such story-tellers as Gissing, Galsworthy, Arnold Bennett, or Mr H. G. Wells, or as Henry James or Howells, may present an aspect of social conditions or

[1] The French *conte* and *récit* have a like derivation, from the act of recounting a history of events.

personal relations through a series of commonplace events;
whilst a novel may be close-packed with incident, and keep the
reader on tenterhooks until curiosity and suspense are satisfied
by a thrilling climax or a surprising revelation; yet it may still
be a novel, the depiction of a world or an era of action, or of
a life, chequered by passions, dilemmas, and dramatic events.
The story is the history of something that has taken place; the
novel, unless it be merely a story on the large scale, is a portrayal
of life as actually going on.[1] Things are shown as they come to
pass, the very movement of life is reproduced; the characters
are seen in the process of living and feeling and acting, so that
the reader knows them, even without description or analysis,
better in many ways than they know themselves. In
Bergsonian terms, the novel takes a strip of time and unrolls
it, the duration of what is displayed corresponding psychologically to the reading of the pages.[2] But the figures in a

---

[1] Hardy did not recognize the distinction, but used the word "story" for novel,
especially when he was thinking of the general outline. See, for instance, his article,
"The Science of Fiction" (*Life and Letters*, 1891).

[2] Of course, different novels conform to the principle in different ways. The way
of James Joyce is not the way of Fielding, though both are conformists. Henry
James, again, does not employ the cinematographic method of Miss Dorothy Richardson or Mrs Virginia Woolf, though all three are true to the same essential principle.
They vary in the depth of their scrutiny into consciousness, and still more in the
strictness with which they exclude anything exterior to the consciousness on which
attention is focused. To plunge into the stream of consciousness and follow its movement is to fulfill to the utmost the distinctive aim of the novel, though whether
anyone's dramatic belief in what is presented actually gains in intensity from the
scrupulous exclusion of everything outside and beyond may be doubted. At any
rate, the beauty and impeccability of the technique which seems to suppress even the
novelist may well excite admiration. But there are professed novels which do not
conform. Thus, when a novelist goes back and forth in time, and when he describes
and narrates in one sentence and in the next leaves it to his creations to speak and act,
it is not only the mingling of interests, now in character and characters and now in the
thrills and suspense of a romance of adventure, that show such a magnificent work as
Conrad's *Nostromo* to be a confused amalgam of incompatibles, both a story of complicated events and a more or less successful portrayal of life in its fullness and its
infinite variety. For this is confirmed by the author's incessant interventions, to
explain, to correct, as well as to moralize—the interventions of one who was not used
to intervene. It is not often that one of the greatest stoops to a false declaration, and
so risks non-acceptance of the whole consignment. But Stevenson, also, and some
others of his decade, tried to run realism and humour and romance three abreast,
innocently believing that they were doing the same as Scott, who, though a romantic
novelist, was a follower of Fielding and always a novelist, and made the faithful
portraiture of life, past or present, first and fundamental, the plot and the exciting
events being only machinery (see Volume VI. 137). Stevenson, however, did it so
enchantingly that any examiner on the point of stopping him would have shut his
eyes and ears to the truth, and reversed the tale of Ulysses and the sirens.

story are, as it were, projected on the flat [1]; they have done with life and time, and now it is only their acts and experiences and what led up to these that have to be recounted. The story will be a sort of abstract, setting out with some concision the decisive turns of events; its aim will be to make the reader understand all that took place, and believe whilst he is reading that it did take place. History has to be authenticated; events must be shown to be credible, result of the antecedent causes. Hence the characters, being a principal means of elucidating and substantiating what is related, must be recognized at sight as probable human beings, and will accordingly be common types, representatives of social orders and occupations, exponents of tendencies and weaknesses or of moral idealisms and standards of conduct. Any idiosyncrasies they are stamped with will be such as have excited curiosity a thousand times. Thus the salient figures in a story, as distinguished from a full-breadth novel, will be summaries of well-known traits and attitudes; they will have a representative and logical significance, appealing to the intellect rather than to the æsthetic sensibilities. [2] Whereas those in a novel, not being called upon to prove that what is said must be true, since they are standing witnesses to their own actuality, are seized intuitively and accepted without a shade of hesitation: however strange their features, their thoughts or their behaviour, there is no denying that they are real. They are living individuals, whilst their opposites in a story of events, being secondary and subordinate, and, first and foremost, of instrumental value, must needs be something more or something less than individuals. The emphasis will

[1] This, of course, is not the same distinction as Mr E. M. Forster's (in *Aspects of the Novel*, 93–101) between "flat" and "round" characters, two-dimensional and three-dimensional; rather, it distinguishes these from four-dimensional characters, those in which the time-factor has decisive import.

[2] George Moore observes, "The suppression or maintenance of story in a novel is a matter of personal taste; some prefer character-drawing to adventures, some adventures to character-drawing; that we cannot have both at once I take to be a self-evident proposition" (*Confessions of a Young Man*, xii.). Stevenson wanted to have both at once. Henry James in his early essay "The Art of Fiction" (*Longman's Magazine*, reprinted in *Partial Portraits*) repudiates the "old-fashioned distinction between the novel of character and the novel of incident—What is character but the determination of incident? What is incident but the illustration of character?" True, for Henry James; but what about the thousand and one novelists of simple sensation?

be on causation, which must be clear and conclusive; for, instead of a reproduction of life itself, this is a demonstration, an appeal for belief in all that is stated. Hence rare and notable qualities of character will be merely indicated, complications of motive will be kept subordinate. The mental and emotional states of Mr Barnet and the woman he loves, in "Fellow-Townsmen," will be laid open only so far as they issue or fail to issue in acts, which are nipped before they ripen by the blast of fate. So too, "On the Western Circuit" goes just deeply enough into the feelings of the unpremeditating lovers to lay bare the ironical situation which changes and almost reverses the current of two lives. To go further or go deeper is not the story-teller's business; it would be to turn the tale into an incipient novel. The momentous event has occurred, and it has been put on record: life is still going on, always going on; but that is business for the novelist.

There is such a radical difference between the two kinds of *Composite* characterization that they seem like the results of distinct *characters* creative processes. That the characters in *Wessex Tales*, *Life's* *in the* *Little Ironies*, and Hardy's other stories, are of the nature *novels* specified, that they are not merely drawn in frugal lines suited to the brevity of a tale, but are in the other respects true to the economy of a narrative of events, needs no demonstration. But how is it that those in the novels also show at least a mixture with their deeper and more vital traits, adulterating their individuality, of these abstract, logical, purely representative qualities? How is it that so many are concepts, terms in a proposition, rather than, or as well as, imaginative creations? Why are they so slow to emerge as individuals with a spon-taneous life of their own? So many of his foremost figures are little more than representatives of place and time, sex, and attitude to life. Fancy Day, in his first Wessex novel, is but a charming embodiment of feminine fickleness and feminine susceptibility to admiration; Bathsheba Everdene, the same thing with more temperamental vivacity. Elfride, of the blue eyes, and Grace Melbury, in *The Woodlanders*, are mere variants of the same feminine type. Ethelberta is the traditional adventuress; Fitzpiers, Troy, Wildeve, Alec d'Urberville, are

the regulation libertines.   A Knight or a Stephen Smith are
the men we are meeting every day.   There is little to differen-
tiate the generality of Hardy's characters except their situation;
though, happily, some do come to life through the intensity
of feeling which this imparts to beings wrestling with the
unfriendliness of circumstance.   Marty South rises to the full
height of her tragedy; but such greatness cannot be thrust
upon them all.   Too often, as in *Two on a Tower*, the characters
are evidently the offspring of a strange and improbable plot;
and it is not as individuals but as persons reacting to far-
fetched moral dilemmas that they leave any lasting impression.
In fact, many of the lesser people, with very small parts to
sustain, are more sharply individualized than those who are
most conspicuous; this owing to Hardy's instinctive response
to the need for the few trenchant lines giving skin-deep
features to an exterior when there is no call to look further.
His rustics are eminently of this order, and they are among his
artistic triumphs.   Thomas Leaf and Christian Cantle, Joseph
Poorgrass, William Worm, Mark Clark, Cainy Ball, Moon,
Creed, and Coggan, are such minor characters that they might
be regarded merely as so much background, furnishing a racy
comment and rich comic relief to the matters in the forefront;
yet they are by no means drawn as mere bumpkins and clodpoles,
as like as two peas.   Their minds are not revealed; but it does
look as if there really were minds behind those gnarled, weather-
beaten, and merry or sardonic visages.   They are not by any
means an unthinking herd, no mere stage-furniture, but like
Shakespeare's peasants have a droll logic of their own.[1]   And
they impersonate the spirit of place; they are soaked in tradition, the traditions of a primitive class, rooted in the soil, which
it is their function to typify.   They are as eternal as the woods
and fields and heaths; whereas the diffident lovers, the weak
or faithless women, the anguished victims of despair, are symbols
of a present phase of disturbance, restlessness, and maladjust-
ment.   Three of Hardy's best examples of the countryman,

[1] But it is Hardy's wit, not the witness's, in *The Mayor of Casterbridge* (xxxi.)—"I
object to that conversation," interposed the old woman, "I was not capable enough
to hear what I said, and what's said out of my hearing is not evidence."

Oak, Venn, and Giles Winterborne, are only a shade or two superior socially to the rest of these. But they have a real inner life, which raises them to another level of æsthetic existence. There is a genuine greatness in Oak and Giles; it is the result of passion held down by the strength of personality; they are cheerful beings, but they have a certain austerity, a calm acceptance, which comes from instinctive wisdom: they have each their own philosophy of life. Henchard is another of the same order, without the serenity, and without the philosophy; and his inner life is developed on a more grandiose scale. But note that the superiority of the character-drawing in these cases is largely due to the absence of that blighting conceptual element which takes the life out of so many others. When this becomes a main ingredient again, as in Clym Yeobright and Angel Clare, the same deadening effect comes in, and the promise of a flourishing individuality is stifled almost at birth. Hardy is sound enough in his delineation of general characteristics, particularly those which are distinctively feminine. A notable one for insight is the self-analysis and exposure of unconscious envy and jealousy of a loved sister, "Alicia's Diary," in the retinue of tales following *A Changed Man*. His women are true women, though so few have a distinct existence apart from their setting, often, to a marked degree, a romantic setting. Eustacia Vye is an unforgettable figure, a figure outlined in memory for ever against the darkness of Egdon. Her richness, however, is peculiarly that of a type of feeling and mood: she is the decadent, the pessimist, in aimless revolt against her lot. Eustacia, Clym, Wildeve, all in the same book, are factors in a problem, terms in an argument; they are postulates, data, elements in a mathematical calcula-tion that Hardy works out for us, having already found the answer. True individuality is a thing they may arrive at; they do not begin as individuals.[1] Even Tess as a living personality has to fight against the birthmark of the "pure woman" with

---

[1] As M. Fernandez remarks of those of Balzac, "Les personnages de Balzac ont été pensées avant d'être des individus vivants, et une question alors nous vient aussitôt aux lèvres: sont-ils des individus? La réponse est *qu'ils finissent par le devenir*" (*Messages*, i. 67).

which she is stamped on the title-page, as if that summed up the whole meaning of her history.

A comparison with Balzac

The most striking instance in literature of such a blending of the logical and scientific with the imaginative, the vital, the dramatic, is the *Comédie humaine* of Balzac, an instance which has been brilliantly studied by M. Ramon Fernandez, who has analysed the differences between characterization in the *récit* and in the *roman*, on similar lines to those suggested in the preceding pages. His fundamental distinction is that the *récit* deals with what is past and over, the *roman* with that which is evoked, chronicled, and analysed as it is going on.[1] This is not quite the same as the distinction between an event as subject and the continuous process of life as subject; though, to be sure, an event is not an event until it has taken place. Balzac's vast systematic survey in the form of a series of novels is the work of an imaginative creator who is also a sociologist; it is a scientific study of human conditions, as well as a succession of dramatic stories. Hence what M. Fernandez terms Balzac's compromise between the *roman* and the *récit*.[2] Balzac saw his vast progeny as living and acting, but he saw them primarily as units in the mighty concourse engaged in running the social machine. He "fabricated" the protagonists of his dramas, by establishing their civil and historical situation, imagined traits forming the character of each, and described the visible features of their environment, their physical exterior, and even the attire marking their profession and status. It is "a purely intellectual operation, *a priori* so far as the individual is concerned," who is himself determined by the place of his classification in the social order.[3] Hardy's mind, also, was continually swayed by theoretical considerations. His presentment of life was shaped

[1] Le récit fait *connaître* et non point *naître* les evénéments (*Ibid.*, 61).

[2] Il n'aurait pu réussir ordinairement qu'un compromis entre le roman et le récit, qu'une synthèse puissante et artificielle, pénible et géniale, qui ne serait ni tout à fait une œuvre de pensée, ni tout à fait une œuvre d'art. En d'autres termes, désireux de produire un effet saisissant par l'évocation de la réalité concrète, il n'aurait obtenu ce résultat que par des moyens abstraits, soutenant toutes les parties par une armature et des joints conceptuels. Il en résulterait une constante confusion de la preuve esthétique et de la preuve rationnelle, le lecteur ne sachant jamais précisément si le sentiment qu'il a de la réalité d'une scène n'est point une illusion due à la vérité du commentaire abstrait qui l'encadre (*Ibid.*, 66).

[3] *Ibid.*, 68.

by his philosophy of life. It is a shallow mistake to regard his novels as sociological studies, though such secondary issues may come in [1]; they are philosophic statements of the human dilemma. Each embodies an ulterior meaning, each is an argument; several of the finest stand out as definitely polemical. The larger and more telling characters, those deliberately meant to be symbolic, are so clearly exponents of a definite philosophy that any reader could apply the approximate formula, and Hardy, if he were alive, would have to countersign it. The formula is as much in the characters as in the tissue of events in which they are involved.[2] Some have a true personal life, having transcended their conceptual origin. Beginning as theorems, they burst the abstract shell in which they were conceived, and attain the deep temporal life of autonomous, self-existent entities. For that is what they all aim at, the really significant figures. It is essential, of course, not to confuse two distinct questions. The question here is, not why many of Hardy's creations are represented as failing in the struggle for self-realization, in the effort to live their own lives; but why, handicapped with so much abstractness, the characters in his books so often fall short of clear individuality, and live only the life of their author's ideas.[3]

[1] Dr Louise de Ridder-Barzin does this continually; see especially chapter iii.—"La Société"—where *The Woodlanders* is considered as a study of *déclassement*, and *Jude* of the English marriage laws. This is to miss Hardy's central thought completely.

[2] Lionel Johnson was irked by this doctrinaire element in novels which he appreciated as finely as any of the numerous critics who have written since. Though "his books are never fanatical, we are forced now and then to pause, and to discount some phrase or tendency, by saying to ourselves: *The shield has another side.* That is to say, Mr Hardy's prepossessions of a positivist sort are held with so firm a conviction, that all things, from farmyards to the stars, and all men whosoever, are touched by them: his novels are not written for a purpose, to prove the truth of something; but with the prejudice, that it is a proven truth. . . . The art of Mr Hardy," he acutely discerned, "is a logical art" (*The Art of Thomas Hardy* (1923), 172–173).

[3] This is in no way inconsistent with the wholesale assertion of D. H. Lawrence about Hardy's people, the people that count: "They are people each with a real, vital, potential self, even the apparently wishy-washy heroines of the earlier books, and this self suddenly bursts the shell of manner and convention and commonplace opinion, and acts independently, absurdly, without mental knowledge or acquiescence. And from such an outburst the tragedy usually develops. . . . This is the tragedy of Hardy, always the same. . . . This is the theme of novel after novel: remain quite [quiet?] within the convention, and you are good, safe, and happy in the long run, though you never have the vivid pang of sympathy on your side, or, on the other hand, be passionate, individual, wilful, you will find the security of the convention a

Resulting mechanical construction   But the expository and argumentative element inevitably made for a mechanical ordering of character and much else, and the mechanism was bound to show. As M. Fernandez points out, Balzac "adopted the mechanical movement of a rather monotonous dichotomy," [1] and opposed one character to another in symmetrical antitheses. So did Hardy, and is congratulated by some critics for doing it. Eustacia and Tamsin, Wildeve and Diggory Venn, in *The Return of the Native*, are such pairs, and, in *Tess*, Angel Clare and Alec d'Urberville. In earlier novels there are Oak and Troy, Bathsheba and Fanny Robin, Grace Melbury and Marty South, Winterborne and Fitzpiers. This formal contrast, so neat and so pat, betrays the conceptual nature of these suggestive figures; though several have been touched by imagination and have acquired a varying measure of personal vitality, their significance in the initial ground-plan is essentially logical. Hardy plumed himself on this mechanical symmetry. In a letter to a friend who had written discriminatingly of *Jude the Obscure*, he said "It required an artist to see that the plot is almost geometrically constructed." [2] Critics have dilated on the diagrammatic likeness of several of his plots, which they show falling into set patterns, for example, in *Far from the Madding Crowd*, *The Return of the Native*, and *The Woodlanders*.[3]

There is a strict subordination of all the miscellaneous elements to the one dominant idea; everything and everybody

walled prison, you will escape, and you will die, either of your own lack of strength to bear the isolation and the exposure, or by direct revenge from the community, or from both. This is the tragedy, and only this" (*Phœnix*, 411–412). Lawrence would be sure to detect the unæsthetic elements in so many of Hardy's characters; his own creations were never of this abstract construction.

[1] "Qui adopte souvent le mouvement mécanique d'une dichotomie assez monotone" (*op. cit.*, 68).

[2] *Later Years*, 400.

[3] Professor Lascelles Abercrombie (p. 111) turns these "personalities into algebra by putting A^1 for masculine simplicity, and A^2 for feminine simplicity, B^1 for masculine complexity and B^2 for feminine complexity"; and shows in the first of these novels A^1 loving B^2, who loves B^1, who loves A^2; in the second, A^1 loving A^2, who loves B^1, who loves B^2; and in the third, A^2 loving A^1, who loves B^2, who loves B^1. All this is supposed to avouch the "dramatic form" of novels which fulfill "the gravest function of art . . . for the first time," and Hardy's dramatic genius is compared with the greatest of all. But such a dramatist as Shakespeare avoided these geometrical dichotomies, except in *The Comedy of Errors* and *Two Gentlemen of Verona*, where a pointed antithesis was the gist of the juvenile comedy; and the symmetry in *Twelfth Night* is, surely, a blemish.

co-operate to express that: casual hints, premonitions, con-
verging indications repeated or recalled, produce a compulsive
formality, a pattern in which chance is seen working systematically to an appointed end. However intricate the events, the
mosaic is the reverse of perplexing. Hardy was a trained
architect, and carefully prepared the lay-out of his structures
before he started building. More than that, he had an
analytical mind, which was always seeking to impose an
orderly pattern on the irregular features of human life. Conrad
brooded over his experience of life, and imagined a story
illustrating certain general intuitions: casting about for a title,
he called the book *Chance*. Hardy would have evolved a group
of characters, and devised a chain of circumstances, such as
would have shown the world governed by chance, "crass
Casualty," or, when he had amended his philosophy, by some
form of determinism. He often went so far as to tabulate the
cardinal traits in his foremost personages, almost in the manner
of the old character-books. Eustacia, remember, was portrayed
in such a series of pungent phrases, as the representative of
contemporary pessimism; like Clym, another modern, who is a
sentimentalist at bottom and succumbs to the perplexities of
a world which he prides himself on seeing through. Later in
much the same way Hardy presents Angel Clare, the modern
who is not modern enough, Jude, the man of intellect, stunted
and repressed by society; and so on. It will have been noticed
already, in the cases of Fitzpiers, Troy, Boldwood, Knight, and
others, how their mentality, their ruling passions and weaknesses, their little foibles and vanities, are set out as by a
professional reader of character filling in a blank form. The
wonder and the triumph of Hardy are that they come to life at
all, as the eventual result of such an abstract procedure. For,
although there is a pleasing shapeliness in this mechanical
scaffolding, like that of a clear page or a tasteful cover, it is an
external shapeliness, and not by any means identical with the
more profound and vital unity and coherence which he did
constantly attain, in despite of it.[1] In *The Return of the Native*

[1] M. Ramon Fernandez remarks that "Meredith est radicalement et heureusement
incapable de concevoir et de concilier tant bien que mal deux unités distinctes,

and *The Woodlanders*, and in his epical biographies of Henchard,
Tess, and Jude, although he lapsed at times into his favourite
geometrical construction, he achieved a lucid and austere
beauty, by seeing the moral conflict as a cosmic struggle—
humanity, not pitted against each other, but striving with their
chief enemy, nature, the universe, the cosmic process.   The
characters may be homely people, but the drama of their lives
takes ˹this wide sweep.   And that is a higher architecture re-
constructing the fabric of causality, but hardly revealing itself
as architecture.   Hardy's novels, like his poems, deal pre-
eminently with elemental things, the large primary factors and
problems, never with the small change of social intercourse.[1]

"*Tess of* *Tess of the d'Urbervilles, a pure woman faithfully presented*
the d'Ur- (1891), and *Jude the Obscure* (1895), the one preceding, the
bervilles" other following *Life's Little Ironies*, are two more of Hardy's
test-cases, and stand out as the most piteous and heart-rending
of all.   In 1891, *Tess of the d'Urbervilles* read like a pamphlet,
incandescent with indignation; to-day, in spite of obvious
infractions of the right ordinances of literary art, it reads like
a classic.   Hardy always seems to present his tragedies of
human life with a half-repressed fury, which breaks the envelope
now and then, and sometimes confuses the issue.   The tragedy
is always an indictment, an exposure of injustices.   But it is not
quite clear whom he would accuse.   Is it nature, or is it society?
Time after time, he seems to be up in rebellion against a
malignant divinity wantonly interfering with man's purposing:

Life offers—to deny![2]

l'unité vivante des individus et de leur action, et l'unité décorative, l'unité esthétique
en soi et pour soi" (*op. cit.*, 139).   But let a scientist have his say on the question, the
lamented J. W. N. Sullivan.   After explaining that the framework of a work of
literature "is provided by the artist's personal vision of life," he goes on: "This is
the light which pervades the whole work and bestows on it such harmony as it possesses,
a harmony which lies much deeper than anything the artist may achieve by the
technical dovetailing of the elements of his works" (*Limitations of Science*, 267).
See also above, p. 22.

 [1] See above (p. 43) on his contempt for mere manners.   Had he studied them more
carefully, however, he would not have made Lucetta, in *The Mayor of Casterbridge*,
volunteer such a caveat to Farfrae at their first meeting: "You may hear them
speak of me in Casterbridge as time goes on.   If they tell you I'm a coquette, which
some may, because of the incidents of my life, don't believe it, for I'm not."   He
would also have avoided a great deal of stiltedness and lack of nature in the dialogue
of his women in general (c. xxiii.).

 [2] "Yell'ham Wood's Story" (*Time's Laughing-Stocks*, 280).

In the final paragraph, it is said to have been the President of the Immortals that has had his sport with Tess. *Jude the Obscure* gives "the tragedy of unfulfilled aims" [1]; which aims are thwarted by two distinct agencies: first, old-established social prejudices scorning and repressing a poor man's ambitions; and secondly, the man's own weakness of character. The adequacy of either of these causes and impediments is abundantly proved; yet the chief sufferers, Sue and Jude, are conscious also of some deeper and more comprehensive hostility: "They would sit silent, more bodeful of the direct antagonism of things than of their insensate and stolid obstructiveness." Regularly with Hardy it comes down to this. He shows Henchard paralysed by his unhappy temperament, Clym and Eustacia estranged by the incompatibility of their likes and dislikes, Tess treated as an outcast for an offence committed by another; but these tangible causes seem to be only the particular contrivances by which the unseen malevolence has its way. In *Tess*, the resentment is as movingly expressed as the pathos; the accusation vies in force with the tragedy, defying all the canons of artistic reticence. And it is definitely an arraignment of both the divine and the human dispensations. Hardy seems to go out of his way to denounce social iniquities, not only man's unjust justice, the inequality of lot, the blindness and stupidity, the unfairness that lets the man off lightly and blasts the woman, the entrenched conventions and prejudices that hamper the consciences even of the liberal-minded; but also the callousness that tortures and murders "harmless feathered creatures" for sport, and the law that in a final insult flings "unbaptized infants, notorious drunkards, suicides, and all others of the conjecturally damned," into the shabbiest corner of the churchyard, where the docks and nettles grow. Hardy seems to be full of grievances, and continually appears in the guise of a special pleader. But there is no inconsistency in the position he takes up, if the defective human morality is the work of a defective higher morality, whether this latter, as in the earlier novels, be identified with blind chance or wanton cruelty, or, as in the later, with the determinism expounded in *The Dynasts*

[1] Preface by Hardy.

as the operation of the Immanent Will. His satirical diatribes have all along had this dual object, which ultimately resolves itself into one: celestial injustice with man's infirmities as its tool.[1] Hardy's preface deprecates the charge of didacticism or aggressiveness, and repeats "that a novel is an impression, not an argument." But for one who reads the preface, there are thousands who nod assent to such an ejaculation as the one on the shiftless house of Durbeyfield:

Some people would like to know whence the poet whose philosophy is in these days deemed as profound and trustworthy as his song is breezy and pure, gets his authority for speaking of "Nature's holy plan."

One provocative phrase struck a controversial note that was irrelevant, and worse than irrelevant, since it challenged opposition in certain minds and distracted attention from the main charge against divine justice. The question whether Tess was a pure woman is a side-issue, and it was a blunder to put it in the forefront, even though it must be answered in Hardy's sense: Tess was violated. But even some shade of technical guilt would not have invalidated the fundamental idea of martyrdom proper to tragedy.

[1] D. H. Lawrence, in his "Study of Thomas Hardy" (*Phœnix*, 419–420), points out how much Hardy's novels gain in beauty and sublimity by his presenting the little human morality-play against the terrific background of "the vast, uncomprehended and incomprehensible morality of nature or of life itself, surpassing human consciousness," a background symbolized by Egdon Heath, or the woodlands, or the stars. It is a quality which Hardy shares with Shakespeare, and Sophocles, and Tolstoy. But, Lawrence argues, "whereas in Shakespeare or Sophocles the greater, uncomprehended morality, or fate, is actively transgressed and gives active punishment, in Hardy and Tolstoy the lesser, human morality, the mechanical system, is actively transgressed, and holds and punishes the protagonist, whilst the greater morality is only passively, negatively transgressed, it is represented merely as being present in background, in scenery, not taking any active part, having no direct connexion with the protagonist." He instances Œdipus, Hamlet, and Macbeth as violating the unfathomed moral forces of nature, whilst Anna Karenina, Eustacia, Tess, Sue, and Jude are brought down by collision with the established system of human government. Yes; but Hardy does not ignore the vast and incomprehensible morality. He tries to comprehend it, on rationalist principles, and to show the lesser as subsumed in the greater and subordinate to it. He hated incomprehensibility. He essayed this in *The Dynasts*, as well as in occasional glimpses of an outer reality in the novels. His vision of this greater morality did not coincide with that of Lawrence. But his inferiority to Shakespeare and Sophocles is a matter of the quality of his vision, rather than of failure to perceive.

Put side by side with those of Dickens, Thackeray, or Trollope, *Char-* *acteriza-* the leading characters in most of Hardy's novels, as already *tion in* noted,[1] show a certain blankness of feature, are lacking in sharp *this* individualizing lines.   But his aim was so different that no one *final* dreamed of comparing personages standing for general humanity *phase* with those singled out for portrayal on the strength of their humorous, anomalous, or at least remarkable qualities.   Bear in mind Hardy's principle, that any "uncommonness must be in the events" [2]; the people must be as ordinary as possible. That Hardy could seize idiosyncrasy and had humour at command is evinced by his rustics; but he held all that in abeyance in shaping these serious, tragic representations of humanity warring with destiny.   And, if there was a default of individuality, it detracted little from the absorbing force and pathos of their lives as he unfolded them.   If he had chosen uncommon characters for his protagonists the loss would have been immeasurable.   These characters are man, and woman; their importance is in their being representatives of the human race to-day.   It is what befalls them, and their feelings and reactions thereto, that is so piercingly urgent.   We and our destinies are at stake: our fate seems to hinge upon theirs; and we hang upon the event, anxiously awaiting the ultimate issue, which is to settle the agonizing problem, answer the dreadful enigma, save us or damn us.   But into Tess and Jude, and into Sue and some other characters, without in the least diminishing the representative appeal, Hardy now manages to breathe that something which individualizes from the outset.   They are homely creatures: Tess a milkmaid, a child of the lowliest peasants; Jude, a village stone-cutter, of like humble origin. The forgotten aristocratic lineage of the Durbeyfields is only an odd circumstance that accidentally subserves the fatality. Both have their abstract significance; but they are no abstractions; they are live, identifiable beings, like their neighbours, but singled out from them by differences in the grain.   They have a winningness often missing in earlier heroes and heroines; and, further, in spite of their homeliness, the dignity which befits a tragic role.   A humanist imagination cherishing and

[1] See above, pp. 61–65.   [2] See above, p. 30.

tenderly observing its creations has this time got the better of mere logic. And so their fate has wrung the hearts of innumerable readers, in a very intimate and personal way. These two last of Hardy's tragic novels, in a manner unexampled by the others, have become, as it were, historic cases. The barest outline would be superfluous here. *Tess of the d'Urbervilles* has obvious resemblances in plot to *A Pair of Blue Eyes*, which, however, is but a mock tragedy set beside the homelier but truer and sterner tragedy of Tess. The innocent girl becomes the victim of two men's misdeeds, of the sensual brute Alec d'Urberville and of the well-meaning and enlightened Angel Clare, who is, however, like Knight his prototype, not enlightened enough to free himself from the deep-seated prejudices of the old order from which he thinks himself emancipated, nor has imagination enough to save the pearl he has found from the swinish world to which it was flung. Tess is a woman; she is weak, with a touching, almost adorable, feminine weakness. Hardy's sensitive insight brings it out appealingly in her halting confession to Angel Clare. She means to tell him all; but how to begin, and how to go on? So she tries to explain how she was first brought into contact with Alec d'Urberville, the modern usurper of the name.

"But there was trouble in my family; father was not very industrious, and he drank a little."

"Yes, yes. Poor child! Nothing new." He pressed her more closely to his side.

"And then—there is something very unusual about it—about me. I—I was——"

Tess's breath quickened.

"Yes, dearest. Never mind."

"I—I—am not a Durbeyfield, but a d'Urberville—a descendant of the same family as those who owned the old house we passed. And—we are all gone to nothing!"

"A d'Urberville!—Indeed! And is that all the trouble, dear Tess?"

"Yes," she answered faintly.

"Well—why should I love you less after knowing this?"

"I was told by the dairyman that you hated old families."

She has not told. Look at the delicate understanding shown in the incident of the flood, when Angel carries the love-sick dairymaids through the water. It is after this that they all know he loves Tess, and she realizes that she must make her full and final confession.

"You will think of us when you be his wife, Tess, and of how we told 'ee that we loved him, and how we tried not to hate you, and did not hate you, and could not hate you, because you were his choice, and we never hoped to be chose by him."

They were not aware that, at these words, salt, stinging tears trickled down Tess's pillow anew, and how she resolved, with a bursting heart, to tell all her history to Angel Clare, despite her mother's command—to let him for whom she lived and breathed despise her if he would, and her mother regard her as a fool, rather than preserve a silence which might be deemed a treachery to him, and which somehow seemed a wrong to these. [1]

Clare is truly the villain of the piece, the defaulter who brings down the tragedy. Hardy is perfectly clear about that. Alec d'Urberville is but the almost impersonal foulness of the world, the clot of mud by which Tess is accidentally defiled. Angel Clare can talk, like Clym, of "the hobble of being alive," and he suffers from the ache of modernism; but "with all his attempted independence of judgment this advanced and well-meaning young man, a sample product of the last five-and-twenty years, was yet a slave to custom and conventionality when surprised back into his earlier teachings." "The shade of his own limitations" hung over Angel Clare and his trusting wife. But he makes a more consistent and intelligible study of a man who cannot achieve consistency than Clym. Alec d'Urberville was a simpler subject, one of those as easy to present as they are hateful to contemplate. Even his fit of religious mania does not make him anything more than a variety of the same breed as Manston, in *Desperate Remedies*, or Troy and Wildeve. Yet even such a simple portrait is masterly in its own way, as is witnessed by the abuse hurled at it by those who dislike him. Both are repulsive characters, the sort that no one wants to act

[1] Chap. xxxi.

in amateur theatricals; which is usually a tribute to the genius that inspired them.[1]

Still the pictorial style

Nowhere was Hardy's pictorial mode of narration more finely exercised; the contour of his sentences, also, is peculiarly noble and shapely, especially when, as often in this novel, he is in a classic mood. And the working of environment is here a less inscrutable matter than in some of his earlier and more lyrical passages. It is nothing occult that reacts upon Tess in the soft and rich and enervating Valley of the Great Dairies, where she loves Clare, or on the bleak, flinty, soul-benumbing downs where she spends the winter turnip-cutting, and her heart freezes to stone. Clare has the poetic imagination, even if he is less of a man than the average poet.

The mixed, singular, luminous gloom in which they walked along together to the spot where the cows lay, often made him think of the Resurrection hour. He little thought that the Magdalen might be at his side. Whilst all the landscape was in neutral shade his companion's face, which was the focus of his eyes, rising above the mist stratum, seemed to have a sort of phosphorescence upon it. She looked ghostly, as if she were merely a soul at large. In reality her face, without appearing to do so, had caught the cold gleam of day from the north-east; his own face, though he did not think of it, wore the same aspect to her. It was then, as has been said, that she impressed him most deeply. She was no longer the milkmaid, but a visionary essence of woman—a whole sex condensed into one typical form. He called her Artemis, Demeter, and other fanciful names half teasingly, which she did not like because she did not understand them. "Call me Tess," she would say askance; and he did.

Hardy gives him his own transfiguring imagination, the grotesquerie that saw evil as an active, malicious sprite, at the moment when Tess stuns him with her confession:

The complexion even of external things seemed to suffer transmutation as her announcement progressed. The fire in

[1] "Angel Clare is real enough to be odious," remarks Professor Abercrombie (p. 148), who "could bear to have dinner" with Alec d'Urberville. Many cannot practise such detachment, and tumble straight into the sentimental fallacy when confronted with a vivid presentment of a hateful original.

the grate looked impish—demoniacally funny, as if it did not care in the least about her strait. The fender grinned idly, as if it too did not care. The light from the water-bottle was merely engaged in a chromatic problem. All material objects around announced their irresponsibility with terrible iteration. And yet nothing had changed since the moments when he had been kissing her; or rather, nothing in the substance of things. But the essence of things had changed.

It is the ironic comedy at the heart of the grimmest tragedy, for the man who is not equal to the situation. The tragedy of existence reasserts itself when Tess finds herself transferred to the dreary uplands, now not even a wife in name. All that too is rendered in the landscape-painting:

The wide acreage of blank agricultural brownness, apparent where the swedes had been pulled, was beginning to be striped in wales of darker brown, gradually broadening to ribands. Along the edge of each of these something crept upon ten legs, moving without haste and without rest up and down the whole length of the field; it was two horses and a man, the plough going between them turning up the cleared ground for a spring sowing. For hours nothing relieved the joyless monotony of things. Then, far beyond the ploughing-teams, a black speck was seen. It had come from a corner of a fence, where there was a gap, and its tendency was up the incline, towards the swede-cutters. From the proportions of a mere point it advanced to the shape of a ninepin, and was soon perceived to be a man in black, arriving from the direction of Flintcomb-Ash. The man at the slicer, having nothing to do with his eyes, continually observed the comer, but Tess, who was occupied, did not perceive him till her companion directed her attention to his approach.

It is Alec d'Urberville; the final act is now in sight. Cornered by fate, Tess throws up all effort to be herself; and, when she surrenders to d'Urberville to save her destitute kin, he embraces a frame that no longer contains a soul. This is the tragedy of Tess, even more than the further episode, the resurrection of the dead self, her vengeance, and its expiation at Wintoncester.

Jude the Obscure (1895) is a different kind of novel from the rest of Hardy's, and shows some approximation to the subtle and searching study of consciousness characteristic of much Continental fiction. Hardy was acquainted with the works of Tolstoy, but did not aim at a realism so stern, cogent, and uncompromising. It was rather under the influence of Ibsen, with whose plays he was more familiar, that he dealt so frankly with the duel of the sexes and drew his elaborate portrait of an emancipated woman in Sue. There are obvious resemblances in *Jude the Obscure* to *Hedda Gabler*, which he saw performed at least twice, being much impressed, and some also to *A Doll's House* and to the courage and outspokenness of *Ghosts*. He had stated his views, when he was engaged upon *Tess*, in an article "Candour in English Fiction," [1] on the timid and conventional way in which English novelists approached matters of urgent interest, particularly religious and sexual questions. He pleaded for frankness and sincerity; and in *Tess*, and still more in *Jude*, set an example of freedom of speech and honesty such as both the Greeks and our Elizabethans had displayed in their tragedies. Both books challenged current literary prohibitions, by deliberately setting out a tragic problem which raised questions of the divine governance and of the proper relations between the sexes. Though he describes *Jude the Obscure*, in the preface, simply as a "tragedy of unfulfilled aims," the polemical bias is as fierce as ever. It is a protest against the exclusiveness of our class system and against social injustices of various kinds, and a virulent exposure of the anomalies of the marriage laws, and even of any law making marriage permanent in spite of avowed incompatibility. The book is full of jeers and raillery, on the part of the author or of his characters, at the expense of the official tie and of "the average husband and wife of Christendom," and can even be read as a pasquinade on marriage and on Anglican respectability.[2] Jude's mis-

---

[1] In the *New Review* (January, 1890), with articles on the same subject by Walter Besant and Mrs Lynn Linton. As to Ibsen's plays, "Hardy could not at all understand the attitude of the English Press towards these tragic productions—the culminating evidence of our blinkered insular taste being afforded by the nickname of the 'Ibscene drama' which they received" (*Later Years*, 20-21).

[2] Just after the horrible incident of the execution of the children by the dreadful boy "Father Time," whilst Jude and Sue are waiting for the coroner's inquest, Sue hears the chapel organ, and asks what the large, low sound can be. "The organist

adventure in being entrapped into marriage with Arabella, and his cross-entanglements with her and Sue, are an obstacle to his ambitions almost as decisive as his original social handicap. So far, then, *Jude the Obscure* is on all-fours with Hardy's previous novels, at any rate with those of an argumentative tendency. The new elements are this different kind of character-drawing and the elimination of almost everything except the characters and what they are doing and experiencing. It is drama on a stage having the minimum of scenery; the action is, so to speak, exhibited in all its nakedness. Hardy has, without noticing it, abjured his principle that any "uncommonness must be in the events, not in the characters," and that "human nature must never be made abnormal, which is introducing incredibility." [1] Jude is, admittedly, an uncommon character [2]; Sue is exceptional, even if she belongs to a type now becoming prevalent; Phillotson, the man that "no woman of any niceness can stomach," is abnormal; and the dreadful boy, even under the direst modern conditions, would be a prodigy and a portent. Jude and the sensual Arabella, the neurotic Sue, and the unwholesome Phillotson, form a quadrilateral of opposing tensions that must produce the resultant on which the novelist has calculated. The geometry of this specification and of the reversion of both pairs to the original defective union is obvious; Hardy himself called attention to it, as already observed.[3] The story implied is the converse of that of Tess, and with its intricate complications

---

practising, I suppose," Jude replies. "It's the anthem from the seventy-seventh Psalm: 'Truly God is loving unto Israel.'" Two voices are heard in conversation hard by. "They are talking about us, no doubt!" moaned Sue. "We are made a spectacle unto the world, and to angels, and to men!" Jude listened—"No—they are not talking of us," he said. "They are two clergymen of different views, arguing about the eastern position" (vi. 2). There are cheaper cynicisms too; *e.g.* "He [the landlord] was about to give them notice to quit, till by chance overhearing her one night haranguing Jude in rattling terms, and ultimately flinging a shoe at his head, he recognized the note of ordinary wedlock; and concluding that they must be respectable said no more" (vi. 8).

[1] *Early Life*, 194. See also above, p. 30.

[2] The probable "germ of *Jude the Obscure*" was the account of a young man "who could not go to Oxford," mentioned in 1888 (*Early Life*, 272), presumably identical with that of the youth who drove the bread-cart and carried on his studies at the same time, and who asked Hardy to lend him his Latin grammar (*Later Years*, 44).

[3] See above, p. 66. Hardy had indulged his geometry in the cast-iron plot of *The Well-Beloved*, written before *Jude*, though published after.

and the monstrous situations they create makes what might almost be called a general lampoon on existence.[1] Happily, Hardy soon shook himself clear of his geometry, though it is only by fits and starts that the character of Jude struggles clear of his polemical role of the repressed intellectual, to be a living example of man, fighting and yielding, and fighting again, in a hopeless battle. "The Fawleys were not made for wedlock," his aunt tells him. But Jude hankers after wedlock. He is a clean-minded fellow, who succumbs only to a compulsive attack upon his virtue, and after that never recovers equilibrium and respectability. Capable of saintlike renunciations and self-sacrifice, he yet falls a prey to the tempter. Arabella has him on the sensual side, Sue on the intellectual and emotional; for the latter he can be persuaded for a while to suppress the lusts of the flesh. She is really much more of a rationalist than he, for Jude's fixed idea is not a sign of great intelligence. His mind works slowly, far too slowly to keep up with the nimbleness and variability of Sue's, though his staid common sense often corrects her flightiness. The contrast—and the inevitable contest—between this pair is something much more subtle than Hardy's imagination had hitherto conceived. This woman of "tight-strained nerves," this "epicure in emotions," with the "Ishmaelite" inside her, hating Gothic and adoring the "Greek joyousness," yet constitutionally shrinking from fleshly contacts, is Hardy's first unpredictable woman. Like Henchard, she does unexpected things, which are seen on reflection to be true to her nature. "Consistent" it would be impossible to say, for she is consistent only in her "colossal inconsistency." From her chaste liaison with the consumptive student who died when they could not be lovers, to the provocative flirtations with Jude that she will not admit to be flirtations, her wild jealousy of Arabella that seems to contradict her "epicene tenderness," and her sincere efforts to save Jude from himself, without ever failing in sympathy even with his dreams, though she sees his foiled ambition in its true perspective, Sue is a psychological paradox

[1] Dr Hedgcock (246) suggests that it is a dramatic exposition of the ideas of Schopenhauer and Hartmann on the gradual progress of the race towards the negation of the will to live.

of rare interest. She comes fairly near to her incalculable nature in her self-analysis refuting Jude's impulsive charge that she is a flirt:

"I am very much the reverse of what you say so cruelly—O Jude, it *was* cruel to say that! Yet I can't tell you the truth —I should shock you by letting you know how I give way to my impulses, and how much I feel that I shouldn't have been provided with attractiveness unless it were meant to be exercised! Some women's love of being loved is insatiable; and so, often, is their love of loving; and in the last case they may find that they can't give it continuously to the chamber-officer appointed by the bishop's licence to receive it. But you are so straightforward, Jude, that you can't understand me!" [1]

Her seeming wrong-headedness and her obstinacy are at times almost as exasperating to the reader as to Jude: Sue is infinitely better in the pages of a novel than she would be as any man's companion. Hardy shows more insight in these two novels than ever before into his favourite study, the female heart.[2] Nothing could be finer in the one way than Tess; yet Sue is by far the more complex psychological invention. But is she psychologically as true? For her vivid personality often stirs a little doubt. She is alive; but the lifelikeness and the sense of life are not so compelling as in Tess. Tess lives and breathes; we know her completely: Sue thinks, and talks; she is always talking, and never more gushingly than when about her feelings. It is this delight in playing with her emotions that awakens doubt. But this foible is implicit in her nature, and must be accepted with the rest. Arabella, on the other hand, is only too obviously true, more so than that other primitive, Alec d'Urberville. It is interesting that, like him, in one brief episode she gets religion. She found it, the chapel, righter than gin, and "took to going there regular, and found it a great comfort." But the results are evanescent in this case

---

[1] iv. i.

[2] This, in spite of Hardy's declaration that women of talent and interesting women are rare (e.g. *Early Life*, 63): "You may meet with 999 exactly alike, and then the thousandth—not a little better, but far above them. Practically therefore it is useless for a man to seek after this thousandth to make her his."

too; and Arabella's enjoyment of race day and of Dr Vibert's
philandering, when she has left Jude lying dead at their lodgings,
is an uglier stroke of irony even than the cheers heard through
the open window from the theatre where the dons are con-
ferring honorary degrees "on the Duke of Hamptonshire and a
lot more illustrious gents of that sort."

*Hardy
as tragic
artist*
These two gratuitous gibes of Fate exemplify once more
Hardy's addiction to irony of the Sophoclean stamp; Jude, a
little earlier, invoking curses on his own head is obviously
parallel to a famous scene in *Œdipus Tyrannus*. When he was
pupil to an architect, Hardy had had to give up Greek; but he
read the two great Attic dramatists later with mature appreciation, sometimes, in his desultory journal, quoting passages in
the original.[1] *The Mayor of Casterbridge* was a tragedy on
Æschylean lines, and is true to the spirit of Æschylus, inasmuch
as Henchard submits and accepts, whereas Hardy elsewhere
rebels and accuses. The sarcasm at the end of *Jude* is not
aimed at anything external to man, but at Arabella's callous
indifference towards the husband whom she has ruined, and at
the disdainful apathy of a great social institution like the university towards a scholar so far beneath its notice. The jest
in *Tess of the d'Urbervilles* at the expense of the President of the
Immortals may be taken as a mere rhetorical sally,[2] the main
charge in this case being that Tess is the victim of men's
misdeeds and lack of understanding. Henchard's calamities
were due principally to his own folly, but also in no small part
to the spitefulness of circumstances. So it was with most of
Hardy's earlier protagonists. Jude is punished for his excesses,
like Henchard; but he and Sue feel vaguely that there is an
inert antagonism in the things around them, a latent hostility
beyond their comprehension. Hence a certain confusion
and perplexity often arises: Hardy continually seems to be
impeaching alternately man and the gods. Not till he had
thought out a theory subsuming all the agencies that interfere

[1] *Early Life*, 43-44.
[2] Hardy replied thirty years later to a critic who charged him with imputing malice
to an all-powerful being who turns everything to evil, that he meant this famous
outburst allegorically—"the forces opposed to the heroine were allegorized as a
personality . . . by the use of a well-known trope" (*Later Years*, 4).

with man, in the determinism originating in the Immanent Will of *The Dynasts* (1904–1908), did he clear up the perplexity. It almost looks as if he spent his latter years trying to define his philosophy of life, asking himself what he meant exactly in the sacrifice of Tess and other sufferers; for he kept on discussing such questions.[1] The comprehensive view symbolized in the supreme Will and in the human automata who unconsciously fulfill the celestial behests, inasmuch as the final responsibility for what men do, whether good or evil, is transferred to above, at any rate sheds a flood of light backwards over the novels just preceding, and even a welcome twilight over those long anterior. The key which this was to Hardy he had been groping towards for years and years. It co-ordinated his many halting attempts at a deeper comprehension, and even gave a kind of rationality to the hoary old superstitions of hostile or capricious powers which he cherished and half-believed.[2] Those superstitions were the dark side of his Manichæan complexes, which he could now psycho-analyse and explain to himself, as symbolic views approximating to rational ones. Read in the full light of his determinism, the novels grow clearer and more coherent; but, alas! their tragic force is inevitably crippled. For the ordeal through which he passes his heroes and heroines becomes less and less a conflict and more and more a course of suffering imposed on helpless victims, who merely struggle hopelessly in the net. Tragedy loses dignity and beauty in the exact measure that it is the play of alien forces controlling the actions of a mere pawn. The parts of a machine have no autonomy; if they think they can will, it is only an illusion, placed there by the general urge that actuates the machine. Hence the conflict of wills, human and divine, which would be the basis of tragic

---

[1] It was the same with Ibsen and with Wagner, as Mr Bernard Shaw long ago pointed out. "Had Ibsen died in 1867, he, like many another great poet, would have gone to his grave without ever having rationally understood his own meaning. . . . Only simpletons go to the creative artist presuming that he must be able to answer their 'What does this obscure passage mean?' That is the very question the poet's own intellect, which has had no part in the conception of the poem, may be asking him" (*The Quintessence of Ibsenism*, "Emperor and Galilean"; see also *The Perfect Wagnerite*, "Wagner's own Explanation").

[2] Dr Ridder-Barzin is good on the wounding effect on Hardy's soul of his surrender to the belief in universal determinism, though it accounted for those apparently capricious interventions of chance that gave rise to superstitions (pp. 55–56).

action, is only a mirage. What most of Hardy's tragedies exhibit is, not the defeat, but the paralysis of will. There is, moreover, no ethical significance left, such as characterizes genuine tragedy, since personality is at a minimum, and Hardy holds that the Fate which defeats man is "neither moral nor immoral, but *un*moral." [1] The only ethical element remaining is "the noble endurance of pain," which rends the heart and "is the source of much that is best worth having in tragedy." [2]

"The Dynasts," sequel and complement to the novels
With his mythopœic instincts, Hardy was always conscious of an overworld pulling the strings of chance. Behind the veil of superficial appearances he saw inscrutable powers at work, which he constantly dramatized in a mythology of his own. Now it seemed like malice, and now blind caprice; then science taught him to perceive the rule of law—it must be some sort of mechanism, but run for what purpose, if for any purpose? Perhaps "an unpurposive and irresponsible groping in the direction of least resistance." "If it is not mechanism, it can be no other than caprice." [3] In his poem "Nature's Questioning" he runs through what he terms the "fanciful alternatives to several others" [4] : "some Vast Imbecility," "an Automaton unconscious of our pains,"

> "Or is it that some high Plan betides,
> As yet not understood,
> Of Evil stormed by Good,
> We the Forlorn Hope over which Achievement strides?" [5]

---

[1] "The said Cause is neither moral nor immoral," etc. (*Later Years*, 217).

[2] A. C. Bradley, on "Hegel's theory of tragedy" (*Oxford Lectures on Poetry*, 82). Bradley agrees with Hegel that "No mere suffering or misfortune, no suffering that does not spring in great part from human agency, and in some degree from the agency of the sufferer, is tragic, however pitiful or dreadful it may be." He points out that Hegel was "objecting to the destiny-dramas of his own time, and to the fashionable indulgence in sentimental melancholy." "Tragedies which represent man as the mere plaything of chance or a blank fate or a malicious fate, are never really deep"; he instances Maeterlinck's earlier work (*op. cit.*, 80–82). Like tendencies are to be seen in some of Ibsen's plays and in Synge's *Riders to the Sea*, etc. D. H. Lawrence explained the weakness of Hardy's tragedies altogether differently. He says, "There is a lack of sternness, there is a hesitating betwixt life and public opinion, which diminishes the Wessex novels from the rank of pure tragedy. It is not so much the eternal, immutable laws of being which are transgressed [see above, 65, n.], it is not that vital life-forces are set in conflict with each other, bringing almost inevitable tragedy—yet not necessarily death, as we see in the most splendid Æschylus. It is, in Wessex, that the individual succumbs to what is in its shallowest, public opinion, in its deepest, the human compact by which we live together, to form a community" (*Phœnix*, 440). [3] *Later Years*, 166–167. [4] *Ibid.*, 218. [5] *Wessex Poems*, 58.

Long before he had finished his last novels, including that waste "ingenuity," *The Well-Beloved*, his customary relaxation, or the recoil of his brain, between two strenuous efforts,[1] he was preparing himself for *The Dynasts*, in which he projected the conflict of human wills and Necessity on the larger screen of the world-epoch of the Napoleonic wars.[2] This is not a tragedy in the Greek or any other tradition,[3] but a vast moving spectacle of human helplessness under the gods, setting forth his conception of an unseen power working throughout the fabric of the universe and manipulating the human drama. That power determines all the activities of men, who as personalities are reduced to nothing. Even the greatest and most historic dwindle to the same nothingness; they believe themselves free agents, but are only puppets in its almighty grip. Their minds and feelings are pervaded by the Will, which shapes their motives and their actions. The conflict is on a different footing from that in the plays of Æschylus, Sophocles, or Euripides, for the antagonist has his eyes blinded and his arms bound. Nelson, Wellington, Napoleon, and the rest, are only machines, worked from above; their genius and epoch-shaping powers of resolution are ignored, or regarded as simply the specialized ability that makes them useful instruments of the Supreme, detached particles of energy transmitted for the maintenance of the ceaseless and aimless process. Hardy accepts a rumoured saying of Napoleon and gives it central significance:

> "Some force within me, baffling mine intent,
> Harries me onward, whether I will or no.
> My star, my star is what's to blame, not I.
> It is unswervable."

Hence the remarkable dearth of forcible individualities. There can be no great characters in such a world, in spite of historical traits and odd idiosyncrasies allotted to this man or

[1] D. H. Lawrence calls it "sheer rubbish, fatuity" (*Phœnix*, 480).
[2] Hardy thought of the Napoleonic epoch as a subject as early as 1877 (*Early Life*, 150). He contemplated an historical drama in 1881 (*Ibid.*, 191). In 1892 he considered the idea again, and after *Jude the Obscure* threw himself into the preparatory labours of research with his usual earnestness.
[3] He himself described it as a dramatic epic (*Later Years*, 124–125).

that to identify him with his traditional portrait; no sublimities of human nature, beyond the casual heroism of such as Ney and the companions in arms of the chieftains, and the devotion and cheerful endurance of the private soldiers. This has to atone poetically for the absence of personality: it is humanity in the mass that is dramatized, not the individual. The struggle is seen to be a blind contest between mundane hosts who decide nothing.[1] Science has given Hardy the mathematical notion of a neutral world, in which a soulless mechanism operates ruthlessly but evenly, producing good or evil, crushing evil or good, without bias one way or the other. Nature is a vast engine, run by a blind impulsion, a Will that knows not why it acts: it is "only able to work by Law." [2] Science excludes the supernatural, ignores the individual: it would regard a creative will, especially one that was unconscious and controlled by something else, as an absurdity. But Hardy's essentially religious nature, craving for something beyond, could not rest without some approximation to a Divine Artificer, a source of energy, a poetic semblance of biblical monotheism.[3] Yet he

[1] It is interesting to find Hardy in essential agreement with Tolstoy. As George Moore pointed out (*Avowals*, c. vii.), the root-idea of *War and Peace* was "the destruction of the Napoleonic legend, it being unendurable to Tolstoy that a man whose profession was war should stand before the world as a man of genius." Tolstoy was a man of genius, but he would not acknowledge that Napoleon counted for much personally. But Moore apparently did not notice that Tolstoy is just as ironical on the actual incompetence and the illusory popular belief in the decisive generalship of others than Napoleon. Bagration comes off as badly as do the far-sighted strategists in Hardy's *Dynasts*. Before an engagement with superior French forces under Lannes, Bagration rides over the area occupied by his troops, glances at the dispositions made by his officers, never criticizes or suggests the least alteration, but with a quiet smile takes the credit for infallible foresight and so infuses the fighting spirit which wins the day. So much for the heaven-born general! Then the little captain of artillery, posted with his guns at the most dangerous and critical point, goes into battle as if it were a delightful game, and sportingly mows down the enemy's infantry, burns the village that had been the French headquarters, and is the chief agent of a magnificent victory. Hardly anyone, least of all the commander-in-chief, knows how that desperate battle managed to be won. Hence, when Captain Touschine, stammering with shyness, comes before the chief and staff to report, and a cowardly scamp of an aide-de-camp happens to inquire about two guns that had had to be abandoned, the poor fellow hasn't a word to say for himself. The captain, without knowing it, has won the battle: the general, who never had a plan or an order to give, has all the glory.

[2] *Later Years*, 226.

[3] See the "Fragment" (*Moments of Vision*, 482):

"O we are waiting for one called God," said they,
"(Though by some the Will, or Force, or Laws;

could find nothing more divine than his Immanent Will which
"works unconsciously"—

> Eternal artistries in Circumstance,
> Whose patterns, wrought by rapt æsthetic rote,
> Seem in themselves Its single listless aim,
> And not their consequence.

CHORUS OF THE PITIES (*aerial music*).
> Still thus? Still thus?
> Ever unconscious!
> An automatic sense
> Unweeting why or whence?
> Be, then, the inevitable, as of old,
> Although that SO it be we dare not hold!

It is a determinism that manipulates the whole web of causation,
operating within man and not merely on outer circumstance.
Hardy invests the idea with a certain grandeur; but neither
reason nor imagination can find satisfaction in such an empty
conceit, a mere verbal subterfuge for the negation to which he
was being driven.[1] The determinism which thus takes the
place of the Greek Moira is a different kind of Necessity: it is
not ethical, it is not even conscious or in any way responsible,
even to itself. It may seem an awesome idea, this eternal
coercion of our thoughts, feelings, and acts, by influences
entirely beyond our ken. But where is the tragic conflict
when Tess, Jude, Sue, and their fellow-combatants are reduced
to mere automata? For what looked like free psychology in
the novels now proves to have been unfree. Jude, even as
Henchard, was overweighted at the outset with abnormal
excesses of character that menaced and eventually compassed
his ruin; yet he seemed to show fight. But the feelings and
doings of all alike are now seen to have been the result of
something that runs entirely counter to the spirit of tragedy.

> And, vaguely, by some, the Ultimate Cause;)
> Waiting for him to see us before we are clay."

Some such poetic adaptation of the Old Testament cosmogony is the usual shape
adopted by pessimist mythologies, *e.g.* those of Byron, Shelley, and Swinburne.

[1] As Dr de Ridder-Barzin points out, it is not Schopenhauer's will, but a poetic
image for an idea derived from the agnostic philosophy of Huxley and Spencer (168).
Her examination of Hardy's philosophy of life and its sources is lucid and
comprehensive.

Growth of Hardy's philosophy

The wavering course of Hardy's speculations on the problems of the will and of the forces which oppose and counteract men's desires has been indicated in the foregoing account of his successive novels. When he began writing, he was full of the revelations of science then going on, and his outlook widened with his reading and his riper reflection and with the deeper insight that came to him as he wrote. In "Hap," the poem written in 1866, the universe is contemplated as the sport of chance; in *The Dynasts*, forty years later, it is a complete system of determinism. The main trend of his thought was settled by his reading of the utilitarians and Darwinians: J. S. Mill, Spencer, Huxley, and others. He accepted the leading convictions of that age, soon finding himself compelled to abandon his religious faith. Much later on, it was from Clodd that he derived "the idea of the Unconscious Will becoming conscious with flux of time," [1] which he wove into *The Dynasts*. His sense of a Will other and more compulsive than man's was deepened by his study of the Greek tragedians, as the novels attest; he knew these long before he became acquainted with Schopenhauer and Hartmann. The latter came within his field of vision late in life, and it is possible that he never actually read their books, *The World as Will and Idea* and *The Philosophy of the Unconscious*. But their philosophies were in the air at that time, and he may well have obtained a fairly clear idea of their theories from articles and reviews and from lectures that he is known to have heard. He owed to Schopenhauer some of the terminology used in the later novels, poems, and his play, though he did not quite grasp, or at any rate assimilate, the essential features of Schopenhauer's doctrines. Hartmann is vaguely bracketed with Schopenhauer and other philosophers, in the "Apology" prefixed to *Late Lyrics and Earlier* (1922), as one of those who had Hardy's respect, though the poet "forlornly" ventures to hope in spite of them. Possibly he had Hartmann's ideas in mind, that life is not worth living and the only sane plan is to lay it down, when he wrote *Jude the Obscure*. The willingness of Tess to die, the suicide of Father Time, and other incidents or senti-

[1] *Later Years*, 275.

ments may indicate such knowledge. As to Hartmann's theories of the subconscious, subconscious perceptions play so large a part in novels as early as *The Return of the Native*, that it is hardly necessary to suppose Hardy borrowed much from this source when it did come later into his ken. So, too, with Schopenhauer's teaching on diseases of the will, Hardy showed the will failing to dominate environment, failing to come into harmony with the facts of existence: Bathsheba, Eustacia, Henchard, Tess, Jude, are maladjusted internally and externally. These cases seem to tally with Schopenhauer's diagnosis; but it is far from certain that Hardy was conversant with Schopenhauer when he analysed the earlier examples.[1] Nietzsche he did not know to any extent, and doubted whether his philosophy was "sufficiently coherent to be of great ultimate value." He spoke just as slightingly of Bergson, as previously noted. At all events, Hardy was no materialist. He never harboured any leanings towards the practical, economic, hedonistic view which is of so much importance in material life but of so little spiritual consequence. Hardy's regrets at not being able to realize better his innate spiritual aspirations are touchingly expressed in his little poem "The Impercipient," written at a cathedral service:

> Yet I would bear my shortcomings
>   With meet tranquillity,
> But for the charge that blessed things
>   I'd liefer not have be.
> O, doth a bird deprived of wings
>   Go earth-bound wilfully! [2]

---

[1] A suggestive article, "The Modern Consciousness in English Literature" (English Association: *Essays and Studies*, ix.), assumes Schopenhauer's influence in *The Return of the Native*, when there is no evidence that Hardy had begun to be interested in Schopenhauer. It was, to be sure, about this time that the German philosopher, after being wellnigh consigned to oblivion in this country, began to be generally read and discussed (see Cazamian, i. 256–257). He is first mentioned by Hardy in *Tess* (xxv.), where Mr Clare senior's "creed of determinism" is described as "a renunciative philosophy which had a cousinship with that of Schopenhauer and Leopardi." The article is by Barker Fairley.

[2] To the end, as his change of mind over the final stanzas in *The Dynasts* betrays, Hardy was never too sure of himself. Look at his portrait—not the head by Mestrovic which is too stern, but the painting by J. E. Blanche, for instance—and you can see why. A gentle, kindly, far from robust and determined spirit looks out. Henchard was perhaps too wilful and peremptory for such a creator!

Hardy's kin and his disciples   As would be expected, Hardy's enchanting pictures of outdoor life and the scenery of earth and sky set a fashion in country novels embellished with word-painting of natural surroundings. Dozens of imitators promptly arrived, who discovered counterparts of Wessex in this or that corner of Britain, in the neighbouring Somerset, Devon, and Cornwall, in Yorkshire, Lancashire, and East Anglia, in the Lowlands and the Highlands, in the Western Isles and in Wales and Ireland. That charlatan, Hall Caine, was following the Hardy lead when he annexed the Isle of Man as his private appanage. The influence made itself felt still further. There was a notable outbreak of regionalism among American novelists,[1] and all over Europe any province or district markedly stamped with local characteristics was seized and exploited. This was due in the main to the vogue of Hardy even beyond the seas, although the French might allege older exemplars in George Sand's Berrichon idylls, Erckmann-Chatrian's Alsatian romances, Pierre Loti's novels of Brittany, and Daudet's conquests in the Midi; the Germans could have pointed to Auerbach's Black Forest tales and Fritz Reuter's stories of Mecklenburg, and the Norwegians to Björnsen and Lie. But more symptomatic of the age that produced Hardy were the many amateur or trained naturalists who went out into the fields and woods to observe and meditate, and into the farm-yards and villages to watch man at work or at leisure, and to delineate him in a less dramatic but not less philosophical manner than Hardy, as one intensely interesting item in the great pageant of the seasons. These were his real kindred, much more so than those who strove to emulate his novels, when they had experienced their charm or their success at the circulating libraries. Their ulterior ancestry might, indeed,

[1] Regionalism "caught on" at once in America. Here are just a few of the novelists who dedicated themselves to particular areas or brands of people in the United States: it might be largely amplified: Constance Fenimore Cooper—Florida, "Octave Thanet"—Arkansas and Iowa, C. G. D. Roberts—New Brunswick and old Acadie, Kate Chopin—Louisiana, "Charles Egbert Craddock"—Tennessee, G. W. Cable—the Creoles, Harold Frederic—old New York State, Mary Wilkins—Massachusetts and old New England generally, Thomas Nelson Page—Virginia, Mary Foote—California and the waste lands of the West, James Lane Allen, a disciple of Thoreau—Kentucky, Sara Orne Jewett and Mrs Deland, both inspired by Mrs Gaskell—old New England.

be traced further back, for Hardy was not so much an originator as one caught by a native and powerful afflatus, older even than Chaucer and Shakespeare. This wistful and often ecstatic intercourse with nature, this quest of the simple life in the rustic and pastoral world, is an ever-recurring episode in literature, especially English literature. In this sense, Izaak Walton and White of Selborne, Frank Buckland (who was still alive, though an old man), and the poets, Thomson and Collins, Bloomfield and Clare, his countryman Barnes, and above all Wordsworth, were Hardy's predecessors. Among his contemporaries, Hardy's nearest affinity was Richard Jefferies, eight years his junior.

John Richard Jefferies (1848–1887) was not a novelist, though *Richard* a number of his books have a thread of story running through *Jefferies* them and must be put in that category as a last resort in classification. Born on a farm in Wiltshire, he went to two schools; but he was a trying lad, running away from home when he was sixteen, and in after-life showing himself morbidly restless and ineffectual. His best teacher seems to have been his father, who made him an observer and a reader. Journalism, in which he found an outlet for the enthusiasm of his nature-worship and cult of rustic life and character, made him a genuine though a minor man of letters. Probably, the majority of his books originated in contributions to provincial papers and to the magazines, records of his close watch on natural phenomena, set down with accuracy but with an impassioned eloquence that often went off into rhapsody, and affectionate studies of the farmer and labourer, including the "field-faring women," which are often charming examples of charactery, and sometimes take the guise of a little story.

One of his earliest books, *Greene Ferne Farm* (1880), was such a bucolic tale, saved from banality by the authentic touches of rustic character, manners, and the routine of farm life. Earlier than that, he had written for the *Pall Mall Gazette* and then published in volume-form *The Gamekeeper at Home* (1878), *Wild Life in a Southern County* and *The Amateur Poacher* (1879); and later on he wrote *The Life of the Fields* (1884), *The Open Air* (1885), and *The Toilers of the Field* (1892), all of which present the rustic as he is, but rarely with any hint of a story. Chapters like "John Smith's Shanty" or "A True Tale of the Wiltshire Labourer" are not much more than illustrative anecdotes. With *Wood Magic, a fable* (1881), and the sequel, *Bevis, the story of a Boy* (1882), Jefferies essayed something more ambitious, though these were only books for boys. But they are among the most epical and stirring of their kind, for in them Jefferies lived over again in more glorious fashion the adventures of himself and his brother on the reservoir near their farm, transfigured in imagination into a mighty ocean, fed by a Nile, a Mississippi, and other fabulous rivers, on whose waters they fought with wild beasts and savages, won a new battle of Pharsalia and founded a new Formosa—an Odyssey better than Homer's. *The Dewy Morn* (1884), which followed, is a most unconventional novel, more than half a pæan, hymning the purity of nature, and the purity of love as a natural passion and a glorious part of the universal scheme. "This wondrous loveliness purified and freed his soul from the grossness of material existence." The "one-ness" of Felise, and her "nobleness," more than atone for her crimes against convention. But, whilst "the dramatist renders all his characters happy, human life leaves half at least in sorrow." Felise has a rival in Rosa: "the existence of one woman is incompatible with the happiness of another." In the conflict that arises, Jefferies gives vent to a necessitarianism like Hardy's, and dogmatizes in much the same manner on the ways of the universe. Much of the book is a pamphlet. In *The Story of my Heart* (1883), published just before, he had found nothing human or humane in nature. Man's intelligence is his only refuge, his one hope. Yet Jefferies depicts himself as a man intoxicated with the beauty and vitality of nature, yearning for intenser union with all that is alive, yearning with a deeper passion than a man yearns for the woman he loves. But, alas! his aspirations are stultified: Nature is not friendly but hostile. He is a nature-lover who arrives at the opposite conclusion to Wordsworth's. Lyrical ecstasy culminates in his Te Deum; the philosophy loses itself in vague excursions into infinite realms of thought and a life "greater than divinity." In his curious fantasy,

After London, or wild England (1886), he imagines this country
overwhelmed by a cataclysm, and reverting to a state of nature,
the few surviving inhabitants resuming the barbarous arts of
our remote ancestors. *Amaryllis at the Fair* (1887) tries hard
to be a novel, and certainly does present real life, in the only
way Jefferies could compass it, the Iden family going about
their domestic concerns, drawn just as they are, country people
in their habitat, neatly differentiated one from the other, with
their diverse responses to the natural influences with which
they are in daily touch and to their personal relationships. It
is truly "a sketch direct from nature" [1]; but, like the rest, it is
entirely lacking in that life-giving dramatic interest without
which the finest full-length of character makes nothing but a
lay figure. That is his limitation. The moment he sets his
people doing something, or even stricken by an emotion, he can
only provide disconnected anecdotes. Nothing coheres, and
it all ends as inconsequently as it began.

Hudson the novelist must wait for a later chapter; Hudson *W. H.*
the friend and fellow-creature of birds and beasts, the humanist *Hudson*
with a wider and deeper comprehension of the universe, who
when he looks at man or any other being alive sees the object
stereoscopically in a vista of the infinite, is a greater seer even
than Thomas Hardy. His novels, though very different from
Hardy's, were the outcome of this kindred creative vision. It
was a mystical faculty, "animism" he called it, which mani-
fested itself from boyhood onwards. He used to feel like a
person "visited by a supernatural being," "perfectly convinced
that it was there in his presence," "thrilled to the marrow, but
not terrified if he knew that it would take no visible shape nor
speak to him out of the silence." [2] He believed that this
animistic instinct "exists and persists in many persons." Hardy

---

[1] That fine critic Edward Garnett went astray in his estimate of Jefferies (*Friday
Nights*, 163–174), mainly through his irritation at the artificial coincidences and
recalcitrances of circumstance that hamper such a story as *The Mayor of Casterbridge*,
with which he compares *Amaryllis at the Fair* to the latter's advantage. But Hardy's
little finger was thicker than the loins of Richard Jefferies. Imagine Amaryllis and
the rest of them transferred to the streets of Casterbridge. Henchard and Elizabeth-
Jane survive all the improbabilities, on which there is no need to lay any more stress;
but where would the Idens have been? Garnett never did Hardy common justice.

[2] *Far Away and Long Ago*, xvii.—"A Boy's Animism."

had more than an inkling of it when he sensed secret influences radiating from Egdon Heath, and subtly and imperceptibly swaying the lives and destinies of those who dwelt there. But Hudson's animism was not quite the same thing as Hardy's ancestral fetishism, and was nothing like Hardy's obstinate effort to see with the intellect, whilst surrendering unwittingly to subconscious instincts. Hardy was always trying his hardest to rationalize, but could not succeed in ridding his mind of deep-rooted preconceptions in which the true and the false were never clearly separated. Hudson trusted his intuitions, and so attained a serene and unclouded vision, beyond the reach of mere intellectualism and free from troubling incertitudes. It is chiefly in Vaughan, Traherne, and other avowed mystics, and also in Cowper and Wordsworth, that he recognized the faculty at work. In his own case, it enabled him to see men and things in the widest perspective, comprehended in the multitudinous life of all creation, linked together in a universal system of interrelationships; and thus he seized deeper and more pregnant truths, untroubled by any agnosticism. He, in short, saw clearly what Richard Jefferies felt obscurely. Like a few others, including Jefferies, he studied nature, not by the process of separating and abstracting, but by refusing "to divide man's life off from nature's life." [1]

Some other writers on nature The poet Edward Thomas might have gone as far had he lived; others, such as the two who christened themselves "George Bourne" and "John Halsham," went a little way in the same direction. George Bourne Sturt (1863–1927), in *The Bettesworth Book* (1901), *Memoirs of a Surrey Labourer* (1907), and *Lucy Bettesworth* (1913), wrote out as master the philosophic ponderings of his man, a poor labourer, self-taught and thinking for himself, whom he asserts to be one of a shrewd, reflective class of whom there exist far more than is commonly supposed. This, accordingly, is a kind of literature which is not fiction, but almost literally fact, with a certain amount of comment and interpretation. Thus

[1] Edward Garnett, *Friday Nights*—"W. H. Hudson's Nature Books," p. 30. Garnett continues, Hudson employed "all the old emotional tools—his sense of mystery, love of beauty, poetic imagination, and human love—to supplement and vivify the 'impassive' truths of Science."

the author says, "I had read of adventures: this man had lived adventurously. While I had sat at the window looking out upon existence as at a lion in the street, Bettesworth had met it face to face every day; he had been at death-grips with it, and had come off victorious." He is a man full of anecdotes, and his talk is alive with racy phrases and "words fat with meaning." A lovable and estimable personage, who takes delight in his job—"I know well that to-day his interest in my garden is more affectionate than my own"; his success is not only a comment on the alleged ignorance and indifference of the country labourer, but has also moulded his self-respect and given him a sort of personal equality with his employer. There is no story; but Bettesworth talks and talks; and talks sense, if more drowsily, even under the influence of beer, the poor man's inspirer and restorer.

Doubtless the beer had not helped to clear it—his speech; but beer or none, it was the usual straightforward practical sense that he talked, animated by good-temper and vivid interest in his subject.

The *Idlehurst* (1898), *Lonewood Corner* (1907), and *Old Standards* (1913), of "John Halsham," or G. Forrester Scott, form a similar blend of charactery, the raw stuff of fiction, with the random musings of one from a more sophisticated world, seeking refreshment among rustic simplicities. All three works are made up of articles contributed to the *Saturday Review*, and together compose the desultory autobiography of a literary man rusticating in the Weald of Sussex. Bits of reinvigorating converse with nature, observant rambles over the downs and the forest, light character-sketches of villagers and gentry, interspersed with scholarly reminiscence and the dreams of "a backward-looking idiosyncrasy," with the merest shadow of a connecting story, make up what is no more a novel than *The Complete Angler* was, a book which these three continually recall with their mingling of quiet reverie and the tonic air of out-of-doors.

The poet Edward Thomas (1878–1917) tried his hand at a

novel, four years before a promising life was cut off. In *The Happy-go-lucky Morgans* (1913) he registered half-forgotten moods and dreams and friendships, in a manner not unlike the foregoing, with an old suburban house as the stage. But he belongs to this group of visionary naturalists chiefly by such a book as *The Heart of England* (1909), in which he applied the poetic imagination to the visible scene, especially to those aspects of it which are usually dismissed with half a glance. It is not fiction in form or intent; but a potential story, even a potential novel, seems latent in many of the sketches of people met. The colloquy with the watercress-man, for instance, is in the manner of George Borrow, who was a novelist, if at all, only by such accidents. Thomas was engagingly modest: "I know nothing of literature," he writes, "I am a journalist."

Hardy's imitators   It may seem that all this is leading a long way from Thomas Hardy. But George Bourne, John Halsham, and Edward Thomas were more authentically akin to him than were the majority of his followers, who were apt to copy the accidental without penetrating to the essential spirit of his art. Perhaps it would be illusory to try and trace even unconscious emulation of *Under the Greenwood Tree* and *Far from the Madding Crowd* in the later novels of such an old hand as R. D. Blackmore (1825–1900), who had made his name by the frank romanticism of *Lorna Doone* (1869), combining arts assimilated from Wilkie Collins with as much as he could learn from Scott. But *Cripps the Carrier, a woodland tale* (1876), *Christowell* (1882), a Dartmoor novel, and *Perlycross, a tale of the Western Hills* (1894), have at least surface resemblances to some of Hardy's novels, not excluding *Desperate Remedies*; and *Springhaven* (1887) weaves in similar rustic material with the same sort of memories of the Napoleonic terror as Hardy often played with, notably in *The Trumpet Major*. Baring-Gould was another miscellaneous romancer who vied openly with Hardy, in melodramatic novels of passion among peasant folk or country yeomen and squires of an old tyrannical stamp, such as *Mehalah, a story of the Salt Marshes* (1880), *John Herring* (1884), *Red Spider* (1887), *The Gaverocks* (1888), *Richard Cable, the Lightshipman* (1888), *Urith, a tale of Dartmoor* (1891), *In the Roar of the Sea* (1892), *The Broom-Squire* (1896), *Dartmoor Idylls* (1896), and *Guavas the Tinner* (1897). Scenery was used by Baring-Gould to give local colour, and also to deepen the tragic atmosphere which he liked to conjure up. On a higher level, and nearer in spirit to Hardy, was the lady, Miss Gwendoline Keats, who signed her novels with the pseudonym "Zack." The title-story in *Life is Life, and other tales and episodes* (1901), is of people in Australia, and the philosophy implied in a tale of calamity following on calamity is summed up in the pithy sayings of the patient old woman, who hammers it in that life is life. *On Trial* (1899) and *Tales of Dunstable Weir* (1901) are about Devonshire country folk; *The White Cottage* (1901) and *The Roman Road* (1903) are also stories of fishermen and country people and the dramas that hinge upon a guilty conscience. Zack was a not unworthy disciple of the Wessex master. Lastly, among the host of territorial novelists, most of whose works appeared in the nineties, the following were the most prominent. It is noteworthy that they were nearly all born soon after 1850, and the fact that they started novel-writing so late in life is good evidence that it was due to some external stimulus, no doubt the vogue of Hardy's novels.[1] "James Prior" (James Prior Kirk, 1850–1922) took Sherwood Forest and the neighbourhood as his district, in *Forest Folk* (1901) and other novels; Walter Raymond (1853–1930) wrote novels and short stories of Somerset, *Two Men o' Mendip* (1899) being a very respectable effort in the Hardy vein; Joseph Henry Pearce (*b.* 1856) annexed Cornwall, Howard Pease took

---

[1] Mr Eden Phillpotts began his long career with a number of stories and novels that challenged comparison with Hardy's Wessex series, e.g. *Children of the Mist* (1898), *Sons of the Morning* (1900), *The Good Red Earth* (1901), *The River* (1902), *The Secret Woman* (1905), and *The Portreeve* (1906), to take but a few. On no one was the Hardy influence more drastic. There is an elemental philosophy of life latent in the commentary, and a fatalism is ofttimes expounded by certain wiseacres among the rustic characters; but the author rejects fatalism as a creed. Oldreive, in *The River*, is just one of Hardy's men, who finds excuse for his misdeeds in the theory that his nature is different from other men's and compels him to act so. "Born to failure he be, an' 'tis vain to tell about free will when you'm face to face wi' the likes of Oldreive. His history be written 'pon his evil face, an' in his eyes, an' under 'em—writ in his jaw an' scowl. But whether his Maker, or his master, the devil, had the planning of his days be beyond man's wit to fathom." "Let fall upon the fire by his father when he was drunk," sounds like an echo of Hardy, and, again, "Her justice ban't ours seemingly." "No; flout her, and somebody's got to sling for it, though it may not always be the sinner."

Northumbria, Robert Murray Gilchrist (1868–1917) the Peak
of Derbyshire, Joseph Smith Fletcher (*b.* 1863) and Halliwell
Sutcliffe (1870–1932) the West Riding of Yorkshire, the Irish-
woman "M. E. Francis" (Mrs Francis Blundell, *d.* 1930)
Lancashire and then Dorset, whilst William Edwards Tirebuck
(1854–1900) aspired to be the novelist of Wales.   The literary
genealogy of Mary Webb (1883–1927) is a little more complicated; she learned from George Eliot and Mrs Humphry
Ward, and probably also from Mrs Gaskell and even Maria
Edgeworth.   Something must be said about her interesting
novels, published late in the first quarter of this century, much
further on.   Here it is enough to observe that her sensitive
use of scenery from the Welsh marches is strongly reminiscent
of Hardy, whose pictorial mode of narration she caught and
overdid, however, so that often in her novels the story is told
in pictures—pictures of scenery, of houses, of waters, pictures
of savage men, seductive women, and the like.

CHAPTER III

MARK RUTHERFORD AND OTHERS

THE writers coming next in view form a somewhat indefinite group, associated rather by the atmosphere of gloom and melancholy they exhale than by any moral or æsthetic attitudes or doctrines. Mark Rutherford, as he is best known, was not really and truly a novelist; Gissing wrote his novels out of loathing and indignation; Moore was a devotee of art, who first found congenial exercise for his realism in those ugly and shady avenues of life by which the other two were horror-stricken. Realists they were, all three, but each in his own sense of the word, not with the dull uniformity of the novelists of mean streets who took up the parable after them. Gissing and Moore, exponents of naturalism or neo-realism, began in the age of the æsthetes, when, from the deference paid to Art with a capital letter, the subject, the raw material, was deliberately rated as of minor account in comparison with the treatment, in a studied, often an over-studied, effort at artistic integrity. It was an obviously self-conscious effort, though each one made it a point of honour to sink himself and his feelings in the quest for truth of art. Hence, while Mark Rutherford and Gissing transmit the liveliest sense of pity and indignation, the more punctilious realists abjure pity and indignation, and claim to have observed and to have reproduced with utter impartiality. Imperturbable veracity was the watchword: the novelist must have a soul impenetrable as marble.

Readers will not go far astray if, with certain reservations, they recognize Mark Rutherford, whose character and mental history are the theme of *The Autobiography of Mark Rutherford* (1881) and *Mark Rutherford's Deliverance* (1885), as the double of his creator, William Hale White (1831–1913), at one time assistant director of contracts to the Admiralty, who preferred to go by that name in literature. Though not entirely corresponding in matters of fact, as four later volumes of collections show, these two books clearly reveal the man, and recount with some variations of circumstance the cardinal incidents of his mental and spiritual career. They are also an eloquent and moving exposition of the philosophy of life in which he at length found peace, in default of consolation. Hale White was born in Bedford, the sleepy market-town of the east midlands which rests unnamed in the novels, and was brought up by his parents, who were well-to-do shopkeepers, for the Dissenting ministry. When, though a man of strong religious instincts, he found it intellectually impossible to accept and preach the doctrines inherited from the past and still strictly enjoined by the Independents of that day, he was forced out of the communion, in a manner as humiliating as that of Rutherford's dismissal. The stages of his emancipation from the narrow dogmas of the Calvinist sect in that obsolete world, far too ignorant and complacent to pay any heed to biblical criticism from Germany or to sceptical English philosophies, and afterwards from the anguish of doubt, regret, and fear, of the man deprived of a creed, are faithfully set forth in these two narratives, which he gave to the world a few years after his translation of Spinoza's *Ethics* (1877).

The "Autobio-graphy" He did not absolutely identify himself with Mark Rutherford. On the contrary, there is a further disguise, in the friend, Reuben Shapcott, who is supposed to have edited the *Autobiography* and put together the *Deliverance* from Rutherford's notes. Mark, like Zachariah and Miriam in the two subsequent books, is indeed represented as not of the same mental calibre as his author, but of rather middling intelligence, for the particular object was to show the unwisdom and danger of speculating beyond one's depth. Nevertheless, the history in its main lines is that of Hale White's struggles and distresses and ultimate deliverance. And, taken together, the two books form an introspective history heralding the modern psychological novel. For it is on the adventures and agonies of a soul that Mark Rutherford is always intent; even the commonest story—and those of Mark and Miriam and Zachariah are far from common—is given the depth and intensity of tragic life. Mark could take no interest in the long prayers at the chapel where he went with his parents. Looking back, at the time when he wrote his autobiography, he could see that "nothing was falser than the long prayer"; it is "a horrible hypocrisy." "Direct appeal to God can only be justified when it is passionate." These people misunderstood the Bible: not till long afterwards was the Bible really opened to him, to become the most precious of books. During the first two years at college his life was purely external; his heart was untouched. But in the third year he picked up a copy of the *Lyrical Ballads*, and this wrought a change in him "only to be compared with that which is said to have been wrought on Paul himself by the Divine apparition." Wordsworth re-created for him his Supreme Divinity, "substituting a new and living spirit for the old deity, once alive, but gradually hardened into an idol." But the result for the young preacher was that his efforts to explain in intelligible terms such doctrines as the Atonement were criticized, in that he did not rest in the simplicity of the Gospel. He made many enemies, especially when the congregation dwindled, and the deacons, who were tradesmen, saw their custom falling off. The worst was Mr Snale, the draper, who was "so very genteel compared with the other draper," a great red man, who "hung things outside his window." He and his wife had had their portraits painted.

Both were daubs, but curiously faithful in depicting what was most offensive in the character of both the originals, Mr Snale's simper being preserved, together with the peculiarly hard, heavy sensuality of the eye in Mrs Snale, who was large and full-faced, correct like Mr Snale, a member of the church, and cruel, not with the ferocity of the tiger, but with the dull insensibility of a cart-wheel, which will roll over a man's neck as easily as over a flint.

Domesticity at the Snales', at the Dorcas meetings especially, is caustically touched in, though Snale, like other of Mark Rutherford's more odious figures, is only a mask for qualities he could not penetrate, only stand bewildered. No wonder Mark begins to have his fits of hypochondria. "Often, with no warning, I am plunged into the Valley of the Shadow, and no outlet seems possible; but I contrive to traverse it, or to wait in calmness for access of strength." Snale attacks Mark Rutherford's simply human interpretations of the Gospel, in an anonymous letter to the local paper, the writer of which Mark at once recognizes, being confirmed in his conjecture by an extraordinary personage whom he comes across at this juncture and makes his friend. Mardon is a free-thinker, yet a man of the purest and finest character, whom negative criticism, conjoined with the virtues of cheerful self-denial and patience, has taught to live without illusions. From Mardon and Mardon's daughter, Mary, an example of the same heroism "in a russet dress," Mark begins to see "the folly of this perpetual reaching after the future," though it is not till years later that he himself attains to their serene joyfulness. Meanwhile, the lonely man pines for a home, and nearly marries a commonplace girl who could never have made him a real companion. He is saved from this by his chance rencontre with another superior soul, Miss Arbour, who finds out his predicament, and reveals that she had been the wife of a narrow-minded egotist, who had made her "wretched beyond description," till she had the courage to leave him. The little episode reveals also Mark Rutherford's power of conveying tragedy in half-a-page of vivid dialogue. "He was confounded. Who could have dreamed that such tragic depths lay behind that serene face, and that her orderly precision was like the grass and flowers upon volcanic soil with Vesuvian fires slumbering below?"

Thrown out by the Congregationalists, Mark for a while occupies a Unitarian pulpit; but his congregation, though it had a free-thought lineage, was a petrified set. There was one exception, in a woman whose "prompt decisions were a scandal to her more sedate friends." Mrs Lane shows a great spirit and stupefies her unimaginative neighbours in divers incidents. Her husband, however, would have lost his business but for an honesty "which drew customers to him, who, notwithstanding the denunciations of the parson, preferred tea with some taste in it from a Unitarian to the insipid wood-flavoured stuff which was sold by the grocer who believed in the Trinity." Unitarianism was only a stage, however, in Mark's progress. He has a spell of school-teaching, described with the same ironic brevity. He simply runs away, after another fit of terror and hypochondria. Later he writes,

I know the causelessness of a good deal of those panic fears, and all that suffering, but I tremble to think how thin is the floor on which we stand which separates us from the bottomless abyss.

He is in London when the *Autobiography* breaks off, a London "*Mark* to be depicted in the same sombre colours by Gissing a year or *Ruther-* two later. Mark Rutherford had the advantage of encounter-*ford's* ing and recognizing a few characters of rare beauty and modest *Deliver-* saintliness, who, with Wordsworth and Spinoza, enabled him *ance*" to accomplish the Deliverance recorded in the volume by "Reuben Shapcott." Brilliant, in spite of the usual reticence, is the quarter-length of Theresa, niece of the Darwinist book-seller, Wollaston. Mark is distressed to find himself in love with her at the same time as his love of Mary Mardon continues unabated. She teaches him the folly of self-despisings. "Of all services which may be done to man, I know of none more precious." More of an original is Miss Leroy, "a person whom nobody could have created in writing a novel, because she was so inconsistent." She, when she had become Mrs Butts, lived among them "as an Arabian bird with its peculiar habits, cries, and plumage, might live in one of our barn-yards with the ordinary barn-door fowls." Even London's nether world is not destitute of characters whom it is the sin of sins to despise. Mark and his colleague M'Kay, when they are earning a scanty living by hard labour as reporters in the House of Commons, make a brave attempt at gradually civilizing the squalid denizens of the slums around Drury Lane, by opening a room where they read books and teach an undogmatic Christianity to such as will come. Among their humblest friends is Taylor, one of the lost in the merciless confusion of modern existence.

Porter at some offices near Clare Market, "he was a servant of servants," even of those who were exposed to the petty tyrannies of the clerks. "The head messenger, who had been a butler, swore at him, and if Taylor had 'answered' he would have been reported." "A little more of such a life would have transformed him into a brute." John was an old man who had begun as a potboy, when ten years old, and now, saddled with a drunken wife, was trying in an alley where "not a square-inch of sky was visible," to bring up his little son decently. Cardinal, a burly Yorkshireman who had been a thriving commercial traveller but had come down, was adrift with his eccentric wife, a pair whose peculiarities were the "necessary result of the total chaos of a time without moral guidance." Like Gissing, Rutherford paints a London which was truly a "City of Dreadful Night"; both seem to echo Thomson's lines:

> The world rolls round for ever like a mill;
> It grinds out death and life and good and ill;
> It has no purpose, heart or mind or will.[1]

But Rutherford's soul was of a different mettle from Gissing's. Superficially, the epicurean calm and content with what is given him in which the latter's Henry Ryecroft ends his days, when after his labours and privations he comes into his little legacy, seem much the same as Mark Rutherford's quietism and resignation to the fact that "one-fourth of life is intelligible, the other three-fourths is unintelligible darkness; and our earliest duty is to cultivate the habit of not looking round the corner." Gissing, too, invokes the shades of Spinoza and Marcus Aurelius, and declares himself a Stoic. But this is the comforting pose adopted by the hard-worked literary man who has lost hope, and tries, in all sincerity, to show how he would make the most of it if a last glint of sunshine were accorded him. Mark Rutherford reaches his tranquillity of soul by living through the worst, and at length realizing the futility of questioning when there is no answer.

The greatest part, far the greatest part, of our lives is spent in dreaming over the morrow, and when it comes, it, too, is

[1] Thomson's poem had appeared in 1874.

consumed in the anticipation of a brighter morrow, and so the cheat is prolonged, even to the grave.

Let us renounce such brooding over the insoluble, bearing in mind our limitations and that the insoluble exists. From the Book of Job, on which his commentary is appended to the *Deliverance*, Mark Rutherford learned two things. "One is, that God vouchsafes to Job no revelation in order to solve the mystery with which he was oppressed. There is no promise of immortality, nothing but an injunction to open the eyes and look abroad over the universe. Whatever help is to be obtained is to be had, not through an oracle, but by the exercise of Job's own thought." The other is that "God reminds us of His wisdom, of the mystery of things, and that man is not the measure of His creation. The world is immense, constructed on no plan or theory which the intellect of man can grasp." Hence, when Mark nears the close of his pilgrimage, he puts away the riddles of death and immortality that once drove him wellnigh insane.

I cannot tell how, but so it is, that at the present moment, when I am years nearer the end, they trouble me but very little.

Life has solved his problems, so far as they can be solved. Very late, but not too late, he rediscovers the woman whom he once loved, now a widow with a little daughter; and they marry. Not long after, he dies of heart failure, the result of a violent rating by his brutal employer. The book ends abruptly, for it is not a novel, not art but truth. And yet there is an art which gives a more poignant life and authenticity to such a record than are to be found in more than one or two of the most faithful biographies, and in very few novels indeed.

Hale White had a good deal of the right endowment, but he would never have been much of a novelist even had he tried. He could tell a short tale perfectly; "A Mysterious Portrait," appended to the *Deliverance*, and "Michael Trevanion," to *Miriam's Schooling*, are masterpieces of singular beauty. But he had no structural ability whatever. He dispenses with anything of the nature of plot, and even the outlines of his

"The Revolution in Tanner's Lane"

stories are broken and discrepant. The *Autobiography* is
dropped when the pen falls from Rutherford's hand; the
Deliverance takes up the narrative at a different point, autobiography being relinquished for memoirs by another. Hardy
was clumsy enough in his transitions [1]; Mark Rutherford
ignores the art entirely, and rambles on from one striking
incident to the next in the most fortuitous way. He will even
introduce a new character or two in the last couple of pages, as
in *Miriam's Schooling*. True, this absence of any formal plan
tends to communicate a sense of fact, for of course this is how
things happen. But it is all so abrupt and inconsecutive that
the reader is often confounded, especially when he fails to
recognize the Ellen whom Mark once thought it unwise to
marry in the older Ellen who at length gives him happiness,
or when the author forgets, in *Catharine Furze*, that the worn
furniture and shabby carpets and the portraits of the Virgin
Mary and of George IV, which the lady of the new house
relegates to the garret, had all been burnt when the former
residence was gutted by the fire. Such an oversight is perhaps
unpardonable. For this was in what purports to be a novel.
His other books did not purport to be anything of the sort.
They were designed, rather, on the model of personal reminiscences, confidential recollections, of a troubled epoch in social
and religious history; and nothing is more unmistakable in
the principal figures than that they were taken from life.
They may perhaps have an unfinished look; they may come
in abruptly and disappear before their features have been
properly scrutinized; but there is a firmness and solidity in
them which guarantees the impression that Mark Rutherford
must have been in the closest contact with their originals. As
Herman Melville says, "The symmetry of form attainable in
pure fiction cannot be so readily achieved in a narration having
less to do with fable than with fact. Truth uncompromisingly
told will always have its ragged edges; hence the conclusion of
such a narration is apt to be less finished than an architectural
finial." [2] This applies accurately to Mark Rutherford's first

[1] That is what George Moore is driving at in his strictures on Hardy's inability to
handle "a sequence of events" (*Confessions of a Young Man*, xii.).　　[2] *Billy Budd*.

three books. All our greater novelists have been great social historians: Fielding, Scott in his best, that is, the Scottish novels, Thackeray, Dickens, George Eliot, and Meredith, not to mention those of yesterday, have had this in common with Shakespeare. But they did not set their minds to the task with the earnestness of Mark Rutherford, or show his grasp of the philosophy of history. It is a pity there have not been more Mark Rutherfords, to trace and comment on the epoch-making changes in other eras, to show them actually going on, with the hopes and disappointments and sufferings which were their personal accompaniment, illuminated by the insight and reflections of an earnest and compassionate thinker. *The Revolution in Tanner's Lane* (1887) is an admirably graphic portrayal of such a critical epoch in the evolution of the modern world; it is also a flagrant instance of Mark Rutherford's disregard of structural consistency, being practically two books in one pair of covers. The story of the years 1814–1817 and the doings of the agitators in London and Manchester ends with the death of Major Maitland, that debonair patriot from the upper classes, and with the rout of the misguided Blanketeers and the execution of the heroic Caillaud. After telling of Zachariah's two years in prison and of the death of his wife, the author in a postscript intimates that Zachariah married Pauline and lost her, being left with a little child; and then begins what is to all intents a new story, in the new environment of Cowfield, a little town in his favourite east midlands, with new characters for the most part, except that Zachariah eventually reappears to form an accidental link with the previous subject. All this has little more to do with that modest champion of almost forgotten struggles for the right to live than has *Miriam's Schooling*, a story also laid in Cowfield. Yet the Tanner's Lane affair actually gives the book its title— another bit of carelessness! The schism in the old Calvinist chapel makes excellent satirical comedy, but is a foreign body so far as the history of the social revolution is concerned.

This latter, which of course precedes the other, is probably *Two* the most moving picture extant of those bitter times, and is *stories* stamped with Mark Rutherford's palpable authenticity. It is *in one* as if he were in it himself, as he was in the excruciating experiences of the former books. Zachariah Coleman, a Byron-reading Calvinist printer, is another of his commonplace figures, an average man of the people, who is drawn into momentous affairs and is a foil to characters much more remarkable, such as the exiled revolutionary Caillaud, who meets an ignominious death with the majesty of true heroism, and his adopted daughter, the brilliant Pauline, child of the unmentionable woman who bearded Couthon during the Reign of Terror and saved the man who had deserted her from the guillotine. The scenes of horror and brutal oppression by the Government and the ruling classes are relieved, yet by no means weakened, by the humours of odd and incompatible characters. Particularly charming are the glimpses of the Colemans' modest household, ruled by that physically and morally spotless woman Mrs Coleman. "The sight of dirt gave her a quiet kind of delight, because she foresaw the pleasure of annihilating it." Only the impeccable Major can enter her prim lodgings with impunity without wiping his boots. As to Pauline, daughter of a wicked woman who had shown herself a heroine, Mrs Coleman has listened with cold, prudish ears to the tale of humble magnanimity.

> She stood like a statue while Pauline put on her hat.
> "Good night, madam," said Caillaud, slightly bowing.
> "Good night, madam," said Pauline, not bowing in the least.
> "Good night," she replied, without relaxing her rigidity.
> As soon as they were in the street Pauline said, "Father, I abhor that woman. If she lives she will kill her husband."
> Mrs Coleman, on the other hand, at the same moment said, "Zachariah, Pauline and Caillaud cannot come to this house again."
> "Why not?"
> "Why not, Zachariah? I am astonished at you! The child of a woman who lived in open sin!"

Mark Rutherford knew how people learned political economy in those days:

> The men and women of that time, although there were scarcely any newspapers, were not fools, and there was not a

Nottingham weaver who put a morsel of bread in his hungry belly who did not know that two morsels might have gone there if there were no impost on foreign corn to maintain rents, and if there were no interest to pay on money borrowed to keep these sacred kings and lords safe in their palaces and parks.

The terrorism with which the hungry Blanketeers, who innocently thought they had only to march to London and lay their grievances frankly before the Prince Regent to have justice done forthwith, are mown down and scattered is described with appalling exactness. Mark Rutherford subscribed to Gissing's belief in outspokenness: "An honest and wise man should have a rough tongue. Let him speak and spare not!" [1] He does not mince matters when he comes to George the Fourth himself:

And yet, when we call to mind the THING then on the throne; the THING that gave £180 for an evening coat, and incurred enormous debts, while his people were perishing; the THING that drank and lied and whored; the THING that never did nor said nor thought anything that was not utterly brutish and contemptible—when we think that the THING was a monarch, Heaven-ordained, so it was said, on which side does the absurdity really lie?

If that is mere declamation, take this incident witnessed by the fugitive Zachariah, when he seeks a night's lodging at a roadside inn, and finds a dozen decent-looking men smoking and drinking round the fire. He is told there is no bed for him; and just then a poor, emaciated weaver comes in, whose wife was down with the fever, and his family all starving.

"Ah," said the overseer, "no work, and the fever, and starving; that's what they always say. I'll bet a sovereign you've been out after them Blanketeers."

"It's a judgment on you," observed the parson. "You and your like go setting class against class; you never come near the church, and then you wonder God Almighty punishes you."

"You can come on your knees to us when it suits you, and you'd burn my rick to-morrow," said a third.

---

[1] *Henry Ryecroft*, "Summer," xiii.

"There's a lot of fever amongst 'em down my way," said another, whose voice was rather thick, "and a damned lot of expense they are, too, for physic and funerals. It's my belief that they catch it out of spite."

"Aren't you going to give me nothing?" said the man. "There isn't a mouthful of food in the place, and the wife may be dead before the morning."

"Well, what do you say, parson?" said the overseer.

"I say we've got quite enough to do to help those who deserve help," he replied, "and that it's flying in the face of Providence to interfere with its judgment." With that he knocked the ashes out of his pipe, and took a great gulp of his brandy-and-water.

Compared with that, the tale of religion as it was in the forties in such a place as Cowfield, and the events that led to the abdication of the bloated, gormandizing, ignorant, and hypocritical Mr Broad, with his unspeakable son, is the transition from old to new, witnessed by Mark Rutherford, seen now from another side, and described in lighter vein. But if this is Hale White at his most entertaining, it is none the less serious satire, and the historical diagnosis of a first-hand authority.

"*Miriam's Schooling*," etc. A comparison with George Eliot is repeatedly challenged in these three books; it is still more to the point in *Miriam's Schooling* and *Catharine Furze*, the one a story, the other a novel, concerned with the ordeals by which character is schooled. Both writers were deeply versed in philosophic theory, both apply it to the problems formulated in the lives of their characters. Hale White seems to do this with a lighter touch, a finer art, but quite as unerringly; it is obviously a science that he has made part of himself by living as well as learning it. In the story he takes the critical portion of a young woman's life, and makes it a parable that interprets itself. Miriam, a very original, self-centred, thinking girl, escapes from the dead-alive Cowfield, but in London meets with one misfortune after another, and comes home again beaten. She cannot find her proper sphere. She has had one sharp moral awakening, when after a dangerous illness, brought on by want and exposure, she finds bending over and tenderly nursing her the very Miss

Tippett whom she had once derided as a narrow-minded old frump, and, worse still, whom she had left in the lurch when almost at the point of death. That incident roused her: "she must do something for her fellow-creatures." But nursing in a hospital proves not to be her vocation; she gets her dismissal. Back in her native place, she drifts in the usual way into marriage, which speedily bores her. Yet it is the dull and unresponsive husband that completes her education, for she accidentally discovers that he too is a personality, with merits and interests of his own, practical and material forsooth, but good enough to sweeten life, for him and why not for her? The vicar is an astronomer, and introduces her to the stars. The dull husband has already been inducted. He, the village carpenter, made the cabinet for the instruments, a piece of faultless workmanship. He now, to please the vicar and also his wife, constructs an orrery. Miriam has been musing over the lines,

> But bound and fixed in fettered solitude
> To pine, the prey of every changing mood,

when her sky clears. It is a talk with Fitchew, the jobbing gardener with the hard-faced wife, and his rejoinder, "We are as we are, and we must make the best of it," on a serene evening after storm which imperceptibly to herself fills her with a Wordsworthian calm, that finishes Miriam's schooling and reconciles her with existence.

Appended to this is a short story, "Michael Trevanion," of *Michael* an earnest Calvinist father who commits a sin to prevent his *Trevanion"* son's marrying a worldly young woman, and suddenly finds that he has made a fearful blunder. He was misled by that verse of Paul's, "I could wish that myself were accursed from Christ for my brethren, my kinsmen according to the flesh." "What did Paul mean?" "What *could* he mean save that he was willing to be damned to save those whom he loved?" Mark Rutherford rejoiced in such pieces of casuistry, as in the former story when Miriam is ready to swear a doubtful oath to exculpate a man charged with arson, simply because she does not like to think him guilty. Trevanion leaves a letter open, from which it appears conclusively that the girl is no better than she should be. The poor lad is stricken as by the poisoned tongue of Iago; and when the old man goes to his little office he finds a note:

"I have left for ever.—Your affectionate son, Robert."

Has he drowned himself? Michael walks by the shore. He longs for death, but suicide is forbidden by his creed. Why not let himself drown? He throws off his clothes and enters the water. In utter indifference he lets himself get out of his depth. It is Robert's girl who saves him, at the treacherous eddy where Robert had saved her only the other day. Not by a mere revulsion of feeling, but by tokens that can be neither defined nor contradicted, he recognizes that the girl is one of the best. Posting after his son, he reaches Plymouth an hour before the boat leaves for America; and there on the Hoe he falls on his son's neck, to the wonderment of all the bystanders. But that night, as the reconciled pair sit and watch the Eddystone light, Robert turns to his father, and finds the old man dead. It is as beautiful a tale as the earlier one, "A Mysterious Portrait," of the lady with the exquisite face whom a man catches sight of at moments of stress in his affairs, and who disappears mysteriously before he can speak to her. It haunts him, that face, and it haunts the reader, like a musical strain which is, simply, beauty. And Mark Rutherford believed that music has "the power to chase doubt from the mind," for what is doubt but despondency? That is Mr Cardew's argument, in *Catharine Furze*, and it is a bit of mysticism that no one who feels the spell of pure beauty will be inclined to question. For minds spiritually awake, like Mark Rutherford's, intimations are all about us. He ends the account of a beautiful day, in *Catharine Furze*, with the sentence, "It was a day on which to believe in immortality."

"Catharine Furze," etc. This was his one novel, or at least his nearest approximation to the accepted form. It has coherence and continuity; it has most of the ordinary ingredients, such as love-interest, satire of the vulgar cult of gentility, and the charm of his own favourite heroine; but those ingredients are refined to a rarer spiritual standard. Yet it might just as well be called a morality, or a stern though gentle criticism of life. Matthew Arnold would

have given it cordial approbation. For an ethical philosophy permeates every incident and every situation, and goes to the root of the matter in the passages of dialogue that carry the story forward. It is a rider to the philosophic lesson taught by Mark Rutherford's history: the folly and the peril of dreaming and theorizing on what lies outside our everyday life and our personal limitations. Catharine has an intelligence not to be hoodwinked by the pretences and little hyprocrisies which are the current coin in middle-class life. She is frank and down-right: her conventional parents are in daily terror of what she may say or do next. But Catharine has not yet found her way in a world of perplexities. And, unfortunately, while she is still wondering, she comes under the spell of the Rev. Mr Cardew. Cardew's eloquence and imaginative vision carry her away. He dwells in spheres of spiritual exaltation far from the workaday world, and he has a notable talent for evolving sublime ideas and dressing them up in seducing images. The wife who adores him, a pattern of unselfish devotion, can never put her feelings into words; so he thinks her empty and commonplace, and has long ceased to expect true sympathy, or that which he conceives love to be, from one so unresponsive. He would even have welcomed criticism if she could have understood him.

Mistaken mortal! it was her patient heroism which made her dumb to him about her sorrows and his faults. A very limited vocabulary is all that is necessary on such topics.

Cardew hugs his solitude, and is all the more liable to be tempted by the lure of a kindred soul. Hence he and Catharine find themselves passionately in love: the young girl and the married clergyman hover on the brink of a mutual declaration, which would be as fatal to their own happiness as to that of all who trust them. Such is the position in which they stand, aching to cross the unseen line, but each withheld by the impossibility to an honest soul of a crime against those who love them. It is another and a more searching study of the problem of marriage, which is the simple one of the divergence of temperament and interests that most people experience

when they find themselves wedded, and most learn to put up
with. As that sage stoic Dr Turnbull says:

A man marries a woman whom he loves. Is it possible that
she, of all women in the world, is the one he would love best if
he were to know all of them? Is it likely that he would have
selected this one woman if he had seen, say, fifty more before
he had married her? Certainly not; and when he sees other
women afterwards, better than the one he has chosen, he
naturally admires them. If he does not he is a fool; but he is
bound to check himself. He puts them aside and is obliged
to be satisfied with his wife. If it were permissible in him in
such a case to abandon her, a pretty chaos we should be in.

This is only common sense; but the insight with which Dr
Turnbull diagnoses what is wrong with Catharine, and also
with Cardew, is far from common. Cardew is a remarkable
man, and a stimulating thinker, "but his thinking is not
directed upon life." The doctor tells his patient:

Nothing is more dangerous, physically and mentally, than to
imagine we are not as other people. . . . Never, under any
pretext whatever, allow yourself to do what is exceptional. . . .
For one person, who, being a person of genius, has been injured
by what is called conventionality—I do not mean, of course,
foolish conformity to what is absurd—thousands have been
saved by it, and self-separation means mischief. It has been
the beginning even of insanity in many cases which have come
under my notice.

Had Catharine not been thrilled by Mr Cardew's discourses
she would probably in the end have married the humble but
sterling Tom Catchpole, whose tragic adoration, and the
persecution it stirs up in the snobbish Mrs Furze and her
compliant husband, form a subsidiary thread of interest. The
plot to discredit Tom, hatched by Mrs Furze and the rancorous
Orkid Jim, is a melodramatic device, but it brings in some
pages of acute analysis, as when Mrs Furze satisfies her conscience by simply refusing to reflect on the possibility of perjury
on Jim's part.

Refusing to reflect on it, she naturally had no proof of it; and, having no proof of it, she had no ground for believing that she was not perfectly innocent and upright.

Tom is exculpated and restored to his old place of trust, when he saves Jim in the flood and Jim makes plenary confession.

It is not that picturesque incident of the flood alone that *Affinities* reminds one continually in this book of *The Mill on the Floss*; *with* Catharine is another Maggie Tulliver, though not drawn at *George* the same full length. George Eliot's Dutch painting is in- *Eliot* fallibly brought to mind in the glimpses of Mrs Bellamy's housekeeping in the Thingleby farm:

Mrs Bellamy's mind, unoccupied with parental cares, with politics, or with literature, let itself loose upon her house, her dairy, and her fowls. She established a series of precautions to prevent dirt, and the precautions themselves became objects to be protected. There was a rough scraper intervening on behalf of the blackleaded scraper; there was a large mat to preserve the mat beyond it; and although a drugget covered the stair carpet, Mrs Bellamy would have been sorely vexed if she had found a footmark upon it. If a friend was expected she put some straw outside the garden gate, and she asked him in gentle tones when he dismounted if he would kindly "just take the worst off" there.

There is more caustic, as a rule, in Mark Rutherford's satire; it is more like Thackeray's, and sometimes like Jane Austen's [1]; yet there is a sweetness in it too. That sweetness often becomes a very beautiful tenderness, as in Catharine's last moments with her dying mare:

The brave animal which she had so often seen, apparently for the mere love of difficulty, struggling as if its sinews would crack. She looked at its body as it lay there extended, quiet, pleading as it were against the doom of man and beast, and tears came to her eyes as she noted the appeal—tears not altogether of sorrow, but partly of revolt.

[1] *E.g.* the subdued satire in Mrs Furze's plan unfolded to her torpid husband for moving to the Terrace and conquering Eastthorpe society, in what is said and the more left unsaid, is perhaps too reminiscent of the Dashwoods' debate on how much of the legacy shall be allotted to the mother and sisters (see Volume VI. 76) to be quite accidental.

Rutherford's keen perception of the good-heartedness and fellow-feeling of the poor is always coming out:

The sympathy of the agricultural poor with one another is hardly credible to fine people who live in towns. If we could have a record of the devotion of those women who lie forgotten under the turf round country churches throughout England, it would be better worth preserving than nine-tenths of our literature and histories. Surely in some sense they still *are*, and their love cannot have been altogether a thing of no moment to the Power that made them!

Catharine and Mr Cardew never avow their love till she is on her deathbed, the untimely result of a night spent in watching over the dismissed servant-girl, Phœbe, dying of phthisis. She asks to see him.

"Mr Cardew, I want to say something."
"Wait a moment, let me tell you—*you have saved me.*"
She smiled, her lips moved, and she whispered—"*You* have saved *me.*"

By their love for each other they were both saved. The disguises are manifold which the Immortal Son assumes in the work of our redemption.

All Mark Rutherford's fiction put together would hardly exceed in bulk George Eliot's *Middlemarch*. He worked not so much on a smaller scale as with a finer pen, and, with a suggestive word, left to the imagination what she would have dwelt upon for page after page. Perhaps he left too much to the imagination: *Catharine Furze* could have been expanded to much advantage. Comparison is inevitable; their themes, their characters, and both their problems and their solutions are so similar, and they all but coincide in their times and places. It would be absurd to deny that in weight and creative fertility she was his superior. But the converse, entirely unqualified, would be just as absurd. Two writers who must needs be compared were never a clearer instance of the futility of scales of merit.

Mark Rutherford gave his bent for casuistry full fling in *Clara Hopgood* (1896), which is also a novel, of somewhat ramshackle construction. He says, at a crucial moment, "It *Clara* is much more important to believe earnestly that something *Hop-* is morally right than that it should be really right." Moral *good"* convictions must not be tampered with, even for the most laudable reasons. The whole plot revolves on a point of casuistry. Clara's sister Madge—they are both young women of the better classes, and brought up on strict Calvinistic principles—through a momentary weakness becomes a mother, but firmly refuses to marry a man whom she knows to be mediocre and a materialist. One of Mark Rutherford's most striking characters and another of his incarnations of spiritual ideals is Baruch, half a Jew, the Clerkenwell diamond-cutter, whose irresistible dissipation is reading Maimonides. He has the magnanimity to espouse Madge with her child. The time is that of the Chartists and the Corn Law agitation, and Mazzini appears in the last chapter, one of the refugees in London hatching the Risorgimento. In fact, he takes Clara to Italy, where she bears her part in the struggle for freedom.

Whilst Mark Rutherford was meditating his autobiography, *Others on* a young girl in South Africa was brooding, not without pangs *the* and tears, on the mystery of the universe, and drafting a novel, *religious* which she practically completed about 1878, but continued to *question* revise, until, with the commendation of Meredith as official reader, it was published in 1883. *The Story of an African Farm* was half autobiography, and dealt with other vexatious problems, such as the claims of the sex to equality with men in the affairs of life, besides the religious question—problems soon to be taken up strenuously, especially by women novelists. This dread alternative of faith and doubt had been racking serious minds long before Mark Rutherford dramatized his memories of sectarian discords and disruptions. It was, as has been seen, a latent or an active element in Hardy's poems and fiction, the earlier of which were contemporaneous with that manifesto of disbelief, *The City of Dreadful Night* (1874). *The Outcast* (1875) of W. W. Reade (1838–1875), a poor novel by the nephew of a more famous novelist, told of the persecutions endured by a man whose theism was unorthodox, a subject that takes its due place also in his conspectus of human history,

The Martyrdom of Man (1872). That of religion was usually bound up with the condition-of-England question, in novels and poems, and also in more prosaic literature, or non-literature. There is no need to summarize again the large crop of such writings that synchronized with the Oxford Movement.[1] Kingsley, in *Alton Locke,* and Mrs Browning, in *Aurora Leigh,* dealt with the problem in contemporary terms.

"*John Ingle-sant*" The strangest feature of the *John Inglesant* (1881) of Joseph Henry Shorthouse (1834–1903), which came out the same year as *The Autobiography of Mark Rutherford,* is that it takes the form of an historical romance of the time of Charles I and the Great Civil War. *John Inglesant* has been hailed as "The one great religious novel of the English language." [2] This is to overlook Bunyan as well as Mark Rutherford. But it is the work of a rare spirit, a Quaker who had joined the Anglican Church, and who wrote some others but will always be known as the author of this one book; and it has literary merits surprising in a man not used to writing, whose days were occupied in the management of the family chemical works. Inglesant is just such another as himself, a mystic, who is immersed in and at times led astray by worldly affairs, but, guided by saintly counsellors and his own inner light, devotes himself to a sacred mission, that of reconciling the Anglican and Roman communions. That which was a question of the hour during the Oxford Movement is thus transposed to the seventeenth century, when it was, verily, a question of practical politics. It is by no means the only historical parallel in the book, which is enriched with living pictures of that age, such as the famous diorama of a papal election and the one of the plague at Naples. The murder of his brother sends Inglesant in pursuit of revenge; he is launched into the turmoil of European politics. It is an absorbing story, in spite of the flagrant lack of humour.[3]

---

[1] See above, Volume VIII. 164–166.

[2] Paul Elmer More: *Shelburne Essays,* iii. 227. Possibly, More was thinking of Cardinal Newman's novels (see Volume VIII. 165), or even of such as the Rev. J. M. Neale's historical tales, e.g. *Theodore Phranza* (1857), or Canon Farrar's *Julian Home* (1859) and *Gathering Clouds* (1896).

[3] *John Inglesant* has been severely and very learnedly criticized by Dr Polak (52–71) for innumerable plagiarisms; much of it is a patchwork of material from various

The more permanent interest of *John Inglesant* is its philosophical or rather its introspective and mystical character.
Shorthouse was not a humanitarian like Mark Rutherford.
To him religion was the cult of personal holiness. Inglesant
listens in silence to the Inner Voice, and strives at a perfection,
a spiritual beauty, which is the realization of a divine ideal.
Religion should be an art: "the end of existence is not the
good of one's neighbour, but one's own culture, provided
that culture is based upon knowledge of and communion
with Christ, in which case one will benefit one's neighbour
more truly than one could do by uncultured altruism." Shorthouse was a Platonist, and discerned behind the visible warfare
the conflict between the educational influences of Plato and
Aristotle. The Church of England, he argued, offers both to
man, in a measure meet for each individual. Hence it is better
than the Church of Rome, with its glorification of authority.
Molinos and the Quietists exemplify the most beautiful life
for such as are worthy and capable of it, by strength of mind
and knowledge. There is a similitude and also a contrast here
with the teaching of Pater in *Marius the Epicurean* (1885),
which would make art a religion, fostering it for the sake of
beauty.[1]

When Olive Schreiner (1855–1920, by marriage Mrs Cron- "*The
wright) published *The Story of an African Farm* (1883), those *Story
self-reliant, solitary souls, Waldo and Lyndall, nursing a pro- *of an
found affinity which never discloses itself to them as love, *African
reminded many of Heathcliff and Catherine; and the scenery *Farm*"
of the veldt, the loneliness, and the resourcelessness of Waldo
and Em engaged in working out a creed, symbolizing the

historians. The historical inaccuracies and misconceptions of historical facts are
a graver charge (see especially pp. 72–106). But, whilst all this detracts seriously from
Shorthouse's achievement, it leaves the importance of the book undiminished. The
sincerity of the man and his spiritual fervour are self-evident. It is his own life
and quest for the truth put in a romantic dress; it is autobiography, though in
another sense than Mark Rutherford's.

[1] The novels with which Shorthouse followed up his resounding success are of
trifling value comparatively, though they overflow with the same mysticism. *The
Little Schoolmaster Mark* (1883) draws upon Jung-Stilling's autobiography (1750);
Sir Percival (1886) and yet more *The Countess Eve* (1888) make, as it were, palpable a
spiritual world which is obviously real to the author; *A Teacher of the Violin, and
other Tales* (1888), and *Blanche, Lady Falaise* (1891), are thinner tricklings from the
same spring.

solitude and helplessness of man confronted by the inscrutable might of nature, deepened the resemblance. But the book is clumsy and inchoate in contrast with the concentrated energy of *Wuthering Heights*. It begins with the budding rationalism of a small boy, discomfited when his sacrifice is not consumed by fire from heaven. "I love Jesus Christ," he exclaims, "but I hate God." Waldo grows up a sensitive, harassed soul, something like Heathcliff in his strength though not in his weakness. His dreams are interpreted for him by a stranger who comes on the scene, only too accidentally. "This thing we call existence is it not a something which has its roots far down below in the dark, and its branches stretching far out into the immensity above, which we among the branches cannot see? Not a chance jumble: a living thing, a whole, *One*." The stranger's allegory of Truth is a great piece of prose-poetry.

He who sets out to search for Truth must leave these valleys of superstition for ever, taking with him not one shred that has belonged to them. Alone he must wander down into the Land of Absolute Negation and Denial; he must abide there; he must resist temptation; when the light breaks he must arise and follow it into the country of dry sunshine. The mountains of stern reality will rise before him: he must climb them; *beyond* them lies Truth.

After the first volume and the childhood of Waldo, Em, and Lyndall, an idyll of real beauty and power, the novel becomes more and more a philosophical pamphlet. But it made a strong appeal, for it had the distinction of introducing the New Woman to the world. The humour is mostly childish: Bonaparte Blenkins is a mere harlequin, though the affectionate old Boer housekeeper, Tante Sannie, may pass.[1] Olive Schreiner's *Dreams* (1891) and *Dream Life and Real Life* (1892) poured out her theosophy in gnomic stories and fables; her *Trooper Peter Halket* (1897) was a tract called out by the imperialistic movement initiated by Rhodes, and demands, "What would Jesus Christ say if he came to Mashonaland?"[2]

[1] One cannot help wondering why Doss, the little dog, never seems to grow any older. Amateur novelists often forget that chronology is a real thing.

[2] Her posthumous novel *Undine* (1928), written between the ages of sixteen and twenty-one, was meant to be destroyed. But it is a "human document," throwing

Robert Elsmere (1888), by Mrs Humphry Ward (1851–1920), "*Robert Elsmere*," etc. made still more noise, and the authoress kept up her gentle disturbance of drawing-room views of religion with a string of novels having this question in the background if not in the forefront.[1] Elsmere succumbs to scepticism after he is well launched on the labours of a parish rector, and, what is more tragic for readers of Mrs Humphry Ward, long after he and his wife have formed what seemed a perfect union, based on the rock of the old evangelical faith. Their estrangement and her heartbreak are the dolorous strait from which there is no deliverance consistent with the ethics recognized by Mrs Ward and her readers. In *The History of David Grieve* (1892), the claims of two women upon the hero illustrate two sides of the problem of marriage; but that of man and God is also opened up by the course of free-thinking which leads him to a unitarianism of his own brand. *Helbeck of Bannisdale* (1898) varies the situation: Helbeck is a devout Catholic, married to an agnostic girl. In *Eleanor* (1900) and *The Case of Richard Meynell* (1911) there are threads of religious interest; the one is a study of modern Italy, reviewing the changes and the oppositions of political and clerical life, and the antagonism between the new State and the Papacy; the other forms a sequel to *Robert Elsmere*, Meynell, a modernist clergyman, marrying Elsmere's daughter. In every one of these novels, the drama of faith and doubt is identified with the personal drama. This was at once Mrs Ward's strength and her weakness.

light on the genesis of her first book. Greatness of soul is patent in even the most absurd incidents, as when the destitute Undine nearly kills herself with overwork to support the crippled Diogenes, or gives back the five shillings that she desperately needs to the bumptious negro. The whole theory of individuality is propounded: "The path through life in which each soul must tread is single . . . no two walk abreast . . . where one soul stands, never has stood, and never shall stand, another . . . each man's life and struggle is a mystery, incomprehensible and for ever hid from every heart but his own." The Bible is full of cruelty. "I don't want to go to heaven, and, if God wants to, He can send me to hell and I will never again ask Him not to, *never*. I know I'm very wicked, but I'm not half so wicked or so cruel as He is. Nothing is—not even the devil. The devil is glad when we go to hell, but he did not make us on purpose to send us there, and he did not make hell, and he did not make himself, and I'm sorry for him."

[1] *Robert Elsmere*, it is interesting to remark, appeared the same year as *John Ward, Preacher*, by the American Mrs Deland, another and much closer follower of George Eliot. Her bigoted Calvinist, whose religion is "grounded on damnation," has an agnostic wife. It is a study of conscience, and Mrs Deland's sympathies clearly lie with the wife's cheerful rationalism.

The parties to the strife are invariably drawn as incapable
of the common foibles, and high-minded enough to accept the
sternest sacrifices of self, an idealism which fascinated her
readers. But this meant that she regularly solved their
theoretical entanglements by a process of sentimentalizing
doubts and beliefs. She enhanced the charm of these triumphs
over intellectual and moral crises by her mellifluous description
of the various settings for the drama, the sequestered dales of
Westmorland, the gloomy recesses of the Peak of Derbyshire,
and the like. Mrs Ward had mastered the literature of all the
controversies, and was qualified to give a most instructive
course on the subject. Thomas Hill Green's Hegelian interpretation of Christianity is admirably expounded in *Robert
Elsmere*. Grey is his representative, whilst the squire stands
for Edmond Scherer, and Langham for the æstheticism of
Walter Pater. Edward Manisty, in *Eleanor*, may be identified,
at least in his views, with W. H. Mallock, Lord Dufferin is
recognizable in the ambassador, and the affair of Dr Schell in
that of Dr Benecke. Mrs Ward, in short, was a popularizer of
recent religious history and the speculative differences underlying it; she knew how to make the history of ideas interesting
to those who liked to think they were following intellectual
and moral arguments when they were only treading the
measures of an ordinary sentimental dance-tune. A course in
this subject of the day was a vital part of culture in the circles
which she knew so well how to depict; and, if her studies of the
conflict are of minor philosophical importance, their great
vogue is an interesting historical fact.[1]

*Refer-
ences in
Gissing,
etc.*
Mrs Lynn Linton, a novelist of domestic life and character
with a large vogue at the circulating libraries, introduced the
religious dilemma in at least two of her books, *The True History
of Joshua Davidson, Christian Communist* (1872), and *Under
which Lord ?* (1879). But those of Shorthouse and Mark
Rutherford are the only studies of the subject that have the
least chance of permanence.[2] Gissing raised the issue repeatedly,

[1] Firmin Roz is too generous in his study of Mrs Humphry Ward, in *Le Roman
anglais contemporain*, 109–163.
[2] "John Ackworth" (Rev. Frederick R. Smith) wrote a number of tales, probably
encouraged by Mark Rutherford's lead, characterizing the Methodists in Lancashire

however, in his portrayals of men and women who were thinkers, and he was singularly clear-headed, in spite of agnostic bias; his candid analysis of states of mind went to the root of the matter. The best example is *Born in Exile*, in which his Godwin Peak, a confirmed rationalist, is guilty of deliberate hypocrisy and proposes to enter the Church. But Peak is guilty with his eyes open; he is perfectly honest with himself, and does not confound the motives which are his private justification with apologetics. There is no sentimentalism or sophistry to betray or confuse: Gissing's intellectual honesty was of the strictest. Helen Norman, in his first novel, though the daughter of a minister, throws over dogma for Darwin, Schopenhauer, and Haeckel. Bunce, in *Thyrza*, is another working-class agnostic, who takes up a deplorably aggressive attitude towards the old school. Much later on, Mary Webb, who was an eclectic in her fealty to various guiding stars, followed some little way in the path mapped out by Mrs Ward. Her favourite theme, however, was the reaction of narrow religious principles on character; and her own chosen faith was a pantheism learned from Blake and Wordsworth:

The human mind, unless it is to remain nescient, must have itself, must develop and explore itself. The more vital, the more awake it is, the more it must turn inwards. For within, deep in the tenebrous recesses of subconsciousness, man hopes to find God. Not in churches, not in his fellows, not in nature will he find God until he has seen all these things mirrored in that opaque and fathomless pool, lying within his own being, of which, as yet, we know nothing.[1]

villages, e.g. *Clogshop Chronicles* (1896), *The Scowcroft Critics* (1898), *The Minder* (1900), biography of an operative called to the ministry, and the more ambitious novel, *The Coming of the Preachers, a tale of the Rise of Methodism* (1901).

[1] *The House in Dormer Forest*, c. x. In all Mary Webb's novels, such a theosophic quest is intwined with the other motives, especially the love-matters; in this one it is much more explicit than elsewhere. Miss May Sinclair's novel, *The Rector of Wyck* (1925), is not concerned with controversy, but gives the pathetic history of a parish priest who holds that Christianity is less a creed to be stated than a life to be lived.

CHAPTER IV

GEORGE GISSING

MORE even than Mark Rutherford's, and in a totally different way from those of Shorthouse and Olive Schreiner, the novels of George Robert Gissing (1857–1903) were composed out of his own personal experiences. They are the fullest exposure extant in English of the hideous realities underlying modern civilization. If, when he began to write, he nursed some faint hope of promoting reform or paving the way for revolution, he quickly abandoned it in despair, and persuaded himself that in this business of writing for the circulating libraries to which he was reduced for a living he was using his fund of intimate knowledge solely as artistic material: to paint a true picture was the purpose that had to satisfy a very sensitive conscience. He belonged to the time though not the company of the æsthetes, and so was led to subscribe to the doctrine of art for the sake of art, which Wilde, Crackanthorpe, George Moore, and the rest, derived from Walter Pater. But the real motive that sustained him, as transparently emerges from a thousand pages of his agonized presentation of the tragedy of existence, is his hatred of the chosen subject, and his burning resentment at the lot of himself and his like. He saw no remedy; he disbelieved in progress; but he was resolute to tell the truth, and make no concession even to the readers on whose favour he depended for his livelihood. Not for him to palter with his own integrity, and stoop to the popular methods that brought success to a Milvain, the literary time-server in his *New Grub Street*. He was content to be the chronicler of misery. And, not only was the material to be used that which he had accumulated in the stress of his own sufferings, but from first to last, from *Workers in the Dawn* to the recollections of his Henry

Ryecroft, the foremost exponents of the tragedy and the mouth-pieces of such philosophy as he could wring out of it were men, or sometimes women, caught in his own predicament, exiles from the spheres to which they belonged by right of mind and taste, fighting unavailingly for a tolerable life, and filled with his own idealism and the consciousness that it could never be realized. Arthur Golding, in his abortive first novel, Waymark in the second, Kirkwood, Kingcote, Reardon, Godwin Peak, and Harvey Rolfe, are all impersonations of Gissing; and a number of his finer women characters, such as Helen Norman and Marcella Moxey, represent himself, his ideals, and his failures, almost as closely.[1] The whole crowd of defeated serfs, potential men of letters slaving for a bare subsistence, in *New Grub Street*, are drawn in his own lineaments, and variously illustrate his grim conscientiousness and his own disasters, together with his hopeless and unresigned outlook upon the world. It is not strange that the best-qualified friend to write the biography of a man who systematically took himself as his own subject should likewise make Gissing the hero of a novel retailing the same facts, with names and places and titles of books thinly disguised.[2] Gissing knew that he would have been in his right place as a professor of classical literature at one of the Universities. This was not the empty aspiration of a Jude the Obscure, though he behaved no less absurdly

---

[1] This must not be taken too much *au pied de la lettre*. Thus Gissing says of one of the most significant, "Waymark is a *study of character*, and he alone is responsible for his sentiments," correcting his brother's impulse to "take Waymark's declaration of faith as my own" (*Letters*, 140).

[2] Morley Roberts: *The Private Life of Henry Maitland* (1912). The best monograph on Gissing is by Mr Frank Swinnerton (see "Select Reading and Reference List" at end). I read it after writing this chapter, and found that we were not in accord on Gissing's circumstances, particularly in the latter part of his life. The view given above he would call "the legend of Gissing's poverty." Mr Swinnerton's chief authorities were the late George Whale and Thomas Seccombe, both of whom I knew intimately, and frequently heard talking about Gissing. But at that time it never occurred to me that I might have to write on the subject, and I kept no notes. Mr Swinnerton and I have discussed the question, and he tells me that the late Mr Pinker said that Gissing in his last years was making at least a thousand a year—a fortune in those pre-War days. On the other hand, Mr Morley Robert writes, in answer to my inquiries: "From about 1877 to 1880 was perhaps his worst time. But till he left Smith Elder and went to Lawrence and Bullen, though not actually often starving he was always in what most would call extreme poverty. At his very best in later years his precarious income never exceeded something like £700. You can read between the lines in *Henry Ryecroft* and also in what I have written of him."

at the outset of serious life. His father was a pharmacist at Wakefield, who died when George was thirteen; but he was a man of culture, and had time to teach his son that the finest of pleasures and relaxations was to be had in the enjoyment of literature. The boy won an exhibition at Owen's College, Manchester, and distinguished himself by carrying off the prizes in Latin and Greek, and also in English language and literature. And then, still hardly more than a youth, he committed the quixotic folly of marrying a girl of the streets, with the immediate consequence of wrecking his prospects and laying up for himself years of unspeakable wretchedness. All else failing, he bound himself to the literary mill, and like his Reardon and Biffen managed to keep just alive by the output of novels which never had the success they merited till just before and just after his too early death. Not long freed from this first marriage, he entered upon another, equally ill-omened. Yet, even when half starving, Gissing constantly found in renewed study of the classics a refuge from his daily hardships, and often sat up till the small hours after a day's toil on a novel, to read a Greek poet or scan a mighty chorus. When he had no other friends, he found all the society he wanted in Shakespeare, Catullus, Homer, or the Greek playwrights and lyric poets. His poor hack-writers did likewise: they were reflections of himself. His obsessing desire was "to escape life as I know it and dream myself back into that old world which was the imaginative delight of my boyhood." Much of the tremendous force in his accounts of slum life and the barbarous pleasures of the lower classes was the result of hatred and repugnance: this was the antipodes to the enchanted landscapes of the poets, and a melancholy contrast to the dignity and humanism of his beloved prose-writers. If for no other reason, he could not have helped making the characters that engaged his sympathies scholars and thinkers, and at least potential gentlemen.[1]

Gissing's subject was the same forlorn depths of the nether

---

[1] His devotion to the classics, his very respectable scholarship, and the frequency of his classical allusions, fully justify the special study by S. V. Gapp: *George Gissing, classicist* (Phila., 1936).

world as Mark Rutherford's; their pictures of Clerkenwell *His* streets and slums in the City may be compared in detail; much *world and* of it coincided also with that of Dickens, though treated in a *his* very different spirit. The colours are as sombre as Ruther- *attitude* ford's, or more so; and, though Gissing's philosophy was *thereto* radically at variance, it was as austere. Here are two passages that might be as plausibly guessed to have come from the one as from the other: they are actually from *Mark Rutherford's Deliverance*.

At the doors of the houses stood grimy women with their arms folded and their hair disordered. Grimier boys and girls had tied a rope to broken railings, and were swinging on it. The common door to a score of lodgings stood ever open, and the children swarmed up and down the stairs carrying with them patches of mud every time they came in from the street. The wholesome practice which amongst the decent poor marks off at least one day in the week as a day on which there is to be a change; when there is to be some attempt to procure order and cleanliness; a day to be preceded by soap and water, by shaving, and by as many clean clothes as can be procured, was unknown here. There was no break in the uniformity of squalor; nor was it even possible for any single family to emerge amidst such altogether oppressive surroundings. All self-respect, all effort to do anything more than to satisfy somehow the grossest wants, had departed. The shops were open; most of them exhibiting a most miscellaneous collection of goods, such as bacon cut in slices, firewood, a few loaves of bread, and sweetmeats in dirty bottles. Fowls, strange to say, black as the flagstones, walked in and out of these shops, or descended into the dark areas. The undertaker had not put up his shutters. He had drawn down a yellow blind, on which was painted a picture of a suburban cemetery. Two funerals, the loftiest effort of his craft, were depicted approaching the gates. When the gas was alight behind the blind, an effect was produced which was doubtless much admired (chap. ii.).

I did not know, till I came in actual contact with them, how far away the classes which lie at the bottom of great cities are from those above them; how completely they are inaccessible to motives which act upon ordinary human beings, and how deeply they are sunk beyond ray of sun or stars, immersed in the selfishness naturally begotten of their incessant struggle for existence and the incessant warfare with society. It was an awful thought to me, ever present on those Sundays, and haunting me at other times, that men, women, and children were living in such brutish degradation, and that as they died others would take their place. Our civilization seemed nothing but a thin film or crust lying over a volcanic pit, and I often wondered whether some day the pit would not break up through it and destroy us all. Great towns are answerable for the creation and maintenance of the masses of dark, impenetrable, subterranean blackguardism, with which we became acquainted. The filthy gloom of the sky, the dirt of the street, the absence of fresh air, the herding of the poor into huge districts which cannot be opened up by those who would do good, are tremendous agencies of corruption which are active at such a rate that it is appalling to reflect what our future will be if the accumulation of population be not checked. To stand face to face with the insoluble is not pleasant. A man will do anything rather than confess it is beyond him. He will create pleasant fictions, and fancy a possible escape here and there; but this problem of Drury Lane was round and hard like a ball of adamant (chap. v.).

The date of this, as of Gissing's companion pictures, is within the memory of people now alive, though, on the material side, at all events, the state of the London poor is so incredibly better. With such horrors under his eyes, Gissing could never be impartial. He recoiled from them in disgust, but at the same time they inflamed his indignation. It was not the poor that he blamed, though their very pleasures were abominable: they were not responsible for their degradation. What stirred his ire was the selfish, stupid, complacent, still more sordid character of those a step or two higher, his own class, in fact, though he knew he was essentially unlike them.[1] The baseness and vulgarity of this lower middle class was infinitely irksome to his over-sensitive nature, and the passionate

---

[1] "They are willing enough," he writes of *The Spectator* and well-to-do readers, "to admit that I have drawn blackguards well when those blackguards are of the poorer classes: the existence of blackguards elsewhere they won't recognize. 'O Scribes and Pharisees, hypocrites!'" (*Letters*, 81).

resentment it kindled stood to him in the stead of that zest and that delight in mere living which are the incentives of most imaginative artists. Reardon speaks for Gissing, in *New Grub Street*, when he avers that the follies and paltry shams and self-deceptions around him only rouse him to inextinguishable laughter. It would have been the laughter of scorn and disgust, the mirthless laughter of desperation, not of comedy. Gissing was destitute of humour.

That is clear enough from his monograph on Dickens,[1] *His* which is so revealing of his limitations that it should satisfy the *mono-* most hostile critic who wished "O that mine adversary had *graph on* written a book!" He begins by detecting "class feeling" in *Dickens* the proprietor of Gadshill's hatred for his memories of a squalid boyhood. Later on, he regrets that Dickens did not treat landlordism, that "curse of English life," on a much larger scale: it will remain a curse "until the victims of house-owners see their way to cut, not the hair, but the throats, of a few selected specimens." Dickens was not quite sincere: Gissing deplores his lack of "veracity in fiction." He let theatrical plots divert him from the plain motives of human life and the "simple probabilities." Gissing was annoyed also by the contempt shown for classical education, which he attributes to the soreness felt by Dickens at having gone only to a London day-school. Mr Feeder, B.A., Dr Blimber, and Dr Strong, who "potters in an imbecile fashion over a Greek dictionary which there is plainly not the slightest hope of his ever completing," exasperate Gissing. But insight and gusto fail him altogether when he contemplates outstanding Dickensian creations merely as so many dreadful specimens of his own most hateful types of ignorance, brutishness, and vice. They are not fantasies, not extravagances; it was "a time of ugliness," but they still exist. The sentimentality of Flora Finching had been "fed upon songs and verses congenial to the feeble mind"; but "born thirty years later, Flora would have been led to a much better taste in that direction, with the result of greater self-command in all." "Her character is in truth a very strong plea for the fair education of

---

[1] *Charles Dickens, a critical study* (1898).

women." As to others of her sex, many are simply "social pests."

Women who might well have wrecked homes, are shown as laughable foils for the infinite goodness and patience of men about them. Justly, by the by, a matter of complaint to the female critic. Weller and Varden, and Snagsby, and Joe Gargery are too favourable specimens of the average husband; in such situations, one or other of them would certainly have lost his patience, and either have fled the country, or have turned wife-beater.

Mrs Bumble exhibits her true self for her husband's benefit, and, so far as we know, does not repent of her triumphs as an obese virago. . . . Mrs Varden . . . typifies a large class of most respectable wives. . . . She is not incapable of good-humour; but so much value does she attach to the gleams of that bright quality, that not one is suffered to escape her until her household has been brought to the verge of despair by her persistent sourness and sulkiness. . . . It is an odd thing that evolution has allowed the persistence of this art, for we may be quite sure that many a primitive woman paid for it with a broken skull. Here it is, however, flourishing and like to flourish.[1]

"Mrs Gargery shall be brought to quietness; but how? By a half-murderous blow on the back of her head, from which she will never recover." As to Mrs Nickleby, "she is ubiquitous, and doubtless always will be: we must endure her, as we endure the caprices of the sky. An ultimate fact of nature, and a great argument for those who decline to take life too seriously." But Gissing could not take life anywise but seriously. He had no humour, and, which is almost as fatal, he had no philosophy, beyond the elementary hedonism forced upon him by the necessities of his own case, which was also the case of many of similar metal. That philosophy could be reduced, in its practical application, to the all-importance of money, the wherewithal to avoid the last straits and procure those little pleasures of body and mind which would have saved a Biffen

[1] *Charles Dickens*, 135–137. Mr Morley Roberts has made much the same remarks, but explains that Gissing wrote the book at Siena "as a pot-boiler, and did it purely for the money" (*Henry Maitland*, 140).

from suicide.[1] Otherwise, it was only the despairing philosophy of Schopenhauer used eclectically to support his
temperamental convictions.[2]

Gissing was intent, in the first place, on rendering in fiction *The*
the life of the masses, on portraying by some sweeping method *natural-*
the teeming and repulsive population of the slums. This *istic*
would be straightforward work, a kind of demographic art *back-*
based on systematic observation, for it was not the lowest *ground*
classes that he knew at first-hand—he had to study them. But *psycho-* *and the*
equally important to Gissing, nay, far more important, was the *logical*
dreary lot of individuals like himself, forced into contact with *drama*
the brutal herd, obliged to live like them, yet striving all the
while to keep their souls intact, and realize their own aims in
spite of overwhelming handicaps. This is the truly momentous
drama that engrossed him, and compels sympathy and apprehension, in such novels as *Demos*, *Thyrza*, *The Nether World*,
New Grub Street, and *Born in Exile*. The squalid streets and
houses and their wretched inhabitants form only the stage,
the imprisoning arena in which the real contest is fought out,
the life-or-death struggle for personal integrity or some self-
abnegating mission. Though he said that fiction must "dig
deeper, get to untouched social strata," he gave only the
exterior physiognomies of his denizens of the nether world,
those which any keen-eyed observer who went among them
could see for himself. To him they were too repellent to
tempt a friendlier intimacy; he does not draw them with any
warm sympathy, usually quite the reverse. Look at one of his
most Zolaesque figures, Clem Peckover, in *The Nether World*:
it is evident that he has seen her, she is terribly real and alive;
but she remains a monster, one of those infesting the abyss, to
be got rid of by fair means or foul, as he recommended in Mrs
Gargery's case—a human being perhaps, but one who has lost

---

[1] Gissing was a reader of Butler; he knew *Erewhon* and *Erewhon Revisited*, and his
views on money coincide with those laid down in *The Way of all Flesh* (see especially
chapter lxviii., on the desirability of establishing "professorships of speculation" at
Oxford and Cambridge).

[2] Whether he ever went to Germany as a young man to study Goethe, Haeckel, and
Schopenhauer, as is stated in the *Cambridge History of English Literature* (xiii. 457),
is much disputed, *e.g.* by Gapp, 82–83. It is accepted by, and perhaps based upon,
Mr Frank Swinnerton, in *George Gissing, a critical study* (1912).

all trace of humanity.   Dickens, or any of the great imaginative
geniuses, would not have left her at that.   On this side,
Gissing is the inferior of Mark Rutherford, with the waifs and
strays he and his compassionate friend rescue from the wilderness
of Drury Lane, and also of George Moore, who made a show of
abjuring pity, but drew Esther Waters and that affecting sketch
of Emma, the lodging-house drudge, in *Confessions of a Young
Man*:

> To know of nothing but a dark kitchen, grates, eggs and bacon,
> dirty children; to work seventeen hours a day and to get
> cheated out of your wages; to answer, when asked, why you
> did not get your wages or leave if you weren't paid, that you
> "didn't know how Mrs S. would get on without me."

Gissing rarely goes so deep or comes so close to the brink of
tears, at least when he is merely concerned with the "human
cattle, the herd that feed and breed."   "With them it was well."
But when he turned to "the few born to a desire forever
unattainable," it was very different:

> The gentle spirits who from their prisoning circumstance
> looked up and afar, how the heart ached to think of them!
> Some girl, of delicate instinct, of purpose sweet and pure,
> wasting her unloved life in toil and want and indignity; some
> man, whose youth and courage strove against a mean environ-
> ment, whose eyes grew haggard in the vain search for a com-
> panion promised in his dreams; they lived, these two, parted
> perchance only by the wall of neighbour houses, yet all huge
> London was between them, and their hands would never
> touch.[1]

Foreign   Gissing learned from Zola, much more than from Dickens,
influences his art of depicting the masses; but he failed to acquire much
that Zola could have taught him.   He did not fail to recognize
the pre-eminence of Balzac, but somehow was antagonized by
that writer's sternly uncompromising method, in many ways,
he seemed to think, inferior to the kinder way of Dickens.[2]
Instinctively, however, he himself felt a closer affinity to
Flaubert, the Goncourts, and Maupassant, who had style, and

[1] *The Crown of Life.*   [2] *Dickens*, 217–219.

who fell little short of Balzac in illustrating how characters, not so primitive as the common herd, may be anatomized and exhibited in the act of facing those dilemmas which may make them or break them. But their exquisitely objective art was beyond him; he could never quite succeed in making the drama enact itself. The author was always intruding in his studies of the conscience at bay, to elucidate the thoughts and half-conscious motives, to trace the process of causation determining issues, even in its most trivial and sordid shapes. As time went on, Gissing showed that he was far from untouched by the spirit of Dostoevsky, that inexhaustible fellow-feeling which was at home with the souls even of the criminal and the outcast.[1] Dostoevsky's example was probably influential in his studies of ruined girls who keep their souls clean, despite the foulness in which they are plunged. Perhaps it helped also to confirm the faith that imagined so many profound and inspiring friendships among Gissing's most forlorn and poverty-stricken wretches. But, again, such sympathetic insight was reserved rather for those whom he recognized as his fellows, the victims of the social order whom he pitied, the final proceeds of the determinism which he, with Schopenhauer, saw as the law of existence. Towards the mob he was as coldly scientific as the naturalist who made a fetish of his detachment, except when inflamed with his animosity against such a blot upon the human world. Thus it might be said that his naturalism in any one of his novels was concerned with the body, the social environment; the soul of the book was the moral history of his chosen individuals and their moments of crisis. His Dantesque evocations of gloom and terror were impressive enough; but the other and the finer accomplishment was his intensive analysis of states of mind, the urgings of passion and the scruples leading to decisions which might be epoch-making in the life of more than one.

Gissing's first novel, *Workers in the Dawn* (1880), which was actually finished when he was twenty-two,[2] tells how a young *Earliest novels*

---

[1] See Weber (65–67) for a discussion of Gissing's debts to Zola, and to Dostoevsky and other Russian novelists.
[2] *Letters*, 49.

man, out of the best motives, marries a woman of immoral life; it also tells of the emancipation of Helen Norman from orthodox dogma, through the study of Darwin, Strauss, and Schopenhauer. Helen dies; the ameliorative projects of both come to naught. Waymark, in *The Unclassed* (1884), also acts upon the conviction that a woman who has led the worst of lives may remain good and pure in herself, and capable of the highest altruism in happier circumstances. The history of Ida's and Sally's reformation is recounted with optimistic aplomb; but when Gissing republished the novel in 1895 he had to admit that it was the dream of a very young man. *The Unclassed* is particularly interesting as marking the stages of his progress from the design of exposing evils and pointing out remedies to the attitude of the artist pure and simple. He said to begin with:

I mean to bring home to people the ghastly condition (material, mental, and moral) of our poor classes, to show the hideous injustice of our whole system of society, to give light upon the plan of altering it, and, above all, to preach an enthusiasm for just and high *ideals* in this age of unmitigated egotism and "shop." I shall never write a book which does not keep all these ends in view. [1]

But he soon changed his mind, and announces:

I am by degrees getting my right place in the world. . . . My attitude henceforth is that of the artist pure and simple. The world is for me a collection of phenomena, which are to be studied and reproduced artistically. In the midst of the most serious complications of life, I find myself suddenly possessed with a great calm, withdrawn as it were from the immediate interests of the moment, and able to regard everything as a picture. . . . In the midst of desperate misfortune I can pause to make a note for future use, and the afflictions of others are to me materials for observation. This, I rather think, is at last the final stage of my development, coming after so many and various phases.[2]

He saw that fiction and sociology do not run well together; he

---

[1] *Letters*, 83.   [2] *Ibid.*, 128–129.

was not going to follow the same path as Kingsley and Besant.[1] Already, he found himself too hopeless to think of being a reformer. It is true that Gissing often has the air of stating a case; much of his reporting sounds like the indictment of a prosecutor. The man simply could not control his feelings, and thus often forfeited the note of authenticity in Mark Rutherford's testimony, as well as the impression of calm veracity left by the purely objective manner of the finest naturalism. Rutherford was so matter-of-fact in recalling his bitterest experiences that the reader does not think of him as a novelist, but accepts it all as genuine autobiography, whilst recognizing the latent artist. How incapable Gissing was of detachment can be seen in his savage portraits of women, such as Clem, who thirsted for "someone who showed fight— someone with whom she could try savage issue in real tooth-and-claw conflict." He wove about them a congenial atmosphere of dread—the jungle with the beast in it. Gissing, at any rate, thought he was practising legitimate artistic methods. It is in *The Unclassed* that he talks of "digging deeper," since "the novel of everyday life is getting worn out." And he goes on:

Not virginibus puerisque will be my novel, I assure you, but for men and women who like to look beneath the surface, who understand that only as artistic material has human life any consequence. . . . Art, nowadays, must be the mouthpiece of misery, for misery is the keynote of modern life.

"It is horrible," Waymark exclaims, and Waymark stands for Gissing—

"often hideous and revolting to me, but I feel its absolute truth. Such a book will do more good than half-a-dozen religious societies. If only people can be got to read it. Yet I care nothing for that aspect of the thing. Is it artistically strong? Is it good as a picture? There was a time when I might have written in this way with a declared social object. That is all gone by. I have no longer a spark of social

[1] Dr Anton Weber, in *George Gissing und die soziale Frage*, 1932 (see especially pp. 53–57), disposes of A. Rotter's contention, in *Der Arbeiterroman in England seit 1880* (1929), that Gissing had similar aims in his novels of the nether world as Kingsley's in *Alton Locke* or Besant's in *All Sorts and Conditions of Men*.

enthusiasm.   Art is all I now care for, and as art I wish my work to be judged."

Such a remark could have been made with much more justice of George Moore's *Esther Waters*, which appeared ten years later.   Gissing keeps but a loose hold on his realism in both these books, even in depicting the hideousness of the life from which his idealized young women are rescued; and the organic improbabilities of their conversion are dissembled.   Had he painted the life from which Ida is rescued with half the realism applied to the repulsive Mrs Casti, and the horrors of Elm Court and Litany Lane, the formidable nature of the problem he solves so easily would have appeared at once.

"*Demos*"   *Demos, a story of English Socialism* (1886), Gissing's first mature novel, shows what he had now come to think of practical schemes for regenerating society.[1]   It is intellectually the sequel to *Workers in the Dawn*, *The Emancipated*, and the slighter *Isabel Clarendon*, published earlier the same year (1886). In this last, the debate between atheism and agnosticism had been resumed, and Gissing had introduced one of his duplicates of himself, in the refined, sensitive, pessimistic Kingcote, tortured with jealousy of Isabel's apparent lightness. This time, his pseudo-hero is a demagogue of the working-classes, who suddenly inherits a fortune, and starts establishing the millennium, by equipping the Wanley mines with all the machinery for alleviating the lot of the workers, and by ear-marking the profits for the furtherance of the socialist cause.   But Mutimer is now a capitalist, and the determinism of commercial rivalry forces him into much the same position of a master of wage-slaves as he used to denounce; he begins to preach an attenuated form of his fiery old socialism.   The crash arrives when a will comes to light depriving him of the whole estate.   Thrown back into the ranks of labour, he sets up as a professional agitator and founds a co-operative society. But he runs undue risks; there is a deficit, and at a meeting of the enraged comrades, when he tries to exonerate himself from the charge of fraud, Mutimer gets knocked on the head.   The

[1] He thought of it as "rather a savage satire on working-class aims and capacities" (*Letters*, 172).

novel appeared about the time of the famous riots in Trafalgar Square, and reaped the benefit of the interest in socialism aroused at the time. Gissing's scheme was to write a "scientific novel," studying the effects of the socialistic programme on different characters and capacities, and trying to show the good and the bad in it. George Moore, like many others, was talking glibly of "the idea of a new art based upon science, in opposition to the art of the old world that was based on imagination, an art that should explain all things and embrace modern life in its entirety, in its endless ramifications." [1] Gissing was aiming at the same thing, but not quite attaining it. The fact is, he hardly pretended to be neutral; his prepossessions were altogether hostile, and the result of any such inquiry or experiment might be predicted. There is some show of scientific impartiality, as when, to explain Mutimer, he draws up what he calls "a tabular exposition of the man's consciousness," and sets forth the motives impelling or restraining his ambitious democrat, who is on the point of breaking with Emma Vine, the girl of his own class, and marrying the genteel Adela. This is a cruder instance of the educated working-man's craving to mate with a woman of breeding, to be more finely studied in Godwin Peak's case, in *Born in Exile*.[2] Adela Waltham, to be sure, is Gissing's own aspiration, the antidote to his repugnance to the basic covetousness and meanness of the poor. It was partly this in Mutimer. But Mutimer " could not regard his nature as a whole; he had no understanding for the subtle network of communication between its various parts." It did not occur to him "that in forfeiting his honour in this instance he began a process of undermining which would sooner or later threaten the stability of the purposes on which he most prided himself." So, in the tabular exposition, "he told himself that the genuineness and value of his life's work would be increased by a marriage with Adela Waltham; he and she

---

[1] *Confessions of a Young Man*, vii.

[2] Gissing himself felt acutely the social privations that were his inevitable lot, his circumstances being what they were. Many a time, no doubt, he had the same longings as Mutimer and Godwin Peak (*Born in Exile*) for a wife who was his intellectual equal. "I suppose the day will never come for me when I shall have intimate acquaintances among people of ordinary family life. Yet it would be pleasant in its way" (*Letters*, 182).

would represent the union of classes—of the wage-earning with the *bourgeois*, between which two lay the real gist of the combat." This is a dull and abstract method of telling a story; and, apart from that, it lays Gissing open to the fallacies of special pleading. Mutimer's disloyalty is at variance with previous expositions of his character, which was said to be singularly straightforward. To prove his case against socialism, Gissing had to show Mutimer slowly but surely changing for the worse. The whole subsequent course of the tale hangs upon this act of perfidy; hence the weakness of the psychological links here has far-reaching reactions. Mutimer, at any rate, secures his woman of the upper classes, and the reader secures the truer and more interesting study of her revulsion when she awakes to the fact that he is "a man of birth and breeding altogether beneath her," and that "a whole world of natural antipathies was between him and her." Sidwell Warricombe might have made a sympathetic mate for Godwin Peak, who was intellectually even her superior, and frankly avowed the motives for his one act of equivocation. For Adela there is no peace of mind till, after Mutimer's violent death, she marries her equal, Hubert Eldon. In sum, the finest parts of the book are not those tracing Mutimer's deterioration or anatomizing the evils of socialism, nor the vivid portraits of party-leaders and mob-orators, but the incidental studies of the frictions and disparities of class and class; in other words, this, like others of Gissing's books, is best as a study of manners and morals. Old Mrs Mutimer's translation to a new sphere, when she is utterly unable to give up her old habits, insists on doing the housework, and still keeps her faithful watch against poverty, though the incentive has gone, and her brave censure of her son's jilting of Emma, are amongst the finest passages. Gissing has no faith in Demos, for he is convinced that democracy is an insurrection of lower forces. He puts his riper views into the mouth of old Parson Wyvern:

One of the pet theories I have developed for myself in recent years is, that happiness is very evenly distributed among all classes and conditions. It is the result of sober reflection on my experience of life. Think of it a moment. The bulk of men are neither rich nor poor, taking into consideration their habits and needs; they live in much content, despite social imperfections and injustices, despite the ills of nature. Above and below are classes of extreme characterization; I believe the happiness assignable to those who are the lowest stratum of civilization is, relatively speaking, no whit less than that we may attribute to the thin stratum of the surface, using the surface to mean the excessively rich. It is a paradox, but anyone capable of thinking may be assured of its truth. The life of the very poorest is a struggle to support their bodies; the richest, relieved of that one anxiety, are overwhelmed with such a mass of artificial troubles that their few moments of genuine repose do not exceed those vouchsafed to their antipodes. . . . Go along the poorest street in the East End of London, and you will hear as much laughter, witness as much gaiety, as in any thoroughfare of the West. Laughter and gaiety of a miserable kind? . . . A being of superior intelligence regarding humanity with an eye of perfect understanding would discover that life was enjoyed every bit as much in the slum as in the palace.

It is a pity Gissing forgot these excellent words when he reproved Dickens for his light-hearted attitude towards poverty. There follows an eloquent tirade against the doctrine of progress. In spite of this equality of distribution, the old parson believes that "the sum total of happiness in nations is seriously diminishing." He is with the socialists in their denunciation of the capitalists as "the supremely maleficent."

"Monstrously hypocritical, they cry for progress when they mean increased opportunities for swelling their own purses at the expense of those they employ, and of those they serve; vulgar to the core, they exalt a gross ideal of well-being, and stink in their prosperity."

"What is before us?" asks a listener.

"Evil; of that I am but too firmly assured. Progress will have its way, and its way will be a path of bitterness. A pillar of dark cloud leads it by day, and of terrible fire by night. I do not say that the promised land may not lie ahead of its guiding, but woe is me for the desert first to be traversed."

Gissing's hopelessness was complete: he saw no rescue for the modern world from one side or the other. No wonder if his finest eloquence was called out by the sight of an East End graveyard:

> Not grief, but chill desolation makes this cemetery its abode. A country churchyard touches the tenderest memories, and softens the heart with longing for the eternal rest. The cemeteries of wealthy London abound in dear and great associations, or at worst preach homilies which connect themselves with human dignity and pride. Here on the waste limits of that dread East, to wander among tombs is to go hand in hand with the stark and eyeless emblems of mortality; the spirit fails beneath the cold burden of ignoble destiny. Here lie those who were born for toil; who, when toil has worn them to the uttermost, have but to yield their useless breath and pass into oblivion. For them is no day, only the brief twilight of a winter sky between the former and the latter night. For them no aspiration; for them no hope of memory in the dust; their very children are wearied into forgetfulness. Indistinguishable units in the vast throng that labours but to support life, the name of each, father, mother, child, is as a dumb cry for the warmth and love of which Fate so stinted them. The wind wails above their narrow tenements; the sandy soil, soaking in the rain as soon as it has fallen, is a symbol of the great world which absorbs their toil and straightway blots their being.[1]

"Thyr- Before realizing his life's dream of visiting Italy and Greece,
za" and Gissing finished two somewhat lighter novels, *Thyrza* (1887)
"A Life's and *A Life's Morning* (1888). He was at his most idealistic
Morning" and poetical in conceiving his Thyrza, the factory-girl imbued with Ruskinian teaching; her love-story, though terminating in renunciation and death, is a relief after the tragic sternness of *Demos*. A lofty act of self-sacrifice, when Emily Hood renounces the man who loves her because her father's suicide might disgrace her future husband, is also the crowning incident in *A Life's Morning*, a tragedy transmogrified with a happy termination because James Payn thought the general reader would not stand the distressing end which was the rightful issue. The dialogue with her lover and the colloquy with

---

[1] *Demos*, xvi. Gissing was gratified at John Morley's singling out this passage as "one of the most beautiful in modern literature" (*Letters*, 185).

herself in which Emily reasons out the question, "Could she move on over her father's body to a life of joy?" is Gissing's ethical casuistry at its most exalted. "Not with impunity could a life be purchased by the death of a soul." It is lamentable that Payn should have been allowed to wreck such a promising forecast of retributive injustice. Gissing had saved enough to pay for a visit to the classical lands he longed to see. In a first tour in 1888, planned on the thriftiest lines, he managed to get as far as Paestum, and next year he went to Greece. Perhaps there is a greater frequency of classical allusion in the novels that appeared now; naturally, there is plenty in *New Grub Street*. Two books were the special outcome of these trips and of another in 1897–1898: the long-meditated account of his journeys, *By the Ionian Sea* (1901), which made readers experience his own raptures, and the unfinished romance, *Veranilda* (1904), an attempt to depict the Roman Empire in its last struggle with the Goths. It was a respectable effort in the manner of *Salammbô*, and the archæology, at any rate, was carefully done. But, though his enthusiasm was anything but shallow and his learning considerable, this was a digression from his truer subject, the one that haunted and depressed him.

The Nether World (1889), that gloomy panorama of the misery, squalor, and savagery of the lower classes of Clerkenwell at the end of the eighteen-eighties, is Gissing's equivalent for *Les Misérables* of Victor Hugo.[1] Not by accident, his portrait of Clem Peckover forms a sort of frontispiece to the book. For he had to lay bare, not only the incapacity of the social organism to provide for common human needs, but also the existence among the dregs of the populace of a brutish, criminal, and probably irreclaimable element which was an evidence of active corruption. He did not believe in progress; but he could discuss the pros and cons of socialism or any other theory, with a self-deceptive show of impartiality. These products of a defective social system, however, were a proof to him that the system was inherently corrupt, and he believed they were going to predominate more and more in the future. Clem is eating

"*The Nether World*"

---

[1] He gives dates in this case.

her supper in the kitchen-parlour, and in the intervals of "conveying pieces of sausage to her mouth by means of the knife alone," she scolds and torments the unfortunate little slavey, Jane Snowdon, who is scrubbing hard at the frying-pan. Then, "with her Red Indian scent," she hits on a brilliant idea. In the next room there is a dead body, waiting to be buried. "The proximity of this corpse was a ceaseless occasion of dread and misery" to the poor child. Clem orders her to go into this back kitchen to fetch the matches.

Jane was blanched; but she rose from her knees at once, and reached a candlestick from above the fireplace.

"What's that for?" shouted Clem, with her mouth full. "You've no need of a light to find the mantelpiece. If you're not off——"

Jane hastened from the kitchen, Clem yelled to her to close the door, and she had no choice but to obey. In the dark passage outside there was darkness that might be felt. The child all but fainted with the sickness of horror as she turned the handle of the other door and began to grope her way. She knew exactly where the coffin was; she knew that to avoid touching it in the diminutive room was all but impossible. And touch it she did. Her anguish uttered itself, not in a mere sound of terror, but in a broken word or two of a prayer she knew by heart, including a name which sounded like a charm against evil. She had reached the mantelpiece; oh, she could not, could not find the matches! Yes, at last her hand closed upon them. A blind rush, and she was out again in the passage. She re-entered the front kitchen with limbs that quivered, with the sound of dreadful voices ringing about her, and blankness before her eyes. Clem laughed heartily, then finished her beer in a long, enjoyable pull. Her appetite was satisfied; the last trace of oleaginous matter had disappeared from her plate, and now she toyed with little pieces of bread lightly dipped in the mustard-pot. These *bonnes bouches* put her into an excellent humour; presently she crossed her arms and leaned back.

Clem is drawn better, from sheer repulsion, than those who are meant to inspire sympathy; and she does not by any means stand alone. In portraying her like, Gissing is a sad-eyed

Dickens, incapable of the humour, the melodrama, or the abounding zest of the expansive and optimistic genius that made an *Oliver Twist* out of just such materials. He takes the horrors far too seriously for joking, and fails to see the comedy even when it is going on before his eyes. But a good half, at least, of his novels are compounded on the same general prescription as those of Dickens. The Peckover clan form one group of characters, the decent and better-educated Hewetts form another; then there is Kirkwood and others who are only too self-consciously trying to live up to high principles, and even attempt something for the betterment of their downtrodden neighbours. All these, a pretty numerous crowd, are linked together by a plot, which revolves round one of Gissing's abortive schemes for social regeneration, but also has many features in common with the novels of intrigue and sensation then in unabated demand. Another element also is no novelty, the vivid painting of externals, especially of the grim surroundings of streets and alleys; but how considerably this differed in Gissing's reproachful hands from the scene-painting of his predecessors may be judged by a short passage describing a railway journey across this limbo of human neglect and desolation:

Over the pest-stricken regions of East London, sweltering in sunshine which served only to reveal the intimacies of abomination; across miles of a city of the damned, such as thought never conceived before this age of ours, above streets swarming with a nameless populace, cruelly exposed to the unwonted light of heaven; stopping at stations which it crushes the heart to think should be the destination of any mortal; the train made its way at length beyond the utmost limits of dread, and entered upon a land of level meadows, of hedges and trees, of crops and cattle.

The fellow here to Waymark and Kingcote is the intellectual working-man Kirkwood, who was to have married Clara, the handsome daughter of the Hewetts; but she runs away, lured by more paltry ambitions. When Jane Snowdon's grandfather comes home from Australia with a fortune, with which he proposes to found an institution for rescuing the reformable among the victims of poverty and vice, it looks as if Kirkwood

Another abortive social scheme

and Jane, now grown up, would be exactly fitted by character and experience to be the ministrants of his philanthropy. Their affection and respect for each other and for each other's ideals seem to be ripening into love. But such a happy and logical solution had no appeal to Gissing. On the contrary, he seems to raise hopes only to administer an extra dose of disillusionment. It is a gratuitous slap in the face, the reader feels; but it is only Gissing's morbid conscientiousness, his dread of the least concession to optimism. When old Snowdon unfolds his plan, Gissing makes both Kirkwood and Jane analyse themselves to the last fibre of their consciences. But, though this fine art of his was developing, it was not yet infallible; his Kirkwood does not always ring true. It is by a feat of moral gymnastics rather than by stern self-examination that he girds himself to renounce Jane and the mission which they could have carried to fruition, though he loves her and believes she loves him. And all from two inadequate motives: as a working-man he scruples to take Jane with her fortune, and he tells himself that he is still responsible for Clara Hewett, who jilted him and has long disappeared, and now after a questionable life on the music-hall stage, in which her beauty has been horribly disfigured by a rival star, allows herself ungraciously and ungratefully to become his wife. It is hard to forgive Clara, even after Gissing's apologetic argument for "this girl of the people, with her unfortunate endowment of brains and defect of tenderness." She felt that she was inherently a lady, and she went her own path with callous disregard for the feelings of others. Many others from that pit of demoralization are drawn with the same alert insight and a terrible lifelikeness. The corruption of Bob Hewett is a typical example of depraving influences. More complex is that of Scawthorne:

Pity that some self-made intellectual man of our time has not flung in the world's teeth a truthful autobiography. Scawthorne worked himself up to a position which had at first seemed unattainable; what he paid for the success was loss of all his pure ideals, of his sincerity, of his disinterestedness, of the fine perceptions to which he was born.[1]

[1] Gissing was not above noticing the little grievances which are so irksome to the poor: "Had the British Museum been open to visitors in the hours of the evening,

But in the crucial case of Kirkwood and Jane there is some slurring of motive, a foreshortening of states of mind. Gissing rarely had those divinations which are so superior to mere rationalist exploration. In a word, the psychology is forced. Hence Jane, instead of being left in a position to be a providence to hapless women with burdens too heavy to bear, finds herself again a penniless worker, and widowed of her hopes of a comrade and helpmate in Kirkwood. Old Snowdon has destroyed his will, and dies before he can make a new one. And so the latter pages are enlivened with the sour comedy of his rediscovered son, Jane's father, who hopes, and is justified of his hope, to come in for all that unexpected wealth. This man's wilier marriage with the wily Clem, his clandestine relations with Scawthorne, who had been implicated in Clara's disappearance, and the plots of Bob Hewett and Clem to murder him before he can get away with the plunder to America, provide an exciting finish, and also a well-merited discomfiture for Clem.

But, again, although this is the novel that plunges deepest *Lack of* and drags up from below the largest collection of the degraded *sympathy* and brutalized, it is not an enlightening study of these poor *and* wretches. The reason is that Gissing's warmest feeling for *under-* them is only that they are poor, abandoned wretches, even in *standing* their contemptible joys, such as the imbecile pranks and base *again* pleasures satirized in his account of a bank-holiday at the Crystal Palace. He has no understanding whatever of the subtle self-adaptation of the poorest to what seems an intolerable state of existence, of their invincible vitality and even cheerfulness amid surroundings and privations that appal a man like himself. He depicts their ways and habits and squalid pretences like an onlooker at some hideous and grotesque procession of the dregs of mankind, without the slightest inkling of what they themselves thought and felt. He could not read beneath their outward physiognomy, for they thought in another idiom than his. He gave it up; it was not a kind of existence that his sensitive soul could stand. Gissing's imagination was limited. His exploration of this alien world stopped

or on Sundays, Bob Hewett would possibly have been employing his leisure nowadays in more profitable pursuits." Gissing spoke feelingly, from his own experience.

at a certain point. In short, he hated it and all that pertained
to it, whereas Dickens went into it with a universal love of
his species; and without such love and such power of self-
identification there could be nothing but the superficial
knowledge of an outsider.

"New Grub Street" *New Grub Street* (1891) presents Gissing's own world of
struggling authors, living in garrets and basements, often too
poor to afford a fire, slaving daily at the British Museum for an
uncertain pittance, never sure of their next meal; and in
Edwin Reardon it gives the history of his own martyrdom, his
days of agony and gnawing anxiety and nights of insomnia, his
fits of sterility, and the ceaseless strain to be honest and not
lapse into the facile vulgarity that brought others success with
a half-educated public. It is not tragedy, unless there be such
a thing as perpetual tragedy, misery without hope and with no
end but death. Reardon eventually dies of under-nourishment
and exposure without proper clothing or any home comforts;
Biffen calmly takes poison when there is nothing left to live for.
The world of small literary men, who write for a living and not
from inspiration, is a worse sphere than the underpaid clerk's
or the humblest working-man's; a slough of despond, a ceaseless
nightmare, out of which the unfortunate never escapes even in
his dreams. There is none of Hardy's poetic joy in life here,
of that which gives dignity to suffering. Such momentary
glimpses of nature as thrill Reardon, who with his last coin has
run down to Brighton to see his dying child, when he wakes to
hear the soft and continuous murmur of the tide and fancies
himself on the boat amid the Ionian Isles, only deepen the
Stygian gloom. It is nearly always fog or rain or filthy snow in
Gissing's London; and yet this was the London of Dickens and
Thackeray not so long before.

Characters like himself The book is packed with authors. Besides Reardon and his
foil, Jasper Milvain, there are the optimistic Whelpdale, with
the ideal woman he is always meeting, a rare bit of comic
seasoning; the excellent Biffen, who in an exciting serio-comic
chapter rushes upstairs in a burning house to save the manuscript of "Mr Bailey Grocer," and all but loses his life; the
fine old scholar Yule, mismarried, and soured by drudgery and

spiteful reviews; his daughter and Milvain's sisters, not to mention a crowd of anonymous helots. The futility of all this parasitic labour is the first idea that emerges: the Museum drudge "kept asking herself what was the use and purpose of such a life as she was condemned to lead. When already there was more good literature in the world than any mortal could cope with in his lifetime, here was she exhausting herself in the manufacture of printed stuff which no one even pretended to be more than a commodity for the day's market." The next idea is the wasted sincerity of a Reardon and the debasing sycophancy of those who succeed, like the scurrilous Fudge and the time-serving Milvain. It is easy enough to please popular taste and be sure of prosperity:

"The art of writing for such papers—indeed, for the public in general—is to express vulgar thoughts in a way that flatters vulgar thinkers and feelers. Just abandon your mind to it, and then let me see it again."

It is the pliable and cynical Milvain who thus corrects his sister Maud's lapses into good sense. But the majority are worn down and condemned to be the slaves of ignoble tastes; whilst the honest craftsman, a Reardon or a Biffen, each "a personality wholly unfitted for the rough and tumble of the world's labour-market," is starved or driven to suicide. Biffen talks good worldly sense to a degree that in another man would have made him protest, for he had not enough of this commodity to save himself from disaster. When remonstrating with Reardon for not trying to make it up when Mrs Reardon who has left him comes in for a legacy of £10,000, he sagaciously observes:

"The art of living is the art of compromise. . . . Genial coarseness is what it behoves men like you and me to cultivate. Your reply to your wife's last letter was preposterous. You ought to have gone to her of your own accord as soon as you heard she was rich; she would have thanked you for such common-sense disregard of delicacies."

Biffen, exponent of "absolute realism in the sphere of the ignobly decent," plus Reardon, "psychological realist for the more cultivated," would together make a Gissing, who, often in the same book, leaned now to one side and now to the other.

Gissing deals with character rather than characters, his Reardons, Milvains, Amys, and Marians being, at least primarily, examples of qualities or defects which are tested and inevitably compared in the battle of life. Without Hardy's formal geometry, there is an obvious contrast between the two men and between the two women, though it comes out only when the story is well advanced. At the beginning, both Reardon and Milvain have good points: Milvain's cheerful efficiency shows to advantage in contrast with Reardon, whose "strong but somewhat pedantic individuality" was "ceaselessly at conflict with unpropitious circumstances" and could never adapt itself. This, of course, is Gissing to the life, who also felt it to be "the unpardonable sin"—"to make a trade of an art," and knew that he "was rightly served for attempting such a brutal folly." Reardon, like Gissing, was too fastidious: he should have kept out of Grub Street at all costs. Milvain understands the situation thoroughly, for to him it is simply and solely an economic problem, that of demand and supply; and he has the moral obtuseness that always accompanies this sort of sharpness. The essential difference between the two women is longer in showing itself unmistakably. Amy marries Reardon when he seems to be a promising novelist, breaks with him when he gives up the struggle and takes a clerk's job at a pound a week, is reconciled in a fit of sentimental repentance, and at last becomes the wife of Milvain, whose journalistic enterprises she finances with her legacy. Amy had never been sure of herself, and, long before, had dallied with the plausible adventurer. The union of such a well-matched pair is a good ironical finish, and Gissing dismisses it with a smile of contempt. Her opposite in character, Marian Yule, does not come off so happily in the worldly sense. She had been the original object of Milvain's attentions, and was at first fascinated, till her honesty and his slipperiness came into hopeless conflict. One of the most remarkable love-scenes in fiction is his proposal to the clear-sighted girl, who is in love, yet cannot be sure that he loves her as she requires to be loved. Why, she asks, does he

talk about "daring" to aspire to her? This is the language of
books, not of the heart.

"Because I have enough of old-fashioned thought to believe
that a woman who is worthy of a man's love is higher than he,
and condescends in giving herself to him."

His voice was not convincing; the phrase did not sound
natural on his lips. It was not thus that she had hoped to hear
him speak.

He goes on with his platitudes. Marian keeps silence. He
explains that it is imperative he should have money, with an
implied defence of his backwardness in not having proposed
before she came into her little fortune.

"Now suppose I had said to you, My one aim and desire in
life is to win your love. Could you have believed me? Such
phrases are always untrue; I don't know how it can give anyone
pleasure to hear them. But if I say to you, All the satisfactions
I have described would be immensely heightened if they were
shared with a woman who loved me—there is the simple truth."

Marian's heart sank. She did not want truth such as this;
she would have preferred that he should utter the poor,
common falsehoods.

She is still too much in love not to accept him; but it is
morally certain that he will betray himself one day, and then
calamity—for her. Marian, who has been warned against
Milvain's mercenary nature by her father, whom she thinks
prejudiced, reflects hourly on his conduct. It is she, not the
author, who anatomizes this specious young man, and it is
torture for her. She shrinks from penetrating too deeply: her
delicacy would have been offended if another girl had made so
many allowances.

In her own case she could indulge to the utmost that
practicality which colours a woman's thought even in mid
passion. The cold exhibition of ignoble scheming will repel
many a woman who, for her own heart's desire, is capable of the
same compromise with her strict sense of honour.

She has to make sure of her father's motives, and of the
reasonableness or the mere selfish infatuation of his efforts to

induce her to devote her legacy to founding a review for him to edit. She has to watch Jasper Milvain's behaviour when that legacy is reduced to a mere nothing. Like Reardon, she has flashes of profound insight. When at length she tells Milvain that he does not love her and it would shame her to marry him, and he talks of sacrifices to give her the happiness she deserves, "Deserve!" she repeats bitterly. "Why do I deserve it? Because I long for it with all my heart and soul? There's no such thing as deserving. Happiness or misery come to us by fate." And there is Gissing's own conclusion, expressed by a character that has more of his better self and his wisdom in her, more by far, than has the unhappy Reardon.

"Born in Exile" Intellectually, *Born in Exile* (1893) is Gissing's strongest novel; commercially, it was one of his failures. It looks like a discussion novel, so much of it consists of long conversations, debating questions of personal and social ethics, the religious problem and other discursive subjects. This is because it is the inner history of a man whose integrity, rather than his happiness, which cannot be divorced from his integrity, hinges upon those questions. Incidentally, it subsumes many of the most engrossing controversies of that chequered period of thought. A hard-headed young rationalist, born of the lower middle classes, and morbidly conscious of his origin and of the gulf between him and those in easy circumstances at the college of his native town, failing to make his mark as a scientist, and ambitious of the equality that he is sure would be his if he married a woman of birth and breeding, goes against his deepest convictions and prepares to take Orders. He throws up his post, disappears from all his acquaintances, and makes some progress towards his goal, including the refined wife. But it comes out that he was the author of a notorious article attacking those worthy people who thought they could blend some agnosticism with enough orthodoxy to save their souls; and the lady's brother paints his alleged hyprocrisy, and his duplicity towards a respectable family, in the basest colours.

Sidwell Warricombe Sidwell Warricombe scarcely dissembles her love; yet Godwin Peak cannot prevail upon her to become his wife, even when, like Gissing's Henry Ryecroft, he becomes possessed of a competence. A defeated man, he goes travelling, catches malaria, and dies abroad. Sidwell is Gissing's most elaborate portrayal of the woman who would be a proper mate for his intellectuals and social idealists. Like Marian Yule, she has a sensitive heart as well as a mind. That she is such a long time liberating herself from her father's anxious trust, the same as Tennyson's, that modern science and the Bible are not incompatible, is part of her feminine charm, of her tender loyalty to the ageing pietist. But she not only condones Godwin's fatal error, for it was out of love for her; she lets him see that if he had honestly avowed his incredulity at the outset she would have come half-way to meet him. This is the irony that embitters Godwin's failure, after he has violated his own self-respect, been estranged from his friends, and shown up by Sidwell's implacable brother. Gissing's love-scenes are never commonplace. Peak and Sidwell have to thrash out their own personal question, and also the vital one of his honesty or dishonesty in trying to reconcile knowledge and truth with doctrines whose only justification in his thinking is that they may elevate the masses and purify the morals and ideals of such as crave supernatural sanctions. But they are in love with each other all the time, and the debate is tense with subdued passion and their sense of all the rival claims on both —her compassionate affection for her father, and his gnawing anxiety to justify himself to her as well as to himself.

Almost as badly as *The Nether World* and *New Grub Street*, this novel is overcrowded with characters, many of them having but a distant bearing on the life of the man "born in exile." The best that can be said for them is that a number are persons of strong intellectual and moral interests, with their own lives to live in the circumstances of the time, and an earnest resolve to live them according to their highest convictions. For the little freaks of individuality Gissing had but an inattentive eye: his concern was with higher things. The unfortunate result is that many of these people are embodied problems or embodied consciences, and little else. Marcella Moxey, for instance, is an engrossing psychological study, with her hopeless passion for Godwin Peak, so magnanimous that she leaves him her

Various exponents of modern tendencies

money, when she knows he is in love with another woman and will use it to free himself from drudgery and marry her rival. Marcella is a great spirit; but she lacks all the feminine graces, and without charm she runs the risk of leaving the totally inadequate impression of a disappointed old maid. Godwin Peak is contrasted with the suave and shallow successful cleric, Bruno Chilvers, as Reardon was with the successful Milvain. Chilvers is a caustic portrait that everyone will recognize. On the other hand, the mercurial and effusive Malkin is an attempt at a Dickensian character, and talks like one. When the widow whom he has befriended with the hare-brained project of educating the elder of her two little girls to become his wife wants to marry him, the result is farcical:

"I got there at five o'clock, and found that the girls were gone to have tea with some young friends. Well, I wasn't altogether sorry; it was a good opportunity for a little talk with their mother. And I *had* the talk. But, oh, ass that I was!"

He smote the side of his head savagely.

"Can you guess, Earwaker? Can you give a shot at what happened?"

"Perhaps I might," replied the other, gravely.

"Well?"

"That woman asked you to marry her."

Malkin leapt from his chair, and sank back again.

"It came to that. Yes, upon my word, it came to that. She said she had fallen in love with me—that was the long and the short of it. And I had never said a word that could sug-gest—— Oh, confound it! What a frightful scene it was!"

"You took a final leave of her?"

Malkin stared with eyes of anguish into his friend's face, and at length whispered thickly:

"I said I would!"

"What? Take leave?"

"Marry her!"

Malkin's only chance is to flee, as the sagacious Earwaker points out, and at last persuades and almost forces him to do. It is better fun than the tame affair of Moxey's disillusionment, by the Laura whom he has waited and sorrowed for during ten bitter years and, when her tyrant of a husband dies, finds to be a fool.

Gissing did nothing better, at any rate, than the psycho- *Godwin* logical portrayal of Godwin Peak: his awkwardness when he *Peak—a* comes in contact with his social superiors; the intense pleasure *reflection* this born "rebel, the scorner of average mankind, the con- *of* summate egoist," experiences when he finds himself a favoured *Gissing* guest at the house of the well-to-do Warricombes; the sudden birth of his scheme, so unpremeditated, so like an inspiration, for entering the Church, the only way a man of his antecedents can place himself on an equality with a woman of that order, and possibly win her for his wife. The arguments which he resolutely applies to his act must, surely, have been imbibed from Nietzsche:

He was learning to review with calmness the course by which he had reached his now steadfast resolve. A revulsion such as he had experienced after his first day of simulated orthodoxy, half a year ago, could not be of lasting effect, for it was opposed to the whole tenor of his mature thought. It spoilt his holiday, but had no chance of persisting after his return to the atmos- phere of Rotherhithe. That he should have been capable of such emotion was, he said to himself, in the just order of things; callousness in the first stages of an undertaking which demanded gross hypocrisy would signify an ignoble nature—a nature, indeed, which could never have been submitted to trial of so strange a kind. But he had overcome himself; that phase of difficulty was outlived, and henceforth he saw only the material obstacles to be defied by his vindicated will.

For Godwin Peak is not to be understood simply as a faulty, egotistic specimen of emancipated rationalism, who inevitably comes to grief; he is as complete a representative of Gissing's personal attitude as Waymark and Kirkwood and Reardon all put together, and he has gone through similar privations and desperate struggles for a life to satisfy his native tastes and his intellect. Gissing, too, was born in exile, and was similarly always contending, though not so fiercely and unscrupulously, for leisure and opportunity to realize his genius. Gissing was an aristocrat, evicted from his place and sphere, a superman without the strength to maintain his natural privileges; and in Godwin Peak's case he gives the Nietzschean programme of self-realization, whatever the cost, full scope. Hear Peak on the vulgar middle-class crowd who are now the arbiters of taste and of current opinion, and it is obviously Gissing himself who is speaking:

"My own experience," pursued Godwin, "has been among the lower classes of London. I don't mean the very poorest, of whom one hears so much nowadays: I never went among them because I had no power of helping them, and the sight of their vileness would only have moved me to unjust hatred. But the people who earn enough for their needs, and whose spiritual guide is the Sunday newspaper—I know them, because for a long time I was obliged to lodge in their houses. Only a consuming fire could purify the places where they dwell. Don't misunderstand me; I am not charging them with what are commonly held vices and crimes, but with the consistent love of everything that is ignoble, with utter deadness to generous impulse, with the fatal habit of low mockery. And *these* are the people who really direct the democratic movement. They set the tone in politics; they are debasing art and literature; even the homes of wealthy people begin to show the effects of their influence. One hears men and women of gentle birth using phrases which originate with shopboys; one sees them reading print which is addressed to the lowest million. They crowd to entertainments which are deliberately adapted to the lowest order of mind. When commercial interest is supreme, how can the tastes of the majority fail to lead and control?" [1]

It is prophetic: the fatal tendency has now gone to lengths that would have driven Godwin Peak to suicide.

Gissing's problem novels   Such are Gissing's serious and heartfelt versions of the tragedy of modern life. As if he had exhausted the main theme, he now applied himself to minor problems, such as sex or the superfluous woman, the aimlessness and inanity of existence to-day, or the fatal spell of social ambitions, in novels that have proved mostly ephemeral. The full tale of his work

[1] Pp. 269–270.

represents an heroic output, in the circumstances with which he was always fighting. But many of these later productions are merely controversial fiction of a dull, pedestrian order. Already, in *The Emancipated* (1890), he had marshalled for inspection a miscellaneous crowd of free-livers, self-questioners, and others of both sexes who had repudiated the ordinary restraints of morals or religion; and now, in *Denzil Quarrier* (1892), he selects a special case, the woman who leaves a husband convicted of felony and enters into an irregular union with the man she loves. *The Odd Women* (1893) is a whole collection of studies, imperfectly combined into a novel, of women who have proved marriage a failure, or who denounce marriage on principle, or who are condemned by circumstances to forgo all hope of wedlock. There are far too many women to go round. Gissing discovers tragedy in the fate of Monica Madden, tied to a jealous elderly man, and hounded into secret drinking; fanatical idealism in Rhoda Nunn, sworn foe of the opposite sex; sound sense in Mary Barfoot, who, almost in spite of her author, declares "It's better to be a woman, in our day"; and what has to be accepted as humour though it is only a rudimentary form of verbal wit, in his elephantine frolicking with the dull Mrs Poppleton, who could not understand a joke, and the boring wife, Mrs Orchard, Miss Nunn's illustration for the riddle, "Why will men marry fools?" Gissing's dialogue was always too neat, too bookish, too uncolloquial; and the more he particularizes, the heavier his touch, often approximating to the style of a report by a special commissioner.[1] The sense of social distinctions survives even the harsh climate of the slums. Gissing thinks fit to discuss it gravely when, for instance, John Hewett, in *The Nether World*, takes umbrage at his ne'er-do-well son's espousing poor Pennyloaf Candy. "For his refusal to recognize Pennyloaf he had absolutely no grounds, save—I use the word advisedly—an aristocratic prejudice. Bob had married deplorably beneath him; it was unpardonable, let the character of the girl be what it might." He is not quite

[1] Henry James rightly castigates Gissing for overdoing dialogue—"the ostensible report of spoken words," whilst admitting that this is a general abuse in English and American novels of that time (*Notes on Novelists*—"London Notes," July 1897, p. 349).

so ponderous on the superiority Bob feels towards Jane Snowdon, who had been a slavey.

"I should think you might find better friends than a girl as used to be the Peckovers' dirty little servant."

Bob turned up his nose and sniffed the air. And Pennyloaf, in spite of the keenest distress, actually felt that there was something in the objection, thus framed! She herself had never been a servant—never; she had never sunk below working with the needle for sixteen hours a day for a payment of ninepence.

"The Whirl- pool"

In the Year of Jubilee (1894) and *Eve's Ransom* (1895) again satirize the vulgarity and essential barbarism of the middle classes, or, rather, strip them naked, the topical theme in the former, which is full of the cantankerous types of women that Dickens treated so amiably, being British philistinism. Then, in *The Whirlpool* (1897), Gissing renewed his old strength and clear-sightedness in solving moral complications, as in *New Grub Street* and *Born in Exile*. Instead of the robust Godwin Peak or even the well-intentioned Kirkwood, however, his own representative, Harvey Rolfe, is a man without much backbone, rather feebly loving the ideal, and feebly aiming at a life of culture. But this time Gissing went as far outside his own experience as he had gone previously, in the opposite direction, in depicting the nethermost classes. His object was to show up the rottenness of an over-civilized society and the snares of fast life in London; and the person caught in the vortex who eventually perishes in the depths is Rolfe's wife, Alma, daughter of a speculator who had shaken the financial world with his failure and then committed suicide. Twice her age when they marry, Rolfe finds out too late that she is vain and selfish, lacking in principle and in elementary consistency. When, primed by adulation which he sees through, she prepares for her great début as a violinist, he refuses even to be present at the concert-hall, though he is as yet far from suspecting that she is playing with fire. But, though she never sins in the technical sense, Alma finds it difficult to avoid compromising relations with Dymes, the musical impresario; and the libidinous millionaire, Cyrus Redgrave, makes dangerous advances.   Now comes the melodramatic central incident.   Foolishly visiting Redgrave at his wicked bungalow at Wimbledon, Alma is found there by the jealous husband of her erstwhile dearest friend; he mistakes her in the dark for his wife, and kills Redgrave, being subsequently given two years for manslaughter.   She hopes against hope that it will never come out that she was alone with Redgrave at the fatal moment.   But henceforward hers is a life of agony—fear of such a revelation, and jealousy of her old friend, Sibyl Carnaby, whom she believes to have been Redgrave's mistress.   It is a curious kind of jealousy:

She had never loved Redgrave, had never even thought of him with that curiosity which piques the flesh; yet so inseparably was he associated with her life at its points of utmost tension and ardour, that she could not bear to yield to any other woman a closer intimacy, a prior claim.   At her peril she had tempted him, and up to the fatal moment she was still holding her own in the game which had become to her a passion. It ended—because a rival came between.   Of Sibyl's guilt she never admitted a doubt; it was manifest in the story made public by Hugh Carnaby, the story which he, great simple fellow, told in all good faith, relying absolutely on his wife's assertion of innocence.   Saving her husband, who believed Sibyl innocent?

Instead of letting sleeping dogs lie, Alma drops innuendoes that come to the ears of her formidable rival; and, in seeking confirmatory evidence, she is outwitted by the society procuress Mrs Strangeways, and, after a duel of mutual recrimination at long range, is contemptuously dismissed by Mrs Carnaby, whom she has ventured to caution in person.   There is a painful scene when Sibyl brings out her accusation, and even her husband's common sense seems to be in revolt against Alma. She feels herself cornered, and that night takes an extra dose of the "draught of oblivion."   Obviously, Alma is a sentimentalist, and her husband not much better; hence both the chief actors in the tragedy, though Gissing did not mean both, are alike examples of the moral deterioration which he is showing up.   And Rolfe's uncertainty whether or not to welcome the muscular programme of Kipling's *Ballad-Room Ballads*, "the voice of the reaction," of the revolt against "the softness and sweetness of civilization," does not mend matters; for he recognizes also "the brute savagery of it," "the very lingo," "the tongue of Whitechapel blaring lust of life in the track of English guns"; and prophesies more truly than he knows the dire results of British imperialism.[1]

Lighter novels and short stories
The well-named volume *Human Odds and Ends* (1897) and *The House of Cobwebs, and other stories* (1906), consist of sketches of people and manners and the ugliness of life under modern conditions: they are hardly dramatic enough ever to amount to a story. That was not what Gissing was aiming at. *The Town Traveller* (1898) was an attempt at the conventional bright story with a plot, enlivened with Cockney humours. *The Crown of Life* (1899) tells how one of the elect misses that most precious thing, love. In *Our Friend the Charlatan* (1901) Gissing tried to write like Meredith, whose influence was also perceptible in earlier studies of temperament, particularly in *A Life's Morning*; but the cynicism is neither Meredithian nor truly his own. It is the sort of comedy that makes everything and everybody look extremely unpleasant; satire the objects of which cannot be recognized as real. Lashmar, the political charlatan, the sentimentalist Mrs Woolstan, the strong-minded woman, Constance Bride, and the amused spectator, Mrs Toplady, are clever illustrations of social hypocrisy, shallow culture, and the lack of either religion or morals; but the satire hardly hits any mark. *Will Warburton* (1905) was a commonplace though unwontedly cheerful novel of such humdrum people as a ruined merchant who saves his respectability by opening a grocer's shop in Fulham, marrying the girl he loves, and providing a home for his mother and sisters.

By far the most interesting of Gissing's later books, *The*

---

[1] Henry James confessed that *The Whirlpool* "was in a manner a grief to me"; yet its emotion "makes me, to the end, stick to Mr Gissing": "He seems to me above all a case of saturation, and it is mainly his saturation that makes him interesting —I mean especially in the sense of making him singular. The interest would be greater were his art more complete; but we must take what we can get, and Mr Gissing has a way of his own." He goes on to discuss Gissing's anatomizing of the vulgar, and to distinguish it from the special case of Dickens (*Notes on Novelists*— "London Notes," pp. 347–348).

Private Papers of Henry Ryecroft (1903), was intended as self-revelation, although it is not autobiography and certainly refrains from analysing his inmost self.[1] It is a dream-story of what he would like to have done with himself had he not missed his vocation. A defeated literary man comes in for a legacy, and settles down in the country to enjoy life in his own quiet way, observing nature and ruminating on books, people, and himself. Ryecroft sometimes meditates on the tombs, striking the attitude of a Mark Rutherford and choosing a text from Spinoza on death. But, on the whole, it is an exposition of Gissing's own hedonistic philosophy; Ryecroft is determined to get the most he can of modest pleasure out of the years that remain after his long struggle. Though obtrusively self-conscious and over-literary, the book shows Gissing to have been no mean essayist, and the mellowness and well-sustained buoyancy are a pleasing contrast to the querulous tone of most of his fiction.

Was Gissing aware of the besetting weakness that impaired so *Some last* much of his work? In *Henry Ryecroft* there is one long dis- *comments* quisition on the much-discussed question of art, beginning, "It has occurred to me that one might define Art as an expression, satisfying and abiding, of the zest of life." The zest of life: that is precisely what he lacked. A man's art may, possibly, be pessimistic through and through, and yet triumph. But it was all very well for Gissing to say, "In truth I think of very little but Art, pure and simple, and all my work is profoundly pessimistic as far as mood goes." [2] The trouble was that he allowed the pessimism to dominate his art. He let the misery which was his chosen theme prey upon his mind and blind him to all else. How could be possibly find any gusto in life? It was his art that should have dominated. Did he not himself say, "Only as artistic material has human life any consequence"? But he should not have immediately added, "Art, nowadays, must be the mouthpiece of misery." [3] This was illogical; it would make art, not master of its own subject, but subsidiary

[1] "I did not put my innermost thought into *Henry Ryecroft*": so he said to his friend the English chaplain at St-Jean-de-Luz, three days before he died (*New Statesman*, 13th April 1929).
[2] *Letters*, 193.   [3] See above, p. 133.

to some sort of humanitarianism or to the bitterness of the pessimist. He was devoid of zest, and he was incapable of detachment: Gissing's pathetic face is always there, full of reproach. He said in his letters, people might if they wished call him "brutal and egotistic," in the final stage of his artistic development.[1] But the truth is, he rarely assumed and never sustained for any length of time the brutal, Nietzschean attitude in art which Godwin Peak maintained in his intellectual life. Both Gissing and George Moore were apt to chatter glibly about artistic detachment and the ruthless objective method of using life as material, and then in their actual work to let their feelings run away with their pens. So much the better, no doubt, for Moore; otherwise *Esther Waters* would not have been such a human book as well as a masterpiece of realism. The results of the discrepancy between theory and practice, or, rather, of intermittent obeisance to theory and inadvertent self-surrender to feelings that did him no discredit, were more unfortunate in Gissing's case. Still more unfortunate for the quality of his work was his compulsory restriction to an old-fashioned pattern and the kind of fiction this implied—the three-volume novel of mid-Victorian England, with its artificial plot, multiplicity of characters, and arbitrary scheme of suspense and surprise. The majority of his novels would have been infinitely bettered had he confined himself to the theme which obviously possessed his mind; but this was not permitted. He had to make this obsolete and cumbrous equipage the vehicle for new ideas, new values, and new conceptions of character and moral complexities. Hence his novels were clogged with masses of otiose and laboured detail, redundant characters, superfluous incidents, and interests that competed with each other and confused the issues, together with a network of connecting links that contributed less than nothing to organic coherence. As soon as this was allowable, Gissing fell in with the new fashion of the one-volume novel; but his more important work had then been done. George Moore had the advantage of beginning when fiction was becoming enfranchised from this

[1] *Letters*, 129.

hampering convention. Gissing was delighted with the change:

> One volume is becoming commonest of all. It is the new school, due to Continental influence. Thackeray and Dickens wrote at enormous length, and with profusion of detail; their plan is to tell everything, and leave nothing to be divined. Far more artistic, I think, is the later method, of merely suggesting; of dealing with episodes, instead of writing biographies. The old novelist is omniscient; I think it is better to tell a story precisely as one does in real life, hinting, surmising, telling in detail what *can* so be told and no more. In fact, it approximates to the dramatic mode of presentment.[1]

Hatred of democracy and of science

He was consistent, at any rate, in his hatred for democracy; Henry Ryecroft does not wish for a nearer acquaintance even with the country folk around him. "Every instinct of my being," he writes, "is anti-democratic, and I dread to think what our England may become when Demos rules irresistibly." "To think that at one time I called myself a socialist, communist, anything you like of the revolutionary kind!" "Democracy is full of menace to all the finer hopes of civilization, and the revival, in not unnatural companionship with it, of monarchic power based on militarism, makes the prospect dubious enough." [2]

As to the universe, it was enough for him to acknowledge that ultimate causes were inscrutable, though he entertained ideas that brought him into close neighbourhood with Hardy. "Rather must I apprehend that man, in some inconceivable way, may at his best moments represent a Principle darkly at strife with that which prevails throughout the world as known to us." [3] "Of all theological systems, the most convincing is Manichæism, which, of course under another name, was held by the Puritans themselves." [4] And he continued to regard science as "the remorseless enemy of mankind":

---

[1] *Op. cit.*, 166.

[2] *Henry Ryecroft*, "Spring," xix. He goes on, with almost uncanny prescience: "There has but to arise some Lord of Slaughter, and the nations will be tearing at each other's throats"; and proceeds to relate examples of the curse of militarism, from Germany and from his own schooldays.

[3] *Op. cit.*, 187.   [4] *Op. cit.*, 280.

I see it destroying all simplicity and gentleness of life, all the beauty of the world; I see it restoring barbarism under a mask of civilization; I see it darkening men's minds and hardening their hearts; I see it bringing a time of vast conflicts, which will pale into insignificance "the thousand wars of old," and, as likely as not, will whelm all the laborious advances of mankind in blood-drenched chaos.[1]

And yet he loved to think that his was a scientific art, at any rate, an art based on science, such as George Moore had described [2]; and he was almost perversely loyal to what he took to be the circumstantial truth. This conception was answerable for a good deal, since it led by an easy fallacy to his besetting vice of making his art "the mouthpiece of misery."

[1] *Op. cit.*, 268–269.　　　　[2] See above, p. 135.

CHAPTER V

GEORGE MOORE

OF English descent, though born at the ancestral home in *Seeking*
Ireland, George Moore (1857–1933) plumed himself on never *a person-*
having really found out that he was an Irishman till, at a late *ality*
date, Yeats and Synge brought the fact to his notice. His is *Moore*
one of the oddest cases in literature of different styles and the *finds his*
art
doctrines and methods of opposite schools brilliantly exemplified
in one and the same writer. Only in the first of his literary
phases does he show any near affinity with Gissing, born the
same year, to justify his being put in immediate succession to
this brother realist—the naturalistic phase for which he got his
training in France, where he went to learn, not novel-writing,
but painting. To say that at this period Moore was one who
would have to be dismissed without a character is scarcely an
exaggeration, for his history is that of the successive influences
which formed him; only with the most liberal allowances can
he be said to have formed himself. No human being was ever
more plastic. "My soul, so far as I understand it," he begins
his *Confessions of a Young Man,* "has very kindly taken colour
and form from the many various modes of life that self-will and
an impetuous temperament have forced me to indulge in.
Therefore I may say that I am free from original qualities,
defects, tastes, etc. What is mine I have acquired, or, to speak
more exactly, chance bestowed, and still bestows, upon me. I
came into the world apparently with a nature like a smooth
sheet of wax, bearing no impress, but capable of receiving any;
of being moulded into all shapes. Nor am I exaggerating when
I say I think that I might equally have been a Pharaoh, an ostler,
a pimp, an archbishop, and that in the fulfilment of the duties
of each a certain measure of success would have been mine."

And so on to the same effect; for nobody knew what there was, or was not, in Moore better than himself. When he left Oscott, after a repressive schooling that he hated, he had learned next to nothing. As to convictions, prepossessions, or definite ambitions, his mind was apparently a blank. It was a clean sheet of paper, a sensitized film, to receive whatever impress had the strength or the magic to arrest a wayward fancy.[1] He was always critical, however, in his egotistic fashion, and prone to be recalcitrant. Egotism and a certain fastidiousness were among the few positive contents, if they can be termed positive, of such personality as Moore had at this preliminary stage.[2] Almost by accident, he drifted to Paris: he thought he would like to be a painter, and Paris, he had been told, was the only place where he could learn. He stubbornly attended the studios, but he did not become a painter. Nevertheless, after watching and hobnobbing with Manet, Degas, Pissarro, Renoir, Sisley, and Monet, he learned all about the art, and was able to write those authoritative as well as entertaining reminiscences in the *Confessions*, and later on the appreciations in his more solid work, *Modern Painting* (1893). Moore, at this juncture, might be described as an accomplished dilettante, a typical decadent, with no convictions except his belief in art; and also as more than half a Frenchman, for he had all but forgotten his own language; how to write it, at any rate. And, not only was he thoroughly at home with the impressionist painters, he

[1] "It always interests me to hear him [Edward Martyn] say that I began myself out of nothing, developing from the mere sponge to the vertebræ and upwards" (*Vale*, 81). In Paris, "myself was the goal I was making for, instinctively if you will, but still making for it; I felt that I must think out life for myself," etc. (*Ibid.*, 132).

[2] The dialogue with Conscience, in the *Confessions*, is illuminating, *e.g.*: "*Conscience*, 'You were glad, I remember, when your father died, because his death gave you unlimited facilities for moulding the partial self which the restraining influence of home had only permitted, into that complete and ideal George Moore which you had in mind.'" The catechism goes on: "*I*, 'There I join issue with you. Have I not drawn the intense ego out of the clouds of semi-consciousness, and realized it? And, surely, the rescue and the individualization of the ego is the first step.' *Conscience*, 'To what end? You have nothing to teach, nothing to reveal. I have often thought of asking you this: since death is the only good, why do you not embrace death? Of all the world's goods it is the cheapest, and the most easily obtained.'" Again, "You have failed in all you have attempted, and the figure you have raised on your father's tomb is merely a sensitive and sensuous art-cultured being who lives in a dirty lodging and plays in desperation his last card. You are now writing a novel. The hero is a wretched creature, something like yourself. Do you think there is a public in England for that kind of thing?" (chapter xiii.).

GEORGE MOORE 163

was equally well versed in modern French literature, in the
work of Balzac, Gautier, Flaubert, the Goncourts, Zola, and
the poets, Mallarmé, Villiers de l'Isle Adam, Verlaine, and
Baudelaire. The living ones were his personal friends; at
least, he liked so to persuade himself and his readers; though
Zola, for one, was stand-offish, especially when Moore began
to criticize the famous notebook method. Moore's peculiar
deities up to this date were, first, Shelley, then Gautier, and for
a while Zola,[1] from whom he imbibed his idea of "the art based
on science" already discussed in relation to Gissing.[2] When
he came back to England, on the stoppage of the larger part of
his Irish income through the anti-rent campaign, he realized
that his likeliest way to earn money was by writing, and the
writing must be either journalism or fiction. He had amused
himself with a few poetic trifles so far, and that was all. But
the first thing was to learn to write English, and he was fastidious
enough to mean this with the most exemplary seriousness. If
a dilettante, Moore was capable when he chose of the most
intense application. Genius, it has been said, is the art of
taking infinite pains: Moore said it is "merely the power of
assimilation; only the fool imagines he invents."[3] In due
time appeared *A Modern Lover* (1883), *A Mummer's Wife* (1885),
A Drama in Muslin (1886), *Spring Days* (1888), and *Esther
Waters* (1894). These sum up his first literary phase, naturalism or neo-realism in English, *The Confessions of a Young Man*
(1888) being his desultory record of the years in which he was
unconsciously assimilating an art of fiction. Flaubert, the
Goncourts, and Zola were his teachers, in the first four; but
he went back to their great master Balzac in *Esther Waters*;
and then it is clear from the *Confessions* that he was deeply
thrilled by the decadent æsthete, Des Esseintes of *À Rebours*,
and by the Durtal of *Là-Bas*, avant-couriers of *En Route* and
La Cathédrale, in which Huysmans makes his Durtal turn away

[1] Hone, 74. Hone, and of course the *Confessions*, make it clear that Moore, after
a spell of Flaubert, came back to Balzac; these two were a much greater influence than
Zola in *Esther Waters*.
[2] See above, p. 135.
[3] *Sister Teresa*; cp. Buffon's "Le talent est une longue patience," as quoted by
Maupassant (*Pierre et Jean*—"Le Roman").

from the sensualism and diabolism of *Là-Bas*, to be drawn to religion by its artistic spells, consummating his transfiguration, in *l'Oblat*, by becoming a monk of La Trappe.[1] In *Evelyn Innes* (1898) and *Sister Teresa* (1901) Moore traced the history of a parallel case. But he was always an eclectic; and the effects of his close study of Flaubert, and still more of the methods of Edmond de Goncourt in chronicling sensations and their reactions on the soul, are as apparent as the debt to Huysmans. Moore eventually ejected these two novels from the canon of works acknowledged as of permanent value. For there was a whole sequence of George Moores, several of his unsatisfactory avatars being repudiated when he branded *A Modern Lover*, and, among other works, the original form of *A Drama in Muslin*, as not up to the mark, and assigned the twofold life of Evelyn Innes to his inferior self, "Amico Moorini." So much for this intermediate phase.

His final avatar— the artist Thus far, he had been a disciple, an interpreter, the self-appointed envoy of certain French schools to the English. He had consorted with French decadents before he found himself among English ones. The ultimate George Moore was the result of two events—his introduction to Pater and Pater's artistic prose, and Yeats and Synge's introduction of Ireland and the possibilities of an Irish literature to Moore. Pater gave him a new standard of prose as an art, of fiction also and of self-interpretation, both as fine arts. What he sought and cultivated in his Irish stories, as will be seen anon in *The Untilled Field* and *The Lake*, was the folk element, on which he discourses at large in *Avowals*.[2] His long training, and the superfine criteria accepted from Pater, enabled him to evolve a purified and perfected form of the primeval mode of story-telling, essentially the oral mode, which could be used both in epic narrative and in a more transparent and more spontaneous kind of mental analysis than he had been able to realize in the introspective study of Evelyn Innes. His aim was at an art that could compete with nature. "My only affectation," he says, in *Avowals*, "is complete naturalness."[3] With the self-

[1] Durtal subsequently enters the Benedictine abbey of Solesmes.
[2] Especially chapter vi. [3] P. 275.

consciousness which was the correlative to the missing ego, he was succeeding in his lifelong effort at self-creation, at establishing a personality of his own. One part of the long process is represented by the long tale of his autobiographical writings. How much he owed to the impressionists in paint and in literature can easily be traced in the *Confessions*. But *Memoirs of my Dead Life* (1906), *Hail and Farewell!* (1911–1914), and *Avowals* (1919), with their various recensions, are the record of other influences and other efforts. They are a novel kind of biographical literature, weaving his recollections of the life he had lived and the life he had observed into a limpid narrative, according to the laws of beauty rather than the mere obligations of fact; they are as unique as their nearest analogue, the methodical reconquest of his past by Proust.[1]

Moore was intensely egotistic, the usual foible of those like him. As Chesterton said, he lived in a "house of looking-glasses": "We feel as if we were being shown through a gallery of really fine pictures, into each of which, by some useless or discordant convention, the artist had represented the same figure in the same attitude. 'The Grand Canal with a distant view of Mr Moore,' 'Effect of Mr Moore through a Scotch mist,' 'Mr Moore by Firelight,'" and so on.[2] "He was enveloped," says his biographer, "like a silk-worm in its cocoon, in an isolating dream, his dream of literary perfection."[3] There was nothing insincere or counterfeit in this attitude, however artificial; on the contrary, Moore always preferred to shout his secrets from the house-tops. He spent an appreciable part of his life sitting to various painters, and most of it after his youth sitting to his potential biographer, pursuing the job in public with the most elegant effrontery. The many instances on record of his incorrigible manners are merely proofs of his utter inability to see anything that concerned himself from any other point of view.[4] And yet he did not

---

[1] Proust did not, however, appeal to George Moore; he was "without a sense of artistic selection" and Moore was "not in sympathy with Proust's generation" (Hone, 370).

[2] *Heretics*, 131. Chesterton remarks also that whilst Stevenson found some sort of philosophy to live by, "Mr Moore is always walking the world looking for a new one."

[3] Hone, 125.

[4] See, *e.g.*, Hone, 232–233.

mind inserting a piece by one of his acquaintances in his own autobiographical writings, if it happened to fit.[1] At all events, he had created, as his literary biographer puts it, "out of the void, it seemed to his friends, the George Moore known to the world." [2] He had moulded himself, as a sculptor models a statue; he had at the same time moulded a perfect style. Himself and his last works were alike the result of this un-deviating process. His persistent effort to co-ordinate his instinctive feelings and impulses, likings and repulsions, bore fruit, on the one hand, in the resolute man of pleasure, the con-firmed Cyrenaic, poetizing if not spiritualizing his sensations, making of the cult of the senses an art, a glorified paganism, and celebrating it in his idealized reminiscences of as many loves as Casanova's; and on the other, in the unprecedented beauty of *The Brook Kerith* and *Héloïse and Abélard*. And what makes his own story of his successive phases peculiarly interesting is that they form a book of illustrations to the history of English literature during that epoch; and at the same time contain, not a body, but a mass of criticism and doctrine, which is all the more apposite from the self-conscious—and sometimes self-contradictory—manner in which it was given to the world.

"A Modern Lover" No wonder Moore afterwards gave up *A Modern Lover* (1883), and even excluded the rewritten version, *Lewis Seymour and some Women* (1917), from the canon representing his mature standards. The book is an historical fact, however; and, as it was hailed by Arnold Bennett as "the first realistic novel in English," the first, in other words, to follow Flaubert, the Goncourts, and Zola,[3] it was also an historic event. Moore's lover is a bad artist, who deserts the modern school because the road is too difficult, and succeeds only through the influence of a woman: he is elected an A.R.A. as the result of an intrigue. A good-looking, effeminate, sensual creature, he invariably takes the path of least resistance, slides from one erotic affair into another, and lives on his mistresses. Though it buzzes

---

[1] See the curious anecdote of the lady-friend who found herself unexpectedly the author of several pages in *Vale* (*Ibid.*, 115).

[2] Desmond Shawe-Taylor, on "The Achievement of George Moore" (Hone, 465).

[3] Maupassant was still young as a novelist; he had not yet written *Bel-Ami*, for instance.

with talk about artists and theories of art, the book is not a satire on the profession or on the Academy; all this is the art talk of a period, the shallowness and fallacy of which are nowadays obvious. But what of the claim that it is a realistic novel? Moore and many of his contemporaries made the elementary mistake of confounding subject and method, as if realism could not be applied to any subject whatever. Since novelists had hitherto shrunk from the ugly and repellent, realism for them was simply that which stressed just those aspects of existence. Someone asked Harding why he always chose such unpleasant subjects.

"We do not always choose what you call unpleasant subjects, but we try to go to the roots of things; and the basis of life being material and not spiritual, the analyst inevitably finds himself, sooner or later, handling what this sentimental age calls coarse. . . . The novel, if it be anything, is contemporary history, an exact and complete reproduction of [the] social surroundings of the age we live in. The poem, on the other hand, is an idealization, and bears the same relation to the novel as the roast beef does to the rich, ripe fruit which you savour when your hunger is satisfied."

This is as inadequate and even untrue as it is clumsily put. Contemporary history? No, the novel is an interpretation of life, not the photographic record of a passing and perhaps inconsequent phase of life; and is not to be opposed to poetry in this haphazard fashion. The real difference is that, being prose, it is an intellectual, a rationalized interpretation, which may be understood and judged as the reader watches what is going on and observes the author's hints and annotations. His method here is not quite this. The novelist thought he could secure realism by massing detail, relevant and irrelevant, rather than by the simple intuition of character and motive—the kind of recognition all may exercise through sympathetic insight into the people round about, who are in the main people like ourselves—the perception that comes from mutual likeness and togetherness. Thus Moore thinks he can give the mental attitudes of his two leading women, the society beauty who falls in love with the flabby artist, and the older lady jealously watching her manœuvres, by elaborate descriptions of the house-party, the younger people engaged in tennis, and the older in looking out for scandal. Hence pages after pages about a trivial game of tennis. Why in so-called realistic novels should the author be eulogized for having achieved a brilliant circumstantial account of some sport, business, profession, art, religious sect, peculiar people, or what-not? This is to mistake the aim of art, and tempt the novelist to get up a special subject, as Zola did, and empty out for readers who may or more probably do not want it the contents of encyclopædic notebooks. Moore worked up many of his subjects—or got someone else to do it for him. Though a man of such wide and varied interests, he could not always rely on genuine personal experience. But that is neither here nor there. This sort of thing is extraneous and irrelevant. Assuming it to be his duty to empty out sackfuls of miscellaneous facts, simply because they are facts, the novelist is only too prone to neglect the essential, the accurate reading of character and conduct. Maupassant, four years later, was to asseverate the need for comprehending and explaining the various tendencies of the most contrary temperaments; to deny the rightness of the realistic motto, "Nothing but the truth and the whole of the truth"; and to point out that the great artists are those who impose their own particular illusion of life and truth upon humanity.[1] Moore's drama fails in clarity and clinching logic. He vaults over improbabilities, leaving the behaviour of his characters at crucial points often incomprehensible. He fails either to make his mimic life a fabric of causes and effects, or to put the reader into such intimate contact that the characters can be read as easily as we read our fellow-beings in actual life. It is impossible to believe, on the strength of what Moore vouchsafes, that the society lady would have fallen so helplessly in love with the bad artist, or that an educated man could be such a numskull as Lord Senton.

A Mummer's Wife (1884) is Moore's *Madame Bovary*; but in the meticulous application of realistic detail, largely super-

---

[1] "Rien que la vérité et toute la vérité" (Preface to *Pierre et Jean*, 1887). Moore, anyhow, never went to Zola's extremes: he had studied Flaubert's methods too intelligently (see the criticism in *Confessions*, viii.).

fluous, he was competing, not with Flaubert, but with Zola, to "*A* whom he wrote when it was finished to report his steady progress *Mum-* in the right direction.[1]   Kate Ede, wife of a dull, asthmatical, *mer's* unsympathetic shopkeeper in Hanley, in the Potteries, *Wife"* fascinated by the vivid and hearty personality of Dick Lennox, manager of a travelling company of actors, goes off with him. Sentimental fiction of the *Family Magazine* stamp has been her only mental food, and she is not much of a conquest.   But she is not less alive than Dick, a good average specimen of a capable business man, whose very obtuseness to ideas, combined with a brimming vitality and warmheartedness, ingratiates him, and even inclines one to pity him rather than Kate when she becomes a shrewish dipsomaniac.   Her decadence begins in wild fits of jealousy.   She thinks that every woman in the troupe is after Dick, now her husband.   Though she has a good voice and takes some important parts successfully, she has to be dropped out of the programme on account of the scenes she makes at rehearsals.   Thus she is left to spend long hours at the lodging-houses on their tours, and gets into the habit of solitary drinking.   She falls deeper and deeper, and the progress of her degradation is traced with a stern yet merciful pen, Moore refraining from such irony as Flaubert's.   His portraiture is admirably efficient—the dull home at Hanley, the irritable patient and the strict, sabbatarian mother-in-law; the motley theatrical crowd; the eccentric rich poetess, who hires a theatre for Dick's company, in the hope of seeing her worthless tragedy produced.   Moore regards himself, not without reason, as an expert on women.   Take this analysis of the feminine attitude, enlarging on the idealizing attachment of the poetic Montgomery to his friend's wife:

To a woman there is always an infinite charm in the society of a man to whom she never can, never intends to, give herself. The power that this platonic affection exercises over her is scarcely less ardent than the strongest sensual passion; it is the best poetry her nature is capable of, and for it many women will risk compromising themselves in their husbands' eyes.

Though other influences were working in him, Huysmans'

---

[1] Hone, 105–106.

"*A Drama in Muslin*" and "*Spring Days*"

and Flaubert's especially, Moore was still faithful to Zola, whose example was wholesome in these and the next two novels in sustaining him against the slightest concession to sentiment. He kept up his reports of progress to the master whilst he was in Dublin, during the winter of 1883–1884, writing *A Drama in Muslin* (1886), which had the sub-title "a realistic novel"; it was afterwards recast, and the title cut down to the simple word *Muslin* (1915). This "awful mummery in muslin" is the artificial life of the young women in Irish society, in the days of the Land League and the Phœnix Park murders, the period, that is, from 1879 to 1882. Whilst the nobility and gentry are expecting ruin at any moment, mothers are shown fishing for coronets, daughters prepared to accept anything in the shape of a husband, bachelors and widowers preying on the ignorant and innocent.

The picture is painted as far as possible as seen through young women's eyes, refined, virginal, regarding men—or pretending to regard them—as "obscene animals." Moore had been snubbed by the Castle, when he sought an invitation, as a novelist out for local colour, to a viceregal dinner; and the idle, empty, wasteful society people and hangers-on, such a contrast to the terrorists, are none the more amiably rallied. Without some allowance for satirical intent, the picture would appear heavily overcharged; and the satire is not by any means undisguised. There are summaries of the present state of "civilization" in Ireland in the very tone of Gissing; and the long disquisition contrasting Alice Barton's good sense and Lady Cecilia's neurotic impulsiveness, under the head of their respective "corporeal and incorporeal hereditaments," is in the style of that novelist when he was most sociological.[1] This and the next novel are naught as stories: they are admirable impressionist paintings of a society. It was remarked by Mr Wilson Steer that "Moore's landscapes are based on pictures rather than nature."[2] In this novel, many of the portraits, and such pictures as that of the farewell prize-giving at the convent school, might have been based on Manet or Renoir, so cunningly sensuous is the drawing and colouring of the girls

[1] Chap. iv.   [2] Hone, 205.

and the millinery distinguishing the occasion. The irony has not yet emerged.

Olive's hair was the colour of primroses. Her face, with its pronounced nose, was full of all the pseudo-classicality of a cameo. Now the action of listening had distended the limbs, and the skirt was cast into folds that made clear the movement of the body; the arms and bosom were moulded into amorous plenitudes, and the extremities flowed into chaste slendernesses, that the white stocking and loose convent-shoe could not distort. In the beautiful framework nothing was wanting but a mind. She was, in a word, a human flower—a rose—a carnation that a wicked magician had endowed with the power of speech.

Moore omitted *Spring Days* (1888) from those works republished when Vizetelly was sent to prison for bringing out Zola's novels in English. He did not care for the book, till A.E. and other admirers persuaded him to change his mind. Moore told himself that he was going to "recreate Jane Austen's method in *Spring Days*" [1]; but he was informed, in rather too censorious terms, that he had "failed horribly."[1] For this is an excellent example of quiet, literal, unrefracting realism applied to an utterly commonplace subject, without satire, without irony, without any insinuation of the author's private view of it whatever. It is strictly objective. Yet this petty world of the shoddy, second-rate people inhabiting a residential place near Brighton, with its bumptious adults, ineffectual young men, and frivolous, flirting girls, is shown up in all its banality; and, without any jokes, the result is as good as *Punch*. Not its significance, but its insignificance, is the drift and point: it is a cut from life, and, with all its reticence, a criticism of life.

If he had written nothing but *Esther Waters* (1894), Moore's name would have been on the roll of English novelists. This life of a poor kitchen-maid, wronged and deserted, who goes through the worst pangs and privations in order to bring her boy up honourably, is the unvarnished truth, if such a thing was ever written. There is very little of Zola in *Esther Waters*; Moore had gone back to his first master, Balzac. The book is

"Esther Waters"

[1] Letter to the Marquise Clara Lanza (Hone, 148).

crammed with detailed realism presenting sides of life that are
not familiar to everyone; but the most prominent of these,
that which, apart from the enthralling dramatic interest, gives
it characteristic colour, the book-making, the spying, the
intriguing, the general demoralization going on regularly in the
household of a racing squire, and in the public-houses and every
spot remotely connected with the race-course, was not a subject
requiring much research on Moore's part; the turf had been
his native element, the daily round at his father's house in
County Mayo.[1]   Nor was there anything very abstruse for him
in the setting of other episodes, such as his inside view of a
lying-in hospital.   The proof that all this is not the same thing
as Zola's encyclopædic naturalism is that these minutiæ of
unfamiliar aspects of life hold the reader's attention with the
intensity of personal and vital interests.   A man's salvation
may depend on the running of a horse, a life's happiness on the
result of a bet.   Moore descends into regions of the nether
world left unexplored by Mark Rutherford and Gissing, and
he goes deeper than Gissing ever tried into the hearts of the
more debased.   The savagery of Clem Peckover is not more
fearfully true than the brutal and callous egotism unveiled in
Esther's effort to comfort her downtrodden mother.

"I dunno, dearie; 'tis hard to say what he'll do; he's a 'ard
man to live with.   I've had a terrible time of it lately, and them
babies allus coming.   Ah, we poor women have more than
our right to bear with!"

"Poor mother!" said Esther, and, taking her mother's hand
in hers, she passed her arm round her, drew her closer, and
kissed her.   "I know what he was; is he any worse now?"

"Well, I think he drinks more, and is even rougher.   It was
only the other day, just as I was attending to his dinner—it
was a nice piece of steak, and it looked so nice that I cut off a
weany piece to taste.   He sees me do it, and he cries out, 'Now
then, guts, what are you interfering with my dinner for?'   I
says, 'I only cut off a tiny piece to taste.'   'Well, then, taste
that,' he says, and strikes me clean between the eyes.   Ah yes,

[1] "It was out of that press (the daily bustle and excitement at Moore Hall) that
Esther Waters came, out of the stable-yard and out of the heart" (Vale, 25).

lucky for you to be in service; you've half forgot by now what we've to put up with 'ere."

It is as relentlessly truthful as the most outspoken naturalism, and yet the realism is kind and sympathetic enough, without the least stress on feeling, to make it a great human document. Moore repressed himself; but, happily, had not yet accepted the Nietzschean formula of stern impassibility. At all events, he never goes out of his way to manufacture pathos—far from it—the strict rule is to tell the truth, and the whole truth; to spare nothing. The result is a piteous, a harrowing book. It requires a stout heart to read it, without breaking down at some of the most affecting passages; it required a stout heart to write it. Did Moore entirely suppress his feelings? Well, no; for here is a paragraph which is not the only one dwelling on the inherent pathos, in a manner that some of the stricter exponents of naturalism would have sneered at as a bad example of running with the hare:

The avenue was full of wind and rain; the branches creaked dolefully overhead; the lane was drenched, and the bare fields were fringed with white mist, and the houses seemed lonely by the bleak sea, and the girl's soul was desolate as the landscape. She had come to Woodview to escape the suffering of a home which had become unendurable, and she was going back in circumstances a hundred times worse than those in which she had left it, and she was going back with the memory of the happiness she had lost. All the grief and trouble that girls of her class have so frequently to bear gathered in Esther's heart when she looked out of the railway carriage window and saw for the last time the stiff plantations on the downs and the angles of the Italian house between the trees. She drew her handkerchief from her jacket, and hid her distress as well as she could from the other occupants of the carriage.

Esther Waters appeared the same year as Hardy's *Tess of the d'Urbervilles*, comparison with which is not only unavoidable but of the utmost service in bringing out the opposite drift of the two books. It is all the difference between simple and complex, the homely and the romantic, the primitive and the highly modern conception of one of life's commonest and

The difference from Hardy's "Tess"

sternest trials. In the wrong done to the innocent Tess, Hardy symbolizes the whole iniquity of the universe in its dealings with the individual. Tess is damned through the wanton act of d'Urberville; the love between her and Angel Clare is blighted as soon as born, and the hopelessness of her lot is clinched by her enforced return to her seducer. It is a well-staged contest with destiny, embracing the overworld that prearranged circumstances to thwart Tess in her natural impulses to live a pure woman. Moore, on the other hand, had no metaphysical axe to grind; his is the history of a straight, deadly fight with a materialistic, ruffianly, and ruthless world, the human world of that day. It is the history of an heroic adventure,[1] out of which, after tragic experiences, Esther comes off victorious, and, in a measure, secures happiness. She is a homely girl of the same humble origin, of the lowest class that can be called a class. The part allotted her is not that of a poetic heroine, though Hardy himself might have made her a theme for one of his saddest elegies. But, if her story is but the common prose of life, in the ultimate ratio her case and that of Tess are exactly alike. She has the same right to be called "a pure woman." "There aren't many such good women in the world as you, Esther," are the impulsive words of that "quiet, instinctive Englishwoman," Miss Rice, after she has heard her tale. When tragedy is hanging over both, she prefers to bear it alone rather than tell her darling boy the shameful secret of his father.

The noble instincts which were so intrinsically Esther Waters' told her that it were a pity to soil at the outset a young life with a sordid story, and though it would have been an inexpressible relief to her to have shared her trouble with her boy, she forced back her tears and courageously bore her cross alone without once allowing its edge to touch him.

Esther, in all her plainness of soul and her humility, has the makings of a saint; and no fairer end for her life of trouble could have been wished for than to find a home at last, when

[1] "Hers is an heroic adventure if one considers it: a mother's fight for the life of her child against all the forces that civilization arrays against the lowly and the illegitimate" (chap. xx.).

she has brought up her son to be a man to be proud of, with that other saint, another of the Plymouth Brethren, Mrs Barfield, once the much-enduring wife of the racing squire. She it is who tells Esther, "Helping others, that is the only happiness." Not that George Moore sows his pages with fine sentiments; but the impassible realist is human, and cannot always remain impassive. But he is never polemical like Hardy. Gissing would have liked to dispatch the obdurate society woman, Mrs Rivers, who advertises for a wet-nurse but objects to Esther's natural desire to go and see her own baby:

"Next time I engage a nurse, I'll try to get one who has lost her baby, and then there will be no bother."

"No bother," Esther answered; "two innocent children murdered so that a rich woman's child may be brought up. I'm not afraid of saying it, it's the truth; I'd like everyone to know it."

At the word "murdered" a strange look passed over Mrs Rivers' face. She knew, of course, that she stood well within the law, that she was doing no more than a hundred other fashionable women were doing at the same moment; but this plain girl had a plain way of putting things, and she did not care for it to be publicly known that the life of her child had been bought with the lives of two poor children. She was inclined to temporize. The difficulty was how to control her temper, and when Esther said that she would like the whole world to know what she thought of this murdering of innocent babies, Mrs Rivers incautiously let drop the word "Bastards."

"Say nothing against my child, he's human flesh and blood, and a good deal wholesomer flesh and blood than your little mite —he shall not be killed like the others. Mrs Spires shan't have him, no, she shan't. I understand it all now. Fine folk like you pays the money, and Mrs Spires and her like gets rid of the poor little things. Change the milk a few times, a little neglect, and the poor servant-girl is spared the trouble of bringing up her baby and can make a handsome child of the rich woman's little starveling."

At all events, Moore puts his eloquence into the right dramatic mouth, and is too scrupulous an artist to turn even a paragraph of a novel into a tract. It was not any controversial animus that provoked W. H. Smith & Son to reject *Esther Waters*.[1] After accepting *A Modern Lover*, they had discovered that it was "unsuitable reading for young girls," and banned it. There was a violent outbreak in the Press over *A Mummer's Wife*. And now, although Mudie had accepted *Esther Waters*, the other autocrats of the circulating libraries condemned a work that might reasonably have been made compulsory reading for everyone of either sex who had reached the age of puberty. The firm gave in when Mr Gladstone approved of the morality of the book, and Moore had the gratification of learning from an accountant that Smiths' had made a net loss of £1500 through their refusal to soil their hands with it. *Esther Waters* was selling in many thousands of copies.[2]

"Evelyn Innes" and "Sister Teresa"   Moore amid his bric-à-brac and his python fed with live guinea-pigs, in the Rue de la Tours des Dames, was too much like Huysmans' Des Esseintes in his palace of art not to salute his æsthetic brother: both *À Rebours*, that famous study of decadence in its last stages, and the sequels to *Là-Bas* stirred his competitive instincts. But it was not because the conversion of Durtal required two and eventually three sequels that the life of Evelyn Innes took up two volumes. It is one book divided into two novels for convenience in publishing. Though among his most popular works, Moore was not long in perceiving the vein of flashy romanticism, and perhaps the tepid character of the love-business, and both dropped out of the canon. Daughter of a music-master at Dulwich, Evelyn teaches the viola da gamba, but secretly longs to develop her voice and become a great singer like her mother. So she is inclined to respond to the rich musical amateur, Sir Owen Asher, who falls

[1] The writer remembers being taken to see Mr Faux, W. H. Smith & Son's manager, at the very time this quite commonplace business man was red-handed from the slaughter of *Esther Waters*, and an individual much in the public eye.

[2] Moore realized at leisure, *i.e.*, five years after it appeared, "that *Esther Waters* was not such a bad book as he first thought it." He enjoyed reading it after that long interval, and also the good it had done. "A harmless joy, the reading of *Esther Waters*, truly, and it is something to think of that the book itself, though pure of all intention 'to do good'—that is to say, to alleviate material suffering—has perhaps done more 'good' than any novel within my generation. It is no part of my business nor my desire to speak of the 'Esther Waters' home—I am much more concerned with the evil I know the book to have done than with the good " (*Ave*, ii.). The Home was for homeless children, and was founded by a hospital nurse who had been deeply affected by the narrative of Esther's struggles to bring her child up decently.

in love and offers to take her abroad to be trained as a future prima donna. Though a Catholic, she goes off with him; and after six years on the Continent returns to England a famous woman. But an Irish poet and mystic—Moore seems to have had first Yeats and then A.E. in his mind's eye when he drew Ulick Dean [1]—fascinates Evelyn; and the shock of finding herself with two lovers, along with a revival of her father's influence and the stern though tactful appeals of a priest, throws her off her balance. She attempts suicide, but finds peace with a sisterhood at Wimbledon and becomes a postulant. She does not take the veil; but she will not marry the middle-aged baronet, now hers body and soul. Evelyn at last settles in a country place and devotes her life to good works. Such is the conclusion that now stands, supplanting one in which she takes the final step and becomes a nun; Moore even coquetted with the idea of suicide in the convent pond as a termination. He told the story in a straightforward way, a way as old as *Moll Flanders*, circumstances and events going hand in hand with the conflicts of feeling and motive that determine them. Evelyn's vacillations are set forth at great length: it is a reflex of the spiritual passion anatomized by Huysmans, though the psychological elaboration had been just as characteristic of the Goncourts. Nay, since Moore parades his veneration for Balzac, it is not surprising if he adheres to the earlier writer's system of exhaustive analysis and explanation of the characters and their mental postures, oftener than to the simple course of showing the struggle going on and leaving comment and generalization to follow. Evelyn is a typical woman of sensuous instincts and strong emotional nature, well and truly drawn; her honesty towards herself and to the world is what is most attractive in her. The other characters are more shallow: her father almost a nonentity, the Irish lover a splendid talker who often collapses into a mere stage figure; and the baronet himself has very little in him beyond the average sensual temperament, though sympathy is demanded for his sufferings

---

[1] Hone, 216 and 234–237. The two strands of Moore's life are said to be symbolized by Owen and Ulick—his social phase in the one, and his returning to poor Ireland in the other.

on the loss of his mistress.   The dashing and cynical airs and
the sartorial extravagances of the man of fashion in Paris are
obviously stage effects.   Any finer touches of characterization
are expended on the inmates of the Wimbledon priory.   It is
difficult to follow Moore when he represents the love-lorn
baronet so desolate at the idea of losing Evelyn to the priests as
to put natural jealousy aside, and encourage his rival Ulick to
"prove to her the futility of her endeavour to lead a chaste
life," exhorting him to save her by "an appeal to the senses."

"They have got her, and her mind will be poisoned.   She
will get the abominable ascetic mind.   The pleasure of the
flesh transferred!   What is legitimate and beautiful in the body
put into the mind, the mind sullied by passions that do not
belong to the mind.   That is what papistry is!   They will
poison that pure, beautiful woman's mind."

Sir Owen Asher comes up to his part better when he is talking
music, and trying to carry out the Wagnerian programme.
For this is one of the big æsthetic novels; it is a good deal more
than another *En Route*, though a good deal less as a study of a
tortured and penitent soul.   And the length is no doubt due
to this dual character.   Moore follows the example of the
notebook realists in pouring into it masses of erudition.   Not
that he worked the subject up expressly for the purpose, as the
worst offenders, including himself, sometimes did.   He loved
music, and was an enthusiastic Wagnerian, although doubts
have been thrown upon his technical competence.[1]   The story
turns largely upon musical and especially operatic experiences.
Evelyn lives in her own soul the parts of Iseult and Kundry,
and yields to her lovers through the compulsive spell of Wagner's
erotic motives.   It may reasonably be compared with *Consuelo*;
though, even if the evocation of musical effects, Evelyn's
singing of Schubert's "Ave Maria!" for instance, rivals George
Sand's, the musical affairs are not integrated so artistically
into all the rest as in that history of a similar career.   Then
the writer's familiarity with Roman doctrines, observances,
and pastoral methods gives some sort of equivalent for the

---

[1] See, *e.g.*, Hone, 131–132, and *Ave*, 199, on his "rudimentary ear."

spiritual motives of Huysmans, though it is a point of cardinal importance that Huysmans was converted and George Moore was not. A good deal of this strays beyond the bounds of relevance at certain points; but, at any rate, is not a mere excrescence, like the lengthy account of Sir Owen's hunting adventures in the Sahara. The citation of Darwin, Spencer, and Huxley, as the fatal enemies of religion is a reminder that this is a period novel, and that the problem has long since changed its ground. Of deeper and more lasting interest is the conflict in Evelyn's mind, the conflict of the world and the soul, focused in her haunting sense of "the lack of agreement between her outer and inner life."

Owen Asher used to think that intellectual conversation kindled the soul; so it does in a way; and great works of art enkindle the soul and exalt it; but there is another exaltation of soul which is not discoverable in the intellect, and I am not sure that it is not the greater: the exaltation of which I speak is found in obedience, in submission, yes, and in ignorance, in trying—I will not say to lower oneself—but in trying to bring oneself within the range of the humble intelligence and to understand it.

Moore has a gift for epigram, but does not let it betray him:

"When I'm a bad woman I believe, when I'm a good woman I doubt."

He drew an amusing picture of the prima donna's husband, the fellow who waits with a scarf ready to wind it round the throat of his musical instrument; the fellow who is always on the watch lest someone should walk off with his means of subsistence.

Here he is as pertinent as he is pithy, as again in the casual epigram, "I suppose that the temptation that we yield to is *the* temptation." But his hesitation over the alternative endings confirms the feeling of a great lack of inevitability in the story, and its exclusion from the canonical books has evoked no protest. It would be a pity to lose them; and Moore did not forbid the future reprinting of these two novels from the original editions, though they must go into the apocrypha, whereas such inferior articles as *Mike Fletcher* (1889) and *Vain Fortune* (1892), his plays, and the two volumes of verse, *Pagan Poems* and *Flowers of Passion*, can be issued, if at all, only "as the work of a disciple"—"Amico Moorini" was the name he suggested.[1] Yet Moore admitted that the writing of *Evelyn Innes* and *Sister Teresa* had been useful to him, inasmuch as if he had not written them he could not afterwards have produced *The Lake* or *The Brook Kerith*.[2] His everlasting discussion of all that constitutes the work of art was a sign of hesitation over his own handiwork; it made him experiment, and throw away the results of the experiment or work upon them again: he was a long time attaining certainty and perfect self-confidence. Even after *Esther Waters*, he was not sure of himself. That, too, had to be revised later on; and almost every page he wrote, afterwards as well as before, went through a more or less drastic process of recasting or revision, till the last few years of his life. Fortunately, he came to feel a repugnance for the subject of these two novels,[3] and then he left them alone: they were not to be discarded for a new version written in a refractory frame of mind.

Ten years in Ireland   With a London behind him rendered intolerable by English fire-eating over the Boer war, and with Yeats, Edward Martyn, and A.E. beckoning from the other side, Moore crossed St George's Channel and settled in Dublin early in 1901, not to come back to England for good till 1911. Henceforward, there was an end of experimenting; and, though he never ceased altering and correcting and rewriting, the march towards perfection was in a straight line, his self-confidence as much as his tenacity being a lesson to fellow-craftsmen. *Sister Teresa* and a revised *Evelyn Innes* signalized the date of his arrival in Ireland. He had been evolving steadily; now his progress was

[1] *Epitaph on George Moore*, by Charles Morgan (12–13). Mr Morgan acutely observes that Amico Moorini was "far from being George Moore's disciple or his friend. He was his enemy who, though beaten down a thousand times, always rose up from under his feet." Mr Morgan says of the rejected novels, "They mark a relapse between that masterpiece [*Esther Waters*] and the final struggle to recreate himself which began in his going to Ireland at the time of the Boer War and resulted instantly in *The Untilled Field* and *The Lake*" (*Ibid.*, 21).

[2] "The writing of *Evelyn Innes* and *Sister Teresa* was useful to me," etc. (Preface to *The Lake*, viii.).

[3] Morgan's *Epitaph*, 21.

by giant's strides, and there is a broad gulf between his early
and middle period and the later. If *Esther Waters* is a masterpiece and not to be lightly disparaged, it was of a nature, or,
rather, an artistic species, different and even remote from *The
Untilled Field* and *The Lake*, which are not radically distinct in
æsthetic method from *The Brook Kerith* or *Héloïse and Abélard*.
Moore's highly original autobiographic miscellanies, beginning
with *Memoirs of my Dead Life* (1906), are nearer akin to the
novels and stories of his ultimate period than to the earlier
Confessions of a Young Man, emancipated as even that book
had been from the reticences and false modesty of the average
memoir. It is hardly too much to say that all he had written
so far was only a preparation, a discipline, a testing of alternatives. But he had been learning all along; his course was
always forward; and the difference between the old and the
new is to be put down only in part to the creative urge that
came from renewed contact with his own land and people.
Certain literary influences are definitely traceable in his mature
work, those of Landor, Walter Pater, and Turgenev, in particular.[1] They were not altogether new, if the effects only
now appear unmistakably. He relates in the *Confessions* what
he had felt in reading *Marius the Epicurean*, the first book in
English prose "that procured for me any genuine pleasure in
the language itself." [2] But Pater and Landor, whom he
venerated no less, had hitherto been high and remote literary
patterns, among those laid up in heaven; they had given him
standards and principles, rather than practicable goals; for he
knew that his time was not yet ripe. But they had helped him
to ripen. As to Turgenev, it was characteristic that of all the
Russians Moore put him first; he cared little for Tolstoy,[3] his
contrary in temperament and outlook, wilfully misapprehended
Dostoevsky, whom he said he knew "to be little more than

[1] "Three great influences are perceptible in it: the majestic austerity of Landor;
the translucence of Turgeniev, whose stories are shaded by none of the mists that
trouble other men; and Pater's doctrine that sensation is the touchstone of value, a
doctrine which Moore, having less moral prejudice than the author of *Marius*, was
able to accept more fully than Pater himself" (Morgan's *Epitaph*, 37).

[2] Chap. xii.

[3] "A Jeremiah of the Steppes," a hater of beauty, "not a natural tale-teller," etc.
(see *Avowals*, vi.).

Gaboriau with psychological sauce, and that of an inferior kind." [1] Moore was a sure critic of what came within his own range, but apt to make the worst of all that lay outside it. He had read Turgenev in the admirable French translations, at a time when he had not finished assimilating those French influences which served him so well up to this turning-point, and which, indeed, he never forgot or put aside—he had assimilated them too deeply. But for Turgenev he felt such a kinship, and now discovered they had such a common ground of inspiration, that he learned from him subconsciously a great deal more than the art derived from the folk element, on which he dilates critically in *Avowals* (1919). He speaks of the art of *Anna Karenina* and *War and Peace* as "cosmopolitan"; it "represents in art the scientific ideas of Taine, Herbert Spencer, and Darwin." To a certain extent, Tolstoy authenticated his realism with this folk-lore element, which Shakespeare had not failed to catch—"In Shakespeare we find culture and folk side by side." [2] Turgenev captured and interpreted it with perfect mastery. At this very instant, Synge was tapping his source for it in Wicklow or in the Aran Isles, and gathering material for his inimitable portrayal of the men and women of his western world. The Irish movement was in full swing. So Moore with some misgivings gave in to John Eglinton's injunction that he should do for Irish life what Turgenev had done for Russian, [3] and the prompt result was "The Wedding Gown," one of the prettiest stories, with one of his most delicate touches of solemnity at the end when the dying old woman lends the wedding dress treasured all these years to the grand-niece who seems to reincarnate her own youth and beauty of sixty years ago. All Ireland was eventually brought into the microcosm of *The Untilled Field* (1903), which, in spite of

---

[1] *Impressions and Opinions*, "Turgueneff," 48. On his obligations to "Tourgué-nieff"—the spelling is indicative of which renderings he had read—see preface to *The Lake* (vii.) and *Salve*, x. It was *A Sportsman's Sketches* that gave him the plan of *The Untilled Field*. Mme Cazamian thinks she can discern the influence of Dostoevsky's compassionate art in *Esther Waters*.

[2] *Avowals*, vi.

[3] *Salve*, x.

certain rearrangements and substitutions, is still a set of thirteen stories.

Moore's preface relates that Martyn, who with Yeats was "*The striving* to establish a realistic theatre in Dublin, had said to him *Untilled* years before, "I should like to write my plays in Irish." Whilst *Field*" Dublin was still looking forward to *The Well of the Saints*, Synge was in County Wicklow listening through chinks in the floor to the rich talk of the peasants. But Moore was as much in love as Synge with their "pretty idiom"; he even had passing regrets that, as a child, he had not learnt Irish from the boatmen in Mayo. The next best thing seemed to be a book of stories that could be translated into Irish, which they were as fast as written, the first published form of *The Untilled Field* being an edition in the native language printed in Dublin (1902), the year before the English one. Moore convinced himself that Synge derived the racy and poetic idiom of his *Playboy of the Western World* from the Anglo-Irish of *The Untilled Field*, which "with becoming modesty" he describes as thus "a landmark in Anglo-Irish literature." [1] Only one tale was of any length, "The Wild Goose," telling of the patriot Ned Carmady, who marries the ravishing Ellen Cronin, then plunges into secessionist politics, using her money to undermine her Church, not from any dishonourable motive but in sheer thoughtlessness; and then in a fit of Irish idealism leaves her and their child to enlist with the Boers, when the wild geese flying south give the signal. Some are grave in tone, like this, some gay; but most are a lifelike mixture of both. What these tales are not is a renovated form of the traditional Irish story, that battered old commodity, a cunning or clumsy blend of the laughable and the touching, seasoned with the exaggeration which was fondly supposed to be a racial prerogative. Moore did not try for effects like the point of an epigram; on the contrary, readers are assured of the truth by the very absence of anything paradoxical or bizarre: the stroke that electrifies which is the commonest end and aim of a story never tempts George Moore. It can be soberly affirmed of these stories that they seem to tell themselves, so natural, so seemingly

[1] Preface to edition of 1914, vii.

artless and even careless is the telling. Every one, almost, is as
simple and straightforward as the title, "So on he Fares," of
one of the shortest would suggest, the tale of the little boy who
runs away from a mother that dislikes him, and drops in upon
her in after-life to find that she dislikes him as much as ever.
For, if any general aim and purpose is to be read between the
lines, it is character, the mentality displayed in acts and
attitudes. That unmotherly mother is worth a great deal
more as treasure trove than any lucky hit of poetic justice.
Such pieces as "Home Sickness" or "Some Parishioners" are
just such portraiture of dispositions and physiognomies, or of
native manners and idiosyncrasies. The charm and quiet
pathos of "The Exile," likewise, are in this self-revelation of
the peasant mind: it is the simple tale of a girl who loves the
brother of the man who had loved her. Getting married, in
the west of Ireland, is the subject of "Patchwork," in which the
old priest irritably refuses to perform the ceremony at the price
offered, and then is at his wit's end to save the pair from the
state of wickedness to which he has unintentionally consigned
them. There is more about getting married in "Julia Cahill's
Curse," the tale of a woman who put the parish under a ban,
told with such conviction that the man who reports it "believed
the story, and for the moment I, too, believed in an outcast
Venus becoming the evil spirit of a village that would not
accept her as divine." A manner as smooth and instinctive as
the spontaneities of reverie is well illustrated by the recollection
of a gift to a blind beggar in "Almsgiving," with its beautiful
little epilogue:

A soft south wind was blowing, and an instinct as soft and as
gentle filled my heart, and I went towards some trees. The
new leaves were beginning in the high branches. I was sitting
where sparrows were building their nests, and very soon I
seemed to see farther into life than I had ever seen before.
"We're here," I said, "for the purpose of learning what life
is, and the blind beggar has taught me a great deal, something
that I could not have learnt out of a book, a deeper truth than
any book contains. . . ." And than I ceased to think, for
thinking is a folly when a soft south wind is blowing and an
instinct as soft and as gentle fills the heart.

But it is in "The Window" that a still finer poetry triumphs over what in older hands would have been merely farcical peasant eccentricities. Poor old Biddy M'Hale makes life a burden for the parish priest, intent on getting his church built, worrying him about the window that is to be her very own. "Sorra penny of my money will he be getting all the same to build the walls of his old church." She has close on a hundred pounds, and it is all to go for the window. Long before the glass is put in she can see the picture that has grown up in her mind: Our Lord "in white on a throne, placing a golden crown on the head of the Virgin kneeling before Him, and all around the women that had loved Him; and with tears rolling over her eyelids the old woman said she was sorry she was not a nun, but perhaps God in his goodness might not think less of her; it couldn't be helped now; for as far as a mortal sin she could truly say she had never committed one." At last the window is fixed, and Biddy contemplates it in ecstasy; her look was so enraptured that Father Maguire "began to wonder if paradise were being revealed to her." She listens to music inconceivably tender; she sees the saint's fingers moving over the harp-strings, playing a little tune of six notes. Next Sunday, at mass, she hears the little tune again, and it seems even more exquisite.

The only difference between to-day and yesterday was, that to-day all the saints struck their harps, and after playing for some time the music grew white like snow and remote as star-fire, and yet Biddy heard it more clearly than she had heard anything before, and she saw Our Lord more clearly than she had ever seen anybody else. She saw Him look up when He had placed the crown on His mother's head; she heard Him sing a few notes, and then the saints began to sing. Biddy was lifted up into their heavenly life, and among them she was beautiful and clad in shining garments. She praised God with them, and when the priest raised the host, Biddy saw Our Lord look at her, and His eyes brightened as if with love of her. He seemed to have forgotten the saints that sang His praises so beautifully, and when He bent towards her and she felt His presence about her, she cried out: "He is coming to take me to His arms!" and fell out of her place, pale as a dead woman.

The clerk went to her, but she lay rigid as one who had been dead a long while.

In "Fugitives," Moore welded two earlier stories that did not satisfy him into one, and the transition is rather clumsy from the account of Lucy Delaney's sitting nude for Rodney's statue of the Virgin, and her pious brethren's revenge in wrecking the studio and everything in it, to her adventures in London, when she is ready to go off with one or other of his artist friends, but ends by marrying her mathematical-instrument maker from Chicago. He, like Dick Dewy in *Under the Greenwood Tree*, accepts her as all that she should be. But no irony is intended. "Lucy wanted life," says Rodney; and Harding rejoins, "She is the stuff of which great women are made, and will make a noise in the world yet." It is in the longest story, "The Wild Goose," that Ned Carmady philosophizes on the three periods of married life: "a year of mystery and passion, then some years of mystery without passion, and a period of resignation, when the lives of the parents pass into the children and the mated journey on, carrying their packs." It is a very natural reflection on what he has gone through. But the author himself never intrudes in these tales, in which a consummate art is perfectly dissembled.

"*The Lake*" It proved too long to be included in the same volume, but *The Lake* (1905) was originally one of the same batch of stories, the root-idea of which was to picture the untilled field that Ireland now was, with the best of the population gone to America, and those that remained having neither the numbers nor the means and energy to utilize the resources that once made Ireland great. The land was priest-ridden too, though Moore shows that it is often the parish priest who alone stands between the poverty-stricken and desperation, keeping the lazy at it, helping the weak and ailing, organizing effort, and obtaining Government grants for roads, often unwanted, and other relief works, and charity from Dublin or America. Father MacTurnan, in "A Letter to Rome," actually conceives the brilliant idea of abolishing celibacy, and letting the priests furnish 4000 first-class infants a year to save the country. The wise and tactful Father Stafford, who has to keep a tight hand

on his irascible nephew, Father Maguire, is a shining light
among the representatives of religion. These stories of priests,
and *The Lake*, with its soul-searching of Father Gogarty,
coming as they do close upon the spiritual history of Evelyn
Innes, indicate whither George Moore's interests were tending.
His next novel, if novel it is to be called, was *The Brook Kerith*;
but a whole decade, and much writing of a varied and far from
unworldly sort, were to intervene. In *The Lake* he came close
home. Moore Hall stood on the spit of land running into the
lake in County Mayo, and the beauty and deep feeling per-
meating the descriptive passages had the best possible warranty,
his earliest associations. So far as material events are concerned,
no story could be simpler; but it leads into infinite complexities
of thought and feeling. A conscientious young priest drives
a girl from the parish, and then comes to realize that it was
jealousy, and not impersonal morality, that dictated the act.
His meditations and heart-burnings are poetically blended
with the beauty and loneliness round about him. The lake
becomes a symbol, of all that is deep and inscrutable in himself,
as well as in the inexplicable universe. For this is a journal of
self-exploration, and Moore's new method enabled him to
expose Father Gogarty's mind without the breach of continuity
and the cumbersome passages of analysis that are the bane of
psychological fiction. "Wagner," he said, "discovered that an
opera had much better be melody from end to end, and the
realistic school following on Wagner's footsteps discovered
that a novel had much better be all narrative—an uninterrupted
flow of narrative." So it all goes into one unbroken reverie,
although Moore had to hark back to things that were really
antecedent. Father Gogarty reviews the whole history in his
retrospective musings, in the most natural way imaginable:
the birth of his aspirations to be a priest, the uneventful course
of his life till he made the acquaintance of Nora Glynn, the
incidents that made no impression till now that he looks back
upon them; and, after he has caused her to leave the village,
the urgent question whether any of the parishioners had noticed
his habit of solitary wandering by the lake ever since he spoke of
her in his sermon. He had not perceived what was the matter

with him when he preached on chastity and "the displeasure
sins against chastity cause to God." Even when he comes to
rigorous self-examination, he is slow to realize what has taken
place in him. "She has always been associated with the lake
in my thoughts, yet she escaped the lake. Every man," he
continued, "has a lake in his heart." He had not sought the
phrase, it had come suddenly into his mind. Yes. "Every
man has a lake in his heart," he repeated, and returned to the
house like one dazed. There follow the long confessional talk
with Father O'Grady, and the exchange of letters with Nora,
which leaves him as helpless and uncertain and as weary of
life as ever, yet unknown to himself has delivered him from
bondage. And at last, when he has swum the lake, leaving his
clothes behind as a token that he has been drowned, and
dressed in the others which he had hid on the other side is in
the train for Cork and a new life in America, "There is a lake
in every man's heart," he says again, "and he listens to its
monotonous whisper year by year, more and more attentive till
at last he ungirds." [1] "Every man," as Jesus says in *The Brook
Kerith*, "is behoven sooner or later to seek himself." So the
story ends, in symbolism and suggestion; how much Moore
had learned from Mallarmé is patent here, as in many stories in
The Untilled Field.

*Moore's
autobio-
graphical
writings
and his
style*
        "Difficulty overcome is a joy to the artist, for in his conquest
over the material he draws nigh to his idea," wrote Moore in
one of his prefaces to *The Lake*. Elsewhere he speaks of "Art
as I understand it—rhythmical sequence of events described
with rhythmical sequences of phrase." In *The Untilled
Field* and *The Lake* he had achieved what he neatly described as
"the melodic line," fluidity and continuity, smooth mastery of
transitions, a style that gives both outer and inner by keeping
to the same concrete simplicity. It looks, not like art at all,

[1] Moore's habit of dictating, and re-dictating from the manuscript, laid him open
to occasional discrepancies. In one letter to Nora, Father Gogarty speaks of having
returned one of hers; but there is no previous allusion to this. Nor did she invite
him to Rome, only to Munich. Apparently, some letter he had dictated was afterwards dropped out, and the cross-references forgotten. The double negative was no
doubt a similar oversight in the sentence, "Taste for learned studies did not preclude
abstinence from those sins which in his ignorance of life he had associated with
worldlings!"

but nature pure and unadorned. For visible artistry is at a
minimum. It is the art that conceals art without making the
least fuss about it. Perhaps it would be truer to say that it
has become second nature, almost unconscious and automatic.
For the melodic line is now the refined and sensitive medium
for everything that Moore writes, becoming lively and colloquial at will, without the least swerving from a natural gait.[1]
It was the perfect vehicle so often sought and so rarely found
for the ups and downs and the level stretches of autobiography,
and its aptness for saying much through what is left unsaid had
ample room here for all vagaries. Moore's open-mindedness
made him an excellent impressionist; all he ever had to learn
from that school was to make the most of what in his case came
perfectly natural. And his curiosity about the enigmas of
character and the privy clues to personality inclined him to
treat himself as the theme of a novel, or an exploratory work
very like one. That is why his autobiography in many volumes
with many titles has been ranked with Rousseau's *Confessions*.[2]
He unified them by dint of a literary imagination enriched by
his lifelong observation of the fine shades in all sorts of temperaments and mentalities; he was a specialist in psychological
subtleties and aberrations from the commonplace, with a zest
for all sorts of life and an hilarious malice that never ran dry.[3]
He began them six years before *Esther Waters*, with his *Confessions of a Young Man* (1888), which reads very like a novel, the
boundary between plain fact and the fact re-dressed by art
being indistinguishable. This was simply the first volume of

[1] The ease of his style and disregard, or rather contempt, for everything constrained
and artificial is evinced negatively by his split infinitives: Moore was unprincipled
enough to split them on principle. The fact is, his grammar is far from impeccable:
he was too autocratic to worry about rules. But what does that matter? His
rewriting and recasting, cancelling and substituting, are an example to his profession.
It is also the final testimony to his artistic conscientiousness, his intolerance of everything but the perfect. "A man can only have one form of conscience," Hone
reports him as being wont to say (309), "and mine is a literary one."

[2] *E.g.* by Charles Morgan (*Epitaph*, 1).

[3] James Huneker says of them: "Mr Moore said things every hour in the day, and
in less than six days he had sown for himself a fine crop of enemies. To 'get even' he
conceived the idea of writing a series of novels, with real people bearing their own
names. That he hasn't been shot at, horsewhipped, or sued for libel thus far is just
his usual good luck. *Vale* is largely a book of capricious insults " (*Unicorns*, "The
Reformation of George Moore," 263).

a garrulous memoir that went on, if only by way of revisal, right down to his death. In the volume most closely emulating the *Sentimental Journey* of Sterne, *Memoirs of my Dead Life* (1906), the pictures called up from a vanished past are, almost undisguisedly, those which a fond recollection has adorned, or at least cleansed of any crude or discordant specks and flaws; hence that delectable bit of nympholepsy, according to the modern rules of the game, "The Lovers of Orelay," may be accepted as veritably the past seen lyrically, through a temperament. Whoever inquires to what maximum or minimum extent it is to be taken as literal and circumstantial truth runs some risk of misappreciating the candour of Moore's self-avowal. Let him take to heart a saying in the same book: "It is only those who have freed themselves from all prejudice who get close to life, who get the real taste of life—the aroma as from a wine that has been many years in bottle." Moore's memories were no doubt very much improved, in a sense that should appeal to the connoisseur, and by a natural and honest process, through being kept a long time in bottle, even if the most piquant are the three instalments of *Hail and Farewell* sent forth whilst he was in the thick of it, or very soon after. He republished the *Confessions* in 1904, inserting a letter of somewhat patronizing appreciation from Walter Pater, whose "consideration of means rather than of ends" had been a large theme in the book. But it was only now or very recently that Moore clearly set before himself and went a long way towards realizing Pater's aim, "to raise literature to the condition of music." The *Confessions* and all the sequels to that book teem with critical ideas, which are often none the less welcome and refreshing for a dash of perversity. One of the rightest was, fortunately, one of the earliest, and one that he took most to heart, that "a greater command of language is required to write in prose than in verse." The very opposite was so widely accepted that it gave Moore almost an unfair advantage to know better, especially as he by no means excepted the novelist from this general rule. What is most pertinent now is that in his consecutive autobiographies Moore was exercising and maturing a style adapted to the utmost refinements of fiction.

To a man like him, writing his memoirs and writing fiction
were very nearly the same art. And, so it happened, henceforth it is in his autobiographical writings that he is at his best,
as a realist or impressionist dealing with his own times and his
own world. For, apart from the transubstantiation of *Celibates*
(1895) into *Celibate Lives* (1927), it is to the realm of the past,
to what had been hitherto the realm of romance, that his later
masterpieces are devoted. "Nature's foresight and versatility
are indeed remarkable," he said in his prelude to *Memoirs of my
Dead Life*. She sent him to France, and all but made him a
French writer, as the *Confessions* recorded. She had brought
him back to England, to play his part in the æstheticism of the
nineties, primed with the naturalism, the impressionism, and
the symbolism, with which he had been in such close and exciting
contact. And then she had ordained that he should return
to the Ireland that he had once hated, and do his duty in the
Irish renaissance, the chronicle of which and the portraits of
the three Mentors to his Odyssey, Edward Martyn, A.E., and
Yeats, are in *Ave*, *Salve*, and *Vale*, the three instalments of
Hail and Farewell (1911–1914). "Out of the wreck and rubble
of my former self a new self had arisen." This new self was
the complete man of letters, equipped with a style all his own,
and now prepared for his return to London early in 1911, and
for the last and cosmopolitan phase that brought forth *The
Brook Kerith* and *Héloïse and Abélard*, and has its intimate record
in *Avowals* (1919) and *Conversations in Ebury Street* (1924).

In *The Brook Kerith, a Syrian story* (1916), he applied the "*The*
subtle and flexible method of which he was now master to *Brook*
a retelling of the old story of the origins of Christianity. *Kerith*"
Profoundly moved by a re-reading of the New Testament,
George Moore, like many sensitive and emancipated minds,
pondered the question, what were the facts behind the traditional record? Perhaps as likely a solution could be arrived at
by devoting the working experience of a versatile novelist to a
rational and sympathetic reconstruction of the circumstances
and events, as by any process of induction and deduction. The
veteran author of *A Mummer's Wife* and *Esther Waters*, of *The
Untilled Field* and *The Lake*, and of all his vivacious histories

of his own time, had qualifications that Renan and Samuel Butler, and even Anatole France, hardly possessed. If any one of them, he was a man of the world; he was steeped in human nature, and very wide awake to its vagaries and self-deceptions. If he was not a philosopher, at all events the unconscious and the subconscious were regions in which he had already done some exploration. And he came to the subject with his usual open mind, without satirical irony, without the complacency such a man as Butler felt in exposing a fable,[1] or the controversial or scientific zeal of a Renan or a Strauss. And his present mood was an assurance that he would approach the supreme point at issue with becoming reverence. Moore had said that writing the history of Evelyn Innes had prepared him for *The Untilled Field* and *The Lake*: assuredly, if he had not altered his whole method and style to write the two last he would never have been able to bring the contents of *The Brook Kerith* into the form and compass of a novel. For a true novel it is, far more so than Pater's *Marius the Epicurean*, which then seemed its nearest parallel. That may have been a yet finer monument of classic English. But, if a novel, it is also something more than a novel: it is the life of a man in his most intimate sensations and feelings: but, beyond that, it is a treatise on theories of life, a balancing of hypotheses and testing of various philosophies and various cultures, in the course of which the concrete essence of fiction is outweighed by abstract thought.

Oral narration *The Brook Kerith* is as genuine a novel as anything Moore wrote; a thoroughly concrete piece of human history, from which Moore's interpretation of the facts emerges as spontaneously as if he had the reader looking on with ingenuous eyes at the events taking place. And as a work of constructive art it may be set beside any other of his novels, perhaps a little higher. Balanced and shapely, part answering to part, as minute examination certifies, it forms a pellucid whole, execution never falling short of bold and comprehensive

[1] Butler's pamphlet, *The Evidence for the Resurrection of Jesus Christ as contained in the Four Evangelists critically examined* (1865), is not now extant, but the substance of it is no doubt embodied in *The Fair Haven* (1873), the ironical and mocking spirit of which is well known.

design. Even when straightforward narrative shifts over to symbolism and suggestion, as it had already in *The Lake*, there is nothing obscure or occult. Moore was, in truth, no mystic. Such is the virtue of this perfected edition of the oral manner of story-telling. Moore's habit of dictating, and dictating again from one draft after another, served him well. The oldest of all modes of narration, it was able to dispense with modern literary devices: simplicity was its keynote. And then, there were personal reasons why this story was a congenial undertaking, and made no inordinate demands on his imaginative invention. He had never forgotten the tales his father used to tell of life in Syria. It was as if those Eastern figures had been his familiars from childhood, as if their stories came out of memory rather than imagination. Paul and the rest are like remembered people, and their doings authentic reminiscences. It was almost a work of supererogation to have made his conscientious journey beforehand to Palestine and the other side of Jordan; it came so natural to him to see them in their own perspective, in their far-off primitive world, where he could feel quite at home, and enter into their simple views of the transient and the infinite. And, accordingly, the warm humanity of *The Brook Kerith* is an absolute contrast to the cold, serene, chiselled perfection of the Landor whom he admired and was in fact emulating; for the "pervading intimacy" of which Moore was conscious whenever he wrote did not fail him now any more than in his tales of the present.[1] So he simply puts his recital in the mouth of Joseph of Arimathea, that deeply interested spectator, and vouchsafes no commentary.

Jesus is a Palestinian shepherd, a member of the ascetic *The new* brotherhood of the Essenes, with a mystic understanding of *story* nature in which he perceives God. Listening in rapture to John the Baptist, he is carried away, and convinces himself that he is the promised Messiah; for which presumption he afterwards feels bitter remorse. And yet "He was astonished he could remember so great a sin and not fear God. But I

[1] "A certain pervading intimacy which I do not seek, but of which I am conscious" (*Memoirs of my Dead Life*, "Euphorion in Texas").

cannot fear God, for I love God, he said; my God neither forgives nor punishes, and if we repent it should be for our own sakes and not to please God. Moreover, it must be well not to waste too much time in repentance, for it is surely better to understand than to repent." Jesus suffers crucifixion, as recorded in holy writ, and after three days is taken down from the cross and laid in the sepulchre. But he is not dead, only unconscious; and Joseph nurses him back to life, hiding him from his enemies, the priests. Jesus in due time returns to the Essenes. The beauty and winsomeness, the exquisite modesty and unfailing charity of the principal character, are a great artistic achievement, the more so that Moore simply records without himself entering into the mystic perceptions of Jesus. It is a restatement of the life of Jesus which would logically entail some reconstruction of Christian theology. But, if there is anything in the least controversial in Moore's attitude, it is only in his resolve to abstain from any dogmatic inference: "Rites and observances, all that comes under the name of religion estranges us from God, he repeated. God is not here, nor there, but everywhere: in the flower, and in the star, and in the earth underfoot. He has often been at my elbow, God or this vast Providence that upholds the work; but shall we gather the universal will into an image and call it God?—for by doing this do we not drift back to the starting-point of all our misery? We again become the dupes of illusion and desire." [1]

Jesus and Paul   The interest culminates, and here Moore is at his most original, when in after days Paul, the bigoted theologian, the Pharisee turned Christian, the preacher of a supernatural Christ risen from the dead without whom there is no salvation, comes across the wandering Jesus and tries to convert him to the new religion. The inherent irony of such a situation would have rejoiced Anatole France. But Moore treated it with the same simplicity. Nevertheless, the concluding chapter, in which Paul indignantly protests that "if Jesus were not raised from the dead our teaching is vain," seeing in Jesus "an evil spirit come to tempt him," yet permitting himself to be set

[1] Chap. xxx.

upon the road to Cæsarea, whilst Jesus quietly reaffirms the gospel truth, is masterly, even as a great piece of dialectic. Jesus is helpless to confute the cherished legend, and Paul departs on his mission to preach it to the uttermost parts of the earth. Moore never lapses from the seriousness appropriate; but he could never do anything by halves, and enlivened this, like any of his narratives, biographical or fictional, with what he called "boniment,"[1] the gossip and chitchat, the casual, inconsequent incident, that so readily serves to convey the very sensation of life, and dissipate any undue abstractness. There was no reason, of course, why humour should be abrogated: it is not intrinsically alien to seriousness. The wrangling of Peter and James about precedence and the question whether their chairs should be on the left or the right of the Master, and the dispute over the flock between Bozrah and Havilah, Havilah from whom "a sensible remark was an event" and "to speak well twice in the same day . . . well-nigh a miracle," are simply those comic touches which are the equivalent to lifelike traits. But it was surely perverse wantonness on Moore's part to depict the Apostles as of much less than average intelligence, and curiously impervious to the ideas with which it was their mission to imbue mankind. And it was his old itch for irritating the strait-laced that no doubt prompted the matrimonial escapade of the virtuous Essenes, with its sardonic results.

Héloïse and Abélard (1921) is another reconstruction of the distant past, in the artistic form of a romance ushering in the famous letters, a romance "composé pour célébrer mon amour" pour Mme X, under the motto "Love is enough." In the previous book, he gave new meanings to the best-known of all stories; in this, he takes one of widest currency in western Europe, the love-story of the famous professor and Canon Fulbert's niece, and retells it according to the rites and ceremonies of the trouvères and the Courts of Love. Moore plunged into his bath of mediævalism with his usual ardour. He was no scholar, and he hated abstractions; yet he made

"Héloïse and Abélard"

---

[1] "Perhaps the French word *boniment* will explain my meaning better" (*Avowals*, i.).

himself so familiar with the points at issue between Nominalists and Realists that he could set his pedants disputing in the most glib and lifelike style. He was bent on rivalling the leisurely, long-winded romances of yore; and reproduced their rambling manner, their naive repetitions and otiose explanations, easy-going digressions and ceremonious episodes. His pictures of old Paris are done in the Kelmscott style, but hold their own with Morris at his best, and they are matched and diversified by the forest scenery of the long journey through Touraine to the port for Brittany, and the rencounters with celebrated trouvères, each with his separate story. He dwells on the course of reading in the Latin poets with which Héloïse beguiles her leisure, till she attains a pitch of learning that even Abélard envies. It is as if Moore had wagered his honour to present the culture and civilization of the early eleventh century in all its manifold aspects. And he succeeded, more brilliantly than Shorthouse in *John Inglesant*, in spite of a few anachronisms, chiefly in the world of thought [1]; and, if he borrowed, as of course he did profusely, he covered his tracks better. Nay, Moore fell short of Pater's *Marius the Epicurean* only on the more philosophic side: as a work of art, *Héloïse and Abélard* can stand the comparison.

An idealistic prose-poem

Admittedly, it is an artificial work, a gigantic piece of make-believe, a calculated effort in an art long since dead and forgotten. But Moore had not forgotten. The artificial romance of the trouvères—for that was itself an artificial cult—was the poetry of his hedonistic creed. He had idealized his theory of life in a manner only a little more like prose in "The Lovers of Orelay." Hence, for him there was a sincerity in such a self-conscious art that redeems it. It is only when the air he puts on of solemn and serious concern for the deeper issues is compared with such historical fiction as Scott's, that it shows only too plainly that Moore was striking an attitude, simulating a romantic mission. Scott could be romantic, when in the mood; but he was always honest to himself and to common sense. His

---

[1] *E.g.* Mother Hilda's saying over her dead husband: "The poor dead require all our thoughts, for they live in us and are only really dead when we cease to think of them," etc. (xxviii.), sounds like a reminiscence of Samuel Butler, or perhaps Maeterlinck, rather than of the eleventh century.

romanticism came natural, when he was excited to view life romantically. For he was not one of those who see the past through coloured spectacles. To him the past, indeed, was always there, even when he was looking at the present: there behind the outward show, an integral element in any comprehensive vision. His instinct gave him as clear an eye as Bergson gained from a metaphysical theory. But the past summoned up by George Moore is not this underlying reality, but an exotic thing, a dream-world to satisfy his heart's desire. And, even so, in his prose-poem he does not maintain his pose of frank acceptance with unfailing consistency; and it is disconcerting when, as in the incident of the devout parrot that prayed without ceasing, although "poor bird, he knows well that himself cannot go into heaven, being but a bird," [1] the simplicity sounds like the badinage of an Anatole France. Whether he was poking fun here at the pardoner's credulity, or at the impostures of that old world, the quip is equally out of key. But there was no repressing Moore's impishness. Except for a few such lapses, however, the story is told in a spirit true to the creed of those to whom the two great lovers were the most illustrious in all their martyrology. And it sticks faithfully to tradition: the famous liaison and the flight of the lovers, with Fulbert's wrath; the secret marriage urged upon Abélard by Héloïse, whose ambition for him is of the very essence of her love; the separation, one to be a novice, the other a priest, when they conspire to enjoy their freedom to love, defiant of clerical restraints and disdaining religious scruples; and, finally, the brutal revenge of Fulbert—or the hostile clerics—and the shattering of their trust in an earthly union. Moore's sensualist philosophy has its counterpart in Abélard's, which is deliberately exalted above ecclesiastical codes and the moralities accepted then or thereafter: "Love is enough." Hero and heroine lie without remorse when lying is opportune: their whole life is a lie, when Héloïse enters the convent as a penitent ostensibly to purify her soul, and Abélard seeks ordination so that as a priest he may be with her again, safe from interference from enemies and scandalmongers. They are vindicated by the

[1] Chap. xvii.

whole implied philosophy—implied, that is, in the story told
in the accents of long ago. For Moore observed all the rules
of artistic detachment. It was his own philosophy of life, the
paganism he always swore by, in *The Lake*, and no less in the
personal freedom asserted in *The Brook Kerith*. On the whole,
he kept a tight hold on himself, and allowed his creed to
transpire through the words that were said and the things that
were done. No one ever dissembled his art more perfectly.
Though the language is carefully studied, and the sound of
every consonant and cadence of every syllable measured
with the finest ear; though it is all a conscious effort of
æsthetic design; it reads like nature, instinctive, impassioned,
unsophisticated.

Moore's
last
works

Neither *Ulick and Soracha* (1926), a story of mediæval
Ireland, nor *Aphrodite in Aulis* (1930) reached the same plane
as *The Brook Kerith* or *Héloïse and Abélard*, though if they had
not been outdone beforehand they might have been greeted as
noteworthy examples of a new genre. The Celtic inspiration
of the one gave it a peculiar charm; but, at his age, Moore
was a little rash to enter into competition with the author of
Pericles and Aspasia, in a novel of Greece five centuries before
the Christian era, and with his own self of fifteen years ago,
author of *The Brook Kerith*. More significant historically is
his final substitute, *Celibate Lives* (1927), for the older and
cruder *Celibates* (1895), which he freely resigned to "Amico
Moorini." It is a further illustration of the ultimate method
attained after so many stages of effort; and, as realism applied
to the least romantic things, it is a book not to be neglected in
any survey of Moore's art. Only one of the original stories
survived, and this had to be rewritten; he refurbished another
from *A Story-Teller's Holiday* (1918), and took over three from
a previous set of tales of celibacy, *In Single Strictness* (1922).
Such weeding-out and ceaseless revision ensured that none of
the five stories finally retained was without the "melodic
line." [1] One tale, liked by some critics, "Hugh Monfert,"
was entirely discarded. Moore had said in *Avowals*,[2] "That
which is firmly and clearly imagined needs no psychology."

[1] See preface, vi.   [2] *Avowals*, 240.

Each of the five is a story of things that happen; they are genuine stories from the memoranda of a connoisseur and collector of the delicate shades of character, of the rarer phenomena of human nature, the memoranda of one who prized and loved all this. For the happenings are those that betray personality, refinements of feeling and motive, the sort of subtleties to be studied still more intensively by Proust, Katherine Mansfield, and D. H. Lawrence. The way with most writers is to take such choice psychological treasures and spread them out for analysis, with an elaborate show of science. George Moore now knew better. He simply tells his story; but the characters are so clearly and firmly conceived that the reader is put in direct contact with them, and goes along with him in intuitive understanding. And this not at the expense of artistic detachment. Moore's artistic integrity kept him clear of all that. He stands scrupulously aloof, bent on telling the truth at all costs, rejecting the lure of poetic justice and of sentimentalism in all its shapes. But he was no speculative explorer of recondite phenomena, like Henry James, who is severely criticized in *Avowals* and elsewhere as a scientist in disguise, like so many of the professors of realism. Moore's absorption in the most enthralling of all subjects, human nature, had grown deeper and deeper. He loved it with a tenderness nowhere more evident than in this book. But, though he was no more impassive now than when he wrote *Esther Waters*, he was too true to his art to take sides, to give any clue to personal feelings, or let them blur the sensitive edge of his insight.

And if Moore knew anything excellently well, it was the *Penetrat-* female sex. These are all studies of women, all but the first, *ing* "Wilfrid Holmes." Wilfrid is the one man in the whole bunch, *studies of* and he is only half a man—poor devil of an ineffectual, living *women* on his aunt's cheque, and nearly dead of under-nourishment when it does not arrive. He has been working for twenty years on the legend of Tristan and Iseult, and has only a few conjectures to show for it. As to his opera, the accompaniments are still unwritten, all but the top line. But Moore does not laugh at Wilfrid Holmes. He and his like, the blind

beggar in "Almsgiving" for instance, have their place in the
human world, if it be only to keep alive "pity and compassion."
Moore divines the whole soul of Emily, in "Priscilla and Emily
Lofft." When her lover will not agree to live with her and her
sister, though Priscilla was to have made up her little fortune to
the amount required by his parents, she dismisses him. And
then Priscilla dies. Everything is told in Emily's long reverie
over the past. Moore's loving insight is like the nervous
comprehension of the living sister for the twin soul that had had
so few thoughts unshared by her. The middle piece, "Albert
Nobbs," is not a comic tale, apart from the farcical incident
when the woman who has earned her living for seven years in
the family hotel in Dublin, disguised as a man, discovers that
the man who has been sent to sleep in the same bed is a woman
too. Moore loved to show off his knowingness and his total
incapacity for being shocked at indecencies. Albert is "neither
man nor woman, just a perhapser," and one of his most appealing heroines. "Henrietta Marr," sole survivor from *Celibates*, is
the history of a "virtuous" woman, who gets all she can out
of her male friends in the Paris studios and at Barbizon, but is
affronted when one of them dies and his mistress accuses her of
separating a faithful couple and breaking his heart. She never
learns: her egoism is proof against the common infirmities and
the common instincts; she is too shallow, and without a qualm
holds her own against importunate lovers, serenely aware that
she is a "good woman." But Etta is not proof against everything. The Comte de Malmédy falls in love with her, and she
extracts a letter promising to marry her if his wife should die.
And the wife presently dies; but he does not marry Etta. There
is nothing left for her but to take a dose of veronal. In brief
abstract, it sounds crude and almost melodramatic. Told in
George Moore's exquisitely natural medium, seemingly a
careless fabric woven of haphazard incidents and scraps of
dialogue between Etta and her suspicious and critical friends,
it is a masterpiece of tragic suggestion. Moore thought his
last tale, "Sarah Gwynn," worthy of Turgenev.[1] The right
comparison is with Dostoevsky, who comes to mind at once

[1] Hone, 380–381.

when the dismissed nun gives her plain but heart-rending account of the underpaid work-girls in Dublin who make up enough to live on by prostitution, and of the Welsh convent which is "just a sweaters' den" for the lay sisters who have no money, and are kept hard at work while the others pray. Here the clear-sighted doctor's cross-examination and the girl's straightforward report are worth pages of methodical realism. Moore gives the truth, and the whole concrete truth, through this "pervading intimacy" and this immediate contact with life; without any gesture of plunging the reader into the stream of consciousness, of showing sensations, thoughts, and feelings impinging all the time, and so reconstituting the individual life. That was the psychology which he disliked. To project mental states on a screen, to construct a sort of psychological graph, he would have said was not art, but an affectation of science. His emphasis is on personal relationships, since it is through these that full individuality is developed. There are two sentences in his *Confessions of a Young Man* which do not altogether coincide in meaning: "Art is not nature; Art is nature digested"; and later, "I am sick of synthetical art; we want observation, direct and unreasoned." In *Celibate Lives*, and indeed in most of his ultimate work, Moore demonstrated the rightness of both sayings.

He was not one of the great creative geniuses; he belonged *A great* to the second order, distinguished by fine qualities of craftsman- *oppor-* ship and readiness at seizing what is useful here and there for *tunist* the development of an art. It is evident, from his own record and the way he developed, that he was an opportunist, and a most skilful and successful one. His peculiar historical importance was largely the result of his very deficiencies, and his indefatigable efforts to make up for them. With his wide and fastidious knowledge of English and foreign writers, and his readiness to experiment in any of the styles then current, he was able in the long run to stretch the capacities of fiction, and to make more technical discoveries on his own account than fell to the lot of any other novelist of his time, except Henry James. It was a time of change, of rupture with a great deal of the past, of the beginnings of new artistic attitudes and

methods. It was largely owing to Moore that English fiction
seems now to make a fresh start, discarding an immense amount
of the cumbrous, old-fashioned make-believe. He remade
the novel to suit himself, and in other hands it pursued the lines
he projected.

CHAPTER VI

ÆSTHETES AND ECLECTICS

GEORGE MOORE was not by any means the only English writer *French* to assimilate and act upon modern French conceptions of the *influences* novel as a work of art, having the right to deal with every *and the* aspect of human existence, and not be tied down to any didactic, *English* moralistic, or other utilitarian purpose. Stevenson, about the *æsthetic* same time, had spent some years in France, coming in contact *movement* with modern painters, and reading Baudelaire, Flaubert, Zola, and other men of letters, who repudiated every restriction on the scope and method of their art. But Stevenson, probably from his origin and upbringing, always had an anxious sense of the writer's responsibilities. In an early essay on "The Morality of the Profession of Letters" (1881) he reflects, "We have it in our power either to do great harm or great good"; and, whilst he recognizes that telling the truth is the supreme duty, he feels "there are certain classes of fact eternally more necessary than others, and it is with these that literature must first bestir itself." [1] His attitude in this essay is diffident and tentative, and to the end he was very wary in his choice of subjects, avoiding, like Henry James, the risky and suggestive— the very opposite of such aggressive champions of the pre-rogatives of art as Swinburne and Oscar Wilde. The artist has his rights; he has also certain duties to society. But a year later, in another essay, "Fontainebleau," he is most insistent on the artistic impulse prompting a man to write, and scornful of those who "prate to him about the lofty aims and moral influence of art." It is "the love of words" and "the love of form" that mark the vocation of the writer and the painter.[2]

[1] *Fortnightly Review* (April, 1881), reprinted in *Essays in the Art of Writing*.
[2] Collected in *Across the Plains*, etc. (1892); it was a rejoinder to Besant's lecture, *The Art of Fiction*, given in April, 1884. It should be noted that Moore's novels *A Modern Lover* and *A Mummer's Wife* came out in 1883 and 1884 respectively.

204 HISTORY OF THE ENGLISH NOVEL

There is a good deal of beating about the bush in "A Humble Remonstrance," which contains as many fallacies as flashes of brilliant insight; but this essay also is emphatic on the main point, that the novel is a work of pure art, and that the method to be followed in any particular novel depends upon the character of the subject chosen from that "inexhaustible magazine," the life of man. Over and over again, as in "A Gossip on Romance," Stevenson puts the claims of art foremost. "Conduct is three-parts of life, they say; but I think they put it high." And if moral dilemmas and moral decisions come into view, as they inevitably must, they are to be treated as so much dramatic material, not as themes for edification. Henry James maintained the pure æsthetic doctrine consistently, when some native tendencies to moralism had been corrected and his riper views brought him into agreement with the great French realists. James was an American, and in his early novels, dealing with the paradoxical situation of various types of American established in Europe, the artistic coincided as regularly with the moralistic point of view as in those of his elder contemporary, W. D. Howells, another New Englander. He was at first repelled by the uncompromising insistence on the claims of art, conjoined as it was with a cynical delight in baiting prudes and puritans, on the part of the French novelists, and he never reconciled himself to their intractable pessimism. But, after he had settled in this country, he was still more repelled by English apathy to art and culture, and the efforts of the strait-laced to put the novelist in a strait-jacket. Though he had said many unkind things about Flaubert and the Goncourts, the art of his second period is a further development of theirs; and the still more subtle art of his final works is the same carried to higher stages of creative and interpretative power— Pater's doctrine of "second intentions" pushed to its furthest reaches. It is noteworthy how many of his novels and stories are concerned with the artistic temperament or with the cruxes of art and life.[1] His essays, prefaces, and of course his novels, enunciating and illustrating a theory of fiction based upon and

---

[1] E.g. *The Madonna of the Future, The Lesson of the Master, The Figure in the Carpet,* "The Author of Beltraffio," *The Tragic Muse,* "The Death of the Lion."

amplifying that of Flaubert and his school, form a body of doctrine, and of the scrupulous and felicitous application of that doctrine, fuller and more exhaustive than those of George Moore and Stevenson put together, and have had more effect upon the work of novelists of yesterday and to-day. It will be necessary to return, later on, to his technical refinements, and the lessons in discipline and artistic integrity which he had for his fellow-craftsmen. Besides these greater novelists—and it must not be forgotten that Meredith and Hardy, not to mention Gissing, who subscribed to the æsthetic creed, were writing novels all through the period when the æsthetes were campaigning, or that they held the same general views on the rights of the creative imagination—there were lesser writers too, such as Dowson and Crackanthorpe, who preferred French models, especially in the short story, and left some choice examples of that genre. French standards of style, and of artistic economy and structural integrity, were widely and frankly accepted by such as took their art seriously. When Hardy was charged with violating British taboos in *Tess of the d'Urbervilles* and *Jude the Obscure*, he did not try to justify himself on moralistic grounds; he simply stood on his right to give artistic form to such trains of events as occur in actual life. A scrupulous regard for the basic principles of fine art was now the best guarantee of a writer's sincerity; and most intelligent people now assented to the view that the novel is not merely a cheap article of popular amusement, which may pass the censor if it is proved to be wholesome and edifying, but a work of art to be assessed by totally different canons.[1]

But, though Moore's experimental career from *A Modern Lover* to *The Brook Kerith*, and *Celibates*, and his critical manifestos from *Confessions of a Young Man* to *Avowals*, seem almost to epitomize the æsthetic movement, especially if James and Stevenson's amplifications of the doctrine are taken into account at the same time, it was not these disciples of French æstheticism that initiated the English movement, though in

The revolt from circumscribed views

---

[1] As Swinburne saw, some novels are works of art, the great bulk nothing of the sort. Gosse states (*Life of Swinburne*, 227) that he "explained to me that he did not regard current novels as literature but as life."

the end English and Continental theories of the novel came into close conformity. There was bound to be a protest and revolt sooner or later against the repressive ordinances that had kept both poet and novelist in leading-strings. Blake and Coleridge, Keats, Shelley, and Byron, had asserted the rights of the intellect and the imagination; but what they had won, or thought they had won, was lost in the half-century following. Literature, especially imaginative literature, and more especially the kind of imaginative literature that would appeal to the crowd, had become the bond-slave of a narrow utilitarian social code. A mutiny was long overdue against the bigoted didactic view of literature and of art in general. Though French exemplars helped to give the revolt a positive direction, it was this negative pressure that at length provoked the outbreak. Carlyle had placed the poet and man of letters among his heroes, but expressly as the destroyer of "Scepticism, Insincerity, Mechanical Atheism"; moral instruction and inspiration was the paramount office of literature and of art in general. Even Matthew Arnold could not free himself from this preoccupation with ethical motives in literature, when he preached the higher culture as a remedy for the prevailing anarchy. But he did insist on the virtue of disinterestedness; he characterized with deadly precision the crass materialism which under specious disguises was the taskmaster and dictator in literary and artistic as well as economic and social affairs; and he invented the useful word "Philistine" to define the enemy from that time to this. Ruskin did more still to awaken his countrymen to the appeal of beauty and art, and open their eyes to the ugliness of a land and people in the grip of the industrial system. Yet Ruskin would have scouted the idea that art had a scheme of values entirely its own. He gave beauty an ethical and even a religious interpretation: the doctrine of art for art's sake could have had no more uncompromising foe. A true disciple of Carlyle, he judged literature by its power of teaching and inspiring. Novels were demoralizing through their "over-wrought interest"; only a few were free from this pernicious tendency. Even Thackeray, he was afraid, might induce readers "to despise humanity"; and for his own part he would exclude, not only Thackeray, but also George Eliot, Kingsley, and Swift, from the hundred best books that could be put safely into the hands of the common reader,[1] When Millais, Holman Hunt, and Rossetti formed the Pre-Raphaelite brotherhood, in revolt from the pseudo-academic school of painting, and were afterwards joined by Morris and Burne-Jones, Ruskin gave them a welcome as leaders in the return to nature which he had been preaching, and wrote a book on *Pre-Raphaelitism* (1859) which expounded their objects in a way they would hardly have put it themselves. The Pre-Raphaelites were the immediate predecessors of the æsthetes; Rossetti was an artist practising the theory of art for art's sake without actually adopting it ; Morris, without any theory, made it his mission to spread the gospel of beauty and of joy in life. Holman Hunt was the only one among the number who was actuated by any didactic tendencies. And now Swinburne, who in his first series of *Poems and Ballads* (1866) had transfused into English verse the very spirit of Baudelaire's *Fleurs du Mal*, and had turned and rent his pharisaic critics in *Notes on Poems and Reviews* a few months later, Swinburne, the bitterest and ablest fighter in the rebellion against puritanical restrictions on the arts, thought he had discovered the germs, and a good deal more than the germs, of a lofty ideal of art as a vital activity of man, having no ulterior purpose, but free and autonomous, in short, the doctrine of "Art for art's sake first of all," in the writings of William Blake.[2] He took Blake as his text for the fullest exposition yet published in English of the æsthetic creed. Should art humble herself and compromise with the principle of doing good, "she is worse than dead." The one important thing is "to have her work supremely well done, and to disregard all contingent consequences." [3] In the same book, he

---

[1] See *Sesame and Lilies*, 76–77. Frederic Harrison mentions Ruskin's objections to Lubbock's choice of the hundred best books (English Men of Letters—*Ruskin*, 112).

[2] How far Swinburne allowed himself to be led astray here is clearly demonstrated by M. Georges Lafourcade (*La Jeunesse de Swinburne* (ii. 332–342)—"L'Essai sur Blake: les sources de la théorie esthétique ").

[3] *William Blake, a critical essay*, 100. Blake's contemporary Coleridge expressed what are approximately the same views, derived from the Kantian theory of an ideal world in which beauty is supreme, and of the imagination as a faculty whose activity pertains to the æsthetic not the moral sphere. In the *Biographia Literaria* (c. xxii.) he takes Wordsworth to task for assuming the role of moral philosopher, for example,

spoke of Balzac, the greatest of the French novelists, as "a prose
Shakespeare." Gautier's example and witty pronouncements
on the matter at issue between artist and philistine he was
always citing. But, with perfect consistency, Swinburne
condemned *Les Misérables* of Victor Hugo, whom he passionately admired, for violating the fundamental principles of art,
being avowedly written to further certain moral and humanitarian aims; and for the same and other reasons he reprehended
the grosser naturalism of Zola. But, though he repudiated any
didactic purpose, Swinburne did not reject moral issues as a
subject for art. "From the man who falls to artistic work
with a moral purpose," he goes on after the declaration quoted
above, "shall be taken away even that which he has—whatever
of capacity for doing well in either way he may have at starting."
Art has nothing to do with morality as an end or purpose; but
it has everything to do with morality as an inescapable portion
of its main subject, life, human nature. In fact, the moral
issues in any drama or story are the most pregnant of all and the
most absorbing. To that principle he adhered unswervingly.[1]

*Few of
the
æsthetes
wrote
novels*

The leading æsthetes were not novelists, except as it were by
accident. Swinburne himself, in his youth, was the author of
a series of imaginary letters, *Love's Cross-Currents* (1905), which
he described as "a compromise between a story and a play,"
but which is little more than an exchange of sentiments and
opinions held together by the thinnest biographical thread.
John Davidson, Ernest Dowson, and Aubrey Beardsley threw
off a few stories, and even attempts at novels, as interludes in
their chief occupation. But the main body of the æsthetes
were artists on other lines; the majority were poets or playwrights, or both, and the remainder, painters, illustrators,
printers, and decorators. The fact is, Moore's novels are the

in his verses on the Leech-gatherer. This is to ignore the fundamental distinction
between a poem and a work in prose, between philosophy and a work of fiction,
"inasmuch as it proposes *truth* for its immediate object, instead of *pleasure*." A
philosophic basis for the æsthetic creed can be found in Kant, as, later on, Pater and
others found one in Hegel. But it is not to be supposed that Swinburne sought any
such metaphysical sanction, for views originating in the reaction of common sense
against the restrictions forced upon poet and novelist, upon imaginative creation in
general, by the prevailing insensibility and prejudice.

[1] His views in this respect coincide practically with those of Baudelaire, and, thus,
are in conflict with Gautier's (see Lafourcade, *op. cit.*, 340–342).

best that can without challenge be called novels, emanating
from anyone closely associated with the group. For Stevenson,
Henry James, and Gissing, though they owned allegiance and
warranty to the æsthetic code, were only friendly allies, who
gave to the movement more than they owed it, which was still
more the case with Meredith and Hardy. The position of
William Morris was different again. His versatile genius, at
home in all the word-crafts as in various handicrafts, simply
changed the measure when it listed, and poured out its inventions in prose—a prose often not distinguishable from verse
except by the absence of metre. To count Morris among the
novelists sounds absurd. Yet his prose romances have their
place in the history of the novel, if only for having led the way,
in conjunction with Stevenson's revival of less antiquated forms
of romance, to the new varieties of historical fiction, the novel
of adventure, the fairy-story, and the semi-poetic tale of
mystical experience, that for a while enchanted the public,
and distracted attention from the novelists who were employing
a semi-scientific realism and the fearless, subversive criticism of
Samuel Butler in a stricter reckoning with actualities, and even
to very drastic solutions of the problem of society. Some of the
latter came dangerously near undoing the work of the æsthetes,
and turning fiction into the agent of a new utilitarianism, a
perspective of contrary principles at work, an object-lesson in
social theory, though they were now too honest and too
respectful of the claims of art to fall into the superannuated
ruse of poetic justice: they let their imaginations stand for
what they were worth.

George Moore's burst of enthusiasm on first reading *Marius* *Walter*
the Epicurean, recorded in suitably mellifluous terms in his *Pater*
Confessions of a Young Man,[1] will not have been forgotten.
"Well I remember when I read the opening lines, and how
they came upon me sweetly as the flowing breath of a bright
spring. I knew that I was awakened a fourth time." Shelley,
and then Gautier and Balzac, had revealed aspects of the world;
Zola, Flaubert, and Goncourt had captivated him with theory,
or workmanship, or brilliant adjectival effects. Pater, however,

[1] Chap. xii. See also above, p. 181.

not only led him back to the genius of his own tongue, but even
made a new dawn in his brain, by showing him "the beauty
of mildness in life, and how by a certain avoidance of the
wilfully passionate, and the surely ugly, we may secure an
aspect of temporal life which is abiding and soul-sufficing." [1]
Pater did this for his age.   At a time of doubt, disillusionment,
and agonizing unrest, of the turmoil of ideas and experiences
that stunned and bewildered Hardy,[2] he announced a panacea
in art, not simply in the making or in the contemplation of
works of art, but in the extension of the artistic activity to life
itself.   He promulgated an art of life.   He showed his Marius
receiving "a lesson in the skilled cultivation of life, of experience,
of opportunity"; he told of minds "made perfect by the love
of visible beauty." [3]   In this new Epicureanism, life was to be
an æsthetic experience; and, "not the fruit of experience, but
experience itself, is the end." [4]

Out of the wreckage of religious and philosophical values, he
built for himself this refuge on the only absolute he could find,
the æsthetic experience, life lived as a fine art.[5]   Walter Pater
(1839–1894) had announced the new way of life in his famous
conclusion to *The Renaissance* (1873), a final chapter withdrawn
in the second edition but afterwards reinstated in a slightly
amended form.   "We are all under sentence of death, but

---

[1] *Confessions of a Young Man*, c. xii.

[2] See above, pp. 14–16.   It must not be forgotten that during the "romantic
nineties," "the Beardsley period," the "*fin-de-siècle*," Tennyson and Browning were
still the great poets of the age.   Browning died in 1889, Tennyson in 1892.   The
Idylls of the King, in their complete and final form, and also *Œnone*, appeared in 1892.
Thomson's *City of Dreadful Night* dates in its magazine-form from 1874, but did not
come out as a book till 1880.   It was regarded as one of the most impressive of contemporary poems, and Davidson's various "Testaments" were in a sense its sequels.
Much of the work of W. E. Henley, Lord de Tabley, Francis Thompson, and other
pessimist poets, not to mention Swinburne's and Stevenson's, were contemporary
with the work of Pater, Oscar Wilde, and their associates.   Meredith and Hardy were
steadily writing; and, on the other hand, Messrs Bernard Shaw and H. G. Wells
had made much more than a beginning.

[3] *Marius the Epicurean*, iii.

[4] *Renaissance*, conclusion.

[5] For the metaphysical bases of Pater's æsthetic solipsism, see *L'Idée de l'art pour
l'art dans la littérature anglaise pendant la période victorienne*, par Louise Rosenblatt
(Paris, 1931), which is the clearest account extant of the thought and work of the
æsthetes.   Lafourcade (*op. cit.*) deals admirably with the history of the movement in
relation to Swinburne.   The second volume of Madeleine L. Cazamian's survey,
Le Roman et les idées en Angleterre (1935)—"L'anti-intellectualisme et l'esthétisme,
1880–1900," is also principally concerned with the movement.

with a sort of indefinite reprieve. . . . We have an interval, and then our place knows us no more." "Our one chance lies in expanding that interval, in getting as many pulsations as possible into the given time."

Great passions may give us this quickened sense of life, ecstasy and sorrow of love, the various forms of enthusiastic activity, disinterested or otherwise, which come naturally to many of us. Only be sure it is passion—that it does yield to you this fruit of a quickened, multiplied consciousness. Of this wisdom, the poetic passion, the desire of beauty, the love of art for art's sake, has most; for art comes to you professing frankly to give nothing but the highest quality to your moments as they pass, and simply for those moments' sake.[1]

He and the other æsthetes had travelled a long way from Matthew Arnold's idea of culture, a synthesis of the three great streams—Hebraism, righteousness; Hellenism, beauty and art; Aryanism, knowledge, science. They were also as far from the reverent delight in beauty as the sign of all that is noble and divine into which they had been initiated by Ruskin. In this new culture, spiritual and moral considerations were eliminated, except so far as some measure of altruism and sympathy was a sentiment that refined and tranquillized the soul—of the elect individual. It was a self-conscious and a self-centred scheme of culture, for Pater's philosophy concentrated on the personal life—a serene and scientific egotism —for himself and a few like him.

Marius the Epicurean (1885) is a book cast in the elementary form of a novel, or at least of fiction; but its historical importance is in its being a manual of æsthetic doctrine, applied to the art of living, and a sacred book to those who profess and practise it. The mental and moral history of this young Roman under Marcus Aurelius is a projection into another sphere and another epoch of Pater's own inner history. He himself followed the same philosophic itinerary, went through the same phases of mental experience, and arrived at the same conclusions. The sensuous temperament, the susceptibility to impressions, the

"Marius the Epicurean"

---

[1] Dated 1868 (1888 edition).

habit of dwelling on their emotional effects, studying his successive states of soul, were the author's own characteristics. There was also a strain of mystical feeling in Pater, the liturgical, the ethical, and the spiritual elements in religion giving him something akin to the ecstasy he had from the æsthetic experience. To this was due a termination to the story of Marius that remains enigmatic. Was he leading his wanderer to the Christian fold, when he abruptly ended his narrative, or merely symbolizing his sense of the inscrutable surrounding our physical existence, and of a revelation to be hoped for after death? At any rate, all this seems to represent a long journey from the doctrine of cultivating the present moment laid down with such eloquence and serene resignation in the conclusion to *The Renaissance*, and in earlier passages of the present book. Seeking beauty and harmony, and aiming to realize them in his daily life, Marius, who has been brought up in the simple religion of Numa, comes successively in contact with various ideologies, the stoicism of Marcus Aurelius, Lucian's scepticism, and systems of thought opening up speculations whether there is a world beyond that known to the senses. At one stage, it is the cult of "the human body in its beauty, as the highest potency of all the beauty of material objects." But, even then, it seemed to him "to be matter no longer, but, having taken celestial fire, to assert itself as indeed the true though invisible soul or spirit in things." [1] For Marius has ever a sense of "the *hiddenness* of perfect things, a shrinking mysticism, a sentiment of diffidence," [2] which he likens to the tremulous hope of Psyche in the child to be born of the husband whom she has never seen. After the death of his friend, the young Flavian, "an epitome of the whole pagan world, the depth of its corruption, and its perfection of form," Marius arrives at a conception of culture, derived from the master of the Cyrenaic doctrine, aiming at "not pleasure, but a general completeness of life." "From that maxim of *Life as the end of life*, followed, as a practical consequence, the desirableness of refining all the instruments of inward and outward intuition," of straining "towards the vision—the 'beatific vision,' if we really cared

[1] Chap. vi.   [2] *Ibid.*

to make it such—of our actual experience of the world."
Hence Marius comes by natural stages to admire and to be
profoundly touched and attracted by the early Church, though
he never fully accepts its belief or is joined to the communion.
And it happens that this *anima naturaliter Christiana*, by taking
the place of his friend Cornelius at his own risk, suffers martyrdom.   But he resigns himself to his death, obscurely aware that
he is on the brink of a great disclosure.   "For still, in a shadowy
world, his deeper wisdom had ever been, with a sense of economy,
with a jealous estimate of gain and loss, to use life, not as the
means to some problematic end, but, as far as might be, from
dying hour to dying hour, an end in itself:—a kind of music, all
sufficing to the duly trained ear, even as it died out on the air."
Yet, "throughout that elaborate and lifelong education of his
receptive powers, he had ever kept in view the purpose of
preparing himself towards some possible further revelation
some day:—towards some ampler vision, which should take up
into itself and explain this world's delightful shows, as the
scattered fragments of a poetry, till then but half-understood,
might be taken up into the text of a lost epic, recovered at
last." [1]   Hence an ambiguity, an inconclusiveness, a suggestion
of transcendental possibilities, such as was implicit in Pater's
own attitude.   He transposed religious into æsthetic values,
but they were never fully absorbed.[2]   It is a great essay in
fictitious biography, with more of the essay in it than of
biographical creation; and it is a weighty synopsis of contemporary currents of thought.   In *Imaginary Portraits* (1887) and
in two of his *Miscellaneous Studies* (1895) Pater pursued the
vein of biographical interpretation, in the latter with more
creative freedom; and in the unfinished romance, *Gaston de
Latour* (1896), he made an elaborate beginning to the history
of a mind intent on the things of the spirit, amid the religious
wars, massacres, and intrigues, of sixteenth-century France.

Pater's gentle reasoning was the very opposite to the con-*Belliger-*
troversial methods of the other æsthetes.   Most upholders of *ent*
the sacred prerogatives of art, though they were on the defensive *æstheti-*
in a world of enemies, adopted the Gallic policy of shocking *cism*

[1] Chap. xxviii.   [2] *Ibid.*

and bewildering a muddle-headed and conservative public, putting their arguments in the most provocative shape. Gautier revelled in flippant exaggerations of the doctrine of art for art's sake; his quips and paradoxes infuriated the opposition. Swinburne was just as bellicose, though not so cynically regardless of moral values. He violently repudiated the general assumption that it is the poet's duty to teach a lesson, and carried the war into enemy country with his ridicule of the cant and prudery that detected the snares of the Evil One in any honest effort to face grave issues. In this guerrilla warfare he was supported, though he quarrelled with the man, by a witty sharpshooter who had attached himself to the Pre-Raphaelite group, the American painter, James McNeill Whistler, sworn enemy of Ruskin and the didactic views of art that Ruskin stood for. Swinburne's invectives were not more deadly than Whistler's arrogant statements of the artist's independence and immeasurable superiority to the common herd, and his witty travesties of the case for the other side, those "for whom there is no perfect work that shall not be explained by the benefit conferred upon themselves."

Humanity takes the place of Art, and God's creations are excused by their usefulness. Beauty is confounded with virtue, and, before a work of Art, it is asked: "What good shall it do?" [1]

Oscar Wilde was to borrow a good deal of his ammunition from the Whistler arsenal; but it did not fit the bore of his guns, and as often as not went wide of the mark. This was the heyday of the artistic temperament, to which the band of young men who acclaimed Walter Pater as their lawgiver accorded sovereign privileges, to the indignation of the man in the street, to whom they replied with calm assurance that they could do no wrong with such an original endowment and such authority behind them. But, though they issued two organs, *The Yellow Book* and *The Savoy*, besides essays and articles, stories and novels, poems and plays, and apparently wished to justify themselves in the public eye, they signally failed to

[1] "Mr Whistler's 'Ten O'Clock'" (*The Gentle Art of making Enemies*, p. 137).

make converts. Like their predecessors, they were immensely outnumbered by hostile critics and a recalcitrant public; and, assuming the same defiant and exasperating attitudes, they roused first curiosity and amazement, and eventually the same violent denunciation. At heart, they hated the average man, and the hatred was warmly reciprocated. Oscar Wilde pushed himself to the front and claimed to be Pater's mouthpiece, though he was recognized as leader of the movement only by himself—and a marvelling world. Probably, the young artist, Aubrey Beardsley, whose decorative designs were a manifesto in plastic line both of the principle of art for art's sake and of the æsthetes' defiance of the ban on certain subjects, was potentially the greatest talent produced by the group. But he died under a cloud at the age of twenty-six, and his drawings are still inadequately appreciated except by the few. His incidental novel, *Under the Hill*, is a playful illustration to his work in the other medium, rather than the customary reverse. Perhaps the poets belonging to the group received their due, such as it was. Certainly those more loosely attached, such as Francis Thompson and W. B. Yeats, did not fail of it. Davidson and Dowson wrote novels or stories as well as poetry, Dowson's not inferior to his verse. Wilde wrote fiction, which is as palpably a manufactured article showing a scholarly acquaintance with the best authors as any of his work; and several other occasional novelists will have to be considered a little later. Whistler took the æsthetes under his wing, and joined in the fray. Pater's other disciple, George Moore, fervently declared his devotion to the cause, but was too considerate of his own quiet and well-being to share in their polemics, except for occasional covert satire and innuendo. Wilde was a loose thinker, and his risky corollaries to Pater's doctrines, and still more the gibes at the philistines borrowed from Matthew Arnold and the paradoxes which he stole from Whistler—and edged with a malice that betrayed him into glaring sophistries—brought the whole movement into disrepute, which was confirmed to the satisfaction of his opponents by his personal downfall. But for this untimely reverse, which threw back for a decade or more the triumph of all that was sound in the æsthetic reaction, there would be a very close parallel between this campaign against conservative elements in the British public and that which Mr Bernard Shaw was about to commence in the theatre against the same stubborn opponents. The parallel is all the closer in that Shaw employed the same aggressive tactics, caricaturing his own audiences and laughing their settled opinions to scorn. His ultimate victory was not one of tact, but of sheer intellectual superiority and dogged persistence. Open-mindedness and clear thinking, especially in social matters, were the objects aimed at, rather than a revolution in attitudes to art; and his was a triumph of pure intelligence rather than the higher wisdom, of the Baconian, not the Shakespearian attitude to life.[1]

Oscar Wilde's exaggerated æstheticism   Oscar Wilde (1856–1900) was a young man of lively wit and immense powers of assimilation, who received the same stimulus from reading Pater's *Renaissance* as Moore had from *Marius the Epicurean*, and straightway applied himself to the mission of interpreting and demonstrating the pure æsthetic truth. "The artistic life is simply self-development," [2] he pointedly observed; and, whereas "Marius is little more than a spectator," though an ideal spectator, Wilde was fond of saying that he put his own genius into his life, and only his talent into his literary works.[3] Agreeably with his extension of the doctrine of art for art's sake to that of life for art's sake, he held himself up as a product as well as an exponent of the new æsthetics; and, in spite of being laughed at, imposed himself on a large section of the British public, then on American audiences, who flocked to see in the flesh the almost incredible butt of Gilbert and Sullivan's *Patience* (1881), and even on critical opinion in Paris, where he is still taken at his face-value by Messrs Maurois and Gide.[4] All this was likewise in con-

---

[1] *Widowers' Houses* was presented in 1892 and *Mrs Warren's Profession*, privately, in 1902; but the real campaigning began with *Man and Superman* (1903) and *John Bull's Other Island* (1904).

[2] *De Profundis*, 67.

[3] "C'est que j'ai mis mon génie dans ma vie; je n'ai mis que mon talent dans mes œuvres" (*Prétextes*, par André Gide, 285, n.).

[4] See *Études anglaises*, par André Maurois—"De Ruskin à Wilde"; and *Prétextes*, 265–304—"Oscar Wilde." Madeleine Cazamian also has a very long and highly appreciative chapter (*op. cit.*, 150–204).

formity with the view laid down repeatedly in *Intentions* (1891), that art is, not expressive, but "impressive purely."

For emotion for the sake of emotion is the aim of art, and emotion for the sake of action is the aim of life, and of that practical organization of life which we call society.[1]

With an enormous appetite for sensations and an imperturbable vanity, he undertook to give the world the spectacle of a life like Byron's, though if he had any such creative powers as Byron's he never exerted himself to develop them. For in his stories and his one novel, and in most of his other writings, he took an easier path—he was an adroit kleptomaniac. His æsthetic doctrines came from Pater, and from Ruskin corrected by Pater; the glosses upon them from Whistler, corrected or enlarged by himself; and the ideas on culture from Matthew Arnold, made to agree with Pater's. Wilde's first essay in fiction, *The Happy Prince, and other Tales* (1888), was a charming imitation of Andersen, Ruskin, and other fabulists, heavily adorned with his æstheticism and enlivened by his paradoxical wit. In a later set of apologues, *The House of Pomegranates* (1892), the further influence of Maeterlinck and the symbolists shows through the deft handling and the accomplished style, now richly embroidered and now simple and transparent. In his poems, he wrote in the manner of Swinburne, Rossetti, Morris, Keats, as the occasion prompted, and succeeded in echoing Arnold in "Ave Imperatrix" and "Requiescat," and Gautier, Baudelaire, and Verlaine, in "The Sphinx" and "The Harlot's House"; even "The Ballad of Reading Gaol," though deeply sincere in feeling and as original as anything he wrote, reminds everyone of Hood's "Eugene Aram," and is full of echoes from Tennyson, Meredith, and others. Wilde's novel, *Dorian Gray*, was another of the contemporary anatomies of decadence and its results called out by Huysmans' *À Rebours*, with a plot adapted from Balzac's *Peau de Chagrin* and further effects from Poe and Maturin. He showed the same prehensile ability, and but rarely more than the power to write competently and sometimes brilliantly in the current fashion, in

[1] *Intentions*—"The Critic as Artist."

his plays, stamped though the dialogue always is with his gift for paradox and repartee. The only one that manifests a positive genius for anything else, *The Importance of being Earnest* (1899), is, however, a masterpiece in a domain that Wilde made almost exclusively his own, that of irresponsible nonsense. It would be taking it too seriously even to regard this as a burlesque of Scribe and Augier at their most frivolous. "Lord Arthur Savile's Crime" (1891) was an invention very nearly as free from the fetters of common sense, and may therefore be counted as Wilde's finest prose story.

His theories and "Dorian Gray" Wilde set forth his artistic doctrines in articles for the reviews, of which he collected four of the most daring in *Intentions* (1891). They were startling, and not free from inconsistency and mutual contradiction; so that he ran some risk of stultifying himself when in *The Picture of Dorian Gray*, published almost simultaneously, he proceeded to show how these maxims worked when applied to life and conduct. In his theorizing, he kept well within the empirical sphere, fighting shy of the metaphysical assumptions to which Pater gave due regard; and, with a ready command of impressive phrase, slid smoothly from one proposition to another, without overmuch heed to logical coherence.[1] He arrived at the idea that nature imitates art through misunderstanding Whistler's smart sayings on the imperfections, miscarriages, and disorderliness of the natural world, contrasted with the completeness and perfection which the artist presents, bringing forth "from chaos glorious harmony." "Seldom does Nature succeed in producing a picture," says Whistler; yet "the casual in Nature is accepted as sublime," as may be gathered from the unlimited admiration bestowed on "a very foolish sunset." [2] Whistler knew what he was talking about, and so did Swinburne when he stigmatized the fallacy of regarding the work of art as a means of ethical instruction, though he would not disclaim the artist's moral responsibility.[3] But Wilde, from the non-ethical character of

[1] He was not incapable, however, of consecutive reasoning, as is evinced by his little book, *The Soul of Man under Socialism*, in which he demolished the argument that any kind of collectivism must be incompatible with true individuality.
[2] *Gentle Art*, 143–144.
[3] Rosenblatt, 132 and 135, n.; cp. 158–159.

art, its neutrality, art as unmoral, proceeds to the unwarranted conclusion that "All art is immoral." [1] Art, it is true, simply as art, has no ethical purpose. Art is for art's sake, just as science for science or sport for sport. Yet a novel, or a poem or picture, or a game, or a scientific experiment, may have extraneous effects; and the person responsible for such effects is under the common obligation for the consequences of his actions. The moral and the immoral are equally subjects for art, and art is not called upon to be the agent of the one any more than the other. Art has neither to teach ethics nor to contravene or undermine ethics: its aims are confined to its own sphere. The mid-Victorian wanted to subordinate art and make it subserve morals; Wilde flirted with the idea of subordinating ethics to art. Yet, though he was always striving to eliminate all traces of moralism from his fictions, he could not eradicate inbred predispositions in himself.[2] It was as if the inherent logic of things was too much for him. He felt that man is, after all, a moral animal. Hence *Dorian Gray*, which was meant to have been the breviary of the new hedonism, Wilde's appendix to *Marius the Epicurean* and also to *À Rebours*, the yellow book described but not named in the tenth chapter—*Dorian Gray*, uncompromising manifesto of art for art and of life for art—turns before it is finished into a moral story with an unimpeachable old-fashioned lesson at the end.[3] It is like innumerable novels of self-indulgence and nemesis, except that the sensuous delights of the life of dissipation that sapped Dorian's soul are depicted with the emotional abandonment of one like him. Wilde certainly achieved the impressiveness that he considered the aim of art, in the tragic conclusion, when Dorian stabs the picture with the knife that has killed the painter, and the portrait which had taken on every line and ugly stain of his steady debasement instantly recovers the beauty of his exquisite youth, whilst he drops to the floor dead, a hideous and loathsome wreck. There is an

---

[1] *Intentions*—"The Critic as Artist."

[2] In "The Preface" afterwards added to *Dorian Gray* he reiterated: "An ethical sympathy in an artist is an unpardonable mannerism of style."

[3] It was so accepted by *The Christian Leader* and *The Christian World* (see Rosenblatt, 272).

earlier passage which gives as good an account of what the
æsthetes, or their critics, meant by decadence as can be found
in imaginative literature.   Dorian, who has been listening to
Lord Henry's prescription of a rule of life derived from Pater
but directed solely to the cult of the senses, ponders in the
haunted darkness before dawn upon the many forms he has
tested of passionate experience, and longs for "a world in which
things would have fresh shapes and colours, and be changed,
or have other secrets, a world in which the past would have
little or no place."

It was the creation of such worlds as these that seemed to
Dorian Gray to be the true object, or amongst the true objects,
of life; and in his search for sensations that would be at once
new and delightful, and possess that element of strangeness
that is so essential to romance, he would often adopt certain
modes of thought that he knew to be really alien to his nature,
abandon himself to their subtle influences, and then, having,
as it were, caught their colour and satisfied his intellectual
curiosity, leave them with that curious indifference that is not
incompatible with a real ardour of temperament, and that,
indeed, according to certain modern psychologists, is often a
condition of it.[1]

The novel goes on to tell of Dorian's thoughts of entering
the Roman Catholic communion, and his yearning to taste
new and ever newer forms of experience.   This insatiable and
unscrupulous appetence is practically the same thing as the
boundless curiosity enjoined in "The Critic as Artist," where
even sin is approved as "an essential element of progress." [2]
"By its curiosity Sin increases the experience of the race."
"Without it the world would stagnate, or grow old, or become
colourless."   "Through its intensified assertion of individualism, it saves us from monotony of type.   In its rejection of the
current notions about morality, it is one with the higher
ethics."   "Self-denial is simply a method by which man
arrests his progress."   Pain and sorrow have their function
also, as Wilde shows in *De Profundis* and "The Ballad of Reading
Gaol."   *De Profundis* is like the final chapter in still another

[1] Chap. xi.   [2] *Intentions*—"The Critic as Artist."

novel of moral perversion and chastening retribution. It is
the tragedy of decadence recounted by one who longed to see
himself as he looked to others.[1]

Such work and such a life as Wilde's inevitably bring up the *His short*
question of his sincerity. In a letter to Robert Ross he wrote: *stories*
"Mere expression is to an artist the supreme and only mode of
life. It is by utterance that we live." [2] This should be set
side by side with his account of truth: "Truth in art is the
unity of a thing with itself: the outward rendered expressive
of the inward: the soul made incarnate: the body instinct with
spirit." [3] But what, it may be asked, if the soul is not worth
expressing—if blood and brain, in Meredith's differentiation,
are developed, but not spirit? In much of his work, Wilde
seems to have had no soul to express, but has to sustain his
artistic being on what he can beg, borrow, or steal from those
better off. And, not only did he make free with other people's
belongings, he also, habitually, professed to take things that
were unclean, and refashion them into things of beauty. Life
was important because it provided materials for art.[4] In
"Reading Goal," and perhaps in *De Profundis*, he was so happy
contemplating his own agonies that he grew serious, with the
sincerity of an actor losing himself in his part. But he was
continually losing himself in the part he happened to be playing:
Wilde was incessantly posing, he was "an artist in attitudes";
and yet there was a sincerity even in his attitudes, for they
represented his aspirations.[5] This is evident in many of his
short stories. It is curious that nearly all are apologues, or
close approximations thereto. He could never resist the
fascination of a moral theme; and if the accompaniments of a
tale are often wantonly sinister, and the atmosphere sometimes

[1] Cp. the excellent analysis of decadence in the essay on Huysmans, in *Affirmations*,
by Havelock Ellis, pp. 178–186.
[2] Preface to *De Profundis*, viii.
[3] *De Profundis*, 55.
[4] Again we are reminded of Gissing's, "Only as artistic material has human life any
consequence."
[5] "An Artist in Attitudes" is the title of the short study of Oscar Wilde in *Studies
in Prose and Verse*, by Arthur Symons. André Gide's touching reminiscences,
especially of Wilde's latter days, in *Prétextes*, bring out the man's charm and amiability,
and also the courage which he never lost, any more than his wit, though it often looked
like mere effrontery.

seems to breathe contagion, that was only the reflex of his doctrine of sin: the moral ending is usually impeccable. Even "Lord Arthur Savile's Crime" has the sub-title, "A Study of Duty," though the moralizing is only part of the fun: it is extravaganza in a realistic dress, a paradoxical mixture of tragic and absurd, in which the comic element has the best of it.[1]

"The Happy Prince," etc. This set of stories is in the plain, incisive, sparkling style natural to Oscar Wilde when he meant business, a style based on his brilliant talk: those in *A House of Pomegranates*, a year later, adapted or imitated from the most modern professors of the fairy-tale and apologue, are in matter and manner a polished tessellation of the choicest bits from the most select sources, elegant extracts put together with refined taste. That was one of the ways he lived literature. But there is real feeling in places. Wilde was affected by current socialistic pity for the underdog, so far as he could be touched by altruistic emotion. This was evident in his first set of fairy-stories, *The Happy Prince, and other Tales* (1888). The prince's statue hails a little swallow, and sends him about the city looking for scenes of distress. He also bids him take out the eyes of ruby and the jewels and gold which were the city's pride, to relieve the poor. The mayor and corporation have the shabby thing melted down: "As he is no longer beautiful he is no longer useful." But God said, "In my garden of Paradise this little bird shall

[1] Lord Arthur, on the point of marrying a beautiful girl, learns from a chiromancer that he is fated to commit murder. For the moment he is paralysed with horror. Then he reflects: if it has to be done, it were better done quickly. So he puts off the wedding, and sends a poisoned bon-bon to a dear old relative, Lady Clementina Beauchamp. According to plan, she dies, leaving him an amiable bequest. Lord Arthur was touched, and "the consciousness that he had done his duty gave him peace and comfort." But, as he is preparing for his marriage, it transpires that Lady Clementina had after all died a natural death—she had never touched the bon-bon. The whole business has to be begun over again. An attempt to blow up his uncle, the Dean of Chichester, proves a fiasco. The fated murderer is in despair, and all but resigns every aspiration for his innocent betrothed; when, on the Embankment, he catches sight of the podgy little chiromancer who started all the bother. Without a moment's hesitation, he flings him over into the Thames, and the heading in that evening's paper, "Suicide of a Cheiromantist," assures him that he can now marry Sybil Merton in safety. "The Canterville Ghost" is mostly ironical banter of the American zest for old houses and bric-à-brac, which in this instance includes such effects as an ancestral ghost. In "The Portrait of Mr W. H.," paradox is heaped on paradox: one man commits forgery and then suicide to authenticate his theory as to Shakespeare's W. H.; and the sceptic, who has opened the eyes of the other believer in the fraud, himself presently dies firmly convinced of its truth.

sing for evermore, and in my city of gold the Happy Prince shall praise me." There is something grim and cynical behind the pretty fable of "The Nightingale and the Rose," and "The Remarkable Rocket" is all cynicism. But this serves all the better to set off the tale of the Prince, and "The Selfish Giant," a charming little morality on the power of kindness. So, too, the harrowing glimpses of the poor ground down by the rich, followed by sumptuous pictures of court and palace, make such a moralistic story as "The Young King" sound impressive, till it is noticed that the point on which all turns, the light through the painted windows that robes him and the dead staff that blossoms, is only a solemn trick, like the "I wonder!" which concludes "The Sphinx without a Secret" in the previous volume. One of the best in workmanship is "The Fisherman and his Soul." The fisherman by magic sleights gets rid of his soul, to wed a mermaid, but keeps back his heart. And while he lives in bliss in the depths of the sea, the soul without a heart falls into terrible depravity. But they meet again on the sands, and the soul tempts him away, not revealing till too late that he has now broken the spell. "Once in his life may a man send his Soul away, but he who receiveth back his Soul must keep it with him for ever, and this is his punishment and his reward." It recalls Arnold's "Forsaken Merman"; but the tale as a whole is Maeterlinckian symbolism.

The æsthetes stood aloof from the graver conflicts of ideas *Wilde* and apprehensions then agitating the world, in an insolent *and* rebelliousness of their own: they had no more to do with the *Aubrey* school of doubt and denial than with the school of acceptance, *Beardsley* and only now and then spared a glance for social questions. Wilde played the part of trifler and dilettante, occasionally suffering himself to be thrilled by others' afflictions when they looked picturesque. The backwash of the prevailing pessimism shows, however, in the epicurean concentration on sensual delights, conjoined with a mournful resignation. It was not a very stoical resignation, to judge by the dismal and premature ends of a large proportion of their lives.[1] Aubrey Beardsley

[1] "The age is distinguished by tragedies, in the purely physical sense of the term, among men of letters and artists. Crackanthorpe, Adams, Laurence Hope, John

(1872–1898) was one of those who played or worked themselves to death, failing to realize all that was in them. He and Wilde were not exactly friends; but their conjunction as writer and illustrator and as active participants in the movement dictates some comparison. Wilde was rebellious and defiant, but not aggressive; he indulged in caustic raillery, not in destructive satire. Beardsley was not of the same emotional nature; he was cool in temper, inclined to be cynical, but almost scientific in his clear observation of the world. Bound up in his art, he showed the opulence of his creative genius by his deliberate extravagance and calculated grotesqueries. His almost uncanny insight laid bare the vices and pretences of his day, and his imagination bodied them forth in depraved, voluptuous, baleful figures, a mythology of evil arrayed in the pomp of a sinister beauty—the beauty of corruption. He was the great illustrator of decadence; it was thus he retaliated upon the disingenuous and rancorous puritanism which, with its stolid inhibitions, was ultimately responsible for a reaction that went to dangerous extremes.[1] As to his famous prose story, *Under the Hill, a romantic novel* (1903), it would be absurd to ascribe to it any importance in the history of fiction. The rococo dedicatory epistle is a better jest even than the half mock-heroic, half sniggering account of the Lady Helen's toilet and the fopperies of the Abbé Fanfreluche. It would have been only a quizzical trifle, but for the illustrations which are an integral part of it: the story is simply a frame for these—these are the characters and substance of the whole invention.

Satires on the æsthetes   Of course, *Punch* was always making game of the æsthetes, and Burnand put them into a feeble burlesque, *The Colonel, an æsthetic comedy* (1881). But this had nothing like the success of *Patience*, already mentioned as of the same year: Gilbert's travesty of Wilde as Bunthorne was accepted as hitting off the type to a T. One parody came from a fellow-

Davidson, and St John Hankin deliberately took their lives. Over-indulgence in drink led to the premature deaths, in deplorable circumstances, of Lionel Johnson and Ernest Dowson. And this list could be extended" (*English Literature, 1880–1905,* by J. M. Kennedy, 2).

[1] On Beardsley's revenge upon the Victorians, his counterblast to the Victorian conspiracy of silence and the regular suppression of facts under the pretence of safeguarding morals, see *The Beardsley Period*, by Osbert Burdett, 113–116.

æsthete, the lady with the pen-name of "Vernon Lee," who disliked the extravagances of some of the other disciples of Pater. In *Miss Brown* (1884), Wilde is easily recognizable in the dandified Postlethwaite, along with caricatures of Whistler, Swinburne, and some of the Pre-Raphaelites. W. H. Mallock's attempt at Peacockian satire, *The New Republic: culture, faith, and philosophy, in an English country house* (1877), was too early for the æsthetes, though it caught some of their immediate predecessors, Ruskin, Arnold, and Pater. But it fell woefully short of Peacock's brilliance, coming to the ground between two stools, mere ventriloquism—literal reproduction, the mimicry that often satisfies a contemporary public—and genuine caricature. As a skit it is not skittish enough, and nowadays makes dreary reading.[1] Mallock was obviously one of the philistines. He turns Professor Clifford into middling farce; but Pater is not merely lampooned, he is libelled. Already, the outsider has a morbid suspicion of the æsthetic doctrine, which he thinks must be a cloak for constitutional depravity. Besant was content with broad humour in his fantasy, *The Monks of Thelema* (1878).[2] The satire that did most execution at the time was *The Green Carnation* (1894), by R. S. Hichens. It consists, in the main, of exaggerated versions of Wilde's topsy-turvy epigrams. But, as wit and humour can hardly be caricatured, only reproduced in a mechanical way, a lot of this without a break now tends to fall flat. As the straight and sober-minded young widow who rejects Lord Reggie, Oscar's mimic, sagely observes, "I can never love an echo, and you are an echo." This is all echo, cleverly magnified. It was good journalism then, but is not one of the satires that are read when the original butt is forgotten. Some of Max Beerbohm's pleasantries of the following years, friendly though they seem,

[1] But there is a comic stroke in the remark of a lady, who has been mystified by a Pateresque rhapsody of Mr Rose, not on the Gioconda, but someone like her: "What a very odd man Mr Rose is!" said Lady Ambrose in a loud whisper. "He always seems to talk of everybody as if they had no clothes on" (Bk. IV., chap. i.).

[2] A lively skit on clerical circles at the time of the Colenso case, and on smart society and contemporary frivolities, fads, and humbugs, such as Swedenborgian theosophy, the *Piccadilly* (1870) of the brilliant traveller and war-correspondent, Laurence Oliphant (1829–1888), is not quite forgotten. Oliphant continued his satire of social frauds and the mystical craze in *Altiora Peto* (1883).

are more searchingly critical of the philosophy of life expounded in *Intentions* and *Dorian Gray*; and the dud literary men, Enoch Soames and Savonarola Brown, in his *Seven Men* (1919), call up with biting urbanity the whole atmosphere of the days of Whistler and Rothenstein and the Bodley Head. A lighter, slighter, but more finely ironical satire, *The Autobiography of a Boy* (1894), by G. S. Street (1867–1937), came out the same year as *The Green Carnation*. The boy is a composite portrait, and the satire hits at the pretence of making a fine art of life, offering one's precious self as a work of art. Street let him tell his own story, in the complacent manner of those who know themselves to be a race apart, though they fear it is not really possible for a lower to "grasp a higher mind." [1] Chesterton was more boisterous in his disquisitions on the artistic temperament as "a disease that afflicts amateurs," and on the hampering excess of æstheticism in such as Whistler, who "really regarded Whistler as his greatest work of art." [2]

Æsthetic realism   Realistic transcription of even the uglier aspects of life, without a sigh at their ugliness, was a logical application of æsthetic principles. Various poets and other adherents of the cause practised it in the handy medium of the short story, which was now coming into fashion, largely through French influences. This had not been exactly a rarity in English literature; but it was only now that it began to rival the full-length novel in favour with both writers and readers. Hawthorne and Poe, the two classics in English, had cast their spell on novelists rather than story-tellers; it was their spirit and ideas rather than their compendious craftsmanship that had been the talisman. Bret Harte, Ambrose Bierce, and a crowd of lesser Americans were comparatively little known. No, the models were for the present almost exclusively French. Balzac had been a great master of the short story; but

---

[1] "His theory of life also compelled him to be sometimes drunk. In his first year he was a severe ritualist, in his second an anarchist and an atheist, in his third wearily indifferent to all things, in which attitude he remained in the two years since he left the University until now when he is gone from us." "He desired to be regarded as a man to whom no chaste woman should be allowed to speak, an aim he would mention wistfully, in a manner inexpressibly touching, for he never achieved it" (Editor's Apology, x.–xi.).

[2] *Heretics*—"On the Wit of Whistler."

Mérimée and still more Maupassant were now the fascinating exemplars. Hubert Crackanthorpe was to come as near reproducing the latter in English as anyone would ever do, and to be followed at more or less distance by the two Americans, Henry Harland, editor of *The Yellow Book*, and Frank Harris, Wilde's biographer, and then by "George Egerton," author of *Keynotes*, best remembered of the notorious "Keynote Series," and by Arthur Morrison, Edwin Pugh, St John Adcock, Pett Ridge, and many more slum novelists. The Cornishman, H. D. Lowry, put his village slum-dwellers, Methodists, and miners, into the same sort of frame; and writers as various as the facetious Barry Pain, the sociological Grant Allen, the witty extravaganzist, "F. Anstey," Richard Le Gallienne, loyal friend and apologist of the æsthetes, and Oscar Wilde's belated scion, Ronald Firbank, found this the most convenient standard pattern for their very miscellaneous goods. A much more conscientious artist, Henry James, was to naturalize the short story in England, as a distinct artistic genre, before he naturalized himself; and Stevenson, Conrad, the Scots Kailyard novelists, and the humorist, W. W. Jacobs, were to put most if not all of their best work into this form. Tolstoy had been known for some time in this country: he was the first of the Russians to be translated to any large extent. It was later that Turgenev became a stronger influence, and later still that Chekhov came to exercise such a spell that certain novelists, notably Katherine Mansfield, submitted themselves almost unreservedly to the sway of this great master of the art.

Meanwhile, French models and French criteria amply *Frederick* sufficed. A good instance among the rank and file is Frederick *Wedmore* Wedmore (1844–1921), best known as a connoisseur and professional critic of the fine arts, who for some time had been spending his leisure in writing tales the very names of which show where the inspiration came from—"A Last Love at Pornic," "Yvonne of Croisic," "The Four Bells of Chartres" —all in his *Pastorals of France* (1877). Later, a Provençal idyll gave the title to his *Orgeas and Miradou, with other pieces* (1896). In between appeared *Renunciations* (1893) and *English Episodes* (1894). "The New 'Marienbad-Elegy'" in this last, the Pornic story in the first set, and "The Vicar of Pimlico" in *Renunciations*, have much the same theme—an ageing person, with disarming melancholy, weighing the pros and cons of marriage with someone who would probably say "yes," but would be wronged by such a concession to sentiment. Tough-hearted readers will perhaps agree that the Vicar, for instance, is too much concerned with his own feelings to think of the lady's. Character-drawing is at a minimum; mild satire and mild sentiment are pleasingly blended with the spirit of place. In the "Elegy," the supposed author wonders why he is not chosen to succeed Tennyson as Poet Laureate, and states his private view of Lewis Morris, Alfred Austin, Edwin Arnold, Austin Dobson, Buchanan, and other candidates. But Wedmore discreetly uses a pseudonym in his dig at Whistler —"In force, suggestiveness, unity of impression, Nature, I pointed out to them, had not got much further than Collier's admirable Art."

Ernest And now Ernest Dowson (1867–1900), a charming minor
Dowson poet who wasted his genius and died young, learned as a writer of fiction from both Wedmore and Henry James, and so stands at a double remove from the French who were his ultimate preceptors. Unfortunately, he had time for very little: *Dilemmas, stories and studies in sentiment* (1895), and *Decorations in prose and verse* (1899), are all that he left, apart from his poetry. There is little here of the harsh realism of Crackanthorpe, who had already published *Wreckage*: Dowson was a poet, and too much wrapped up in the inner life to take Maupassant as his model. These are, indeed, studies in emotion, sentiment, conflicting motive, in which the author does not always hold himself absolutely aloof, or at any rate absolutely insensible. The dilemma in "A Case of Conscience" is, as the title suggests, a piece of casuistry: shall Murch tell the girl he is engaged to that he has divorced his wife, now he has learned that as a Catholic she is forbidden to marry a man divorced? Two minds are tortured and perplexed, for Tregellan, who has just told him this, also loves the girl; and Murch protests, "you are no right arbiter here." "The Diary of a Successful Man" is more hopelessly poignant. He

comes back to Bruges at the end of a career in India, and finds out by accident that the woman he loved did not reject him twenty years ago, and that his exile was a useless sacrifice of what would have been the greatest thing in life. Delphine had put the letters in the wrong envelopes; and Lorimer, his old friend and rival, had let him go without confessing that she had discovered the mistake. Delphine takes the veil. She belongs to the Dames Rouges, the strictest, the most austere, and most sternly secluded of all the orders. The lovers hear her magnificent voice rising above the rest, in the Church of the Dames Rouges.

Lorimer was still kneeling with bowed head in his place. Presently he rose and came towards me. "She was there—Delphine—you heard her. Ah, Dion, she loves you, she always loves you ; you are avenged."

"An Orchestral Violin" and "Souvenirs of an Egoist" are vivisections of sentiment or of the cynical converse. The dilemma lies in the unanalysed remainder left in the brilliant prima donna, Madame Romanoff, or in the egoistic soul of the world-famed violinist, Baron Antonelli, listening to an air in the street, and brooding over his callous disregard for Ninette, the little organ-grinder who rescued him when he was a street-arab. Has the sceptical critic who tells the story wronged Madame Romanoff? Should he have gone himself to give her the priceless violin, left by the poor old music-master who had long ago befriended her? Had she been sincere in inviting him, and had he been pusillanimous? It is an insoluble alternative. The Baron has no patience with the people who rant about the "passionate sympathy" of his playing, the "enormous potentiality of suffering" revealed in his music; he knows that he is composed of "vanity and egoism"; but, apparently, Dowson would admit that this is a possible foundation for sentimentalism, to judge by his Lady Greville, one of the "three most cynical persons in the universe." "Yet for all her cynicism Lady Greville, I know, has a bundle of old and faded letters, tied up in ribbon in some hidden drawer . . . that she can never forget or destroy." At all events, it is not cynicism or

sentiment that makes the lover, coming home with his pile
from Chile to marry the girl whom he has loved for fifteen years,
drop himself quietly over the bulwarks one dark night. He,
the man he now is, simply cannot face the woman she has now
become.

The notion of the woman which now she was, came between
him and the girl whom he had loved, whom he still loved with
passion, and separated them.   It was only on our voyage home,
when we walked the deck interminably during the hot, sleepless
nights, that he first revealed to me, without subterfuge, the
slow agony by which this phantom slew him.

Hubert
Crackan-
thorpe
Dowson is neat and workmanlike, but he has not the austere
economy of Crackanthorpe, nor the cold impassibility.   Hubert
Crackanthorpe (1865–1896) was one of those who held forth in
The Yellow Book [1] on the heresy of didacticism, urging that
art, when sincere and truthful, has a subtle morality that need
not be expressed. Of the novelists most heavily in debt across
the Channel, Gissing, George Moore, Frank Harris, Dowson,
Harland, and the rest, he was the strictest observer of the
integrity of his art, and the closest parallel, though on an almost
miniature scale, to one eminent French novelist. He was as
scrupulously objective as Maupassant, and like him could
dispense with analysis, for no one was ever a better proof of
George Moore's dictum, already quoted, "That which is firmly
and clearly imagined needs no psychology." [2]   He never drops
a comment, though the relentless realism with which appalling
truths are set down almost amounts to an indictment of society,
nay, of human nature.   In *Wreckage, seven studies* (1893), he
took a full look at some of the ugliest things at the back of our
civilization.   Crackanthorpe stooped to none of Maupassant's
concessions to the baser sort of reader; but in his two or three
tiny volumes he dealt uncompromisingly with subjects fouler
and more terrible than any faced by Gissing or George Moore,
in their most Zolaesque phases. Impeccable workmanship
and a style of beautiful precision seemed to mark him out as a
great novelist to be. Fortunately, there is no humour in

[1] July, 1894.   [2] *Avowals*, 176.

Wreckage or in *Sentimental Studies*: humour would have been more intolerable than Maupassant's fits of cynical laughter. He did not live long enough to seek and find beauty. It is as impossible to say what Crackanthorpe would have made of his authentic fragment of genius, as to know his state of mind when he threw himself into the Seine at the age of thirty-one. Two of his best studies are of literary men. In "A Conflict of Egoisms," a novelist of "the idealist school," who has inadvertently slid into marriage with another person well past the age of mutual assimilation, and is dumbfounded and helpless when she proves to be a woman with flesh-and-blood instincts, fills his pockets with stones, but drops dead before he can fling himself from the bridge. This man's mental affinity with Crackanthorpe was slight, however; and the writer in "A Commonplace Chapter" in *Sentimental Studies* is branded as absorbed, perhaps, in "a mere literary melancholy, assimilated from certain passages of Pierre Loti." Crackanthorpe rarely allows himself even so much explanatory reference as that, confining himself to a plain, dispassionate statement of the facts. These are both studies of married life, a theme that proves as fertile in tragic oppositions as courtship or illicit love. The "Commonplace Chapter" is lengthy, his nearest approximation to a novel. It traces stage by stage the long and painful, and even at the end only perfunctory, process of mutual adjustment between an ordinary, egotistic man and a girl completely ignorant of life, whom he has married to the astonishment of his smart friends. But it is *Wreckage* that directs the searchlight upon the things which are usually covered up. In "Profiles" are traced with terrible infallibility the irresponsible steps by which an inexperienced girl suddenly finds herself upon the streets. The grim counterpart in a lower sphere is "The Struggle for Life"—there is significance in that "The." This time the tragedy is enacted in the slums and a low Thames-side drinking-den. With what deadly insight Crackanthorpe shows the superfluousness of psychological analysis, when it is instinct and simple incompatibilities that cut the knot! The girl about to be married yields without hesitation and without a qualm to the stranger who appeals to her senses; and when the cheated lover comes to save her, at all costs, from the dreadful occupation that has brought her near death's door, she turns on him:

" Look here," she interrupted almost fiercely. "It's no good your going on about it. I could never marry a man I didn't love. And I don't love you. I thought I did once. But it was all different then."

These are not so much stories, as cross-sections of life, with a story implied rather than told—enough to establish a dramatic crisis, the upshot of which can be logically deduced. There is no cynicism, but sometimes a murderous irony, as in "Dissolving View," where the rich young sensualist, who has been profoundly relieved to hear of the death of his mistress and her babe, returns to eat a hearty breakfast, "for the morning excursion had given him a splendid appetite."

A month afterwards, Gwynnie and he were married. It was a smart wedding. There was a fashionable crowd, and the couple started to spend their honeymoon in Italy.

But the objective method passes safely over far more complex deeps in such a story as "A Dead Woman." This is related almost entirely in the talks between two old cronies, one the bereaved husband, the other the friend who, as he gradually pieces together, betrayed him with her. She was the beauty of the country-side, and now it almost comes to murder between them. But, as time goes on, they see things differently. "Each remembered that she had belonged to the other, and, at that moment, they felt instinctively drawn together: each was conscious of a craving to talk about her, to hear the other mention her name." The second collection should have been called "Unsentimental Studies of Sentiment," not, however, of sentimentality. Such, for instance, is the sombre "In Cumberland," which curiously resembles in idea George Moore's novel, *The Lake*. "Battledore and Shuttlecock," again, is a most unsentimental study of a highly sentimental affair—the innocent amour of an unspoiled youth and a courtesan, grateful to him for such a taste of true friendship.

"Anthony Garstin's Courtship," in the posthumous *Last Studies* (1897), is another small masterpiece. *Vignettes, a miniature journal of whim and sentiment* (1896), shows Crackanthorpe in another light, but still one of the æsthetes. The word-painting of scenery and the seasons, in London and abroad, is done with a strength of vision hitherto held in check. Here is a fragment from a reverie on sunrise, in the twilight before dawn:

> To scout the future; to unlearn the past; and to brood vaguely, as the night broods. . . . To elude desire; to disdain the thrill of hate; to forget the long aching of love, and to commune, in tender serenity, with the grave-eyed Spirit of Rest. And then, while the night slinks away across the hills, to push on towards the sunrise; to watch the marshalling of ruddy heralds across the East, and at last to meet the Great God's dazzling glory, bursting in splendour across the empty land.

Novelists had now resolutely asserted the right to choose their subjects where they listed, and to treat them with the utmost candour. Arthur Morrison chose the same kind as Gissing, in *Tales of Mean Streets* (1894), *A Child of the Jago* (1896), *To London Town* (1899), and *The Hole in the Wall* (1902), diverging into rural Essex in *Cunning Murrell* (1900) and *Green Ginger* (1909). But it was Crackanthorpe and Maupassant who were his artistic patterns. Edwin Pugh [1] (1874–1930) was another follower of Gissing, and of their common master Dickens. The impressionist sketches of people and manners in *A Street in Suburbia* (1895) were followed by *Tony Drum, a Cockney boy* (1898), in which he sought to vie with *Oliver Twist*, and this by the story of a gaol-bird's sturdy and self-reliant daughter, *Mother-Sister* (1900), and a long series of novels very much like Gissing's, except that he tried to rid himself of the dejection that weighed on his rival and to infuse a little humour. *The Spoilers* (1906), *The Broken Honeymoon* (1908), *The Quick and the Dead, a tragedy of temperaments* (1914), and *The Eyes of*

Followers of Gissing, Moore, and Crackanthorpe

---

[1] Pugh has been singled out for a dissertation (1934) by T. E. M. Boll (University of Pennsylvania), which is so thoroughgoing as to have a section on his use of typography.

a Child (1917) are as good as any in his industrious output, which in spite of his efforts is sadly lacking in gusto. William Pett Ridge (1860–1930) was more sentimental and even more prolific in novels of Cockney life, ranging from the slum-folk of *Mord Em'ly* (1898), the lower middle-class people of *Outside the Radius* (1899), and the Hoxton street-arab in *A Son of the State* (1899), to post-war immigrants to Wood Green, in *Well-to-do Arthur* (1920). Arthur St John Adcock (1864–1930) may go with the same group, on the strength of his efforts to give literary form to studies of the very poor, in *East End Idylls* (1897) and *In the Image of God* (1898). It was some years later that the poet Mr W. H. Davies raised a sensation with his *Autobiography of a Super-Tramp* (1908); but it must not be overlooked that Hardy's *Tess of the d'Urbervilles* and *Jude the Obscure* both appeared in the first half of the nineties. The problem of evil, especially social evil, was much to the fore. One highly serious sociological study of the poor as the essential complement to the over-rich, *No. 5 John Street* (1899), by Richard Whiteing (1840–1928), was thrown, not ineffectively, into the form of a novel. And the work of Arnold Bennett and Galsworthy, of Somerset Maugham and Frank Swinnerton, and some of that of H. G. Wells and Kipling, is closely affiliated to this mass of realism applied to the humbler walks of life; several of them, in fact, had already started on these lines. The novels and tales of another sociologist, Grant Allen (1848–1899), stand on a different footing. He was as serious as Whiteing, but he had a lighter touch than most of those of the scientific outlook. *Philistia* (1877) laughed the pioneer socialists out of court; *The Woman who Did* (1895), his bold vindication of free love, actually did more for the emancipation of women than any amount of arguing, by dint of the calm self-assurance with which the doings of his antinomians are recounted and philistine protests made to look foolish. The fact is, Grant Allen had a touch of " F. Anstey's " comic power, though Anstey was a professional humorist, a regular member of the staff of *Punch*, and only once stooped to anything more serious than to laugh divers fads and absurdities out of existence. Anstey's inimitable *Vice-Versa, or a lesson to fathers* (1882), with its change of personality between a boy at school and his father, staid Mr Bultitude, appeared two years before his senior's *Philistia*. It was succeeded but not ousted in popular esteem by extravaganzas with a more definite satirical target, such as *The Tinted Venus* (1885), *A Fallen Idol* (1886), and *The Brass Bottle* (1900); whilst a running fire on modes and manners and passing crazes was kept up in *Voces Populi*. His one serious novel, *The Pariah* (1889), failed of its deserts; after that Anstey never tried to get out of the rut he had worn so deep.

But the most striking and original supplement to the work *Zangwill* of the native slum-novelists came from a writer who was an Englishman indeed, and a Londoner born, but a Jew of the Jews, whose impressive studies of his own people are probably the greatest contribution of modern times to the literature of Jewry. Israel Zangwill (1864–1926), after a first novel that was only clever, found his proper mission when he was invited to write a novel on the Jews of to-day. *Children of the Ghetto, being pictures of a peculiar people* (1892), was a rich portrait of Jews of all classes in London, from the most miserable refugee to the aristocrat of the race, and as sound in the picturing of general as of individual traits. Zangwill was not a creative artist; but he knew his people as intimately as his master Dickens knew his. He was not devoid of humour, as his farces and extravaganzas show; but he also had a tragic grip of essentials that comes out strongly in *Ghetto Tragedies* (1893) and *They that walk in Darkness* (1899). His peculiar endowment, however, was his command of local colour, in the broadest sense of the term; in this he rivalled Kipling, who was making his début about the same time. In *The King of Schnorrers, grotesques and fantasies* (1894), this served him even in a raid upon Jewish beggars and vagabonds of the eighteenth century; whilst in *Dreamers of the Ghetto* (1898) he used his knowledge to paint speaking likenesses of some of the most illustrious of his kindred—Uriel Acosta, Maimonides, Spinoza, Heine, Lassalle. Two non-Jewish novels, *The Master* (1895), imaginary biography of a Nova Scotia lad and at the same time a philosophic study of moral problems, and *The Mantle of Elijah* (1900), a political satire, are able performances; but his best example of local colour and human interest outside his special sphere is the Essex novel, *Jinny the Carrier* (1919).

Some miscel- laneous æsthetes —David- son

Long before his "Testaments," the unhappy and rebellious Scots poet, John Davidson (1857–1909), wrote some strange novels, which proclaim and yet seem to scoff at the individualist philosophy which he had assimilated from Nietzsche. Perhaps the key to them is his lyrical pantomime, *Scaramouch in Naxos* (1889); but it is a key that will leave the average reader more bewildered than ever, the general sentiment being nowhere more distinctly summed up than in the catch sung by satyrs and bacchantes:

> Drink, my gallants; reel and rhyme!
> Though our souls are second-rate,
> We are none the less sublime:
> Drink, and give the lie to fate!

Perfervid, the career of Ninian Jamieson (1890), is best interpreted as a pantomime in prose. The hero—but, as usual with Davidson, only a pseudo-hero—is a Scots provost, of lordly presence and great wealth, derived from whisky, who claims to be the last of the Stuarts. Attended by a farcical squire, Cosmo Mortimer, originally Hugh Smith, who is everlastingly disputing about the fateful significance of names, he sets out on a hare-brained campaign to recover the Scottish crown. It comes to a speedy and inglorious conclusion, mainly through Davidson's inability to keep the ball rolling. He suffered from a curious lack of invention, and had hardly an elementary idea of structure. In the appended tale in the Bunyan style, "The Pilgrimage of Strongsoul and Saunders Elshander," Ninian's son goes on a holy war to reform the world, fights giants and errand-boys, and incidentally rescues an heiress. Davidson's incurable formlessness appears again glaringly in his next fiction in prose, *Baptist Lake* (1894), the salient figure in which is a would-be superman who proves to be a conceited humbug, rehearsing his postures and bons-mots beforehand, and using them on different people until inadvertently he tries them on the same person, and is found out. Some of the less pre-

tentious Scots folk do, however, drop some racy aphorisms.[1]
But the story seems a missfire rather than a skit. *Earl Lavender*
(1895),[2] on which Aubrey Beardsley conferred a frontispiece,
had better also be regarded as a pantomine; it is a burlesque
picture of contemporary decadence, in colours that leave it
doubtful whether the author was satirical or complacent.
Davidson is good reading in patches. Sometimes his Rabelais-
ian humour comes off, too often it falls flat. But he was a poet;
and, if that be remembered, the same sort of elfin beauty will
now and then be recognized in his wilder flights as over and
over again in his ballads and testaments.

Another fantasist, who might almost be paired with the most *Kenneth*
exquisite of all modern tellers of fairy-stories, Lewis Carroll, a *Grahame*
quarter-of-a-century his elder, was Kenneth Grahame; but
there is actually a very important difference between these two.
Both viewed the world poetically, both were inspired by the
ingenuous fallacies and passionate make-believe of the childish
mind. Both rejoiced in the glory of nonsense, and also in the
subtle affinities of sense and nonsense. But, whereas the
author of *Alice's Adventures in Wonderland* (1865) and *Through
the Looking-Glass* (1871), and of the history of *Sylvie and Bruno*
(1889–1893), has always been able to enrapture children of
every age, up to the ripest manhood and womanhood, Kenneth
Grahame's appeal is only to those readers whose intellects have
matured yet have not forgotten the emotions of childhood. In
The Golden Age (1895) and *Dream Days* (1898) the things of
childhood are seen through a mist of dreamy longing: it is
impressionism again. So too, only a grown-up intelligence will
enter into the sophisticated make-believe and the humorous
interchange of the human and the animals' point of view, in
The Wind in the Willows (1908), or even the bubbling lyricism
of the Rat's vision of the great god Pan—"O, Mole! the beauty
of it!" "Such music I never dreamed of, and the call in it is
stronger even than the music is sweet! Row on, Mole, row!

[1] *E.g.* "Whenever you find a man with a hobby you may know he has no soul."
"Baptist was the actor; and it is always the simple-minded who imitate the self-
conscious."

[2] The title has been cut down here to these two words, out of some
thirty.

For the music and the call must be for us." [1] It is a more
playful and fanciful thing than Kipling's *Jungle Books*; but
the imaginative hold upon both the two worlds, the wild and
the human, and the deep sense of their fellowship, are just as
strong, and the fantasy in this case is enhanced with a very
delicate irony. It is almost a satire.

Du Maurier and De Morgan The black-and-white artist, George du Maurier (1834–1897),
who was half-French and bilingual, being born in Paris of a
French father and an English mother and educated in this
country, put a good deal of personal reminiscence of Bohemian
and more sedate society in France and Belgium into his three
novels, *Peter Ibbetson* (1894), *Trilby* (1895), and *The Martian*
(1898), the last of which was written round the dream of a
visitant from Mars and has a utopian flavour, which comes out
in his illustrations to the book. Du Maurier knew Thackeray,
and was one of his minor disciples; he was not uninfluenced
also in his domestic fiction by his admiration for Mrs Gaskell.
Many artists and others of his circle at home and abroad can be
identified among his characters; Whistler was so annoyed at
his portrait in the serial edition of *Trilby* that it had to be cut
out of the book. There were touches of the occult in *Peter
Ibbetson*; and *Trilby*, which had extraordinary success on the
stage, was a story of hypnotic influence over a beautiful girl.
Like many others mentioned here, Du Maurier was a connexion
of the æsthetes only by the accidents of time and place. [2]
Another novelist who would probably never have written had
he not been all his life an enthusiastic student of Dickens was
William de Morgan (1839–1917). This is not to say that De
Morgan was devoid of originality. On the contrary, when at
the age of sixty-six, after devoting half a lifetime to reviving
old processes in making pottery and lustre-ware, he began

[1] It is a pity Grahame blemished this delightful episode with his blunder over the
moon, which rises, traverses the heavens, and sets, all in the space between an hour or
two after ten and the dark before dawn in spring.
[2] As Richard Le Gallienne points out (*The Romantic '90s*, 122), the "yellow" and
"naughty" and "decadent" writers and artists were not so very numerous. "Even
that group of writers most closely identified with this aspect of the '90s was only
accidentally a group, and, being all of them strikingly independent individuals, had
really very little in common. Indeed, when we examine their work, one might
almost say that they had nothing in common but—a publisher"—*i.e.* John Lane.

writing fiction, he had a great fund of the right sort of experience and a whole gallery of characters at the back of his mind, ready to be set in motion in rambling and easygoing stories. He was, veritably, a modern Dickens; but a mild and attenuated Dickens, with much of the goodness and few of the glaring faults, but with little of the genius of his great master. De Morgan was, first and foremost, a character-monger, expert at resuscitating the originals of the London streets in his old days, and the figures of well-loved friends. His novels are full of genuine portraits, admirably lifelike, and flavoured with something that gives them a curious hold on the reader's affection. An original novelist has revelations to make, even if he writes solely about the past. In this sense, De Morgan was irrelevant; he had nothing for his age. A second time he revived a lost art, and offered his contemporaries some admirable gallery-pieces. But his novels are too plainly resurrections: after once enjoying their charm, nobody wants to re-read them— the infallible test. The first was *Joseph Vance, an ill-written autobiography* (1906), a leisurely outpouring of reminiscence, in which the best of a number of odd characters is old Mr Vance, a curious mixture of acute and muddled thinking—the self-made man whose rise to fortune begins with his lucky purchase of a second-hand signboard, and who lets fall such profound remarks as this on practical sagacity: "Only just as much as a man is born with when he's lived among tradesmen all his life." His "picters of Stags before Letters" or "Stags without Words," due to a confused recollection of something played from Mendelssohn, are an unmeant joke not to be forgotten. Joseph's mother, and her successor, the maid-of-all-work permanently known as Miss Dowdeswell, Dr Thorpe and his delectable family, especially Lossie and Jane, are the gems of a brilliant galaxy. Yet they are no finer than Alice, the girl rescued from a dreadful home, in *Alice-for-Short, a dichronism* (1907); or Charlie Heath, a self-portrait, who rescues her; or his sister Peggy. Then, Pope & Chappell, the Catholic and Protestant firm of church-window manufacturers, the pathetic old Verrinder, and the bevy of youngsters, stand out in a medley rich in humour and pathos, whose lives are followed through a quarter of a century. *Somehow Good* (1908) illustrated De Morgan's interest in psychical theories, the plot turning on a man's loss of memory through an accident and the amazing complications that precede its recovery—a theme rather like those in *The Old Madhouse* (1919) and *The Old Man's Youth* (1921), both of which he left unfinished. The long-winded *It never can happen again* (1909) combined two main plots: one the case of a jealous wife and a husband's straying affections, at the time of the Deceased Wife's Sister's Bill, which puts her matrimonial rights in jeopardy; the other a "Little Nell" story of a blind old sailor and his daughter. *When Ghost meets Ghost* (1914) sets in motion a vast complication of circumstance, culminating in the rediscovery of each other by two devoted sisters when they are long past middle age. But in every book it is the wealth of diverse character and the loving scrutiny of motive that fills out the ample framework. Sentiment, more than humour, was the keynote; and nothing makes a wider, or more immediate, and also a less permanent appeal, as those other literary descendants of the Man of Feeling, the Kailyard novelists, were demonstrating almost at the same time.

Ronald   Ronald Firbank (1886–1926) was a belated straggler from the
Firbank æsthetic rearguard, who astonished an innocent second decade of the twentieth century with his revival of the cynical perversions of Beardsley and Oscar Wilde and his own delicately indelicate jests. Like Wilde, he began with an essay in the style of Andersen, *Odette, a fairy-tale for weary people* (1905), about a little French girl who wanders out from a château on the Loire, and rescues a desperate woman from her evil life. But it was ten years later that, with *Vainglory* (1915), *Inclinations* (1916), and *Caprice* (1917), he showed himself possessed of a new and curiously efficient mode of impressionism, rapidly and vividly conveying, without describing anything or telling any story, the attitudes and affectations and the simpering accents of the half-real types in Mayfair society or cosmopolitan pleasure-cities by tropic strands, which were his chosen material. His peculiar object is to evade formal narrative. There is, in truth, no story to tell. The characters, who are so

vaguely outlined that they might be interchangeable, talk aimlessly, and in an absentminded way utter witticisms that are funny without malice prepense: for the most part, in fact, just agreeable nonsense. The scene is evoked by adjectives that are simply dashes of colour. One hears of "a witty frock" which is "a perfect psalm." A lady sits "on a piece of crumbling richness in the long grass." "Miss Thumbler was a mediæval-looking little thing, with peculiar pale ways, like a creature escaped through the border of violets and wild strawberries of a tapestry panel." Then there is the small talk. "You'd never credit it, dear, but we were the same age once." "Never mind, Mr Harvester," Lady Georgia was saying, "I'm sure your play was exquisite, or it would have had a longer run." A lady about to be received into the Roman Catholic Church observes, "I shall need a frock for my conversion . . . and another for my reconversion, in case that's necessary." "My manicurist has left me with such claws," says another. "Poor little soul! When she came to my wedding-finger she just twiddled her rasp and broke out crying, 'To be filing people's nails,' she said, ' while my husband is filing a petition!'" This is from *Caprice*, a pretty little fantasy of theatrical life; the others are gentle quips from *Vainglory*, the tale of an old lady who wants to immortalize herself in a stained-glass window. Firbank had an itch for the suggestive and even the obscene; a little oxygen is wanted for some of the nastiness in *Valmouth* (1919), talked chiefly by women, in a variety of lingos. Life, one of the characters says somewhere, is "an utter hoax."

Prancing Nigger (1925) is a good example of the story that *"Pranc-* enacts itself. A nigger family quit the village where they have *ing* run naked, for the city of Cuna-Cuna, to make their way into *Nigger"* the highest social circles.

From motives of economy and ease, it had been decided that not before Cuna-Cuna should rear her queenly towers above them would they change their floral garlands for the more artificial fabrics of the town, and Edna, vastly to her importance, go into a pair of frilled "invisibles" and a petticoat for the first amazing time; nor, indeed, would Mr Mouth himself "take to de pants" until his wife and daughter should have assumed their skirts.

The real mistress of the situation is Mrs Mouth, who wants the goluptious Miami to "'come out"; her husband, Prancing Nigger, has religion, calls Cuna-Cuna the modern Sodom, and emits groans and exhortations as diverting as those of Mr Burchell. At Cuna-Cuna they see the fairy wonders of the City of Moonstones, but from the back seats, and it is from a distance that they admire the millionaires and duchesses among the birds of passage, and Madame Ruiz and the Archbishop who are permanent grandees in this metropolis of pleasure. An earthquake interrupts the perpetual festivities; and a great intercessional is held in the cathedral, assisted by hired singers from the opera-house; but Miami the débutante is distraite amid the excitements: her lover has been caught by a shark.

"Why you so triste, Chile?   Dair no good at all in frettin'."
"Sho' nuff."
"Dat death was on de cards, my deah, an' dair is no mistakin' de fac'; an' as de shark is a rapid feeder it all ober sooner dan wid de crocodile, which is some consolation for dose dat remain to mourn."

It is like a talking film.

CHAPTER VII

HENRY JAMES

AN exhaustive account of the novels of Henry James (1843– *Henry* 1916) is not called for in a history of English fiction; but the *James* work of the great American has had such a subversive effect upon the methods of other novelists, and even upon the general conception and status of the art, that a number of his stories and novels which have been chiefly instrumental in these results must of necessity be examined.[1] James came early into the field as a champion of æsthetic views. In 1884, a lecture by Walter Besant on "The Art of Fiction" [2] drew a reply from James, maintaining the right of the novelist to choose his subject and deal with it according to his own ideas, free from the obligation to insinuate any sort of lesson. Besant's plea was for the professional dignity of the novelist; he protested against the general view that he was a mere entertainer. But he based his case largely on the "teaching power" and moral influence of fiction. Of all the Arts—

it is the most moral, because the world has always been taught whatever little morality it possesses by way of story, fable, apologue, parable, and allegory. It commands the widest influence, because it can be carried easily and everywhere into regions where pictures are never seen and music is never heard.

James replied that a work of art must be judged solely by its

[1] Henry James became a naturalized Englishman, but this would not justify kid-napping him and making him out to be an English novelist. On the other hand, the editors of the "English Men of Letters" series have thought proper to include volumes on Hawthorne, Whitman, and Herman Melville, and presumably will not spare James.

[2] Published under this title (1885). James's reply appeared in *Longman's Magazine* (September, 1884), and was incorporated in *Partial Portraits* (1888). See also above, p. 168, on Maupassant's preface to *Pierre et Jean*.

artistic qualities, with which these moral considerations have nothing to do whatever.[1] Some, like Stevenson, were troubled by the confusion between truth of science and truth of art, a point debated to much the same effect in "A Humble Remonstrance" and in Wilde's essay, "The Decay of Lying." As James put it, the work of art is not required to be an exact representation of life as seen through a lens: the novelist, or any other artist, is not like the man of science; he is not called upon for a mathematical statement of the facts, such as can be verified by other observers. The truth required lies in the fullness and perfection and the vivid sense of reality with which the artist transmits his personal view of life. And the romantic artist has the same rights as the realist; he likewise succeeds according to the degree of perfection with which his personal vision is embodied in the concrete work. "A novel is, in its broadest definition, a personal, a direct impression of life; that, to begin with, constitutes its value, which is greater or less according to the intensity of the impression." "The air of reality (solidity of specification)" is the supreme virtue. In novels and stories carefully thought out beforehand, in prefaces setting forth his intentions, and in critical studies of other novelists, prose fiction was now definitely annexed to the realm of art, or, rather, it was proclaimed an integral part of that territory; and James proceeded to codify the laws and ordinances holding authority in what had hitherto been a no-man's-land. He gradually developed and formulated a complete science of the art of fiction; although he restricted himself to a more specialized art, or province of that art.

The limits he set himself For James assigned to himself, or found that he must accept, a number of limitations, and refrained from certain modes of realism that he did not deny were just as legitimate. His outlook on life was circumscribed by the nature of his experience, his interests, and his tastes. Personally, he was not greatly interested in man's reactions to external nature; and he never spared a glance for the wider social and the economic problems

[1] "We are discussing the art of Fiction; questions of art are questions (in the widest sense) of execution; questions of morality are quite another affair, and will you not let us see how it is that you find it so easy to mix them up?"

vexing humanity at large. His sphere was the novel of manners, and a curiously restricted novel of manners, concerned with a limited class, the rich and leisured, highly civilized, over-sophisticated, international society, that has no particular country or at any rate easily finds itself at home anywhere. These people he studied from the point of view of the develop-ment of character through the friction, the give-and-take, of social intercourse and personal relations. From the patient observation and analysis of actual life, first American and then European and international, having matured a technique, he went on to imagine modes of life beyond the actual, or, at least, the normal—exotic characters, bizarre situations, strange and complex motives. Finally, on still higher levels of imagin-ative art, he showed characters of finer mould, rare and exquisite but free from these abnormal conditions, involved in dramas of contrary motives that illustrated his ultimate conception of life—exquisite refinements of feeling, a more sensitive insight, higher values, in which the ethical and the æsthetic factors were indistinguishable. Life has indeed become a fine art in the thoughts and feelings that dictate the actions of those self-conscious beings, in the last few of his novels. From beginning to end, the most interesting question in human life, that of right and wrong, was a favourite dramatic motive with James, strictly though he repudiated any purpose beyond that of watching and exhibiting the conflict. He was himself apparently obsessed by an acute and even a morbid sense of the evil openly or stealthily operating against all of us. "If ever a man's imagination was clouded by the Pit," says one critic, "it was James's."[1] But he solved the ethical problem, so far as his work in fiction is concerned, by attaining a region where beauty and goodness melt into each other, and where he felt himself in touch with beings and modes of life that transcend general codes of behaviour. And he remained a realist. For to the very end he wrought upon the artistic principle that the novelist has to produce imaginary creations answering in

---

[1] "Henry James," by Graham Greene, 223 (*The English Novelists*, ed. Derek Verschoyle, 1916). This essay deals especially with *The Turn of the Screw* and other stories of ghostly and other agencies of moral corruption.

feature and action to those moving in the other element, actual space and time, and that by maintaining the rhythm of life he conveys the illusion of reality.[1]

Early novels and tales

James, the son of a wealthy and scholarly American, and brother of the philosophic writer William James, was educated partly at home and partly in Europe, and at an early date began to look upon himself as cosmopolitan. After long hesitation, he made up his mind to pitch his tent in London, in 1877, and to make this the central point of view in his fiction. There is no need to dwell on the stories and novels with American scenes published before 1875, the date of *A Passionate Pilgrim, and other tales*, which are good examples of his international fiction. The title-story here, which had appeared in the *Atlantic Monthly* in 1871, is the tale of a romantic young American who believes himself the heir to an English estate. Anglomania with him is a dreamy, poetic passion. The companion story, "Madame de Mauves," is a more serious study of racial incompatibilities. Madame de Mauves is of American birth but French schooling, and is married to an aristocrat who cynically neglects her for his mistresses. Her portrait is given through Longmore, a New Englander who meets her at St-Germain-en-Laye and straightway falls in love. The French husband is only too happy to give him encouragement; but the lady entreats him to go. The uncompromising ideals of purity and honour which she drank in with her mother's milk, heightened if possible by the romanticism that led to her marriage, are proof against her wrongs and her deep attraction towards her countryman. He must sacrifice his passion to those ideals. Years later, he learns that Monsieur de Mauves came to recognize his wife's magnanimity and beauty of character; but it was too late: she was obdurate, and he blew his brains out. James is himself here a New Englander of the purest water. It hardly occurs to Longmore that he might well face the risks and capture the fortress by storm. The difference between Longmore and Strether, the emissary who, in *The Ambassadors*,

[1] "The Art of Fiction" (*Partial Portraits*, 398). "Catching the very note and trick, the strange irregular rhythm of life, that is the attempt whose strenuous force keeps Fiction upon her feet."

deliberately surrenders to the charm and superlative fineness of the French social economy, is the difference between the early and the later Henry James.

There is a technical anticipation of Strether and others in the "*Roderick Hudson*" riper novels who serve as mirrors and interpreters of what goes on, in the novel published the same year, *Roderick Hudson*. Roderick's benefactor, Rowland Mallet, is the one who has his eye on him and the rest of the company, and it is Mallet's observations and reflections that compose the record. This is a résumé of the strength and the weakness of genius, the artistic temperament at the extreme of its aberrations. It is constructed, however, on old-fashioned lines, with formal introductions and sketches of the characters, and summaries of antecedent events; James had not yet evolved his finer modes of conveying necessary information. Adopted by a wealthy friend, rescued from drudgery in a lawyer's office, and supplied with the wherewithal to study at Rome, Roderick Hudson first makes a flare: his genius achieves two or three works of eminent merit, and it looks as if he will be a great sculptor. But he is exhausted at once; his imagination fails, and his will is not strong enough to revive it. How or why is not made perfectly clear: psychologically this is perfunctory work according to James's later standards.[1] At all events, Rowland Mallet does not understand his protégé, even if James does. The wild inconsequence of Roderick's character now emerges. He has no conscience, except, perhaps, the artistic one, which is sensitive in its peculiar way. He flings himself at the feet of the dangerous Christina Light, outrages the affection of the sterling Mary Garland, his betrothed, flouts his benefactor, and at length sinks into the lethargy of despair, from which death frees him. To Mallet, he seems little else than a beautiful, irresponsible animal; yet he compels pity, if not love, useless as he is. There are depths of character in Mary Garland; but she is eclipsed by the more showy qualities of the adventuress Christina, a creation whose unscrupulousness is matched by her

---

[1] James admitted, in his introduction to this in the collected edition of his novels, that he had telescoped the process of Roderick's going to pieces, and generally neglected the time element (*The Art of Fiction*, 12).

magnanimity: her towering personality was too interesting to be thrown away, and James pursued her career ten years later in *The Princess Casamassima* (1886), a work of much bolder technique.

"*The Ameri-can*" His next big novel, *The American* (1877), was an almost scientific study of internationalism, bringing into a revealing light the differences of manners and breeding, of traditional standards and ideals, and the utter impossibility of reconciling such opposites, even when there is a desire for mutual understanding. The eternal war of the patrician and the commercial classes is embittered by the remoteness of an old-world aristocracy, with its roots deep in the past, from the new nation of shopkeepers across the Atlantic. A self-made American comes over to enjoy his pile. He is admitted to these exclusive circles, and a lady who has him under her wing suggests that he should enter into a matrimonial alliance with the daughter of an ancient house. Newman's wealth opens the door. The family put no obstacles, and he becomes engaged to the beautiful Madame de Cintré. There are dinners and balls, at which the most august representatives of this social world, a world that keeps itself apart and uncontaminated by the ordinary run of mankind, give the outsider a sort of guarded approval. But, almost imperceptibly, a change comes over the scene. The powers that be in this supercilious realm at length deliver their verdict: the alliance cannot be permitted. In love with Newman though she is, the countess will not disobey the family decree. He pleads her engagement, and argues that she is a free agent. She is not free. She is enslaved by the traditions of a caste as rigid as those of Hindustan. When James has recourse to melodrama, and Newman discovers a criminal secret that threatens the head of the house with infamy and ruin if divulged, the only result is a fiercer antipathy; and the lady forestalls the very possibility of changing her mind by entering a Carmelite nunnery. A tragic note sounds in the pages that tell how Claire goes to her living tomb, and her lover mourns impotently outside the grille. But, if not satire, there is humour in the scenes of this commercial person's introduction to the stately Bellegardes and their friends as the fiancé of one of themselves.

The American's pluck and good nature strike amusing sparks in contact with the colossal pride and intrinsic meanness of the old order. Newman's revenge was to forgo his revenge: he, at any rate, the mere plebeian, could afford to be generous. But James came to the conclusion, when he prepared the book for the final edition of his novels, that he had looked at the situation too romantically and misread it: he ought to have made more of the falsity of the Bellegardes. Now that he knew better the meanness of this old nobility, he saw clearly enough that they would have jumped at Newman: they would have swallowed him and his fortune, and then perhaps have let him learn what they thought of him. No doubt, he would have rued it in the long run; but the solution adopted was the wrong one. At any rate, James could congratulate himself on having kept Newman consistent, and imparted a sense of his infatuation, and also of his generous nature "engaged with forces, with difficulties and dangers, that it but half understands."[1] Technically, Newman has too little of the subtle insight and the suppleness required of a good interpreter: he is not a Strether. But James's ultimate method is visibly developing.

Much less serious but possibly more amusing to some is his treatment of the converse situation in *The Europeans* (1878). In this, a brother and sister from Europe, but American by descent, come to visit their relations in Boston, and there are various clashes between their point of view and American rigours. Then, in *An International Situation* (1879), two Englishmen of title visit Newport and two Boston ladies come to London, the social comedy turning on the question whether the dignified younger lady will accept Lord Lambeth, who has paid her marked attentions. At least as interesting, but in a very different way, is the first story, which had appeared six years before in the *Atlantic Monthly*, in *The Madonna of the Future, and other tales* (1879). An American in Florence comes across an aged compatriot who has so pastured his mind on the masterpieces in the Uffizi and the Pitti that he has become infatuated with the ambition to paint like that himself.

Stories and novelettes

[1] *The Art of Fiction*, 37.

He has been talking for years about the great work he is engaged upon, the Madonna studied from a woman of the people who may once have been beautiful but has grown coarse and faded. Actually, he has never put pencil to canvas, but has spent countless hours watching the face of his model and seeing visions; and "one by one, the noiseless years had ebbed away and left him brooding in charmed inaction, for ever preparing for a work for ever deferred." Scarce realizing what he is about, the man who has taken so much interest in the solitary rouses him from his illusion. The awakening is too cruel. The old man feels that he has the brain of a Raphael; it is only the hand that is lacking—the other half of his genius. A few days after the shock he passes away. *Washington Square* (1881) is regarded by many as James's very best delineation of life and manners on the other side of the water; scene, the oldest and stateliest quarter of New York. Perhaps it must be admitted that it is more like Howells than James.[1] But, at any rate, the characters are drawn and their secrets exposed with an accomplished art, and with a kindness that does not preclude irony when that is called for. The theme is the disillusionment of an innocent girl who finds that her lover is chiefly interested in her fortune.

"*Daisy Miller*," etc.

The little novel, *Daisy Miller, a comedy* (1878), made a great noise at the time; Howells alludes in *Silas Lapham* to the reproach of "Daisy Millerism," which was long cast up at the American globe-trotter. It is the tragi-comedy of a sprightly American girl holidaying on the Continent, and getting into scrapes and compromising situations through sheer ingenuousness, her ignorance of and superiority to the elementary rules of propriety. She is a rare example of one without the fine tact of James's pet characters; but he was able to congratulate himself later that such "an outrage on American girlhood," as a Philadelphia critic called it, proved ultimately the "most prosperous child" of his invention.[2] "The Siege of London," "The Point of View," and "The Pension Beaurepas," were further studies of internationalism, the first a little comedy of manners, but none lacking in serious criticism. They appeared

[1] Beach, 228.   [2] *The Art of the Novel*, 268.

in a volume under the first title (1883). "The Author of Beltraffio" and "Pandora" were the best of a dozen *Stories Revived* (1885). The one gives the tragedy of the literary artist whose wife is a philistine. Rather will she sacrifice her son than let him fall a prey to the malign influence of his father's heterodox writings. "Pandora" is an anecdote to be coupled with *Daisy Miller*; it sketches a new product of American society, the self-made girl. The title-piece in *The Aspern Papers, and other stories*, and *The Reverberator*, both of 1888, may likewise be coupled. James was thinking of Shelley when he set his would-be biographer on the track of certain papers supposed to be in the custody of the poet Aspern's old lady-love at Florence.[1] He had a germ of fact, or legend, for his little drama of the American's infinite trouble and address in overcoming the privacy of the lady, and the tactful diplomacy which seems about to be rewarded, when the whole thing proves to be due to a misapprehension. *The Reverberator* borrows its title from an American society journal; the comedy of the young man in love with the pretty American girl in Paris, and his dread that his people will object to her vulgar relatives, is made more piquant by the success of the Paris correspondent in writing up the most intimate affairs of a respected family in this journal.

Many of the stories James was continually throwing off in his middle years, and some of the novels, are not now in the canon —he did not include them in the thirty-five volumes of his collected works. But some of the omitted items are far from uninteresting, especially when they represent stages or experiments in his efforts towards a perfect method. "The Real Thing" (1890) did survive the process of sifting, and apart from a delicate charm, and its subdued pathos, is not without a hint of his own æsthetic attitude. An old major and his wife, an affectionate pair who have come down in the world, offer themselves to an illustrator of society fiction as models—the incident actually happened to Du Maurier when he was doing

Miscellaneous stories of special note

---

[1] "The Coxon Fund" (1894) is a too prosaic study of the shiftless Coleridge. This, be it noted, appeared in *The Yellow Book*. Though the problem of Coleridge was long meditated, it was Dykes Campbell's life of the poet that prompted the story (*Art of the Novel*, 229–231).

his illustrations for *Punch*.[1] They are the real thing; at any rate, they look genuine specimens of smart society. But the artist does not want the real thing: he must have variety, adaptiveness, showy attitudinizing, which he gets from a London street-girl or an Italian ice-vendor. James makes excellent play with their pathetic courage, their inability to conceive his point of view, and the pride of breeding which puts slights to shame. The study of a rare personality, in this instance a butler, in "Brooksmith" (1891), is a trophy of James's untiring quest for preciosities of character. "The Lesson of the Master" (1892) is an ironical story. A man takes the advice of one whom he idolizes, and finds in the upshot that, while he has made the mistake of his life, the other has innocently and unconsciously reaped all the benefit. There is a serious reflection on the common mistrust of analytical appreciation [2] in the banter of "The Figure in the Carpet" (1896) of the pretensions of critics to find esoteric significances in their pet authors. A writer tells how he and another reviewer sought indefatigably the figure in the carpet, the buried treasure, the general intention, in the work of the eminent novelist Vereker, a meaning which Vereker himself said was as plain as a pikestaff but which the knowing ones missed. The older man, by dint of profound cerebration, at length deciphers the secret; but he has now gone to India. He promises to reveal it to another inquirer, a woman novelist, after they are married. He comes home, and they are duly married; but he is killed in an accident almost at once. The lady remains mute. Must the other marry her in turn, to learn the secret that still eludes him; for Vereker too is now dead and has not spoken? She does marry again, this time a rival critic whom the eager inquirer does not love to excess. Then she also dies. He braces himself to cross-question the widower, who does not even know that there was a secret.

For the few persons, at any rate, abnormal or not, with whom my anecdote is concerned, literature was a game of skill, and skill meant courage, and courage meant honour, and honour meant passion, meant life. The stake on the table was of a

[1] *The Art of the Novel*, 283.　　　　[2] *Ibid.*, 227-228.

special substance, and our roulette table the revolving mind; but we sat round the green board as intently as the grim gamblers at Monte Carlo.

"The Death of the Lion" was a contribution to *The Yellow Book* (1894), and James was apprehensive of Beardsley's illustrations, which were, "as illustrations, related to nothing else in the same pages." [1] He escaped this infliction, however, though the clique of admirers gathered round the decadent novelist, who dies of a cold while they are waiting to hear him read his manuscript, would have made an apposite picture. "The Great Good Place" (1900) was a fancy that beguiled him, of a world of rest, a calm and beautiful dream-country, to which an over-driven young man is privileged to escape at intervals, coming back again to everyday things with the feeling that he has been there for weeks and weeks. James himself confessed that "Paste" (1900) was after Maupassant, or, rather, parallel to "La Parure" but turned in the opposite direction. The pearls in James's story, supposed by the giver to be only paste, turn out to be real. But the new line of interest is in the suspicions arising from the discovery of the magnificent necklace among the posthumous effects of a lady of only moderate means.

It would have been remarkable if a novelist so deeply in-*Psych-* terested in every kind of mental experience had not written *ical* stories bearing on mysticism and the occult; and there are in *stories* fact half-a-dozen at least, of varying dates, that group themselves together under the badge of psychical occurrences or more or less deliberate meddling with occultism. Others too, "The Great Good Place," for instance, bring in abnormal states of consciousness. But long before this James tried his hand at a ghost-story, in the very characteristic shape of "Sir Edmund Orme," appended to *The Lesson of the Master* (1892), the vengeful wraith appearing to the woman who had wronged him at the moment when a young man is seeking her daughter's hand. James put this and a number of other stories of the supernatural, or at any rate the supernormal, in the volume headed *The Altar of the Dead, The Beast in the Jungle, The*

---

[1] *Ibid.*, 218–219. Harland also extracted "The Coxon Fund" and "The Next Time" for the same pages (*Ibid.*, 220).

Birthplace, and other tales. "The Altar of the Dead" is a rich and elaborate piece of mysticism. A man founds an altar in memory of his loved ones, and pays them sacrificial rites. A woman also comes and mourns at his altar; and he discovers at length that the person for whom she lights her candles is the old friend who had unforgivably betrayed him. Never again will he visit the church; till, at the very last, he summons up strength and comes creeping back, to be greeted by "the partner of his long worship." They feel as if the place were full of unseen beings: all are there save one. And Stransom, whispering forgiveness of that false old friend, whom she had loved, expires in her arms. "Owen Wingrave" is a highly refined version of the not uncommon tale of the man who sleeps in a haunted room and is found dead. "The Beast in the Jungle" and "The Birthplace," both of which appeared in *The Better Sort* (1903), are psychological inventions of considerable subtlety. In the one, a man's whole existence is embittered by the premonition that he is marked down for a terrible calamity, the nature of which he does not know; and he realizes too late that he has missed the blessing that lay nearest to his hand—there was the calamity, the unknown beast in the jungle. The point of the other story, possibly the most humorous he ever wrote, is the effect upon an honest and cultivated pair, in charge of a literary shrine, of having to retail a legend for which there is very little basis in fact.

"*The Turn of the Screw*," *etc.* "The Jolly Corner," now associated with these, and "The Turn of the Screw," which appeared first in *The Two Magics* (1898), are out-and-out tales of terror, that achieve their effects with unfailing dexterity. The former takes the well-worn experience of the lonely watcher in an empty house, and metamorphoses the customary details. In the other, James utilizes his now regular device of conveying experiences through a brain into which the reader is directly gazing, and so produces the most realistic of ghost-stories, for the ghosts appear, on this almost tangible screen, and appear in broad daylight and free from the ordinary romantic jugglery. They are two evil spirits, beings from hell and only just gone there, who have secured a dreadful grip on the souls of two children, and

initiated them, made them partners and accomplices, in the
abominations of their secret life. He based his tale on a
fragment of anecdote of moral corruption which he had heard
long before, a germ which he developed with great zest, and
without expanding it too much.

It is an excursion into chaos, while remaining, like Blue-Beard
and Cinderella, but an anecdote. . . . I need scarcely add after
this that it is a piece of ingenuity pure and simple, of cold
artistic calculation, an *amusette* to catch those not easily caught
(the "fun" of the capture of the merely witless being ever but
small), the jaded, the disillusioned, the fastidious.[1]

He also took care to avoid the common mistake of vulgarizing
his ghosts, which are indeed not ghosts at all, "as we now know
the ghost," but sheer embodiments of the principle of evil.
"The essence of the matter was the villainy of the evoked
predatory creatures," which he constrained the reader to comprehend by making him "*think* the evil," his own part being to
devise particulars, which he did with an ingenuity that he found
successful beyond his liveliest hopes.[2] James's evident enjoyment of the horrific has led some of his critics to detect in him
a morbid strain. He himself saw in it simply a "spell," of the
same sort as those which drew him in entirely different direc-
tions. To the æsthetes all themes have their attractions,
although "one man's amusement is at the best (we have surely
long had to recognize) another's desolation"; and he confesses
that the ghost-story "has ever been for me the most possible
form of the fairy-tale."[3] Possible, yes; but not easy. The

[1] *The Art of the Novel*, 172. James's remarks here should be carefully weighed,
in considering this and others of his stories of demoniac possession and malicious
agencies of corruption, which Mr Graham Greene believes to be the result of some
moral lesion and consequent obsession (*The English Novelists*, ed. D. Verschoyle
221–223).
[2] *Art of the Novel*, 176.
[3] *Ibid.*, 254. These remarks must be taken into account in considering Mr
Graham Greene's contentions that as the result of some mental lesion or complex—
Mr Greene attributes it to the load upon his conscience of having been a war-shirker
in the struggle between the Northern and Southern States, or else to epileptic and
suicidal tendencies in the family—James suffered from morbid terrors, a nervous
sense of spiritual evil, was, in short, a Manichæan. Hence the vivid sense of moral
corruption in *The Wings of the Dove*, *The Golden Bowl*, etc. (*The English Novelists*,
ed. D. Verschoyle).

very last of his stories, *The Sense of the Past* (1917), the one to which he turned. from *The Ivory Tower*, which he never completed, had been laid aside for fourteen years; its intrinsic difficulties, indeed, all but resulted in its being given up altogether. Not the horrific, but certainly the uncanny, an almost intolerable sense of uneasiness, is shed upon the man himself and those about him when the young American, in quest of the historic past, lives back into it, only to find that he cannot mix and commune as one of themselves with the beings amongst whom he is transplanted.[1]

Some outstanding novels A number of these stories belong to James's later years, or at least to his middle period, in which technical skill and complexity of interest were the dominant characteristics. But his development was not marked by the sudden discovery of new devices or by drastic changes of method, though he was by no means lacking in invention. Talking about the most notable of his devices, the use of "perceivers" or "mirrors," characters so placed as to see what is going on, through whose impressions and reactions thereto the reader has a personal view of it, free from the inevitable though involuntary distortions and the strict limitations of autobiography, James was glad to point out that he had employed it regularly from *Roderick Hudson* at the beginning to *The Golden Bowl* at the end.[2] Newman in *The American*, Isabel Archer in *The Portrait of a Lady*, Vanderbank in *The Awkward Age*, and Fleda Vetch in *The Spoils of Poynton*, are examples variously constituted of such perceivers, some abnormally sensitive and imaginative, some matter-of-fact, some absorbed in their own predicaments, and yet all the better as witnesses known and trusted by the sympathizing reader: they are his chosen intermediaries, just like Densher in *The Wings of the Dove* or Strether in *The Ambassadors*. Their minds are the theatre into which the reader peers, seeing the drama of impressions actively proceeding, with all its reverberations on

---

[1] Edgar, 184–187.

[2] *Art of the Novel*, 70–71. Percy Lubbock is particularly good on the limitations of autobiography (*The Craft of Fiction*, 144–145). On the dramatization of the story in the mind of Strether, see pp. 147 and 159–171. This dramatization of the character who serves as point of view is compared with the pictorial method of narration (pp. 252–257).

such interested observers. Isabel Archer, in *The Portrait of a Lady* (1881), deliberately sets herself to explore life; yet it is not the things that happen so much as her responses, not so much the characters playing a vital part as the reactions which they provoke, that constitute the story. Gilbert Osmond, Lord Warburton, Madame Merle, are amply and vividly portrayed through this living medium. And when James found such a promising figure as Christina Light left on his hands after finishing *Roderick Hudson* he resorted to the same vivifying indirectness in *The Princess Casamassima* (1886), in which she is seen through the eyes of the disillusioned plotter Hyacinth Robinson, to whom she remains to the last a beautiful mystery. Hyacinth's consciousness is the stage, a consciousness haunted by the spectres of the countless victims of the social order; and this romantic light and shade give a vividness to her figure and to her somewhat enigmatic attitude to socialist activities such as James's hazy knowledge of this special subject would hardly have secured in any other way. Even in this novel, there were some reversions to the older, biographical style of fiction: in *The Tragic Muse* (1891), written when a serial was invited by the *Atlantic Monthly*, he went back to the common practice of a multiplicity of centres. Yet, with many characters competing in interest, and in fact with two stories woven into one, he managed to attain some unity and give a good general picture of life going vigorously on. The particular world in which it was going on chiefly was that of the theatre. James felt excited at having, as he said, to write "a story about art": and, not only the scenes of artist life, with their touches of Bohemianism, but also questions of studio and stage, of dramatic illusion, and of the interrelations of the personal life and artistic self-expression, gave him opportunities not to be missed. But it was the exuberant vitality of Miriam Rooth, her sensational stage triumphs, and the perplexities of the man in love with her, that are the memorable features of this novel and made it a popular success.

All this time James's later manner was developing, his elaborate chronicling of the finest and most elusive shades, the labyrinthine reactions of character, the utmost complexities of

The
later
manner
develop-
ing

feeling, the most tenuous vibrations of sensibility. He worked on a generous scale: the amplitude of the picture, as well as its minuteness of detail, was always striking; and yet it tended to grow ampler and still more complex. Such fullness necessarily involved, not merely the omission of everything not strictly relevant, but also a careful pruning away of many technical superfluities, the formalities and conventions, the summaries of past events, the ceremonious introductions of new characters, and other familiar guide-posts for the reader's behoof, who was now called upon, not merely for acute sensitiveness and refined intelligence, but even for close mental application to the problem before him. It was a new etiquette of novel-writing. The mirror or perceiver must have a counterpart in the responsive reader, ready to seize the clue opening up indefinite possibilities, as well as the immediate fact, anxious to experience for himself the last throb of feeling. Else, he would find himself groping in a maze of half-expressed emotions, implied affinities and incompatibilities, reciprocal influences that might easily elude him. He was set, as it were, along with the characters themselves, to trace and determine the nature of intricate and conflicting motives, and to weigh the remote consequence of every act and every utterance. At first, it seemed as if he were being introduced to a world not a bit like the ordinary; the way was bewildering. It was a world, or was tending to be a world, of superfine manners, delicate insight, subtle perceptions, hypersensitive tact; of perfect self-control and sureness in one's dealings with life, full command of one's personal development: such were the ideals, at any rate, bodied forth or at least adumbrated in concrete examples. New sets of values were taken for granted, marking new levels of civilization: new codes were accepted, as in the more prophetic of Meredith's novels. Life itself had become a fine art, more so even than in Walter Pater's finest evaluations.[1] James had arrived at a more intimate, appreciative, responsive scale of social sentiments and relationships, in which his grounding in New England puritanism and transcendental idealism

[1] On Pater's conceptions of life on higher levels, and more particularly on his aim at an æsthetic morality superior to the pragmatic morality of life, see Rosenblatt, 176 and 205.

may be traced, although a mind of extreme sensibility and acuteness had progressed beyond them. His were not like other novels. Compared with the ordinary story of incident, nothing seemed to happen. A gesture, a change of expression, was an event. Incidents were not interesting in themselves, but only in the vibrations they set up. The drama was all internal. True, that is what real drama always is, however violent externally: but here the decisive signals had to be watched for, instead of being conspicuous and electrifying. For the new method aimed at quite different effects from those sought by the ordinary novelist. Having devised a method for himself, James put the reader right into it, into the stuff itself, as he described the proceeding. As soon as it is realized what he is driving at, the reader sees his way, and gets to know the characters, the thoughts, the feelings and attitudes, no matter how recondite, by a direct intuition—or else not at all. Granted, some of James's novels do offer an arduous task. But it is necessary only to learn the language, and the task becomes, not indeed easy and automatic, but absorbing and eager, because animated by a sense of continual revelation. The result is worth all the effort, for at the end we feel as if we had gone through all the dramatic experiences ourselves.

The novels and stories examined and those next to be considered are of peculiar interest, an interest almost outweighing their actual accomplishment; they illustrate James's unremitting efforts towards an adequate method. *Technical innovations—the idea* The mature method was soon to be shown in a minor but perfect work, *The Spoils of Poynton*, and in three full-length masterpieces, *The Wings of the Dove*, *The Ambassadors*, and *The Golden Bowl*. What, then, are the cardinal features of this perfected art? The first thing perceived, after a comparison of any of his novels or tales chosen at random, is that his initial motive in writing them was not merely to tell an entertaining or a surprising story: those popular qualities may be there, but they will be subordinate to something else. That something is not hard to distinguish, though it may be troublesome indeed to define all its implications in a particular case. Each one is conceived and designed to illustrate or embody or elucidate an idea, or a structural situation presenting something of the nature of an enigma. This germinal idea or situation ensures harmony of impression, and is the basis of the design or pattern giving unity amid the complexity, the artistic coherence and integrity which James made a prime object. These, be it noted, are the qualities of a representational work rather than of narrative. And it was less a story that he had to tell, in any given instance, than a picture he was to paint—of a complex of human relations, a group, large or small, of persons reacting to each other. His aim was not primarily realism, for the accuracy and completeness with which he infused the idea into the work and made the work express the idea were much more important to him than the faithful rendering of life as he observed it.

Exploration of motive, etc.

And then, what story there was being but the sum-total of these complex relations and reactions, the task which he set himself was the gradual disclosure of the situation, which could be analysed into characters, feelings, attitudes, and the various personal responses thereto. The characters in a novel of Henry James are engaged at least half the time in finding out exactly where they stand, or where others in whom they are keenly interested stand, in the general complication: accordingly, there is more emphasis on sense than on sensibility. And again, the reader is like one of them, inasmuch as his lot is not to throw himself back in an armchair and listen to a story, but to work away at exploring the entanglement of sentiments, passions, moods and fears, of abstruse, tortuous, and perhaps sinister motives, and to comprehend exactly what is at stake, and the nature of the forces in the shape of different personalities in active or passive opposition. The statical problem of the various tensions will yield a clue to the dynamical problem when the poised forces begin to react. Having mastered the situation, the reader watches it work itself out. As it has been well said, he is not so much listening to a story that goes on and on, as watching the gradual unveiling of a picture.[1] The dramatic suspense experienced is in the question what will next be revealed.

[1] "If you are to use the word story at all in connexion with these novels, the story is not what the characters do, nor how the situation works out. The story is rather the process by which the characters and the situation are revealed to us" (Beach, 41).

It was in the quiet and gradual mode of the revelation that *The James* showed himself most punctiliously the artist, relying, as has been already remarked, on an agency strictly concrete, a single character or possibly two or three, as the mirror or interpreters through which everything is conveyed, even that which may be taken for his own attitudes and ideas. He early abandoned the time-honoured form of direct narration, either with the loose assumption of omniscience or through the mouth of a personal witness. Now and then he might drop into autobiography, especially that revealing form of it the private letter. Sometimes he dropped into that procedure which Conrad favoured, of piecing together a tale told fragmentarily by various witnesses, a procedure that Conrad probably learned from an intensive study of James. Firmly and consistently, at any rate, James held to the "compositional law" of "employing but one centre and keeping it all within my hero's consciousness." Perceiving and conveying through a consciousness was the great principle, for the personal reactions and the faintest vibrations thus at the same time transmitted gave the thing conveyed an immediacy and intensity of effect like that of poetry. The reader peering into the consciousness in which it is mirrored sees, not only the drama itself, but the accompanying drama of impressions and temperamental responses in that consciousness, and thus has a closer and richer awareness of all that is happening than would be enjoyed by a neutral spectator. James's intermediary is no mere reporter, but a personal and vital link between the reader and all that is at issue. Consequently and finally, that unrolling of the web of time which is the essential operation of the novel as a reduplication of life has never been performed with a more perfect coincidence of the general sense of duration with that of the fictitious events and emotions.[1] A vivid illusion of simultaneousness results from this indirect mode of giving out a story; for what is presented is no mere translation of events into literary terms, but the sound and feel of the accents and emotions of someone alive plunged into the events and directly responding to them. Though at a double remove, the reader

The mirrors or perceivers

---

[1] See above, p. 59.

experiences the very sensation of life.[1] The novel has become a stage on which it is proceeding: the apparatus of a theatre has been compressed into a book.

Approxi-   Most of James's stories are genuine stories, as the story has
mations been already differentiated from the novel, however brief.[2]
to drama But there are some, and the next coming into view is a conspicuous example, that are not easy to classify: on the one hand, they obviously give the history of an event, or a complication of events, whence their unity of impression and also the suspense that holds the reader down; yet, on the other hand, character is as much at stake as anything more material, and the individuals engaged are obviously meant to compel, and do compel, an overriding interest in themselves. In every one, James's standard pattern may be recognized. There is the intricate complication, the situation with its opposing stresses to be elucidated. The distinctive feature is that these are soon in violent activity; in every case there is an intense contest of wills. Call them novels or call them stories, it is evident that, fundamentally, these are all dramas, fully equipped for performance in James's pocket-theatre. *The Spoils of Poynton* is the masterpiece of the group, which comprises also *The Awkward Age*, *The Portrait of a Lady*, and, at any rate, *The Sacred Fount*. But the same kind of dramatic conflict is an element in other novels and stories, notably in the long duel of Maggie and Charlotte Stant in *The Golden Bowl*.

"The   Too precise dates are better avoided in trying to mark out
Spoils of the differences between James's middle period and his last and
Poynton" most splendid, that of the three great novels which are universally accepted as the consummation of his genius. At all events, his art was visibly maturing when he wrote *The Spoils of Poynton* (1897); and "The Figure in the Carpet" of the year

---

[1] A luminous article on "The Significance of Henry James" (*Times Literary Supplement*, 6th January 1927) ascribes the truth and illusion of his art to the reproduction of the pattern and rhythm of life. In "The Art of Fiction," he said, "In proportion as we see life *without* rearrangement do we feel that we are touching the truth; in proportion as we see it *with* rearrangement do we feel that we are being put off with a substitute, a compromise and convention." The virtue and the irresistible spell is "its large, free character of an immense and exquisite correspondence with life." The novelist must catch "the very note and trick, the strange irregular rhythm of life, that is the attempt whose strenuous force keeps Fiction upon her feet."

[2] See above, pp. 58–61.

before was a trifle only in its brevity. Before the great three, he busied himself with a number of stories and two novels, *What Maisie knew* (1897) and *The Awkward Age* (1899), which are, pre-eminently, brilliant exercises in technique; and a few others, *The Sacred Fount* (1900) and *The Outcry* (1911), for instance, might be similarly assessed. The principal short stories of these later years have already been looked at. *The Spoils of Poynton* is, indeed, an absolute compendium of James's technique, a perfect example of his use of the intermediary, in Fleda Vetch, the girl who "was only intelligent, not distinctively able," in comparison with the rest of the small group; it is also a striking instance of the comparative triviality of the ostensible theme—the Spoils—and the gradual emergence of a deeper and finer meaning, never formulated, but unmistakably there—the question of immaterial values, the characters themselves, their intrinsic worth and integrity, and what is left permanent when the Spoils have gone up in smoke.

The free spirit, always much tormented, and by no means always triumphant, is heroic, ironic, pathetic or whatever, and, as exemplified in the record of Fleda Vetch, for instance, "successful," only through having remained free.[1]

There are only some two hundred and fifty pages in *The Spoils of Poynton*, which would be rather short for a novel; and it has been suggested that James meant at first to write only a magazine story, but found it grow on his hands. His idea of a short story was the anecdote, which is practically that already adopted here.[2] It is an anecdote that forms the skeleton of the novel or drama, and the anecdote in the shape James embodied it is so pregnant that it must be summarized at some length. Mrs Gereth and her late husband have spent their *The* married life hunting over Europe for objects of art, and *story* Poynton Hall when he dies is a beautiful old house filled with the rarest and costliest things. It was not left to the widow, but to the son, Owen; and Mrs Gereth is torn with anxiety over the possible fate of what she regards as the work of her life. It is at this juncture that Fleda Vetch comes on the

---

[1] Preface to final edition.   [2] See above, p. 58 *et seq.*

264 HISTORY OF THE ENGLISH NOVEL

scene; her fine sensibility is to be the focusing-point of all that
now happens. She has an eye as unerring as Mrs Gereth's.
Beauty is her element. When Owen shows signs of being
fascinated by the bouncing Mona Brigstock, bred in a home
of rich and shameless vulgarity, Mrs Gereth, dreading the rape
of her treasures by such a vandal, takes refuge with Fleda, and
goes so far as to advertise the sense and superiority of her young
friend to the infatuated Owen. There is something ideal,
almost spiritual, in Mrs Gereth's passion for the things. Fleda
can share her feelings, though Fleda's devotion is to other and
loftier values. But the girl undertakes the negotiations with
Owen, who feels sore towards his mother for pushing her very
dubious claims. Fleda is in love with his straightness and
simplicity; and, all unawares, he falls in love with her fineness,
so infinitely above the grasping crudity of Mona. For Mona
has accepted him; but when there is talk of letting his mother
have the pick of the Poynton treasures she delivers her ulti-
matum—with them she will marry him, without them she will
not. The drama now grows tense. Mrs Gereth betakes
herself to Ricks, the small place left her in the will; and, acting
far beyond the amiable understanding arrived at with Owen,
carries off the best of the spoils to furnish it. Owen comes,
but will not face his mother. He talks it over with Fleda, and
lets her know that Mona has postponed the wedding-day
indefinitely. Fleda has three loyalties to preserve: her duty
to Mrs Gereth, who has acted unscrupulously but is to be pitied;
her promise that Owen shall be righted; and, finally, her
determination not to wrong Mona, however grossly Mona
may behave. The struggle going on within her is embittered
by her unconfessed love for Owen, and indeed by Owen's for
her, in no long time openly avowed. But that is a motive she
will not allow to influence her, well aware though she is that
Mrs Gereth would make instant restitution if Fleda were to
be mistress of Poynton.

The dénoue-ment So matters stand, and so for a while they remain. What any
of the four parties will do, or even what they would like to
happen, is more or less an enigma to the others. At length,
that acute, though short-sighted and impulsive lady, Mrs

Gereth, grows aware that Owen and Fleda are in love, and
forthwith jumps to the conclusion that Mona and Owen have
definitely broken with each other, never dreaming that Fleda
has insisted on the point of honour and made Owen keep to
his bargain until his fiancée herself releases him. She thinks
the game is in her own hands, and without hesitation or calcula-
tion performs a showy act of magnanimity. She returns all
the treasures to Poynton. Alas for herself and for Fleda! She
has been too precipitate. She has left certain items out of the
account. Fleda, to whom she announces the fact, feels in her
very bones that the game is not won but lost. If Owen is not
already formally dismissed by Mona, Mona will now make sure
of him and of Poynton with all it contains. And she has an
intuition that to the rapacity of the ordinary sensual woman
has by now been added a keener motive—jealousy of Fleda.
In brief, Owen marries Mona, or, rather, Mona marries him.
Poynton is gone: it is now the property of a tasteless and
stupid philistine. Fleda has but the moral consolation that
she is loved by Owen. But, if she has lost every material thing,
hers is the spiritual victory. She has not yielded a jot of her
ideals: exalted and even quixotic as they are, she has fully lived
up to them. Poynton and all its riches, unappreciated and
unwatched by its new mistress, is burned to ashes—a conflagra-
tion that is not mere irony, but symbolic of the less perishable
beauty of the things of the soul.

Nowhere as yet had James given away such a master-key to *Ethics*
his ethical attitudes, to his identification of the beautiful and *and good*
the good, of taste and morals.   Good taste and a good conscience *taste*
are here in the same category: and it is the same in all the works
of his ripest period—it is not so much the beauty of holiness
that he acknowledges as the holiness of beauty. Fineness of
perception is the root of all virtue—the basis for the delicate
sympathy which he exalts, for self-respect and personal dignity,
for the point of honour—in women as in men. "Good form,"
in its highest sense, is a general expression for the cardinal
virtues. "Ugliness fundamental and systematic" was the
quality of the Brigstocks, "from whose composition the
principle of taste had been extravagantly omitted": ugliness

is only a particular aspect of baseness. Vulgarity is the flesh and the devil. James, with his Swedenborgian father and puritan upbringing, had by now arrived at a position not very remote from Walter Pater's. He had learned something in the past from Hawthorne, on the artistic but not too formal use of symbolism, for instance, and a little possibly on the telling of a story from definite points of view. Hawthorne was loose and uncertain, however, in the latter respect, though he won James's approval by maintaining a concrete standpoint, that of Miles Coverdale, in *The Blithedale Romance*, "the lightest, the brightest, the liveliest" of his unhumorous fictions. Hawthorne continually turned the puritan idea to account, without by any means always adopting the puritan view. He was an artist, though careless and faulty by Jacobean standards. But at any rate "he contrived, by an exquisite process, best known to himself, to transmute this heavy moral burden [of evil and depravity] into the very substance of the imagination, to make it evaporate in the light and charming fumes of artistic production."

Nothing is more curious and interesting than this almost exclusively *imported* character of the sense of sin in Hawthorne's mind; it seems to exist there merely for an artistic or literary purpose. He had ample cognizance of the Puritan conscience; it was his natural heritage; it was reproduced in him; looking into his soul, he found it there. But his relation to it was only, as one may say, intellectual; it was not moral and theological. He played with it and used it as a pigment; he treated it, as the metaphysicians say, objectively. He was not discomposed, disturbed, haunted by it, in the manner of its usual and regular victims, who had not the little postern-door of fancy to slip through, to the other side of the wall.[1]

Emancipation from puritanism But, in spite of his censure of those who, like George Eliot in *Romola*, let ethics submerge art, James was a long time freeing himself from the attitude of the New Englander, and arriving at that purely æsthetic conscientiousness which appears in his handling of Strether, in *The Ambassadors*. Strether acquires enlightenment and the true freedom of a liberal

[1] *Hawthorne*, by Henry James (English Men of Letters, 58–59).

culture through the experiences he goes through in Paris, and
so realizes that he has made the mistake of not living. "Live
all you can" is his advice to Little Bilham, at the end of his
ambassadorial mission from the strait-laced mistress of Woollett,
U.S.A. One of the many deeply significant conversations in
The Spoils of Poynton must be quoted in part, to illustrate the
stage James had now arrived at. Owen is now more than half
in love with Fleda, and ready at a word of encouragement from
her to take Mona's refusal to fix the day as a final rejection.

Owen took it in; then "Oh she's all right!" he laughed. "I
go by Mrs Brigstock's certain effect on her—the effect of the
temper the old lady showed when we parted. Do you know
what she asked me?" he sociably continued. "She asked me in
a kind of nasty manner if I supposed you 'really' cared anything
about me. Of course I told her I supposed you didn't—not
a solitary rap. How could I ever suppose you did—with
your extraordinary ways? It doesn't matter. I could see she
thought I lied."

"You should have told her, you know, that I had seen you
in town only that one time," Fleda said.

"By Jove, I did—for *you*! It was only for you."

Something in this touched the girl so that for a moment
she couldn't trust herself to speak. "You're an honest man,"
she said at last. She had gone to the door and opened it.
"Good-bye."

Even yet, however, he hung back. "But say there's no
letter—" he anxiously began. He began, but there he left it.

"You mean even if she doesn't let you off? Ah you ask me
too much!" Fleda spoke from the tiny hall, where she had
taken refuge between the old barometer and the old mackintosh.
"There are things too utterly for yourselves alone. How can I
tell? Good-bye, good-bye! If she doesn't let you off it will
be because she is attached to you."

"She's not, she's not: there's nothing in it! Doesn't a
fellow know?—except with *you*!" Owen ruefully added.
With this he came out of the room, lowering his voice to secret
supplication, pleading with her really to meet him on the
ground of the negation of Mona. It was this betrayal of his
need of support and sanction that made her retreat, harden
herself in the effort to save what might remain of all she had

given, given probably for nothing. The very vision of him as he thus morally clung to her was the vision of a weakness somewhere at the core of his bloom, a blessed manly weakness which, had she only the valid right, it would be all easy and sweet to take care of. She faintly sickened, however, with the sense that there was as yet no valid right poor Owen could give. "You can take it from my honour, you know," he painfully brought out, "that she quite loathes me."

Fleda had stood clutching the knob of Maggie's little painted stair-rail; she took, on the stairs, a step backward. "Why then doesn't she prove it in the only clear way?"

"She *has* proved it. Will you believe it if you see the letter?"

"I don't want to see any letter," said Fleda. "You'll miss your train."

Facing him, waving him away, she had taken another upward step; but he sprang to the side of the stairs, and brought his hand, above the banister, down hard on her wrist. "Do you mean to tell me that I must marry a woman I hate?"

From her step she looked down into his raised face. "Ah you see it's not true that you're free!" she seemed almost to exult. "It's not true, it's not true!"

He only, at this, like a buffeting swimmer, gave a shake of his head and repeated his question: "Do you mean to tell me I must marry such a woman?"

Fleda gasped too; he held her fast. "No. Anything's better than that."

"Then in God's name what must I do?"

"You must settle that with Mona. You mustn't break faith. Anything's better than that. You must at any rate be utterly sure. She must love you—how can she help it? *I* wouldn't give you up!" said Fleda. She spoke in broken bits, panting out her words. "The great thing is to keep faith. Where's a man if he doesn't? If he doesn't he may be so cruel. So cruel, so cruel, so cruel!" Fleda repeated. "I couldn't have a hand in that, you know: that's my position, that's mine. You offered her marriage. It's a tremendous thing for her." Then looking at him another moment, "*I* wouldn't give you up!" she said again. He still had hold of her arm; she took in his blank dread. With a quick dip of her face she reached his hand with her lips, pressing them to the back of it with a force

that doubled the force of her words. "Never, never, never!"
she cried; and before he could succeed in seizing her she had
turned and, flashing up the stairs, got away from him even
faster than she had got away at Ricks.[1]

In the novel that followed that same year, *What Maisie knew* "*What
(1897), the method of revelation through the brain of an actor *Maisie
in the drama is employed with extraordinary technical skill, *knew*"
for this is "an attempt to print the figure of life as it falls upon
the very acute vision of a little girl." Maisie is the child of
divorced parents who are "carrying on" with other people,
and she becomes the innocent and uncomprehending witness
of one affair after another. It is an unsavoury or, at any rate,
a sordid business, which the reader has to piece together and
realize for what it is through what she sees of it without in the
least understanding the ugliness of half the things she reports.
The irony of Maisie's position as a witness firmly believing in
the goodness of these seasoned evildoers is all the more pungent
from her belief in her own knowingness; the pathos is obvious.

So the sharpened sense of spectatorship was the child's main
support, the long habit, from the first, of seeing herself in
discussion and finding in the fury of it—she had had a glimpse
of the game of football—a sort of compensation for the doom of
a peculiar passivity. It gave her often an odd air of being
present at her history in as separate a manner as if she could only
get at experience by flattening her nose against a pane of glass.

It is a tricksy and fine-drawn variation of the accustomed
expedient of an intensely observant, mature, and penetrating
mind, and one urgently implicated in the drama, as the visible
theatre of events, or of the dramatic perception of events.
James was to go on to put two or three persons of such acuteness
into his foreground, all anxiously intent, not only on their own
feelings, but on finding out all that the others feel, and so to
effect an intense realization on the reader's part of all that is
done or said or felt or surmised, not only by the actor-deponent
but also by the others. *In the Cage* (1898) was an easier
feat, a playful variant, the girl in a telegraph office absorbing

[1] Chap. xvi.

herself in the doings of a higher social world, and spinning romance out of an exchange of telegrams passing through her hands.

"The Awkward Age" But in *The Awkward Age* (1899) James discards his patent method, and lets his story proceed in the scenic manner in favour with other novelists, without insistence on any special point of view; it goes almost entirely into dialogue. It is a social study of a peculiar phase of civilization. "Not a formal association nor a secret society—still less a 'dangerous gang or an organization for any definite end. We're simply a collection of natural affinities,' Mitchy explained." The characters, indeed, are hardly individuals at all; they are tints in a peculiar harmony. Every generation, such is the assumption, outruns the one before either forwards or backwards. "Oh, Harold's talk," protests one of the initiated, "offers, I think, an extraordinary interest; only I'm to say it crushes me to the earth. I've to make at least, as I listen to him, a big effort to bear up. It doesn't seem long ago," he pursued to his young friend, "that I used to feel I was in it; but the very way you bring home to me, dreadful youth, that I'm already not—!" Changes of manners, chiefly for the worse in the eyes of older people, who are themselves no better than they should be, make these aged free-livers seem to themselves almost puritans in comparison with such a coterie of smart decadents. Then there is the way young girls, innocently nurtured, are tumbled into this world of the mature, with their terrible knowledge of good and evil. "Most English talk is a quadrille in a sentry-box. You'll tell me we go further in Italy, and I won't deny it; but in Italy we have the common sense not to have little girls in the room." It is a monstrously clever book, demanding monstrously clever readers to catch the subtlety and elusive charm of many passages. James hardly seems to try to disclose the minds of his characters; what he really does here is to indicate their thoughts, try to make them reveal themselves. And his comment is there, though lurking in the dialogue and the visible doings: it is a shrewd and highly personal comment. The ulterior meanings may require alert imagination to seize them, quickness of intuition. Meredith's obscurities, in *The*

Amazing Marriage, for instance, which was still a recent book, are those of a poet; they are boldly sensuous and imaginative. James's are entirely different; they are more like those of a Persius, more a matter of expression, of compressed allusiveness, pregnant rather than subtle or profound: they puzzle by what they leave out.

The whole gist of *The Wings of the Dove* (1902) can be put in a sentence. Kate Croy and Densher are in love and pledged to each other, but he is only a struggling journalist and their prospects are uncertain; so she persuades him to pay attentions to the American girl, Milly Theale, sickly, and probably sentenced to death in her prime, so that they may enjoy the large fortune which will almost certainly be left him by the tender-hearted girl. But their plot is disclosed only by degrees; the first book is wholly concerned with Kate and Densher's affairs, and the reader is made thoroughly acquainted with the characters and their hopes and fears before the conspiracy is broached. The scheme is Kate's; Densher accepts his part reluctantly, and with more and more remorse as it seems likely to succeed. Kate Croy is one of James's adventuresses, one of the sort ready to seize opportunities when they arise, though perhaps not to contrive them; she has brains, and temperament, and taste: she is not entirely corrupt and unscrupulous, but convinces herself to her own peace of mind that Milly will be none the worse for the fraud, which might even cheer the despondency of the brief time left her. James painted that beautiful soul from his cousin Mary Temple, who died at twenty-four; brilliant, affectionate, captivated with life to the very end.[1] Everyone adored her. "When Milly smiled it was a public event—when she didn't it was a chapter of history." But she is marked for death, before her splendid chances of joy can be realized. And Milly loses the desire to live: she is lacking in will-power, and one thing alone will ever revive that—the reciprocated love of a man like Densher. Kate's plot shows signs of success; how much it is hers and how little Densher's this snatch of dialogue will show:

"The Wings of the Dove"

[1] Edgar, 299–300.

"Ah, she believes she won't die. Not if you stay. I mean," Kate explained, "aunt Maud believes."

"And that's all that's necessary?"

Still, indeed, she didn't break down. "Didn't we long ago agree that what she believes is the principal thing for us?"

He recalled it, under her eyes, but it came as from long ago. "Oh, yes. I can't deny it." Then he added: "So that if I stay——"

"It won't"—she was prompt—"be our fault."

"If Mrs Lowder still, you mean, suspects us?"

"If she still suspects us. But she won't."

Kate gave it an emphasis that might have appeared to leave him nothing more; and he might in fact well have found nothing if he had not presently found: "But what if she doesn't accept me?"

It produced in her a look of weariness that made the patience of her tone the next moment touch him. "You can but try."

"Naturally, I can but try. Only, you see, one has to try a little hard to propose to a dying girl."

"She isn't for you as if she's dying." It had determined in Kate the flash of *justesse* that he could perhaps most, on consideration, have admired, for her retort touched the truth. There before him was the fact of how Milly to-night impressed him, and his companion, with her eyes in his own and pursuing his impression to the depths of them, literally now perched on the fact in triumph. She turned her head to where their friend was again in range, and it made him turn his, so that they watched a minute in concert. Milly, from the other side, happened at the moment to notice them, and she sent across toward them in response all the candour of her smile, the lustre of her pearls, the value of her life, the essence of her wealth. It brought them, with faces made fairly grave by the reality she put into their plan, together again; Kate herself grew a little pale for it, and they had for a time only a silence. The music, however, gay and vociferous, had broken out afresh and protected more than interrupted them. When Densher at last spoke it was under cover.

"I might stay, you know, without trying."

"Oh, to stay is to try."

"To have for herself, you mean, the appearance of it?"

"I don't see how you can have the appearance more."

Densher waited. "You think it then possible she may *offer* marriage?"

"I can't think—if you really want to know—what she may *not* offer."

"In the manner of princesses, who do such things?"

"In any manner you like. So be prepared."

Well, he looked as if he almost were. "It will be for me then to accept. But that's the way it must come."[1]

The symbolism here is to be noticed as well as in the title. The plot proves successful. But Milly becomes aware of it, and it is the last blow. One thing alone can save her, and that only for a happier death: will Densher assure her that there has really been no conspiracy, and that he really loves her? Densher refuses that final treachery, and Milly dies, leaving him her money; but she has left him also the consciousness that she died knowing his designs and yet forgiving him. Between him and Kate it can never be the same again. She tells him:

"Your change came—as it might well—the day you last saw her. She died for you then that you might understand her. From that hour you *did*." With which Kate slowly rose. "And I do now. She did it *for* us."

Densher rose to face her, and she went on with her thought.

"I used to call her, in my stupidity—for want of anything better—a dove. Well, she stretched out her wings, and it was to *that* they reached. They cover us."

"They cover us," Densher said.

"That's what I give you," Kate gravely wound up. "That's what I've done for you."

His look at her had a slow strangeness that had dried, on the moment, his tears. "Do I understand then—?"

"That I do consent?" She gravely shook her head. "No —for I see. You'll marry me without the money; you won't marry me with it. If I don't consent, *you* don't."

. . . .

He heard her out in stillness, watching her face but not moving. Then he only said: "I'll marry you, mind you, in an hour."

"As we were?"

[1] Bk. VIII., c. xxviii.

"As we were."

But she turned to the door, and her headshake was now the end. "We shall never be again as we were." [1]

There is excellent character-drawing in the subsidiary figures: Milly's faithful companion, the New Englander from Burlington, Vermont, for instance; or Mrs Lowder, Aunt Maud, the West End society lady—British respectability at its highest pitch, the car of Juggernaut that grinds human nature to stucco. But the centre of vision rests with one or other of the three principals, with a momentary shift to Susan Stringer; and their picture gradually unites into a complete whole. This novel, also, is more pictorial of external nature than is James's wont. Many scenes are poetized by the beauty around. But the point of this snatch depicting a bright morning after heavy weather at Venice is that it is a great item in Densher's consciousness, as he goes to the station to meet the eminent physician; it is a factor rousing him to summon up "a small make-believe of freedom" in the equivocal position to which he has tied himself:

The weather changed, the stubborn storm yielded, and the autumn sunshine, baffled for many days, but now hot and almost vindictive, came into its own again and, with an almost audible pæan, a suffusion of bright sound that was one with the bright colour, took large possession. Venice glowed and plashed and chimed again; the air was like a clap of hands, and the scattered pinks, yellows, blues, sea-greens were like a hanging-out of vivid stuffs, a laying down of fine carpets. Densher rejoiced in this on the occasion of his going to the station to meet the great doctor.

"*The Ambassadors*" James thought *The Ambassadors* (1903) his masterpiece of shapely and expressive construction; it all centres in one "reflector," the chief ambassador, Strether; and its con-

---

[1] Last two pages. It is difficult to follow Mr Graham Greene in his characterization of Densher and Kate Croy, as "apart from Quint and the Governess the most driven and 'damned' of all James's characters" (*The English Novelists*, ed. D. Verschoyle, 220). James evidently regarded them, not as "incomparable figures of evil," incapable of redemption, but rather as poor devils who persuaded themselves that, as things were, their deception of Milly could do no real harm. That they had a conscience is clear from this last interview.

stituent parts, almost summed up in Strether's perceptions and conclusions, fall into that meet proportion the lack of which he deplored in *The Wings of the Dove*.[1] He rejoiced in having secured a hero of such mature experience, one who had "accumulated character" and had therewith "imagination galore." The germ came from a friend's anecdote, together with a hint of the doctrine which is the general conclusion: "Live all you can; it's a mistake not to. It doesn't so much matter what you do in particular so long as you have your life. If you haven't had that what *have* you had?"[2] It all arose from this. "Nothing can exceed the closeness with which the whole fits again into its germ."[3] But, though all this now stands in the preface, it is not till half-way through the book that the ultimate drift is revealed, when the middle-aged Strether, on his mission to find out what his dear friend's absentee son is up to in Paris, and to try to bring him back home, begins to realize that he himself is now seeing things as they are for the first time, and that the free-and-easy existence which he was sent to curse is the very one to be blessed, as the antithesis to the narrow and unimaginative philistinism of Woollett, U.S.A. Strether is the emissary of Mrs Newsome, the wealthy queen of that New England industrial town, its puritan society and philistine culture. As James confesses, it was his desire to make that lady's presence felt "no less intensely than circuitously" throughout the story: she is not heard, or seen, or even read, though there is mention of cables and voluminous letters; and yet she is a force pervading the background and exercising a corrective hand on her most distant dependants. Chad Newsome, her prodigal son, is in Paris, and will not come home; evidently there is some mysterious entanglement detaining him, which Strether must investigate. So this first ambassador, her confidential secretary, editor, and apostle of her culture, arrives, and ere long by the regular Jacobean methods discovers that Chad is somehow attached to a certain Madame de Vionnet, a lady not yet entirely liberated from an

[1] *The Ambassadors* was written before *The Wings of the Dove*, though published after.
[2] Introduction (*Art of the Novel*, 307).
[3] *Ibid.*, 308.

objectionable husband, but herself an exquisite embodiment of all that is finest in the social genius of France. She has made Chad into one of James's own most perfect men. Strether is not long in coming to recognize this; and eventually it is he who goes counter to Mrs Newsome and the limited outlook of Woollett, and entreats Chad to remain. Other ambassadors arrive to see what is going on: the masterful and indignant Sarah, with her susceptible husband who falls a prey to Parisian temptations, the bouncing Mamie, and the pompous and grandiose Waymarsh. But Strether almost feels as if his own youth had been revived in Chad; it is he who has become emancipated. He all but accepts a charming *émigrée* for himself, but decides to cleave to honour and return to face the music at Woollett.

Not autobi- ography All one's intelligence must be alive and receptive in reading *The Ambassadors*. Strether is the mirror in which everything is seen going on, and his "lifelong trick of intense reflection" is invaluable in bringing out the less obvious significance of what is mirrored; but he is not an autobiographer, and he does not offer statements that compose a simple relation. Far from this, James deliberately shunned both "the terrible *fluidity* of self-revelation" and the danger of smuggling in romance and "other queer matters" by the back door, to which narrative in the first person is perversely liable.

This is not narrative in the first person. Strether is watching what goes on, and trying to find out what has gone on already or is going on where he cannot see it; and the reader is watching Strether. Strether is in the drama with the rest of them, and the same allowances are made for his mind and temperament as for those of anyone else. And even Strether cannot be utilized for conveying some kinds of vital information; hence James has to fall back at times on those subordinate parties that he called "*ficelles*," the most serviceable in this case being Strether's friend Miss Gostrey. This admirable lady keeps the reader posted in previous events and in the hidden bearing of much that is now happening, chiefly in her chats with Strether, for he tells her confidentially what an awkward position he finds himself in.

But he had been for an instant thinking away from this, and he came up in another place. "And yet Mrs Newsome—it's a thing to remember—*has* imagined, did, that is, imagine, and apparently still does, horrors about what I should have found. I was booked, by her vision—extraordinarily intense, after all— to find them; and that I didn't, that I couldn't, that, as she finally felt, I wouldn't—this evidently didn't at all, as they say, 'suit' her book. It was more than she could bear. That was her disappointment."

"You mean you were to have found Chad himself horrible?"

"I was to have found the woman."

"Horrible?"

"Found her as she insistently imagined her." And Strether paused as if for his own expression of it he could add no touch to that picture.

His companion had meanwhile thought. "She imagined stupidly—so it comes to the same thing."

"Stupidly? Oh!" said Strether.

But she insisted. "She imagined meanly."

He had it, however, better. "It couldn't but be ignorantly."

"Well, intensity with ignorance—what do you want worse?"[1]

James thought he had so blended the pictorial and the scenic by this dramatization of one or two consciousnesses, Strether's in particular, that it was as if the reader sat at a performance of the whole affair, and had some other special advantages to boot. He had taken his material "absolutely for the stuff of drama"; and, if the result is not always scenic in appearance, "it may definitely be said . . . that everything in it that is not scene . . . is discriminated preparation, is the fusion and synthesis of picture."[2] Thus to the refractory question of Strether's past, for instance, he had given "a high lucidity and vivacity," such as would be the effect of "an excellent *standard* scene." But the great feat in *The Ambassadors* is to have made Strether at once a spectator and to all intents and purposes the chief reporter of the events going on, and also a chief figure in the drama. Though it is in his consciousness of them that the events are rendered visible, that mind is involved in the events

---

[1] *The Ambassadors*, xxix.
[2] *Ibid.*, 323.

and steadily altered by what he sees. That mind is laid bare, and its every movement watched. And the changes in it at length grow more absorbing than the doings on which it is directed. Strether is intent upon the behaviour of Chad and Madame de Vionnet, and it is the reader who first becomes aware that Strether is a changed man. No wonder James was able to write with such confidence, "I am able to estimate this as, frankly, quite the best, 'all round,' of my productions; any failure of that justification would have made such an extreme of complacency publicly fatuous." [1]

"The Golden Bowl" Yet, in the fineness of the ethical standards tacitly vindicated, which are fundamentally the charity and sympathy and natural affections which make life fair, moral and æsthetic values being thereby identified, and in the tragic poignancy of feeling brought to a dramatic pitch before the ultimate scene of parting and quiet renunciation, *The Golden Bowl* (1905) rises perhaps to still higher levels, and certainly does not fall short in James's most elaborate and refined technique. Like the two others in this culminating group,[2] it is an international novel; and here again the depth and scope of his internationalism is of a comprehensiveness and sensitiveness far exceeding the differences of temperament, manners, and culture which were the theme of earlier novels. A lifetime of international experience had enriched and mellowed his insight and broadened his sympathies. It was not now downright opposites to be reconciled, but differences of native endowment and of social tradition and manners to be absorbed and blended for the shaping of a finer world. New England philistinism had the worst of it in *The Ambassadors*; here it is the converse. A case of moral obliquity that might be put down to loose Continental principles is the disturbing cause that jeopardizes an American marriage. It is rectified by a lofty act of forgiveness and devotion on the part of the American wife, an act that might go to the credit of puritan tradition liberalized by cosmopolitan culture and by

[1] *The Ambassadors*, 309.
[2] Four volumes appeared subsequently: a collection of stories, *The Finer Grain* (1910), *The Outcry* (1911), a novel on the lines of a three-act play, and, posthumously, *The Sense of the Past* and *The Ivory Tower*, the latter unfinished (1917). For *The Sense of the Past*, see above, p. 256.

the imagination that sees things as they are. It is a graver situation altogether. Potentially this is an *Othello* in which vengeance is forgone in favour of Christian forgiveness and another chance for the sinners, overwhelmed and schooled by the generosity of the injured pair. The daughter of the man of millions married to the Italian prince at length becomes morally certain that her husband and the beautiful woman who is now her father's wife—a marriage which she herself had brought about—had been and still are lovers. But Maggie is free from the petty egotisms and the baser jealousies. She is one of those who can bear anything. Mrs Assingham, who is in everybody's secrets and knows all that is going on, finds Maggie wonderful:

"My dear child, you're amazing."
"Amazing—?"
"You're terrible."
Maggie thoughtfully shook her head. "No; I'm not terrible, and you don't think me so. I do strike you as surprising, no doubt—but surprisingly mild. Because—don't you see?—I *am* mild. I can bear anything."
"Oh, 'bear'!" Mrs Assingham fluted.
"For love," said the Princess.
Fanny hesitated. "Of your father?"
"For love," Maggie repeated.
It kept her friend watching. "Of your husband?"
"For love," Maggie said again.

For her it is a sudden awakening, and she only now becomes aware of the nature of her love for her errant husband. She determines to make sure of him, the father of her child. And she has the greatness of heart to forgive both the sinners; she can pity the woman who lost him. So Maggie tells the Prince that she knows all, and leaves it to him to break off with his mistress. Her chief anxiety now is to keep her father unsuspecting. But Mr Verver is equally clear-sighted; he too takes his measures. At the cost of parting with his child, he resolves on the decisive step of giving up his adopted country and going back to America with his wife. Such is the simple course of events, such the tragic complication and its resolution. And, since there is a tacit conspiracy to avoid open charges and recriminations, since the tragic conflict has to work itself out under the surface of an affectionate and apparently felicitous family life, it is only in one or two scenes that the danger-signal is sounded.

A consummate example of James's methods

James never contrived an apter framework for the handling of human passions at issue, or solved an agonizing problem with such uniform suppression of anything violent. There is no case here of glaring misdemeanours, of scandalous doings caught in the very act. There is never any doubt of what is going on, but the only plain-speaking is when those interested friends the Assinghams talk the situation over. The reader moves about, not among categorical facts, but amid the moral certitudes that are so much better than facts. He comes to see, by the same process as Maggie and Mrs Assingham, exactly how the land lies. Nothing is definitely stated, nothing takes place that can be pointed to as marking a decisive change of attitudes and relations between the different pairs; but conviction is borne in by a thousand signs and hints. The reader, and those who have everything at stake, have alike to watch for the tokens that put together may tell a tale. That is what James hints when he pictures Maggie sitting full-dressed in her drawing-room waiting for her husband's return after the day he has spent with Charlotte. She has asked herself many questions, wondered at many odd things, realized at last that her feeling for her husband has "begun to vibrate with a violence that had some of the effect of a strain"; she was "acting up to the full privilege of passion." And she looks back on the course of her wonderments and surprises and perceptions, trying to realize what it all means.

It fell, for retrospect, into a succession of moments that were *watchable* still; almost in the manner of the different things done during a scene on the stage, some scene so acted as to have left a great impression on the tenant of one of the stalls. Several of these moments stood out beyond the others, and those she could feel again most, count again like the firm pearls on a string, had belonged more particularly to the lapse of time before dinner—dinner which had been so late, quite at nine o'clock, that evening, thanks to the final lateness of Amerigo's own advent.

Maggie's intuition is hard at work. "Her grasp of appearances was thus out of proportion to her view of causes; but it came to her then and there that if she could only get the facts of appearance right, only jam them down into their place, the reasons lurking behind them, kept uncertain, for the eyes, by their wavering and shifting, wouldn't perhaps be able to help showing."

The reader is called upon to exercise the same keen intuition, the same careful judgment, and goes step by step, with the Prince in the first half, with Maggie in the second, in realizing the essence of the situation, and the last shade of significance in the attitudes of the characters each to each. But the method is triumphant; his assurance of the truth is perfect—it is as if he were inside the minds of the chief actors or commanded all that takes place from the standpoint of omniscience. He knows all that it is vital to know, and waits quietly for Maggie or her father, or for Charlotte or the Prince, to do the next thing, with all the odds and alternatives and probable consequences clearly realized.

The Golden Bowl is an immensely long novel, and if it seems *Moral* to be lacking in incident it reproduces something like the grain *issues* and texture of life—it is a vast succession of "watchable" *from first* moments. And from the first pages the moral question is *to last* to the fore. Amerigo, the Prince, that astonishing museum specimen, that *"morceau de musée,"* has to bring it up himself. He has noticed how the English, and the Americans, are always unprepared for "any *serious* discussion of veracity, of loyalty, or rather of the want of them." It is a question that has "to be joked about. It couldn't be gone into." Mrs Assingham has it up later with her husband, from another point of view. She calls him immoral, and he objects. "She hesitated. 'I'll call you stupid if you prefer. But stupidity pushed to a certain point *is*, you know, immorality. Just so what is morality but high intelligence?'" This first book, "The Prince," builds up the situation: that easygoing state of things, so perfect by Italianate standards, is indeed the work of Amerigo. The second, "The Princess," is the symmetrical history of Maggie's mastery of it and eventual solution. Amerigo is always prepared to discuss it with his sponsor, his fairy godmother, Mrs Assingham, though the English point of view escapes him. "He might vulgarly have put it that one had never to plot or to lie for them; he might humorously have put it that one had never, as by the higher conformity, to lie in wait with the dagger or to prepare, insidiously, the cup. These were the services that, by all romantic tradition, were consecrated to affection quite as much as to hate." Fanny Assingham is easily checkmated. "Oh, I deny responsibility—to *you*. So far as I ever had it I've done with it."

He had been, all the while, beautifully smiling; but she made his look, now, penetrate her again more. "As to whom then do you confess it?"

"Ah, *mio caro*, that's—if to anyone—my own business." He continued to look at her hard. "You give me up then?"

It was what Charlotte had asked her ten minutes before, and its coming from him so much in the same way shook her in her place. . . . "I think I don't know what to make of you."

The longest sitting of the two Assinghams on the affair is in chapter twenty-four, which from beginning to end is a masterpiece of comedy reading tragedy. To one side of life Fanny Assingham's imagination has been closed, "her sense altogether sealed"; and now Fanny sees it is about to be opened. "To what's called Evil—with a very big E: for the first time in her life. To the discovery of it, to the knowledge of it, to the crude experience of it." Their own safeguard is that they know nothing. They are as innocent as babes.

"Why not rather say," he asked, "as innocent as they themselves are?"

"Oh, for the best of reasons! Because we're much more so."

He wondered. "But how can we be more—?"

"For them? Oh, easily! We can be anything."

"Absolute idiots then?"

"Absolute idiots. And oh," Fanny breathed, "the way it will rest us!"

Well, he looked as if there were something in that. "But won't they know we're not?"

She barely hesitated. "Charlotte and the Prince think we are—which is so much gained. Mr Verver believes in our intelligence—but he doesn't matter."

Maggie dare not broach the subject to her father; she admires his "splendid indifference," all the while wondering how much he knows, hoping he knows nothing. But by almost imperceptible signs it soon grows clear that the wonderful little man, who keeps so isolated in the pursuit of his life's ambition, the connoisseur who knows every gallery in Europe and the whereabouts and value of every piece of marble or canvas destined for his great museum in American City, is the one that knows most. There is the irony: her efforts have been to shield him from the pain of any disclosure, he on his part has been all intent on shielding her. And they keep silence to the end. He without a word of accusation or reproof brings Charlotte to heel. "They, on their side"—the Prince and Charlotte—"thought of everything *but* that," Maggie tells her friend Fanny.

"They thought of everything but that I might think."

"Or even," her friend too superficially concurred, "that your father might!"

As to this, at all events, Maggie discriminated. "No, that wouldn't have prevented them; for they knew that his first care would be not to make me do so. As it is," Maggie added, "that has had to become his last."

Fanny Assingham took it in deeper—for what it immediately made her give out louder. "*He's* splendid then." She sounded it almost aggressively; it was what she was reduced to —she had positively to place it.

"Ah, that as much as you please!"

Maggie said this and left it, but the tone of it had the next moment determined in her friend a fresh reaction. "You think, both of you, so abysmally and yet so quietly. But it's what will have saved you."

"Oh," Maggie returned, "it's what—from the moment they discovered we could think at all—will have saved *them*. For they're the ones who are saved," she went on. "We're the ones who are lost."

"Lost—?"

"Lost to each other—father and I." And then as her friend appeared to demur, "Oh yes," Maggie quite lucidly declared, "lost to each other much more, really, than Amerigo and Charlotte are; since for them it's just, it's right, it's deserved, while for us it's only sad and strange and not caused by our fault. But I don't know," she went on, "why I talk about myself, for it's on father it really comes. I let him go," said Maggie.

The artist's sense of responsibility

Once more, virtue is its own reward, as it had been for Fleda Vetch, for Densher, for Strether. Goodness and beauty are again identified. Following their several guiding stars, these four elect, richly endowed beings are seen consciously busy making their lives a work of art. Even the two Assinghams, whose serio-comic colloquies are a refreshing distraction from the inner and more serious theme, have their place and part in bringing out the latent meanings, the remoter bearings, of what is doing. Idiosyncrasies, the surface accidents and eccentricities of character, were welcome perquisites of the spectator of human nature when they occurred, and James gathered in a picturesque assortment of such casual humours. But these were not his main object. He had little but contempt for the Dickensian view; like George Eliot and Meredith, he looked on life as the sphere for something more serious—for the making and exercise of character. Life is a solemn affair, and the urgent requisites are intelligence, thought, imagination. The primary impulse of the individual is to assert himself—from the core, the vital principle of selfhood, to establish a personality. That is the art of life; the art of the novelist is to mirror this activity and reveal the laws and conditions that govern it. Galleries of droll characters are a frivolous amusement compared with this. Quality not quantity was the mark for the self-respecting novelist. James shows his imaginary beings at work developing themselves as responsible, self-respecting units, asserting their freedom, dignity, and integrity as individual souls, making their own decisions and shaping circumstances and personal relationships to some correspondence with their ideals. It meant in this case again a virtual equation of moral and æsthetic values. Brought up in a puritan environment, James was transplanted to the richer civilization of western Europe. From first to last, his main interest was in the conflict between a narrow and bigoted and a broad and liberal culture in which intellectual and æsthetic interests were given full play. His conception of the personal life as the root of the problem saved him from viewing it merely as a question of dogmatic ethics. Moral attitudes were to be determined by the criteria of personal development in a complete revaluation of life. And, though the artist is not called upon to expound and inculcate a moral lesson, he cannot be blind and indifferent to what is inevitably one of the largest aspects of his appointed subject. James had a profound sense of the responsibilities of the novelist. The sensitiveness of his artistic conscience appears in the strain and exertion he imposed on himself in sticking to his "irrepressible ideal" in the ever-recurring problem of presentation, when it might have provoked little criticism to have taken the beaten path instead of his fastidious indirectness.

Beset constantly with the sense that the painter of the picture or the chanter of the ballad (whatever we may call him) can never be responsible *enough*, and for every inch of his surface and note of his song, I track my uncontrollable footsteps, right and left, after the fact, while they take their quick turn, even on stealthiest tiptoe, toward the point of view that, within the compass, will give me most instead of least to answer for.[1]

On this side, James is the novelist's novelist, setting new and finer standards, as well as employing new methods, and showing himself the most punctilious observer of the new code when obedience was most arduous. He set new standards of craftsmanship, and, of course, new standards of criticism. But it is necessary only to glance at the register of men of letters to be reminded that the serious artist, however much he disclaims the office, cannot help being both a teacher and a lawgiver. Not unlikely, his scope and influence will be in precisely

[1] Preface to *The Golden Bowl.*

inverse ratio to any such pretensions on his own part.   James will, no doubt, have eventually to take his place, and no minor one, in the long row stretching from Carlyle, Dickens, and Tennyson to Kipling, Chesterton, and D. H. Lawrence.   Even those who repudiated the alleged effects of art, such Gallios as Moore and Wilde and Whistler, did not quite escape responsibility.   James's gift to his age was, not only a science of the art of fiction, but also a science of the art of life.   His novels were a contribution to civilization.   Over and over again in them, the conflict is seen going on, puritanism at odds with a higher and richer civilization, which he shows in process of evolution to still higher levels, led by a culture to which puritanism was bitterly and doggedly hostile.   He may have ignored many sides of human activity; but, at any rate, he did not ignore the vital problems; and, as he looked to the future as well as the past and present, he may be of lasting value to mankind as a far-seeing critic and a philosophic guide. Henry James had his "message" as much as anyone.

Influence on other novelists   The results of his revision of the principles of the art have, of course, not yet fully appeared.   The paths he pointed out were too arduous but for the few.   He remains the novelist's novelist—and the critic's.   George Moore learned considerably from James before he wrote *Evelyn Innes* and *Sister Teresa*, but showed better results in those later works in which he saw the problem of statement and presentation in a stricter light and adjusted his practice to a psychological theory of illusion. Conrad, it will be found, studied James to good purpose. Arnold Bennett could not read him.   Galsworthy was probably in debt to James most of all for the lead given in such novels as *The Spoils of Poynton*, which approximate to regular drama. Katherine Mansfield and still more Mrs Virginia Woolf and Miss Dorothy Richardson show further stages, or special developments, of what James called "my preference for dealing with my subject-matter, for 'seeing my story,' through the opportunity and the sensibility of some more or less detached, some not strictly involved, though thoroughly interested and intelligent, witness or reporter."   Such close disciples as Paul Bourget and the American, Mrs Wharton, are not the only

evidences of his remoter influence. One result not to be overlooked is the deeper and wider gulf that now yawns between
the novel of mere amusement, "the novel of commerce," and
that which can be recognized as literature—which is surely
something not to be deplored.

CHAPTER VIII

THE ROMANCERS

Romance and realism in continual reaction

THE object of romance, says Meredith, is "to beguile us"; and in *The Amazing Marriage* he sums it up: "Poetic romance is delusion—a tale of a Corsair; a poet's brain, a bottle of gin, and a theatrical wardrobe"; going on to descant on "the enchanted horse of the Tale, which leaves the man's mind at home while he performs the deeds befitting him." Tired of the sober and serious study of realities, readers thirst for something headier; and writers—mere bootleggers many of them—are speedily found ready with a suitable beverage. When Fielding, Richardson, and Smollett were showing the supreme interest of common human nature and actual every-day life, Walpole in a fit of boredom wrote *The Castle of Otranto*; and, he having shown what inspiration there was in gin and the theatrical wardrobe, Mrs Radcliffe and other teetotal ladies started a lucrative business at the circulating libraries with their spicy concoctions of mystery and terror, dubious history and unabashed sentiment. How the draught was strengthened by the taste and skill of "Monk" Lewis, Maturin, and other adepts is a familar story. They have all been immortalized by literary historians as heralds of rom-anticism, which is, however, something bigger and more impassioned, springing from the deeps of man's nature—a spiritual attitude, a more ardent and penetrating philosophy of life and the universe, a vision that outsoars the logical reason. Nevertheless, these votaries of mere romance did provide Scott with ideas for the romantic novel. But Scott was the contemporary of Jane Austen and Maria Edgeworth; and, when he gave up writing Ladies of the Lake and Marmions for fiction in prose, he showed that romanticism was not simply to be identified with romance or any other prescriptive relaxation or amusement, but is truly an emancipating force, releasing the imagination, creating the world anew. Scott has his place in the company of Wordsworth and Coleridge, Shelley and Keats. The truth is, romanticism asserts itself as readily and abundantly in realistic fiction as in romance, better perhaps, for nothing tends more inevitably to a tissue of conventions than the out-and-out romance. Realism and romance may be opposites, as intimated by Meredith; but there is nothing irrational or inconsistent in pressing realism even into the service of romance—genius finds that they get on very well together. Stevenson, it will soon appear, could make himself a regular Defoe, to authenticate by a stroke of vivid sensation a hazardous flight of originality. Scott's intention in his romantic novels was certainly not merely "to beguile"; his familiar knowledge of the manners and usages and even the lesser events of the periods he chose to write about, and his profound interest in human character, would have saved him from that. The best of them called back to life his own yesterdays or times remembered by people whom he knew, and were as truthful in everything but a few candid alterations of fact as he could make them. Romance was not lacking; but the larger and richer element was their essential veracity.

Scott's influence was immense. He it was that gave the lead to be followed by G. P. R. James, Captain Marryat, Harrison Ainsworth, Fenimore Cooper, Charles Lever, and a large body of European novelists. Then, under the dictatorship of Dickens and Thackeray, romance went into the background or into disguise. Some gin and theatricality might be detected in the melodramatic parts of *Barnaby Rudge* or *A Tale of Two Cities*; but *Esmond* and *The Virginians*, *Barry Lyndon* and *Denis Duval* were compounded of the same realism as the rest of Thackeray's fiction; these were historical novels that seemed to shun the least suspicion of being romantic. Charles Reade's and George Eliot's two most painstaking novels, *The Cloister and the Hearth* (1861) and *Romola* (1863), show the same anxious regard for matters of fact. The most

Scott's successors

romantic historical novels of that period were Lytton's and Charles Kingsley's. And yet over against *Westward Ho!* with its heroic afflatus must be placed *Hypatia* and *Hereward the Wake*, which paraded their documentary claims to accuracy with as fidgety a conscientiousness as even Lytton displayed, rather superfluously, in *Harold*, *The Last Days of Pompeii*, and *The Last of the Barons*. To hear their assurances, they might have been Flaubert writing *Salammbô* (1862), a piece of hard labour and research that did indeed mark an epoch in the application of realism to historical fiction. There was nothing even remotely comparable with it in English till the era of *John Inglesant* (1881) and *Marius the Epicurean* (1885), and of George Moore's reconstructions of the ancient and the mediæval worlds.

Another revival of romance —Blackmore   Two new lines of romance date from the time of the æsthetes, the revival of full-blown mediævalism by William Morris and Stevenson's daring manipulations of what he called "the poetry of circumstance." But the notable outbreak of miscellaneous romance identified with the names of Besant and Rice, Baring-Gould, William Black, Robert Buchanan, and those purveyors of the lurid and blood-curdling for the uncritical mob, Hall Caine and Rider Haggard, may be attributed to the vogue of a novelist who stood aloof from contemporary schools and movements, Richard Doddridge Blackmore (1825–1900), author of that popular classic *Lorna Doone*. Blackmore was rather a solitary, and so far as his work represents a movement he was the only member. His novels were indeed a counterblast to the anti-romantic historical fiction of Thackeray; but this actual effect of them was probably undesigned. Born of West Country stock, and brought up amid the scenes to be immortalized in *Lorna Doone*, he went, like John Ridd, to Blundell's School, and from there to Oxford, becoming a good classical scholar. Love of the subject-matter as well as of the poetry was the motive of his translation of the first two Georgics, published under the title, *The Farm and Fruit of Old* (1862). A legacy having saved him just in time from having to earn his living by the law or as a teacher, he settled down about the age of thirty on a little estate at Teddington, to his lifelong hobby, gardening,[1] and the secondary occupation of writing verses and then novels. *Clara Vaughan* (1864) and *Cradock Nowell, a tale of the New Forest* (1865), were country novels deserving no better fate than they met with. Though Blackmore solemnly prefixed to his first novel the Æschylean watchword δράθαντι παθεῖν, and gave it to be understood that he proposed to naturalize romance amid the complexities of our modern existence, all he had to offer was a medley of sentiment, farce, and melodrama, loosely held together by a plot thick with coincidences. It was an effort in the style of Wilkie Collins and Collins's industrious and immensely popular disciple, Miss Braddon, whose *Lady Audley's Secret* (1862) and *Aurora Leigh* (1863) were then all the rage.[2] It was the same with *Cradock Nowell*. Pages could be singled out in both set off by the gift for wordpainting of landscape, the seasons, and the weather, which readers of *Lorna Doone* were to find so seducing; and he made a bid for distinction also in the lush, euphuistic, highly lyrical and even half-metrical prose, which sometimes has a charm in spite of his disregard of accepted law and order. The best that can be said for his wrestling prodigy Huxtable, in the first, who could fling a horse and man over a hedge, or for the eccentric Parson Rosedew in the second novel, is that they have a certain elementary raciness, like the rest of the rustic worthies who were to be a feature of his novels right to the end. The humour is as broad as the melodrama is crude. Blackmore was evidently courting the suffrages of a very unfastidious class of reader.

All the same, neither these nor *Lorna Doone* (1869) had "*Lorna* any immediate success, though when this third and far better *Doone*," novel did gain recognition Blackmore went on swimmingly.[3] *etc.*

---

[1] He reckoned that in thirty years he "lost some £20,000" by his gardening enterprises, which he tried to make remunerative by having a stall at Covent Garden Market and other means. He was a poor man of business (see *Wilkie Collins, Le Fanu, and others*, by S. M. Ellis).

[2] Blackmore is said, however, to have told my old friend James Baker that *Clara Vaughan* "was written before Miss Braddon was heard of" (Burris, 35). Anyhow, the sensational novels of Wilkie Collins, Sheridan le Fanu, and Mrs Henry Wood, as well as Miss Braddon's, were having a roaring time just then.

[3] The story is that it leapt into fame, after three years of neglect, through the blunder of a journalist who connected it with the Marquesses of Lorne, at the time of the royal marriage with this house in 1871 (Burris, 35).

It was written to the Waverley formula for historical fiction, fortified with the more exuberant brand of romance that Kingsley had infused into *Westward Ho!* A rich and mellow flavour was also imparted by the scenes of old-fashioned life going peacefully on far from the busy haunts of men, a leavening for either romance or realism that both Kingsley and George Eliot had recently been using to great effect. The setting was indeed a most important feature, and as romantic as the doings of Blackmore's stalwart heroes and lovely damsels in distress; in both the descriptions and the narrative the colours were laid on thick. Exmoor and its picturesque fringes, about the time of the battle of Sedgemoor and of the barbarities of Kirke's Lambs and Judge Jeffreys, was the theatre of events; in short, this is localized romance, utilizing facts from local history, but bringing in such outside events only, as it were, by accident. Blackmore's idea of romance was a loose from the trammels of reality: his object was, veritably, "to beguile us." In lieu of the Corsair prescribed by Meredith, he had his robber Doones; and the rest of it was according to a very old formula—the heroine of peerless beauty, imprisoned in the ogre's castle, and rescued by a racier equivalent to the Gawain or Lancelot of tradition, John Ridd, the colossal yeoman of wrestling prowess. Of dulcet sentiment or of poetic justice there was no stint. The opening chapters of *The Maid of Sker* (1872) are laid among fisher-folk in Glamorganshire, where Blackmore had spent some years of his childhood; but the story soon crosses to Devon, where a lonely parish is ruled despotically by the chief landowner, the diabolical Parson Chowne, one of his few unamiable clerical figures, and not a bad substitute for Carver Doone in the previous novel. An historical original has been found for him, as for a good many of Blackmore's worthies or unworthies. This is one of several novels in which abduction is an episode on which the plot hinges. In others, things turn upon a disputed inheritance and the misfortunes of an ancient house, and so on. The situation of Lorna, the persecuted heroine who must be delivered, of course by the hero who wins her hand, is continually repeated, with variations; and Blackmore's plot-work, though ingenious enough, often leaves the reader far from convinced that events would have ended so pleasingly. It was his practice to let the chief person concerned tell the story, a method condemned by Henry James and Stevenson. Though he happened in *The Maid of Sker* to put it in the mouth of the old fisherman, Davy Llewellyn, with the same advantage of a point of view as old Mackellar provides in *The Master of Ballantrae*, he failed to notice the immense superiority of this oblique method, and relapsed into the facile and delusive trick of autobiography. None of his other novels, such as *Alice Lorraine, Mary Anerley, Springhaven,* or *Perlycross,* went so far back into the past as *Lorna Doone.* The fact is, Blackmore wasted himself, and a great deal of pains and skill, on sugary romances and flimsy melodramas, when a man of his literary breeding and genuine talent ought to have done better altogether. Perhaps the seclusion in which he lived, and a lack of self-confidence, were to blame. He shut himself away, and knew next to nothing of what had been going on in the world since the time of Judge Jeffreys. If he did write a novel or two on the days of Nelson or the Reform Bill, it was a daring attempt at modernity—the modernity of his own schooldays. Anyhow, he knew or found out what was popular, and for a time had as good an innings as Wilkie Collins and Miss Braddon. And the sensuous and emotional romancing, historical or non-historical, which he revived and improved to the taste of readers, was closely imitated by those novelists who envied him his success with *Lorna Doone.*[1]

To other novelists, as evidently to Blackmore, romance was *Other romantic* a business proposition, though some of them might have been *novelists* loath to admit that they were simply and solely romancing. William Black, Sir Walter Besant, and Baring-Gould were professional writers who had to satisfy the circulating libraries, and if they had tastes of their own were ready to make them conform to those of the general reader, a composite figure that was now coming to be the recognized autocrat of letters

[1] Blackmore has been accounted worthy of an American university thesis—*Richard Doddridge Blackmore, his life and novels,* by Quincy Guy Burris (University of Illinois Press, 1930), which has already been referred to. It is a sensible and critical piece of work, and does not boost its subject unduly.

—in this commercialized sphere. Such writers really stand, of course, only on the outskirts of literature, though they doubtless cherished higher pretensions, and Besant had the assurance, as already noted, to lay down the law in *The Art of Fiction*, and to draw up a set of "Rules for Novel-writers." The latter, at any rate, formed a useful vade-mecum for the neophyte, insisting upon intelligence and industry, but not going into æsthetic questions except in the injunctions, "Endeavour to be dramatic" and "Avoid the sin of writing about a character." William Black (1841–1898), a Glasgow journalist, struck a remunerative vein when he discovered how enormously the appeal of a happy love-story and of light sketches of Scottish manners and personal peculiarities was enhanced when combined with lyrical word-pictures of Highland glens and mountains and Hebridean seas. His first novel, *A Daughter of Heth* (1871), is probably his best, though he was more ambitious and more effusive when he proceeded to contrast the garishness of society and fashion with Highland simplicities, usually by marrying a hothouse flower from the English metropolis to a brave and dignified young chieftain, as in *Macleod of Dare* (1879), or transplanting an unspoiled girl from a Highland home to fast life in London, as in *A Princess of Thule* (1874), *The Maid of Killeena* (1874), or *Wild Eelin* (1898). Obviously, all this was mainly according to Blackmore's recipe, though Black followed him into the historical field only once, in *Judith Shakespeare* (1884), a feeble romance about Shakespeare's daughter. His scenery was still more lavish; his sunsets over Skye became famous—or a byword. His novels must, indeed, have been a great advertisement, and have brought many thousands of tourists to the Western Isles. Some of them were actually planned on the lines of a tour, and served some of the purposes of a guidebook. Sabine Baring-Gould (1834–1924) did not compete with him, but employed his descriptive powers, as already mentioned in the comparison with Hardy,[1] to deepen the grimness of some tale of passion and crime, or at least to add colour and picturesqueness. He was an accomplished antiquary

[1] See above, p. 95.

and an expert in local history and folk-lore, qualifications exploited to the full in very miscellaneous novels of quiet village life, or unquiet life in more or less distant epochs, the scenes laid in out-of-the-way spots from the salt-marshes of the east coast to Devon and Cornwall. *Urith, a tale of Dartmoor* (1891), *Kitty Alone* (1895), *Dartmoor Idylls* (1896), and *Guavas the Tinner* (1897), did for Dartmoor very much what *Lorna Doone* had done for Exmoor; and Baring-Gould found material and suitable environments for many other romantic reconstructions of the past, from the Continent as well, and from the most ancient times down to the eve of the present.

There was a steady demand for historical fiction all the time *Besant* the æsthetes and the professors of various types of realism were *and Rice* writing and theorizing. The earlier novels of Walter Besant (1838–1901) were written in partnership with James Rice (1844–1882), and several took this popular shape, the title-piece of *'Twas in Trafalgar's Bay, and other stories* (1879), for instance, with the half-legendary tale of old Quebec, "Le Chien d'Or," and *The Chaplain of the Fleet* (1881), a well-informed novel of London, Epsom, and the famous gaol, in the time of George II. The pair had begun with a good, exciting plot-novel, *Ready-money Mortiboy* (1872), followed by *The Golden Butterfly* (1876), this latter invading the sociological field with its half-satirical account of a vast humanitarian undertaking on which an American oil-king expends his millions. Besant was an earnest worker for social amelioration, and played with similar fancies after the loss of his coadjutor, or cheered his optimistic heart with ideas a little more feasible. *The Revolt of Man* (1882) was a pleasantry at the expense of women's claims to be at least equal to men: they are shown in full command, until the men mutiny—and they are right glad to abdicate. *All Sorts and Conditions of Men* (1882) and *The Children of Gibeon* (1886) also attacked the social problem, the one putting forward a utopian scheme, after-wards realized in the People's Palace, in the East End, the other a study of actual conditions in a poor district of London, having something shrewd to say on class distinctions. *Beyond the Dreams of Avarice* (1895), with a suitable mingling of seriousness and humour, dealt with the evils of colossal wealth in unscrupulous hands. But the great bulk of Besant's novels are of the other category, historical fiction substantiated with a sufficiency of hard facts and with the general verisimilitude and the plausibility of character at the command of an experienced novelist, especially one well grounded in Dickens. *Dorothy Forster* (1884), of Northumberland and Bamborough Castle at the time of the Jacobite rising in 1715, comes nearest to *Lorna Doone*; but *The World went very well then* (1887), *For Faith and Freedom* (1888), *The Orange Girl* (1899), *The Lady of Lynn* (1901), and *No other Way* (1902), were animated pictures of bygone times, especially times of domestic unrest or war abroad, not without the proper allowance of gin and the theatrical wardrobe. One historical romance of this period, *The Shadow of the Sword* (1875), by Robert Buchanan, an epical perspective of the Napoleonic era, evidently inspired by *Quatre-vingt-treize* and *Les Misérables*, was a solemn diatribe against militarism. Buchanan's other not quite ephemeral novel, *God and the Man* (1880), is also a grandiose apologue in the manner of Victor Hugo.

Romance according to Stevenson   Stevenson did his best to put romance upon a proper footing, in regard to realism and to art in general. Even from the few remarks already quoted, it is obvious that he was a very self-conscious writer, prone to ask himself questions about his art and the responsibilities it laid upon him. What he wrote on the subject amounts, not merely to an æsthetics of romance, but also to an ethics of the attitudes and intentions of the romancer. The main facts of the life and the brief and crowded literary career of Robert Louis Balfour Stevenson (1850–1894) are too well known to need even summarizing here. He began, apart from an odd trifle or two, as an essayist, or as a meditative traveller in the manner of Sterne, which is much the same thing. It is in his essays *Virginibus puerisque* (1881), *Familiar Studies of Men and Books* (1882), with its "Preface by way of criticism," the papers collected in *Memories and Portraits* (1887), some of those in *Across the Plains, with other Memories and Essays* (1892), and several dating further back and posthumously gathered together as *Essays in the Art of Writing* (1905), that he discussed these questions. What he first sought to frame and then expound was a philosophy of life; but this obsessing topic was gradually succeeded, without being relinquished, by the problem of art, the two being so closely bound up together that they often seem inseparable. In truth, the more Stevenson tried to contemplate his art as an "a-moral" activity—to adopt his own adjective—the more he was thrown back upon his ingrained propensity to moralize. Those scornful sayings of his on "the lofty aims and moral influence of art," and his deliberate preference for "a grace in handling, apart from any value in the thought," [1] seem to affiliate him to the æsthetes: they tally pretty closely, and so does the brilliance of the writing, with Oscar Wilde's pronouncements upon art, "not as expressive but as impressive purely." [2] As time went on, and he put his theories to the test of practice in his novels and stories, he debated still more exhaustively these questions of the nature and aims and methods of art, especially the literary art, and more especially prose fiction. But never to the end of his life did he quite clear up the discrepancies between his repeated assertions that art is purely a matter of form and style, and must at all risks abide by its own canons of perfection, and his acute sense of the moral influence of art and the moral responsibilities of the artist. "I still contend," he said, in writing of "the morality of the profession of letters," "that, in the humblest sort of literary work, we have it in our power either to do great harm or great good." [3] Elsewhere he said, "There is no quite good book without a good morality"; though he added, significantly, "the world is wide, and so are morals." [4] There was an incurable tendency to moralism in Stevenson, who was a born preacher. Colvin relates, as to the four chapters on ethics written in 1879 and now known as *Lay Morals*, that he spoke of ethics as being always his "veiled mistress." [5] A large proportion of his essays are didactic

[1] See above, p. 217.
[2] "Fontainebleau" (*Across the Plains*, etc., 116).
[3] "The Critic as Artist" : this did not appear till 1890, as an article in *The Nineteenth Century*.
[4] *Memories and Portraits*, 238.
[5] See L. Cope Cornford's discussion of this (*Robert Louis Stevenson*, 52).

in matter and manner, and the same may be said of his poems. Since, as he put it himself, "drama is the poetry of conduct," [1] it was right and inevitable that his plays should deal with moral problems, and they cannot be accused of dealing with them didactically. But there are innumerable passages in the novels where his characters get into the pulpit, almost with the express approval of the author; and a number of his most striking tales are thoroughgoing and unimpeachable moralities, for example, "Will o' the Mill," "The Suicide Club," "Dr Jekyll and Mr Hyde," "The Bottle Imp," or "Markheim," not to mention his "Fables." This is not to say that they trespass against his rule that when moral issues arise in the course of a story they must be treated strictly as dramatic material and not used as pegs for a homily. [2] They are among the few of his stories and novels embodying an idea; and, as is likely to happen, it is a moral idea. But at any rate they bring out his continual preoccupation with ethical matters, his unfailing devotion to the "veiled mistress," as unmistakably as does the sermon in "Old Mortality" or the solemn sententiousness of a dozen other essays on life and death and the enigmas of the universe.

Why he chose to write romance
Stevenson may or may not have been seriously perturbed in spirit by the contradictions between his inherited puritanism, along with his sense of the duties of the writer who has "set himself up for a leader of the minds of men," and the æsthetic doctrine of serene impartiality, of the supremacy and absolutism of the claims of art. But as a professional writer he was faced with the dilemma that literature is a business, that he had "to live by his writing," and hence lay at the mercy of public opinion. In considering "the morality of the profession of letters," he subscribed to the obligation of frankness and sincerity at all costs: the writer "must tell the truth as he sees it," "he must express himself and his own views and preferences; for to do anything else is to do a far more perilous thing than o risk being immoral: it is to be sure of being untrue." [3] "Partiality is immoral; for any book is wrong that

---

[1] *Memories and Portraits*, 250.
[2] See above, p. 204.
[3] *The Art of Writing*, pp. 66–67.

gives a misleading picture of the world and life." But the
criteria of truth and candour that he had assimilated from his
contacts with the leading French novelists were pretty sure to
bring him into collision with the prejudices and suspicions
of middle-class opinion in this country—that opinion which
settled the question whether a book would be a financial
success or the reverse. The hampering restrictions under
which the novelist laboured in England have clearly appeared
in the case of George Moore, whose *Modern Lover* came out
in 1883 and *A Mummer's Wife* in the following year, and who
was to be assailed for *Esther Waters* ten years later.[1] Even
such innocent stories as "The Beach of Falesá" and "The
Treasure of Franchard," incredible as it sounds to record it,
were not to escape the charge of immorality from the British
pharisees. Stevenson raised his voice even against the "public
falsehood" practised by journals in garbling news in the
interests of party. As to the serious reader of fiction, he
justified the frank and fearless statement of even the ugliest
truths on strictly moral grounds. "Each man should learn
what is within him, that he may strive to mend; he must
be taught what is without him, that he may be kind to others.
It can never be wrong to tell him the truth." [2] There are,
indeed, excellent reasons for thinking that Stevenson would
have chosen to write realistic fiction had he had a free hand;
he possessed many of the right gifts, which gifts, whilst he
found such a zest in romancing, and was disposed to see things
in a romantic light, proved invaluable for this other purpose.
If he revelled in the poetry of circumstance, no one knew
better how to make the smallest detail vivid and of enthralling
import, if only to rouse insensate terror and loathing. And
he did it by methods that are the stock-in-trade of realism.
Stevenson knew in his heart of hearts which was the solid and
serious and which the false and flimsy, a truthful and comprehensive statement of his personal view of the world or the
mere romance to which he capitulated, cheating himself with
sophistical arguments about the dangers and difficulties of

[1] See above, p. 176.
[2] *Art of Writing*, 58.

sincerity. "With all my romance," he confessed, "I am a realist and a prosaist, and a most fanatical lover of plain physical sensations plainly and expressly rendered; hence my perils. To do love in the same spirit as I did (for instance) D. Balfour's fatigue in the heather, my dear sir, there were grossness ready-made! And hence, how to sugar?"[1] So he fought shy of love as a dramatic motive. It was George Moore's view that both James and Stevenson had surrendered far too much to "the foolish, false, and hypocritical taste of the time." But, whereas the concessions James made "had in little or nothing impaired his talent, the very opposite seems to me the case with Mr Stevenson. For if any man living in this end of the century needed freedom of expression for the distinct development of his genius, that man is R. L. Stevenson."[2] The novel's emancipation from the despotism of bigotry and hypocrisy was much overdue; but Stevenson had not the firm convictions or the resolution of a Hardy, a Gissing, or a George Moore. He chose the safer course, and declined upon romance, which is a tissue of unrealities, and therefore, as he put it, "a-moral" and immune from attack.

Art and the poetry of circumstance For art is, first of all and last of all, a trade. The love of words, and not a novel reading of historical events, mark the vocation of the writer and the painter. The arabesque, properly speaking, and even in literature, is the first fancy of the artist; he first plays with his material as a child plays with a kaleidoscope; and he is already in a second stage when he begins to use his pretty counters for the end of representation.[3]

In this early essay, "Fontainebleau," and in *The Art of Writing* and elsewhere, Stevenson candidly expounded his view that art is a business, the object of which is to provide entertainment; and the artist a tradesman, a man of business, dealing in a certain commodity and living on the proceeds. As to the particular kind of commodity, he had decided that the safest

---

[1] *Vailima Letters*, 174. Mlle Rosenblatt (239, n.) gives a good account of the compromise Stevenson arrived at, "compromis qui l'empêcha de donner toute sa mesure comme artiste, et qui au fond offense l'idéal de l'art pour l'art, tel qu'il l'avait exprimé ou tel qu'un Flaubert l'avait compris."

[2] *Confessions of a Young Man*, xii. 172.

[3] "Fontainebleau" (*Across the Plains*, 114).

for himself was romance. The common hucksters purveying romance were not troubled as a rule with scruples about form and finish. But Stevenson had a conscience; he was determined on supplying only the best quality, and asked himself what was the first requisite of a work of art, of this or any other kind? The answer was, excellence of workmanship, style in the diction and style in every detail—everything in it should communicate the maximum of pleasure.[1] It is Wilde's view of art again, "not as expressive but as impressive purely." Form is the first essential.

It may be said with sufficient justice that the motive and end of any art whatever is to make a pattern; a pattern, it may be, of colours, of sounds, of changing attitudes, geometrical figures, or imitative lines; but still a pattern. That is the plane on which these sisters meet; it is by this that they are arts.[2]

Even realism is under the same requirement:

This question of realism, let it then be clearly understood, regards not in the least the fundamental truth, but only the technical method, of a work of art. Be as ideal or as abstract as you please, you will be none the less veracious; but if you be weak, you run the risk of being tedious and inexpressive; and if you be very strong and honest, you may chance upon a masterpiece.[3]

A work of art is first cloudily perceived in the mind; during the period of gestation it stands more clearly forward from these swaddling mists, puts on expressive lineaments, and becomes at length that most faultless, but also, alas! that incommunicable product of the human mind, a perfected design.[4]

As a corrective to the neglect of form by Zola and other

[1] "So far as it [i.e. literature] imitates at all, it imitates not life but speech" ("A Humble Remonstrance"—*Memories and Portraits*, 283). This was Stevenson's dialectical warranty for putting style first.
[2] *Art of Writing*, 9.
[3] *Ibid.*, 97–98.
[4] *Ibid.*, 98. Cp. Oscar Wilde's view: "For the real artist is he who proceeds, not from feeling to form, but from form to thought and passion. He does not first conceive an idea, and then say to himself, 'I will put my idea into a complex metre of fourteen lines,' but, realizing the beauty of the sonnet-scheme, he conceives certain modes of music and methods of rhyme, and the mere form suggests what is to fill it and make it intellectually and emotionally complete" ("The Critic as Artist," *Intentions*, 200–201).

realists, who aimed simply at the reproduction of life as they observed it, and acknowledged no rule but that of scientific exactitude, this was a timely contention. But Stevenson's idea of form or pattern as the starting-point, the germ of the work of art, is a singularly empty one. He does not speak of "significant form," of a coalescence of some pregnant idea with a form suitable to develop it, as the creative germ. That will come, apparently, in the process of execution, a time of "extreme perplexity and strain."

It is then, first of all, at this initial and decisive moment when execution is begun, that the ideal and the real do indeed, like good and evil angels, contend for the creation of the work.[1]

Stevenson was not a consecutive thinker; he strikes out many arresting phrases, but there are obvious gaps in his train of thought. In his insistence on form and pattern as the first essential, he seems to slight the originative impulse or inspiration; or, rather, he seems to put all such on the same footing, as of equal validity for the further stages of creation. And, in fact, it was thus that he justified his choice of romance instead of realism, which he says "is a matter purely of externals." It is no especial cultus of nature and veracity, but a mere whim of veering fashion, that has made us turn our back upon the larger, more various, and more romantic art of yore." [2] He was much more fair to the finer realism of his day when he wrote, in "A Humble Remonstrance":

And as the root of the whole matter, let him bear in mind that his novel is not a transcript of life, to be judged by its exactitude; but a simplification of some side or point of life, to stand or fall by its significant simplicity.[3]

But having voted for romance, though he wrote some novels, it was not till he half finished *Weir of Hermiston* that he himself managed to infuse this "significant simplicity" into a broad and ample portrait of life. He saw drama as "the poetry of conduct," which would have given him the novel,

[1] *Art of Writing*, 100–101.
[2] *Ibid.*, 96.
[3] *Memories and Portraits*, 297.

and romance as "the poetry of circumstance"; and he decided upon the latter. It does not seem to have occurred to him that there is no sort of equality between conduct and circumstance, or that an affair of mere circumstance is not likely to be an affair of much moment; so that he was virtually assenting to Meredith's animadversion that the object of romance is "to beguile."

Stevenson was always liable to be dazzled and spellbound *The* by the poetry of circumstance, as his essays demonstrate no *essayist* less eloquently than his novels and stories: it is the circumstance in which he arrays them that gives to his pictures of travel and his meandering reveries such a fascination and such a look of incisiveness. The romancer's mind can be seen at work in his *Travels with a Donkey* (1879), *The Silverado Squatters* (1883), and *In the South Seas* (1900), gloating over and treasuring items of the picturesque and the thrilling, noting down idiosyncrasies and spinning yarns on the strength of them, storing up material for romantic tales which the mere dozen years of his literary life did not give him time to write.[1] *The Silverado Squatters*, in particular, which is presumably a veracious account of his gipsy honeymoon in a derelict mining settlement, is almost a novel as it stands.

One thing in life calls for another; there is a fitness in events and places. . . . One place suggests work, another idleness, a third early rising and long rambles in the dew. The effect of night, of any flowing water, of lighted cities, of the peep of day, of ships, or the open ocean, calls up in the mind an army of anonymous desires and pleasures. Something, we feel, should happen; we know not what, yet we proceed in quest of it. And many of the happiest hours of life fleet by us in this vain attendance on the genius of the place and moment.[2]

---

[1] "If Nature had given him health we should have had the most wonderful tales of travel ever written, interspersed with the quaintest character sketches. But good health would not have given him what he did not bring into the world—a sympathetic mind. He was an eye-man, a wanderer, an Autolycus, picking up halfpence and with exquisite craft turning them into guineas" (Moore's *Avowals*, 44). Moore makes Gosse rejoin "A superior kind of Loti," which agrees with the comparison by Henry James of a page in *Weir of Hermiston* to "the tenderest manner of Pierre Loti" (*Notes on Novelists*, 18-19).

[2] "A Gossip on Romance."

The essayist sets down his impressions; the romancer, whom Stevenson dignifies as "the great creative writer," prepares to "show us the realization and the apotheosis of the day-dreams of common men."

His stories may be nourished with the realities of life, but their true mark is to satisfy the nameless longings of the reader, and to obey the ideal laws of the day-dream. The right kind of thing should fall out in the right kind of place; the right kind of thing should follow; and not only the characters talk aptly and think naturally, but all the circumstances in a tale answer one to another like notes in music.

A training for fiction

The essays on falling in love, on marriage, or on truth of intercourse, in *Virginibus puerisque* (1881), were likewise material for, or the next thing to, romance or novel; and the glimpses of his course of self-training and the discourses on modes of invention and composition, in *Memories and Portraits* (1887), are of much more intrinsic interest than the random philosophizing. For Stevenson was no thinker, though he had flashes of insight, and the manner is more impressive than the matter expounded: he was an adept at making a platitude sound magisterial. Physical and mental adventure was as much the lure in his holidays in strange places and his sojourns in more distant lands as the renewal of health which was the ostensible object; Stevenson had to escape from the humdrum of life and from narrow respectability, if it were only to Bohemia—the same things as he sought and the same as he shunned in his romances, and perhaps with a like avoidance of certain moral obligations, such as a more heroic regard for the duller and sterner truths. The disabilities of an invalid cut him off from the full life of adventure for which he professed a violent yearning. But he knew once or twice what it was to experience the call to action.[1] He faced hardships and privations and some personal danger for the lady who became his wife, and showed powers

[1] He showed his chivalry in the affair of the Curtin family in Ireland (1885). The father had been murdered, and the sons and daughters were the object of a savage boycott and threats of vengeance for one of the moonlighters who had been shot. Young Stevenson offered himself as agent, and was prepared to risk living at the house with his wife and stepson (*Letters*, ii., 26–27).

of command in the final days in Samoa. It would be unjust to say that he got to the world of action only by proxy in his romances. Yet these were, in more senses than one, his way of escape from the restraints that irked him.[1] They originated in the stories he read, and those he enacted with himself as hero or desperado, when a lad; those that he wrote in riper years served the same purpose—they enabled him to recapture the zest of boyhood, and escape from reality into a world of dreams. He could escape thither; but, unhappily, he could never quite conquer that elusive realm, for, try as he might, he never created a genuine hero, the nearest he ever got to it being his villainous Long John Silver and that queer compound of gallantry and vainglory, Alan Breck. There was something of Alan in Stevenson himself, as well as a good deal of the over-conscientious David Balfour. There was always more than a suspicion of attitudinizing about him, from the fopperies of dress and carriage that amused the friends of his youth, to the various kinds of pose assumed in his books. His very optimism was an unconscious pose. It was no ignoble thing, and he thoroughly believed in it. But he talked as if it were based on perfectly unchallengeable philosophic foundations; whereas at the best it was simply the instinct of a brave man, and at the weakest, the nervous audacity of one who was sick. No blame to him for that. This irrational optimism sustained him in many dark hours. It was, as Chesterton put it, "the paradox of hope or faith—that the more hopeless is the situation the more hopeful must be the man." [2] It was a temperamental quality that he assiduously cultivated; but in cultivating it he gave it a strongly theatrical tinge. He loved to talk about life as stern and serious, as serious and stern as a game of football. It pleased him to

[1] Richard Le Gallienne never thought Stevenson "a very great novelist, but regretted that he continued to squander his great gifts upon the British boy, who cares as much about style as a pig about asparagus. The comparisons with Scott were, of course, friendly exaggerations, though it is possible that they may have done Mr Stevenson the unintentional ill-service of diverting him from the true path of his genius. Mr Stevenson, like most of us, sought an escape from the grinding material-ism of the day, and he found it, for the most part, in the gallant world already created for him by Scott " (*Retrospective Reviews*, ii. 191–192, 1894).

[2] "The Moods of Mr George Moore" (*Heretics*, 129). "Stevenson understood this," says G.K.C., " and consequently Mr Moore cannot understand Stevenson."

look at its trials and disasters with the eye of a sportsman: we must realize that they are a part of the game and should be accepted in the proper spirit—we should go into battle singing. But such attitudes look a little childish when it is remembered that Hardy, Mark Rutherford, and Gissing were his fellow-fighters. His sincerity was not quite perfect, any more than his intellectual honesty, which let him indulge in the criticism of life whilst repudiating it, wrong-headedly, as contrary to the laws of art, and evade the duties of a serious novelist by expending himself on romance. These evasions and this amiable make-believe were at bottom the natural corollary to his view of art as mere entertainment, or at best the cult of beautiful form for the pleasure it gives, rather than the most powerful embodiment humanly possible of a serious and aspiring vision of realities. But, at all events, Stevenson had much that is sound to say on romance: he was the Coleridge of that secondary province of romanticism. And his dictum, "the poetry of circumstance," not only holds good for himself and the Stevensonians, but is of retrospective validity.

The master of style Hence, too, the pre-eminence of style in his artistic programme. At the expense of what there was to present, he concentrated first on the rites and ceremonies of presentation. And in this he was so brilliantly successful that many of his stories and of his other works will no doubt still be read when they have no other claim to attention.[1] He arrived at his novel-writing equipped with a style fit for anything—impressions of travel, reminiscences, gossip, essays, sermons, fiction. It followed from his doctrine of form as the primal requisite that he is the great and obvious example of those who put style foremost, who look round for something to exercise their art upon rather than do their best with a chosen and urgent subject. His style was not meant to be merely transparent, though it would be unfair to call it a distorting medium. It is like a stained-glass window; it is there to be looked at, as well as to give light. It is a highly self-conscious style. Often

[1] "Il lui a manqué, pour être un des grands auteurs de la période contemporaine, une matière digne de sa manière" (Abel Chevalley: *Le Roman anglais de notre temps*, 116).

he can be detected writing for display, especially in the essays; and writing for display always excites some suspicion: truth may suffer for the sake of point. A veritable Armado he—

> A man in all the world's new fashion planted,
> That hath a mint of phrases in his brain;
> One whom the music of his own vain tongue
> Doth ravish like enchanting harmony.[1]

For style, the prose-unit is the phrase; and Stevenson was an expert phrase-maker long before he made himself a master of rhythm and cadence. Whatever he was writing, it was the poetry of circumstance that inspired the language; hence the substantives that instantly evoke the image, nay, the very sensation, of a physical thing; or, if it be an abstraction, the vivid, concrete adjective that drives it home with the same force. Stevenson never employs the expected adjective. A pet artifice of his was to think of the word that the average person would say expressed the meaning, and put another with a slightly different sense. So he arrived at his "dainty equilibrium," his "tearing divines," "a high-handed debauch," or "quite a little elegiacal synod."[2] Strange and paradoxical adjectives gave a new vigour to nouns long dulled with overuse. There were other heterodox combinations, especially the mixtures of the racy and colloquial with the formal, the trite, the literary. He was an adept at wedding preciosity to the commonplace. *Virginibus puerisque* is full of such bizarre collocations of noun and epithet. The Brownian rhapsody "Æs Triplex," on "the unparalleled disaster of death," and the moral "to live daringly," teems with electrifying phrases, from which it is only a step to the epigram, "It is better to lose health like a spendthrift than to waste it like a miser," or "The complexity of that game of consequences to which we all sit down." Then there is the oft-quoted "Marriage is a subjective affection," and the witty "To marry is to domesticate the Recording Angel." "Pulvis et Umbra," again, an imaginative reading of the facts presented by science, strips off the abstractness and leaves them in all the nakedness of

[1] *Love's Labour's Lost*, Act I. i. 161–164.
[2] Cp. "Two very sad betting men were playing billiards, attended by a moist consumptive marker" ("The Suicide Club").

their horror and paralysing mystery. Here his blind, instinctive optimism lifts him to a finely cadenced peroration:

And as we dwell, we living things, in our isle of terror and under the imminent hand of death, God forbid it should be man the erected, the reasoner, the wise in his own eyes—God forbid it should be man that wearies in well-doing, that despairs of unrewarded effort, or utters the language of complaint. Let it be enough for faith, that the whole creation groans in mortal frailty, strives with unconquerable constancy: Surely not all in vain.

The essayist in his fiction

For the phrase-making was only a stage. Stevenson learned all there is of rhetoric, only to keep it under—though, it must be admitted, he did not always succeed. In his mature style, the paragraph is as well balanced and as musical as a sonnet. In fact, it is rhythm and cadence that determine the larger unities, rather than thought determining construction. And for the very reason that narrative exercised a sort of external control, and saved him from being led astray by the magic of a cadence or the temptation of casual bypaths, the prose in his stories, if not in his novels, is superior to that of the essays. But it was infinitely indebted to the exercise he had given his pen in the essay. After all, fiction and the essay are no very distant relations. Both interpret life; the one aims to give the quintessence by a philosophic commentary, the other by dramatizing what it thinks of life. Again and again, at the climax of a story, Stevenson puts the whole matter into what is virtually a little essay, only half disguising himself, the essayist, in one of the actors. Who believes it is anyone but Stevenson, though he protests that it is Mr Malthus, in the "Story of the Young Man with the Cream Tarts," who lets off these pyrotechnics on fear: "People trifle with love. Now, I deny that love is a strong passion." (That is certainly Stevenson, who never believed in it.) "Fear is the strong passion; it is with fear that you must trifle, if you would wish to taste the intensest joys of living. Envy me—envy me, sir," he added with a chuckle, "I am a coward!" And thus Stevenson's trade-mark is on *The Ebb-Tide*, written in conjunction with Lloyd Osbourne, in Herrick's debate with himself when he fails in his attempt at suicide and at length swims ashore.

To any man there may come at times a consciousness that there blows, through all the articulations of his body, the wind of a spirit not wholly his; that his mind rebels; that another girds him and carries him whither he would not. It came now to Herrick, with the authority of a revelation. There was no escape possible. The open door was closed in his recreant face. He must go back into the world and amongst men without illusion. He must stagger on to the end with the pack of his responsibility and his disgrace, until a cold, a blow, a merciful chance ball, or the more merciful hangman, should dismiss him from his infamy. There were men who could commit suicide; there were men who could not; and he was one who could not. For perhaps a minute, there raged in his mind the coil of this discovery; then cheerless certitude followed; and, with an incredible simplicity of submission to ascertained fact, he turned round and struck out for shore. There was a courage in this which he could not appreciate; the ignobility of his cowardice wholly occupying him.

The *New Arabian Nights* being largely composed of apologues are full of these relics of the essay; but countless instances occur throughout Stevenson's fiction, even in that which is not half-apologue and so half-essay. But his apologues, like everything else of his, were full of the poetry of circumstance, and are romances too. The style is as circumstantial, as concrete, as richly charged with the magic and atmosphere of place, as that of the essays; hardly more so. Narrative with him is visual, descriptive, pictorial; it appeals to the senses; even so is the dialogue. Here is a bit of the talk of the pirates, just before the sensational moment when they hear the voice from among the trees on the uninhabited island:

Silver, as he sat, took certain bearings with his compass.

"There are three 'tall trees,'" said he, "about in the right line from Skeleton Island. 'Spy-glass Shoulder,' I take it, means that lower p'int there. It's child's play to find the stuff now. I've half a mind to dine first."

"I don't feel sharp," growled Morgan. "Thinkin' o' Flint— I think it were—as done me."

"Ah, well, my son, you praise your stars he's dead," said Silver.

"He were an ugly devil," cried a third pirate with a shudder; "that blue in the face, too!"

"That was how the rum took him," added Merry. "Blue! well, I reckon he was blue. That's a true word." [1]

His first stories George Moore speaks of Stevenson's "direct indebtedness to Edgar Poe, and his constant appropriation of his methods." Not so obvious, but perhaps more vital, was the influence of De Quincey, with his sense of "the horror of life mixed . . . already in earliest youth with the heavenly sweetness of life." Stevenson would surely have assented to De Quincey's warning that "The mere understanding, however useful and indispensable, is the meanest faculty in the human mind, and the most to be distrusted." [2] De Quincey was another great master of style; but it is only when Stevenson is at his most solemn and grandiose that there are obvious echoes, as in the sumptuous phraseology of "Æs Triplex," "Pulvis et Umbra," or "Old Mortality." But it is not difficult to find parallels among his stories to some of De Quincey's Radcliffian and Faustian narratives, such as "The Dice," an apologue of the riches that bring damnation, or "The Avenger," on a wealthy young nobleman's career of murder, or those magnificent reconstructions of history or semi-history, "The Spanish Military Nun" and "The Revolt of the Tartars." Often he reminds one of such of the *Suspiria de Profundis* as "Savannah-La-Mar," or "The Vision of Sudden Death," in *The English Mail-Coach*. But the reminiscence is inescapable in "The Suicide Club," exemplifications of Stevenson's creed of "living dangerously" forming the first three of his *New Arabian Nights*. The freakish humour, the sporting with terror, the

---

[1] George Moore's opinion of Stevenson's style must be quoted for the light it sheds on both men. "I aver that Mr R. L. Stevenson never wrote a line that failed to delight me; but he never wrote a book. . . . I think of Mr Stevenson as a consumptive youth weaving garlands of sad flowers with pale, weak hands, or leaning to a large plate-glass window, and scratching thereon exquisite profiles with a diamond pencil. . . . But Mr Stevenson's style is over-smart, well-dressed, shall I say, like a young man walking in the Burlington Arcade? . . . It is not Mr Stevenson's brain that prevents him from being a thinker, but his style " (*Confessions of a Young Man*, xii. 171).

[2] "On the knocking at the door in Macbeth" (*Literary Theory and Criticism*, 389).

impish and ghoulish streak, are the very traits of De Quincey's *Murder considered as one of the Fine Arts*, with its terrific postscript.[1] The *New Arabian Nights* (1882) were Stevenson's first volume of stories, and contain some of his best, such as the first of "The Suicide Club," that of "The Young Man with the Cream Tarts." Pure fantasy is here carried off by lively, matter-of-fact narrative, by what it almost seems too heavy to call realism. There is indeed a deliberate excess of fantasy; the cream tarts, for instance, have nothing to do with the gist of the story, though they are such a picturesque call to attention, and strike the keynote of oddness and absurdity, which then modulates to a cool, business-like tone and an unperturbed detachment from all that is normal. Startling irrelevance, brilliant inconsequence, entrancing horror, are skilfully evoked, both here and in the subaltern tale of "The Saratoga Trunk." The virtuoso of language could make a character talk like a book with the most piquant effect, as in Dr Noel's remarks after his autopsy of the corpse, which practically contain the story:

"I noted a little while ago that you have there, in the corner, one of those monstrous constructions which your fellow-countrymen carry with them into all quarters of the globe—in a word, a Saratoga trunk. Until this moment I have never been able to conceive the utility of these erections; but then I began to have a glimmer. Whether it was for convenience in the slave trade, or to obviate the results of too ready an employ-ment of the bowie-knife, I cannot bring myself to decide. But one thing I see plainly—the object of such a box is to contain a human body." [2]

Of the accompanying stories, "The Pavilion on the Links" is like the ordinary run of ingenious and exciting inventions, except that Stevenson provides a setting of derelict mansion

[1] Is it too fanciful to suggest that Stevenson may have got the name of his Mr Malthus in "The Suicide Club" from the Mr Malthus, De Quincey's "old Sathanas," in the amusing "Notes from the pocket-book of a late Opium-Eater?" (*Suspiria*, etc., 477–483).
[2] There is another "essay" at the end, in Prince Florizel's debate whether revenge is after all worth while. "The existence of a man is so small a thing to take, so mighty a thing to employ! Alas!" he cried, "is there anything in life so disenchanting as attainment?"

guarded by vast solitudes and murderous quicksands, as fault-
lessly in keeping as that of *The Antiquary* or of *The Bride
of Lammermoor*. It was not improved by the introduction of
a sentimental motive; and the moody, incalculable Northmour
was a psychological venture of doubtful success. "A Lodging
for the Night" is a vivid evocation of the distant past, almost
succeeding in bringing the poet Villon back to life, cheek by
jowl with his rascally familiars. It is mostly picture, though
there is incident for colour—for manners and morals, but not
enough for drama. That, however, is not lacking in "The
Sire de Malétroit's Door," the adventure of the forced, but
in the end gladly accepted, marriage—a telescoped love-story
if ever there was one. "Providence and the Guitar" is
another anecdote cunningly manipulated and given the merest
shade of a moral. It is of the same genre as the later "Treasure
of Franchard," an apologue almost in the guise of extravaganza, but true to life at a certain distance, and logically
imparting its lesson—the theft of the treasure "from a man
unfit to be entrusted with its use" sobering and humbling the
would-be philosophic Dr Desprez.

*"Treasure
Island,"
etc.* The genesis of *Treasure Island* was from a map made by
Stevenson as a schoolboy, which took his fancy, with its
"harbours that pleased me like sonnets"; and, when he had
learned something about seamanship, suggested a boy's book
of adventure, something in the manner of "that admired
friend of my boyhood, Captain Reid." No doubt, at the
back of his mind was the idea of seeing what could be made
of a thing so primitive, by the closest attention to detail, and
the perfect style usually lacking in such productions. But, as
Stevenson always retained the spirit of boyhood, his heart was
in it, and the result was the very best of his longer stories,
best for negative as well as positive reasons. It is a story, the
account of an adventure, rather than a novel or an image of
life; though it is distinguished from most of its species by
being very much richer in character. It may be said generally
of Stevenson that he could see and convey temperament and
idiosyncrasy, but not character, in the sense of complete men
or women. *Treasure Island* does not belie this generalization;

for the figures of Pew, Jack Silver, Captain Smollett, the Doctor, the Squire, and the rest, are the regular personnel of such an affair, individualized and rendered very memorable by just these external traits, in other words, set out with appropriate circumstance. Stevenson said himself, "Character to the boy is a sealed book; for him, a pirate is a beard, a pair of wide trousers and a liberal complement of pistols." [1] As to John Silver, he took an admired friend, deprived him of his finer qualities and higher graces of temperament, leaving him with "nothing but his strength, his courage, his quickness, and his magnificent geniality," and expressed these "in terms of the culture of a raw tarpaulin." [2] He put his yarn in the mouth of the boy, Jim Hawkins, letting the Doctor take it up when Jim was absent on his cutting-out expedition. This is not Henry James's dramatic method of "indirection," Stevenson's nearest approach to which is the case of Mackellar, in *The Master of Ballantrae.* In fact, it is the most elementary of all ways of getting a story told. But it works without any serious hitch, Jim being on the spot at most of the decisive turns, and such baleful accompaniments as the tap-tapping of blind old Pew's stick on the frozen road, the "Pieces of eight! pieces of eight!" shrieked by Cap'n Flint the parrot, or the mysterious voice that paralyses the buccaneers hot on the scent of the treasure, losing nothing in being heard and felt by the blood-curdled heart of a boy. The workmanship was impeccable; the style, the finest modernization of Defoe's, with beauty superadded. Here, for instance, is the plain, business-like account of Jim's experience of Ben Gunn's rude coracle:

It is surprising how easily and securely my little and light boat could ride. Often, as I still lay at the bottom, and kept no more than an eye above the gunwale, I would see a big blue summit heaving close above me; yet the coracle would but bounce a little, dance as if on springs, and subside on the other side into the trough as lightly as a bird. I began after a little to grow very bold, and sat up to try my skill at paddling. But

even a small change in the disposition of the weight will produce
violent changes in the behaviour of a coracle. And I had hardly
moved before the boat, giving up at once her gentle dancing
movement, ran straight down a slope of water so steep that it
made me giddy, and struck her nose, with a spout of spray,
deep into the side of the next wave. I was drenched and
terrified, and fell instantly back into my old position, whereupon
the coracle seemed to find her head again, and led me as softly
as before among the billows. It was plain that she was not to
be interfered with, and at that rate, since I could in no way
influence her course, what hope had I left of reaching land?

"Kid-
napped"
and
"Catri-
ona"

Kidnapped (1886) is the same thing in essence; but it was
not a simple attempt to rewrite the traditional boy's story-book
on finer lines. Instead of the one big complicated adventure,
it piles incident upon incident, as if to illustrate all the laws of
psychological effect enumerated in "A Gossip on Romance."
Something even more thrilling has to be invented every time,
with care to avoid an anticlimax. David's narrow escape on
the broken staircase and his kidnapping are followed by the
strange advent of Alan Breck and the battle of the round-house;
then comes the Appin murder, the bit of actual history on which
the plot of both *Kidnapped* and its sequel was to pivot, and after
that the flight in the heather, perhaps the most memorable
episode of all, which does indeed evoke "the genius of the place
and moment" and show magnificently that "there is a fitness
in events and places," making a wild tract of country eternally
"famous with a legend." "The right kind of thing," he had
said, "should fall out in the right kind of place; the right kind
of thing should follow; and not only the characters talk aptly
and think naturally"—notice the order in which he puts it—
"but all the circumstances in a tale answer one to another like
notes in music." [1] Stevenson sought the right kind of scenes
and found them; he also devised the right sort of events; and,
with his seamanship and other accomplishments and his mastery
of language, was able to make his characters say the right thing
at the right time, and talk in the right idiom, whether the
broadest and coarsest or the most refined dialect of the place

[1] "A Gossip on Romance" (*Memories and Portraits*, 255-256).

and time. For it is in these two novels that Stevenson begins his racy use of the Scots vernacular in both narrative and dialogue, with such success that many of the footnotes explaining strange terms have now become supererogatory. By dint of style and workmanship he has turned the tale of adventure into literature. The story goes with a swing; but that is only the pace of it at given moments, the broader movement is neither so rapid nor so self-assured. For *Kidnapped*, as has been remarked over and over again of Stevenson's novels, is, after all, only a congeries of episodes, and *Catriona* is still less a unity. The Appin murder is but a mechanical centre for the events in both, not an organic motive. It actually has nothing to do with either David or Alan. The two books are just miscellanies of adventure, admirably pieced together, not artistic wholes; the second completing the history of David Balfour in a manner which, if it were not so brilliant externally, would be called laboured. *Kidnapped* was meant to be romance of a superior order, but falls short of *Treasure Island* in spontaneity. It may perhaps yield moments of higher satisfaction to the reader, rarer thrills; but the art that prepared them is not so utterly and felicitously dissembled. With the exception of *Treasure Island*, which is a story rather than a novel, and of *Weir of Hermiston*, which is unfinished, Stevenson's masterpieces in fiction are in the briefer and more concentrated genre. He had not the staying power; he was apt to lose his grip in the sustained effort of a novel of full length. He seems not to have visualized his novels as complete wholes, but to have built them up from one episode to the next.

In these two he was further led astray by a diversity of aims. *Character Kidnapped* puts adventure foremost, yet dallies with character *versus* for its own sake; *Catriona* is a novel of character and manners, *adventure* but tries to hold itself together as a sequel giving the final issue of the events. George Moore very wisely pointed out that "the suppression or maintenance of story in a novel is a matter of personal taste," but added, "some prefer character-drawing to adventures, some adventures to character-drawing; that we cannot have both at once I take to be a self-evident proposition." [1] This is in agreement with his remark already quoted,

[1] *Confessions of a Young Man*, xii., p. 157.

"That which is firmly and clearly imagined needs no psychology."[1] There was too much, and much that would hardly stand analysis, in Stevenson's handling of Alan Breck, though nothing like the excess of it that was to wreak such havoc with the more ambitious figures in *The Master of Ballantrae*. That novel was to be the crucial instance of the fallacy of trying to combine preciosities of character and the paradoxes of empirical psychology with a narrative of adventure.[2] To Stevenson, no doubt, the quaint and picturesque character was itself an adventure, something strange yet true, to be accepted as any other providential find, and made the most of. No doubt, too, he thought it was much the same with Defoe's Man Friday and Borrow's Petulengro. And then he had been brought up on Meredith, and had to show off his own virtuosity; hence the over-elaboration of his Alan Breck, the Master of Ballantrae, or the paradoxical Attwater, in *The Ebb-Tide*, that elegant gentleman living in the South Sea isle, dead-shot and Christian revivalist, and such failures as the Master's Friday, Secundra Das, and many of Stevenson's women-folk, especially the younger ones. To the romancer, character is incidental, part of the circumstance that gives colour or the data that carry conviction; and it may well be considered that such passing glimpses as are accorded of people like Simon Fraser, "yon thief of the black midnight," or of Prestongrange or Argyle, or the swashbuckling Duncansby, are more effective for their purposes than the more elaborate portraits in *Catriona*. Catriona herself, in spite of Stevenson's susceptible heart and his dutiful efforts to make her a personable heroine, is not a success. There is a certain glamour about her, but it is intermittent; and for either convincing truth or interest of personality she cannot compare with the elders of her own sex. Stevenson was certainly better at old women than at young ones, perhaps because they were more like men. The weird old wife sitting under a leg of the gibbet who reads in David's brow of "the bonnie lass that has bricht een" and of the "wee man

[1] *Avowals*, ix., p. 176.
[2] He said himself, "It is not character but incident that woos us out of our reserve," and in the same essay, "A Gossip on Romance," condemns "character-studies" in that which aims at the effects of romance.

in a braw coat and a big man in a pouthered wig"; and the
plain-speaking Mrs Ogilvy who asks if he proposes to marry a
girl at the foot of the gallows that has hanged her father, make
very brief appearances but stamp themselves on David's history.
Stevenson might have been thinking of himself when one of
these viragoes remarks, "To your last day you'll ken no more of
women-folk than what I do of sow-gelding." It was, on the
other hand, by such bits of sensational realism that Stevenson
made even romance incomparably vivid: little details come in
that hit one on the raw. In his dedication of *Kidnapped* to
Charles Baxter, he disclaimed "the desire of accuracy." But
there was an accuracy more vital than adherence to historical
records in such descriptions as of David's nocturnal struggle
with the waves when he was flung overboard from the brig:

> Sometimes the whole tract swung to one side, like the tail of
> a live serpent; sometimes, for a glimpse, it would all disappear
> and then boil up again. What it was I had no guess, which for
> the time increased my fear of it; but I now know it must have
> been the roost or tide race, which had carried me away so fast
> and tumbled me about so cruelly, and at last, as if tired of that
> play, had flung out me and the spare yard upon its landward
> margin. I now lay quite becalmed, and began to feel that a
> man can die of cold as well as of drowning. The shores of
> Erraid were close in; I could see in the moonlight the dots of
> heather and the sparkling of the mica in the rocks.

It is the same with Alan and David lying on the bare top
of the crag in Glencoe, "like scones upon a girdle," when
Alan shows himself a true chip of the essayist in his excuse
for David's not being gleg at the jumping: "Hoots! small
blame to ye! To be feared of a thing and yet to do it, is what
makes the prettiest kind of man."

His other boys' book of adventure, *The Black Arrow* (1888), "*Prince*
was mere journeyman's work for Stevenson,[1] and the posthum-*Otto*"
ous *St Ives* (1897), though of higher pretensions, had nothing
but his style to distinguish it from scores of picaresque romances
with an historical setting. He aimed much higher, or at any
rate farther, in *Prince Otto* (1885), written between *Treasure*

[1] "Tush! a poor thing!" he says of it (*Letters*, May 1883).

Island and *Kidnapped*, and also in *The Master of Ballantrae*
(1889), between *Kidnapped* and *Catriona*, without quite
attaining in either novel the objective that floated in his mind.
The former was an excursion in an alien style, which accounts
for the worried way he discusses it in his correspondence, and
for his having to rewrite it several times in whole or part.[1]
Whether he was aware of it or not, it was a Meredithian
attitude that he was assuming in *Prince Otto*, and an ironical
humour that came less natural than the poetry of forest and
garden and rococo palaces with which he bedecked what he
said "is not a romance, nor yet a comedy, nor yet a romantic
comedy, but a kind of preparation of some of the elements
of all three in a glass jar." [2] Meredith's imaginative handling
of mental and moral complications fascinated both Stevenson
and his disciple Maurice Hewlett, neither of whom, however,
was able enough to emulate his cogent analysis. Otto, only
too conscious that he is not born for kingship, marries an
aspiring girl and permits her to reign, whilst he lapses into
the dilettante inaction suited to his temperament. She
despises him, and they become hopelessly estranged. Suddenly,
he awakes from his lethargy, resolved to reassert himself. For
a moment, success seems within his grasp; but with his wife,
love for whom is his real motive, he has no success whatever;
and, since he knows in his heart that he has neither the desire
nor the ability to bear the weight of affairs, he lets himself be
imprisoned by her. But the intrigue has led to a revolution;
the princess finds herself homeless. Now she realizes that her
position has been an empty one all along, and that the real
monarch is the minister Gondremark. Full of compunction
and eager to make amends, she makes her way from the invaded
palace to the fortress where Otto is confined. But he is
already on his way to meet her, and together they flee to a

[1] See numerous allusions in the *Letters*, especially under dates February 1880,
May 1883, and March 1884, with more afterwards on its reception by the reviewers.
[2] *Letters*, May 1883. Mr L. Cope Cornford thinks that "*Prince Otto* should be
twice perused, once for the story and again for the landscape" (p. 176), which is a
doubtful compliment to its artistic integrity. Henry James talks about the forced
pose of hardness and almost inhumanity in the story (*Partial Portraits*, 144). It is
here he remarks that women are out of place in Stevenson's novels of action, and are
therefore omitted, except in *Prince Otto*.

refuge he has secured across the frontier. Now that she has learnt their fundamental equality, the princess also realizes that she loves him. She has been shocked back into primitive womanhood, almost into an Eve before the fall. How the true state of their affections is conveyed from one to the other is the burden of a pretty comedy, which passes lightly over the fate of a people to anatomize the sentiments of two prince-lets. It is an artificial comedy, Stevensonian chiefly in the paradoxical situations that rejoiced his romanticism.[1]

The same bent for the fantastic was allowed full fling in "*The The Master of Ballantrae*, which, like *Catriona*, is half a novel, *Master of* by virtue of such constituents as its serious study of a generous *Ballan-* mind in decay, in Henry Durie, under visitations for which *trae"* it is in no way responsible, and half romance of action and adventure. The dominant tone is too melancholy to compare it with *Kidnapped*; yet merely as a tale of picturesque incident it is in many points superior: it has more surprises and stranger events, and the improbabilities are forestalled with consummate ingenuity. What could be more romantic, in the Stevensonian sense, than the Master's enigmatical character, his repeated resurrections, and such a scene as the fraternal duel by candle-light—that masterpiece of stage-effect and of a witchery remote from the merely Anglo-Saxon mind? Reflecting on such a posture of affairs as when the aristocratic Master turns tailor in New York, to spite his brother, one feels that there is an overstrain somewhere; but it is only in the crescendo of plots and perils and escapes in the Canadian backwoods, when Secundra Das fails to resuscitate the miscreant's corpse, that a finger can be put on the very place. The novel in *The Master of Ballantrae* is, however, far better than the romance. Henry Durie is a real man, studied with thorough penetration; the brother, a figment of the romantic imagination, although

---

[1] He found as usual plentiful scope for his Scots casuistry, *e.g.*, in Dr Gotthold's confession that he is a secret tippler, and that the very books Otto has been praising ought to have been vastly better. Otto good-naturedly asks him, "What matters it how bad we are, if others can still love us, and we can still love others?" "Ay!" replied the Doctor. "It is very well said. It is the true answer to the pessimist, and the standing miracle of mankind. So you still love me? and so you can forgive your wife? Why, then, we may bid conscience 'Down, dog,' like an ill-trained puppy yapping at shadows" (Bk. III., chap. iii.).

he tends to overshadow the true though passive hero of the conflict. The wife at stake between them, except at certain intense moments, is so blank and unresponsive a thing that the latent tragedy does not always show as the bitter human agony it is. But the little chapter entitled "Persecutions" is unmatchable as subtle comedy of the sour kind. Here the dialogue is recognizably Meredithian. Critically, one may question whether Henry would have succumbed so repeatedly, would not have made a stand somewhere, and thus, even by mere inaction and inertia, have loosened the Master's hold upon his will. And the Master's scheme of revenge is, surely, too far-fetched; the motives on both sides are often so subtle and fantastic that it is hard to follow them. It is not Henry James's method of "indirection"; but the device of putting the narrative in the mouth of the old steward, who does not mince matters when it comes to criticism, is immeasurably better than the autobiographic method of previous stories. And old Mackellar himself is a notable instance of moral courage and physical cowardice. He will confront the devil for his master's sake, yet the sight of cold steel throws him into fits. It is a pity Stevenson sought such a multiplicity of interests. The austere strength and dramatic force of the first part is on the level of his great though unfinished *Weir of Hermiston*; but to this the extravagance of the subsequent adventures is almost an anti-climax. The connexion of the two parts is indeed not much more than accidental, and unity is still further dissipated in the capricious trend of events. *The Master of Ballantrae* is thus another example of Stevenson's inability to conceive and execute a work as a homogeneous whole.[1]

More short stories

As would be expected of an accomplished essayist and moral casuist, and also of a writer so good at the episode, Stevenson showed himself a finer artist in the more compact form of the story than in the novel. His stories vary enormously in merit.

[1] In *The Art of Writing*, Stevenson has a chapter on "The Genesis of *The Master of Ballantrae*," from which it appears that the germ was "a singular case of a buried and resuscitated fakir," which he had been told about by an uncle of his. He groped about for "the fable and the character required," and found them in his own memories of a tragic story in the Athole correspondence.

His best are those which are vitalized by some idea, that possesses him and stirs his deepest feelings and is implicit in his general philosophy of life. When the essayist merely fabricates a story that is in essence a little dissertation, as in "Markheim" or "Will o' the Mill," finely wrought as these are, they fall below even such irresponsible fantasies as "The Suicide Club" or such anecdotes cast in a shapely form as "The Sire de Malétroit's Door" or "A Lodging for the Night." There is far too much of this sermonizing in one of his most famous, *Dr Jekyll and Mr Hyde* (1886), which appeared just before *Kidnapped*, and rivalled it in popularity. Admittedly, the horror and mystery of Hyde's criminal doings and of his relations with Jekyll, his other self, are skilfully and powerfully done. But, technically, it is no masterpiece. No less than three narrators have to be called in: Utterson, the confidential solicitor, Jekyll's medical colleague Lanyon, and Jekyll himself in his confession. There is an idea; but it is not thoroughly embodied. The disquisition on the duplicity of man's nature, and the rest of the psychological or philosophical exegesis, are sheer claptrap. And, surely, the opposite elements in man could have been symbolized as impressively in a fashion less thaumaturgical. Or is the weak point in the compromise between thaumaturgy and realism? Henry James was right in objecting that the effervescing powders which effect the transformation are too matter-of-fact a trick. One of the grimmest features is the icy sense of shrinking everyone feels at the mere look of Mr Hyde. But that is nothing compared with the sensations inspired by a glimpse of the Bottle Imp, in a story far superior in logical coherence and moral probability:

Now as soon as that was said, the imp looked out of the bottle, and in again, swift as a lizard; and there sat Keawe and Lopaka turned to stone. The night had quite come, before either found a thought to say or voice to say it with; and then Lopaka pushed the money over and took the bottle.

In *Dr Jekyll and Mr Hyde* Stevenson was writing a "*Jekyll* shocker, and at the same time he wanted to be respectable. *and* He gives in to the purists, and drops realism altogether when *Hyde*" he comes to Hyde's facinorous debaucheries. A Frenchman would have ventured some concrete terms; Stevenson sticks to the general and abstract, and the reader wonders what on earth Hyde could have indulged in that was so awful. A year later, *The Merry Men, and other tales and fables* (1887), had a miscellaneous title that permits some of the best to be recognized as moral apologues without injustice to Stevenson. Such, for instance, is that flawless piece of beautiful fabling, "Will o' the Mill," a parable on standing aloof from life. A man may play his part, and be submerged in the crowd; or he may refrain, and go down to his grave unnoticed. The stately, sensuous, oracular prose is very beautiful; but, again, this is no revelation of eternal truths, and there is little to justify such solemnity of form. Commonplaces are movingly expounded also in "Markheim"; but the profundity and the subjective logic on which Stevenson evidently plumed himself are far to seek. It is the vivisection of a haunted consciousness; the teeming presences Markheim senses in the empty house after the murder taking shape at last in the Devil himself, who listens to the sinner's self-justification, and shows him what it will mean "to make a truckling peace with God." The culprit's eyes are opened: he will give himself up. And, at this decisive resolve, the aspect of the visitant changes; he becomes an angel of light. Reduced to plain prose, however, the course of the argument is a little too like Long John Silver's paltering with both sides when the game is up, in *Treasure Island*. There are instants pregnant with spiritual insight in "Olalla"; but this is long-winded and laboured, a barren theme over-written. It is one of the few cases in which Stevenson tried to deal seriously with love and passion. But the repulsive scene where the werwolf nature of the degenerate mother comes out, and she springs at the horror-stricken lover, is out of key. It is a misguided attempt to combine a traveller's tale of racial aberration with tragic romance. As to the title-piece, "The Merry Men," Stevenson never succeeded better in calling up the glamour of place and the poetry of circumstance; he shows himself here as elsewhere a splendid raconteur; but there is nothing to tell, except certain love-making, and as usual with that his heart was

"Mark-heim," etc.

not in it. Nevertheless, the volume contains two of his finest stories, of contrasted species: "Thrawn Janet" and "The Treasure of Franchard." The latter has been mentioned already. That famous tale "Thrawn Janet" goes with "The Bottle Imp" as another proof of the logical superiority of acceptance in dealing with the supernatural. And there is not a syllable of the exegesis or moralization that attenuates the force, if it does not weaken the illusion, in too many of Stevenson's. Written in the most unmitigated broad Scots, which unquestionably deepens the grimness, it may be regarded as the ultimate and consummate outcome of the stories told to the boy Stevenson by his nurse, Alison Cunningham.

Two others of his best are contained in *Island Nights' Entertainments* (1893), besides the pretty Hawaian fairy-tale, "The Isle of Voices." "The Beach of Falesá" is a good rousing yarn, told with a skill that brings two uncommon persons vividly home to the least imaginative reader, of a plain, honest white man's marriage with a native girl in a South Pacific station, and the diabolical scheme of a rival, one of Stevenson's irredeemable scoundrels, to frighten him or get him ostracized. He is almost convinced that he is under taboo; but discovers that Case has terrorized the natives with a sort of witch's cavern, garnished with sham supernatural images, Æolean harps, luminous paint, and the like, which he contrives to blow up. He and Uma are shot by Case, but only wounded, and he gets his knife home in the villain's body. The loyalty of the oddly matched pair is feelingly brought out. Stevenson never told a finer story than "The Bottle Imp," the terrible moral of which has no need to be stated. The bottle is a talisman which gives the possessor anything he wishes for. But whoever dies possessed of it will go straight to hell. It can be sold only at a price less than was paid for it; and when the wretched Keawe realizes his predicament and that no purchaser can ever be found, for there is no coin lower than the cent for which he bought it, he thinks no more of the Chinese Evil from which it had healed him, but sees himself bound to the imp for time and for eternity, with no better hope "but to be a cinder for ever in the flames of hell. Away

Island Nights' Entertainments

ahead of him he saw them blaze with his mind's eye, and his soul shrank, and darkness fell upon the light." If it was a Samoan folk-tale, Stevenson made this into one of the most fearful apologues in literature.

Novels written with Lloyd Osbourne

Of the three novels written in collaboration with his stepson, the hand of Stevenson can be recognized with fair certainty in large parts of the second and third; but Lloyd Osbourne must have been mainly responsible for *The Wrong Box* (1889), an elaborate absurdity, competently dressed in a realistic outfit. Osbourne's vigour kept Stevenson going in the other two, with few lapses into his digressive tendencies, though *The Ebb-Tide, a trio and quartette* (1894), all but drops apart into two stories. Conrad would have fused the piracy and treasure business more indissolubly into the psychological drama. As it is, however, Herrick, the university man down on his luck, the desperate captain, broken through having lost his ship in a bout of drunkenness, and the loathsome Huish, the little Cockney, a masterpiece of irreclaimable baseness, form a picturesque trio, and their perilous dilemma with the ship they have seized makes excellent comedy of the grim and sardonic kind. The comedy grows more exciting, but at the same time too patently artificial, when the trio becomes a quartet with the addition of Attwater, and the scheme for robbing him of his vast hoard of pearls. It is impossible to believe in Attwater: he is too clearly, as already noted, one of those paradoxical creations, like the Master of Ballantrae, who may have come out of books or out of Stevenson's ingenious fancy, but never had their like on earth.[1] So much for "the ever-to-be-execrated *Ebb-Tide*."[2] As to *The Wrecker* (1892), which came in between, it was to be a counterblast to the purely mechanical ingenuity of detective fiction, moral or immoral idiosyncrasy furnishing mystery enough for the expert to solve at leisure. Stevenson must have done the writing; the style is his. He must also have drawn upon his

[1] Richard Le Gallienne wrote: "The more we read of the insufferable, impossible Attwater, prig and pearl-fisher, university man and evangelist, expert alike with his Bible and his Winchester, the unreality increases" (*Retrospective Reviews*, ii. 146).

[2] *Vailima Letters*, 278; cp. "as grim a tale as was ever written, and as grimy, and as hateful" (*Ibid.*, 274). "A little indecision about Attwater, not much" (*Ibid.*, 322).

memories for the lively pictures of art students in Paris and
at Fontainebleau, whilst Osbourne would have provided
material for the equally vivid pictures of life in San Francisco,
and the gallery of Yankee skippers and sailors, business sharpers
and other scamps. For the realism and motley individuality
of the characterization are as striking as the ultra-romanticism
of the exploits and adventures. There are some of the constituents of a novel of manners in this exciting chronicle of
vast, semi-piratical speculations and the fast and furious contest
for the wreck of the *Flying Scud*. Yet, in spite of Osbourne's
co-operation, it remains a well-knit string of episodes rather
than a novel.

Stevenson was now in his forties, which in the case of most *"Weir of
novelists would have been in mid-career. By insensible degrees, Hermis-
stimulated perhaps by his collaboration with Lloyd Osbourne, ton"
he had been moving from romance to realism; and it is one
of the tragedies of literary history that he was not spared to
finish *Weir of Hermiston* (1896), the existing fragment of which
was published after his death, with an outline of the projected
close. If he could have maintained the confidence and energy
and momentum of this first half, it must surely have turned
out his masterpiece, for he had the right ending in view when
he began, and there is no sign anywhere of his deviating from
the course marked out.[1] He had attained maturity at last.
For *Weir of Hermiston* is a novel. It may well be said to be
the only one of his works of fiction that is genuinely and
uniformly a novel. The romantic element, the poetry of
circumstance, is there sure enough, in the haunted atmosphere
of old Edinburgh and the wild moorlands where Archie holds
tryst with the younger Kirstie. A snatch of verse never came
into prose with more magical aptness than her song of the

> "Auld, auld Elliotts, clay-cauld Elliotts, dour, bauld
> Elliotts of auld!"

The whole of that incident is poetry. "His question was

[1] Colvin related that Stevenson in the last weeks of his life "was sometimes aware
of a tension of the spirit difficult to sustain. 'How can I keep this pitch?' he is
reported to have said after finishing one of the chapters; and all the world knows how
the frail organism in fact betrayed him in mid-effort" (see *Letters*, ii. 367–368).

answered. She was a human being tuned to a sense of the tragedy of life; there were pathos and music and a great heart in the girl." And it is not only Archie but the reader also who is "blendit and glamoured" when the jealous elder Kirstie tells him, "'I have seen ye, and what's to prevent ithers? I saw ye once in the Hags, in my ain howl, and I was wae to see ye there—in pairt for the omen, for I think there's a weird on the place—and in pairt for pure nakit envy and bitterness o' hairt. It's strange ye should forgather there tae! God! but yon puir, thrawn, auld Covenanter's seen a heap o' human natur since he lookit his last on the musket barrels, if he never saw nane afore,' she added, with a kind of wonder in her eyes." But this is the romanticism of a Scott, not of Stevenson in his twenties and thirties. Finished, it might have stood comparison with *The Heart of Midlothian* or *The Bride of Lammermoor*; at any rate, Scott would have approved the grandeur and breadth of portraiture in the rugged figure of old Hermiston, that "man of granite," the deep humanity, the tenderness and beauty, of the older Kirstie, and the winsome girlishness of her niece and namesake. In those two, Stevenson made amends for having failed so often at drawing a woman —or, rather, for having so often shirked the attempt. Like Scott again, he sets down the lineaments of a dour, hard-featured people, in such as the Elliotts, and the Four Black Brothers, who were to play a lawless part in the final chapters never written. He sums them up in one of his pithy asides:

The excuse of their folly is in two words: scarce the breadth of a hair divided them from the peasantry. The measure of their sense is this: that these symposia of rustic vanity were kept entirely within the family, like some secret ancestral practice. To the world their serious faces were never deformed by the suspicion of any simper of self-contentment. Yet it was known. "They hae a guid pride o' themsel's!" was the word in the country-side.

The book is as rich as any in Stevenson's gnomic wisdom, now thrice refined, though now displayed in the nobility of the

general thought and style, or put in the sententious mouth of
such as Lord Hermiston, the hanging judge.[1]

Stevenson's immense vogue and prestige had the effects to *The*
be looked for on writers of fiction. That activity in historical *Steven-*
romance already noticed received a fresh impetus; so did the *sonians*
tale of adventure, the zest for which never runs dry. He had
exalted even the boy's story-book to the dignity of literature;
no one need henceforth fight shy of such a humble department
of letters. The result was that writers of the highest pretensions applied themselves to the novel of incident; or, to put
it the other way round, that new standards of style and workmanship were accepted or exacted. Maurice Hewlett, Anthony
Hope, and Neil Munro were novelists of no mean ability who
put much of their best into the mere romance, like some still
living such as "Q" and Mr Compton Mackenzie. Even critics
of the standing of Sir Edmund Gosse and Andrew Lang [2]
stooped to write *The Secret of Narcisse* (1892) and *A Monk of
Fife* (1895), depicting life as they imagined it in the sixteenth
century or the times of Joan of Arc. But Stevenson's example
was not all to the good. His predilection for such figures as
Alan Breck and the Master of Ballantrae, Pew, Black Dog, and
Long John Silver, or the strange quartet in *The Ebb-Tide*;
his theory that character and idiosyncrasy were only a
picturesque component of romance, joined to the doctrine that
"it is not character but incident that woos us out of our
reserve," and the triumph is when "something happens as
we desire to have it happen to ourselves," when "we forget the
characters," when "we push the hero aside," when "we plunge
into the tale in our own person and bathe in fresh experience," [3]

---

[1] Any apprehensions that Stevenson might have ruined the novel by giving it a
happy ending have been fairly well put to rest by the letter of Mrs Isobel Field,
Stevenson's amanuensis, in a recent number of *The Times Literary Supplement*. As
Colvin stated in his "Editorial note," young Kirstie was to fall a victim to Frank
Innes. Archie kills him at the spot where he used to meet her, is arrested, and
condemned to death by his own father, the Lord Justice-Clerk. Old Hermiston dies
of the nervous strain of condemning his son. Archie is rescued from prison by the
Four Black Brothers, and afterwards escapes to America with the unfortunate
Kirstie. Not much of a happy ending!

[2] Lang had run down Stevenson, as only "a superior kind of Loti," and for "the dry-
ness of his stories" apart from "his own enchanting presence" (Moore's *Avowals*, 44–45).

[3] These quotations are from "A Gossip on Romance," especially pp. 267–268
(*Memories and Portraits*).

had the unfortunate result that certain typical romantic personages figure in conventional roles over and over again, in well-marked types of entertainment, like the costume novel and the romance of cloak and sword, which are played again and again, simply with variations. Few except Hewlett ventured on those psychological refinements and excursions that George Moore had so trenchantly condemned as stumbling-blocks in a story of adventure; but many failed to observe Moore's caution that characters must be clearly and firmly imagined if they are to dispense with psychology. Hence the story might be an excellent one, and the characters look picturesque and perform everything required of them; but yet not be alive. The game of identifying himself with mere automata soon began to pall on the intelligent reader.

Steven-son's combined with other influences Other influences coalesced with this of Stevenson, especially that of the elder Dumas, whom he had hailed with enthusiasm as his master, and that of Scott, whom he acknowledged with a more distant reverence. Stanley Weyman, Anthony Hope, and Agnes and Egerton Castle, to name but a few out of a small army, followed in the track of Dumas very much as Stevenson had done, displaying style and good workmanship. Stevenson convinced himself on various occasions that he had been writing in the fashion of Meredith, though most of what he learned from that exemplar was mislearned. Hewlett drank deeper from this source, the taste of which was not strange to his palate; and, among a good many others, Bernard Capes, whose best novel was the first of a long series, *The Lake of Wine* (1898), acquired and gloried in certain mannerisms of the men of letters' novelist. Then, at a time when realism was regarded as distinctively the modern art, even the historical novelist who felt the call of romance as compellingly as even Stevenson had done might refuse to believe that romance was entirely a matter of distance and glamour, and try to outstrip the mirage and see the thing itself as it is, or was, with the instruments furnished by scientific method. This was the endeavour of Neil Munro, the greatest because the most independent and original of the Stevensonians. Stanley John Weyman (1855–1928) was a closer follower of Dumas than Stevenson was of Scott. The proof of this is not only in the fact that the majority of his romances have French themes which are the very counterparts of Dumas'. In his first, however, *The House of the* Wolf (1890), published a year after *The Master of Ballantrae*, it was not Dumas' fault that Weyman put his story of the Huguenots and St Bartholomew, rather clumsily, in the mouth of his young hero. He was more skilful in *A Gentleman of France* (1893), *Under the Red Robe* (1894), an English Jacobite story, *Shrewsbury* (1898), *The Abbess of Vlaye* (1894), *Chippinge* (1906), a novel of the second Reform Bill and the Bristol riots, and the capital picture of early Victorian times and of a financial panic, *Ovington's Bank* (1922). He was a good story-teller, too fond of coincidences, and almost incapable of presenting a live human being. But he could not satiate thousands of addicts of historical romance, and was rapidly followed up by Hamilton Drummond, S. K. Levett Yeats, "May Wynne," Rafael Sabatini, "Marjorie Bowen," and a host of others, including Sir Gilbert Parker, who had the advantage of Canadian local colour studied on the spot, and S. R. Crockett, who switched off from his homely tales of village folk in his own Galloway to sensational romances of the same and other regions, like *The Grey Man* (1896), *The Black Douglas* (1899), or *The White Plumes of Navarre* (1906). Crockett degenerated into a regular hand of the circulating libraries. Anthony Hope was less amenable and more versatile; he gave a distinguishing note to his emulations of Dumas, first by putting the most out-and-out romance of love or intrigue or peril and escape into a circumstantially modern environment, for the imaginary kingdoms or republics of *A Man of Mark* (1890), *The Prisoner of Zenda* (1894) and its sequel, *Rupert of Hentzau* (1898), and *The King's Mirror* (1899) are such cunning blends of the actual and the fantastic as Prince Otto's State of Grünewald, and may be sought on the same map; and secondly by means of the witty and not quite superficial comedy which the age found so brilliant in *The Dolly Dialogues* (1894). Hope had the name of a trifler and mere entertainer; for some obscure sense of dis-illusionment seems to have pushed him into a half-bantering, half-cynical attitude; but he was more serious than it looked, and no one would question his fundamental sanity. In one of his later novels, *A Servant of the Public* (1905), he was successful in a method almost as thoroughgoing as that of Henry James; and the pretty actress here, brilliantly drawn, may well be the proof and impersonation of a deep current of romantic idealism in Hope.

Neil Munro

In his first book, *The Lost Pibroch, and other shieling stories* (1896), Neil Munro (1864–1930) was a voice of the Celtic movement of his day, of which the chief memorial in prose fiction is the long set of legendary stories put forth under the name of "Fiona Macleod." The Stevenson touch is evident however in the next, *John Splendid, the tale of a poor gentleman and the little wars of Lorn* (1898). *Kidnapped* had raised a competitor not to be belittled, for Munro was a Highlander who knew the savage wildernesses of Argyllshire better than Stevenson did, and could interpret that elusive thing the Highland character more truly, if not with such seductive airs of romance. There is a long episode in *John Splendid* which was evidently meant to rival and beat Alan Breck's and David's flight in the heather. The historical basis is the same as that of *A Legend of Montrose*; but, instead of romantically, the story is told with an exact and almost scientific realism that seizes certain truths beyond the range of Scott's outlook. Scott displays the picturesque and the amusing side of Highland character: Munro strives to give every line and shade, interesting or not. Scott loved the contrasts of rich and poor, wild and civilized life. Munro shows they were all pretty much on a level; Montrose, a Lowlander, is almost the only civilized personage, and he appears only by glimpses. There is nothing to set beside Captain Dalgetty. It is a picture of clan life in all its ugliness—the feuds, the raids, the murderous tribal battle. It is realism, eschewing any romance inconsistent with the facts. Yet in such incidents as the ambush at Dalness, the flight and pursuit, and the exquisitely human episode of the blind widow of Glencoe, emerges that romance which comes from the mating of strangeness with beauty. Munro, with far less charm than Scott, rouses deeper feelings of pity and tragedy. And yet the realist comes to grief in other ways:

he is too modern. Hewlett and Bernard Capes, and even Stevenson, split sooner or later on that fatal rock. When the child of the clansman's daughter is asked why he has not learned his lessons, he replies, "I was too busy living." That is obviously not the voice of the child of nature, but of the psychologist. And it is no Gael of that age who tells the story: the introspection into his own emotions and his penetrating study of John Splendid are anachronisms, and worse, in a soldier of fortune, bold and swift in action but decidedly slow of wit. The inferior in intelligence has to chronicle and criticize the tortuous thoughts and the love-making of the highly sophisticated hero; and of course the thing cannot be done. Further, the seventeenth-century Scot is gifted with a Wordsworthian feeling for nature which he expresses in language of the nineteenth. Such faults marring a fine piece of work are characteristic of these labourers in a field of their own discovery, which lies somewhere between the territories of romance and realism. None of them entirely avoided these fallacies, which are discernible also in Munro's impressive studies of the Celt, *Gilian the Dreamer* (1898), *Doom Castle* (1901), *Children of Tempest* (1903), and *The New Road* (1914), and are absent only where they would have been harmless, in showy romantic tales like *The Shoes of Fortune* and *Fancy Farm*. This is why such unambitious masterpieces of fantasy, with realism confined to the characterization, as *The Lost Stradivarius* (1895) of John Meade Falkner, *Moonfleet* (1898), and *The Nebuly Coat* (1903), are æsthetically much more satisfying.

Maurice Henry Hewlett (1861–1923)—and almost the same thing might be said of Bernard Capes—was a romancer at heart who applied himself to the job of dressing semi-history in the garb of truth. They would take the most romantic characters and events on record, or invent something of a like paradoxical kind, and serve it up in the shape of an intensely realistic novel. Both began writing at the time when Meredith was the idol of the intellectuals, and his mark is on both. Hewlett was a fine scholar, of habits and tastes much the same as Pater's. His series of Italian studies, *Earthwork out of Tuscany* (1895), is a book that must have delighted and

Maurice Hewlett

might almost have been from the hand of the author of *Imaginary Portraits*. Historians have paid tribute to Hewlett's power of calling up in a novel or story the very spirit and atmosphere of an age and a people.[1] It was the imagination of a poet, who would have written plays at the end of Elizabeth's reign but wrote dramatic fiction in Victoria's, that vitalized Hewlett's learning. This was not so evident as later on, however, in his first piece of prose fiction, *The Forest Lovers* (1898), which was an attempt to vie with Malory, to recapture the glamour of mediæval romance, the tale unrolling before the eye of imagination like one of William Morris's richly embroidered tapestries. It was work nourished on literature rather than life. It is in *Little Novels of Italy* (1899) that he violently assails the reader, in a composite picture of Renaissance times, with a realism such as has rarely been concentrated on the reconstruction of a past epoch. It shows life as it went on day by day in the fourteenth century, with the dramatic contrasts of superfine culture and diabolical crime, the swift changes from gaiety to tragedy, that made the epoch so intensely individual. His *New Canterbury Tales* (1901) were a more fanciful or at least more poetical interpretation of the same age in England. But it was in *The Life and Death of Richard Yea-and-Nay* (1900) and *The Queen's Quair* (1904) that Hewlett was most modern and, incidentally, most Meredithian. He undertook to solve the puzzle of the lives of Richard Cœur de Lion and Mary Queen of Scots in this pair of dramatic novels, in which action both on the mental and on the physical plane is kept at a high pitch. Here is a sample of how the narrative goes:

Lying at Coupar-Angus, at Glamis, at Edzell, her spirits rose as she breasted the rising country, saw the cloud-shadowed hills, the swollen rivers, the wind-swept trees, the sullen moors, the rocks. She grew happy even, for motion, newness, and physical exertion always excited her, and she was never happy unless she was excited. No fatigue daunted her. She sat out the driving days of rain, bent neither to the heat nor to the cold fog. She was always in front, always looking forward,

---

[1] See H. Butterfield's remarks (*The Historical Novel*, 94–108).

seemed like the keen breath of war, driven before it as the wind by a rain-storm. Lethington likened her to Diana on Taygetus shrilling havoc; but the Lord James said: "Such similitudes are distasteful. We are serious men upon a serious business." She rode astraddle like a young man, longed for a breastplate and steel bonnet. She made Ruthven exercise her with the broadsword, teach her to stamp her foot and cry "Ha! a touch!" and cajoled her brother into letting her sleep one night afield. Folded in a military plaid, so indeed she did; and watched with thrills the stars shoot their autumn flights, and listened to the owls calling each other as they coursed the shrew-mice over the moor. She pillowed her head on Mary Livingstone's knee at last, and fell asleep at about three o'clock in the morning.

Even as with Meredith, the subordinate as well as the principal characters are of exceptional if not abnormal natures— Bertrand de Born the troubadour, Henry II, Sancho the Wise, the abbot Milo, Bothwell, Rizzio, Murray, Morton, Chastelard, Ruthven, all come into a drama such as would have done credit to an Elizabethan stage, and yet is pre-eminently modern. *Mere-dithian char-acters*

Here is one difference between imagination and fancy, that the first will leap full-fledged into the life of the upper air from the egg of its beginning, while the second crouches long callow in the nest, and must be fostered into plumage before it can take its pretty flights. Here, of these two who had been separate for a week, she had flown far beyond the man's way-faring, and stood upon a height which he could scarcely hope to see. To keep touch with her might call for all his wit. For what had actually passed between them but a couple of snatched kisses in the dark? No more upon his honour, to his sense. For though he had built upon them a fine castle—with the bricks of Spain—he would have been the first to own himself a fool for so doing. But she! Not only had she reared a fair solid house of chambers and courts, but she had lived with him in it, a secret life. Here she had had him safe since the hour he left her in the garden. In her thought he was bound to her, she to him, by sacraments; they were, like all lovers, of eternal eld. No beginning and no end will love own up to. It is necessary to remember this.

Hewlett wrote more studies of distant epochs and some

romantic novels of the present, in which he essayed to clothe
poetic fancies in a similarly realistic garb. *Mrs Lancelot* (1912),
for instance, is a poetic comedy, which combines something of
Meredith, much also of Thackeray and Disraeli, with a dash
of George Borrow, in the story of a certain Duke, not entirely
unrecognizable, and the nymphlike Georgiana Lancelot. A
larger exposition of his unorthodox philosophy of life is the
trilogy *Halfway House* (1908), *Open Country* (1909), and *Rest
Harrow, a comedy of resolution* (1910), in which the Borrovian
gentleman Mr Senhouse, who wanders about England and
Europe with a tent, teaches ladies the wrongness of matrimony,
devotes his days to gardening in desolate places and his nights
to thinking or preaching philosophic anarchism, is a charming
creation, especially when the author does not mean him too
seriously. He is, at any rate, an admirable solvent of social
prejudices. But romance and realism fail to make a sound
amalgam; common sense and truth mix badly with fancy
and mysticism. And when Sanchia figures as the spirit of all
life, it is as if Hewlett had gone out into the streets of modern
London and caught sight of an angel parading there. His
modernizations of the sagas, on the other hand, in *Gudrid
the Fair*, *The Outlaw*, and three other tales, are tolerable; here
he had to keep within bounds.

*Revivals
of medi-
ævalism* There were many other historical novelists whose work
shows more or less the employment of realistic methods. To
this is largely due the vigour and vividness of Beatrice Barmby's
saga-like *Rosslyn's Raid, and other tales* (1903); of *The Long-
shoremen* (1903), and the other stories of "George Bartram,"
who was really Henry Atton (1853–1915), an officer of the
Customs and Excise; of the Northumbrian folk-tales of
Howard Pease; and a great many more. This, however, was
not the special characteristic of the long series of historical
novels by Monsignor Robert Hugh Benson (1871–1914),
brother of A. C. Benson, author of *The Upton Letters*, and of
E. F. Benson, the prolific author of *Dodo* (1893). His long
series of historical novels centring in religious controversies,
persecutions, and martyrdoms, scholarly as they are, cannot be
absolved of some propagandist bias. A cloister story, *The*

Gathering of Brother Hilarius (1901), and *The Roadmender* (1902) of "Michael Fairless" were spiritual biographies of a more peaceful colour. A large proportion of the historical romances enumerated were stories of the Middle Ages, the spirit and art of which had recently been revived in a manner that had but a limited effect upon the novelists, by William Morris and by the collectors and imitators of old Celtic romance. Only two of Morris's stories had much contemporary appeal, *The Dream of John Ball* (1888), in which his account of the Kentish rising in the reign of Richard II was made the vehicle of his socialistic ideals, and the more emphatic announcement of the same gospel, *News from Nowhere, or an epoch of rest: being some chapters from a Utopian romance* (1891). He had done good work in collaboration with the Icelandic scholar, Eiríkr Magnússon, in various translations and adaptations of the sagas, and he was solely responsible for a charming set of *Old French Romances done into English* (1896). The prose romances with which he beguiled not merely his leisure but also the monotonous hours of handiwork, in his latter years, may be regarded as prose counterparts to his earlier metrical romances, *The Life and Death of Jason* (1867), those in *The Earthly Paradise* (1868–1870), and *Sigurd the Volsung* (1877), though the epical strain was now subdued to a quieter note. *A Tale of the House of the Wolfings and all Kindreds of the Mark* (1889), with its sequel, *The Roots of the Mountains* (1890), *The Story of the Glittering Plain* (1890), *The Wood beyond the World* (1895), *The Well at the World's End* (1896), *The Water of the Wondrous Isles* (1897), and *The Sundering Flood* (1898), were long, meandering prose-poems, their themes drawn from a half-mythical past or frankly from fairyland. Hewlett and a few others caught the infection of their glamour; but they had but the slightest influence upon the course even of the historical novel. The revival in Ireland affected the poets profoundly, but except perhaps in the case of Donn Byrne (1889–1928), who will be considered later, left no perceptible traces on the novel. Lady Gregory's magnificent recensions of the Cuchulain and Ossianic cycles, *Cuchulain of Muirthemne* (1902) and *Gods and Fighting Men* (1906), are monuments to stand beside Malory's *Morte Darthur*; whether, however, they have succeeded in popularizing the old literature and reviving its spirit is another matter. A curious incident of the last decade of the century was the popularity secured by William Sharp's versions or imitations of old Gaelic romances, *Pharais, a romance of the Isles* (1894), *The Mountain Lovers* (1895), *The Sin-Eater, the Washer of the Ford, and other legendary moralities* (1895–1896), and several others, which he put forth under the name of "Fiona Macleod." It was some time before it came out that there was no such person, except in the sense in which he insisted upon Fiona's reality, that she was his other self, and would die if the secret were divulged.

Some popular romancers The novelist who courts the widest suffrages must resort to methods of exciting emotion of which he may perhaps feel somewhat ashamed. The reader for mere amusement is not much interested in himself, or in seeing the dull existence of himself or those exactly like him faithfully mirrored. He wants to escape from his dullness, and have the spectacle of life diversified by excitements that seldom come his way. Average life in the Australian colonies was no doubt as monotonously humdrum as in the homeland; but the early Australian novelists had by some means or other to make their honest accounts of it readable. Marcus Clarke (1846–1881), the pioneer of Australian fiction, was transparently honest, and his picture of convict life in Tasmania in the second quarter of the century, *For the Term of his Natural Life* (1874), was on the whole a truthful record, tragic in its presentation of hideous facts. "Rolf Boldrewood," as Thomas Alexander Browne (1826–1915) called himself, in *Robbery under Arms* (1888), *A Colonial Reformer* (1890), *The Squatter's Dream* (1895), and a number of other novels, had to rivet attention by giving undue prominence to the lawless doings of bushrangers and other sensational events that did not happen every day. One of his stories, *The Miner's Right*, is said to be a real contribution to colonial history. He was a plain, common-sense writer, without much literary art, but not a mere sensationalist like Guy Boothby or B. L. Farjeon, the author of *Grif* (1866), a rousing tale of the Gold Rush, with some reminiscences in it of *Oliver Twist*.

No novelist was more popular at home during this period than Sir Arthur Conan Doyle (1859–1930), an Irishman with an Edinburgh degree in medicine, who turned to literature and speedily became an idol of the "general reader." He made himself a novelist-of-all-work, and was equally proficient at the historical romance and the novel of heterogeneous adventure, the tale of mystery and the detective novel. He could season the wildest inventions and make them fairly plausible with a sprinkling of realism, in which his medical knowledge came in handy. Detective fiction had its apotheosis in his amateur thief-taker Sherlock Holmes, who made his first appearance in an early novel, *A Study in Scarlet* (1887), but developed into the being of superhuman penetration and inductive sagacity, whom Doyle kept in harness till the last days of his own literary life, in the trilogy, *The Adventures* (1892), *The Memoirs* (1893), and *The Return of Sherlock Holmes* (1905). Conan Doyle's rivals in popular esteem were "Henry Seton Merriman," or Hugh Stowell Scott (1862–1903), and William John Locke (1863–1930). Merriman was almost as versatile, but kept more within the limits of their common exemplar, the elder Dumas. Adventures by sea or land, in Africa, or Russia, or Spain, Corsica, the Balearic Isles, or anywhere where trouble was going on, including the business world, and of course the world of the past, gave Merriman all he wanted, and he certainly dealt with them in a workmanlike style. W. J. Locke did not go so far afield, and his novels of what he called everyday life in England or at familiar resorts on the Continent, with episodic flights into Bohemia, were accepted by a large and confiding public as a serious and critical view of reality by a wise and humane intellect. *The Morals of Marcus Ordeyne* (1905) and *The Beloved Vagabond* (1906) were accorded the deference regularly paid to the problem-novel; though they were no more profound and no truer to life than *Simon the Jester* (1910), *The Glory of Clementina Wing* (1911), *The Joyous Adventures of Aristide Pujol* (1912), and the rest of the amiable, amusing, and superficial simulations of genuine realism or not quite empty romanticism, of which actually two examples appeared in the year of his death.

Conan Doyle, Merriman, and W. J. Locke

But is it fair to think W. J. Locke meant all this seriously? He may have been simply complying with what Meredith said was expected of the romantic novelist—namely, " to beguile us." It may be hoped that he did not beguile himself.

SELECT READING AND REFERENCE LIST

GENERAL

ALBRIGHT, EVELYN M. *The Short Story: its principles and structure.* 1920.

BEACH, JOSEPH WARREN. *The Twentieth-Century Novel.* 1932.

BENNETT, ARNOLD. *Books and Persons: being comments on a past epoch, 1908–1911.* 1917.

CAZAMIAN, MADELEINE L. *Le Roman et les idées en Angleterre.* 2 vols. 1923–1935.
   I. *L'Influence de la science, 1860–1890*; II. *L'Anti-intellectualisme et l'esthétisme.*

CHEVALLEY, ABEL. *Le Roman anglais de notre temps.* 1921.

CUNLIFFE, J. W. *English Literature during the last Half-Century.* 1908.

DOBRÉE, BONAMY. *The Lamp and the Lute: studies in six modern authors.* 1929.
   Ibsen, Hardy, Kipling, E. M. Forster, Lawrence, T. S. Eliot.

ELLIS, HAVELOCK. *The New Spirit.* 1890.
   Whitman, Ibsen, Tolstoy, etc.

FREEMAN, JOHN. *The Moderns: essays in literary criticism.* 1916.
   Shaw, Wells, Hardy, Maeterlinck, James, Conrad, etc.

GARNETT, EDWARD. *Friday Nights: literary criticism and appreciations.* 1st series. 1922.
   Hudson, Ibsen and the English, D. H. Lawrence, Richard Jefferies, English and American fiction, etc.

GEORGE, W. L. *A Novelist on Novels.* 1918.

HOWELLS, WILLIAM DEAN. *Heroines of Fiction.* 1901.

JAMES, HENRY. *Partial Portraits.*
   George Eliot, Trollope, Stevenson, Maupassant, Turgénieff, Du Maurier, The Art of Fiction, etc.

339

LEGGETT, H. W. *The Idea in Fiction.* 1934.

LOVETT, ROBERT MORSS, and HUGHES, HELEN SARD. *The Story of the Novel in England.* 1932.

MUIR, EDWIN. *Transition: essays on contemporary literature.* 1926.

MURRY, JOHN MIDDLETON. *Discoveries: essays in literary criticism.* 1924.
Tchehov, Proust, The Break-up of the Novel, Flaubert and Flaubart, etc.

MYERS, W. L. *The Later Realism: a study of characterization in the English novel.* 1926.

READ, HERBERT. *Reason and Romanticism: essays in literary criticism.* 1926.

ROZ, FIRMIN. *Le Roman anglais contemporain.* 1912.
Meredith, Hardy, Mrs Humphry Ward, Kipling, Wells.

SCHIRMER, WALTER F. *Der englische Roman des neuesten Zeit.* 1922.

SCOTT, DIXON. *Men of Letters.* With introduction by Max Beerbohm. 1916.

SCOTT-JAMES, ROLFE ARNOLD. *Modernism and Romance.* 1908.
Personality in Literature. 1913.

SYMONS, ARTHUR. *Studies in Prose and Verse.* 1904.
Pater, Stevenson, William Morris, Crackanthorpe, Robert Buchanan, Oscar Wilde, Meredith, etc.
Studies in two Literatures. 1897.
Morris, Pater, Zola's method, Jefferies, Stevenson, etc.

VERSCHOYLE, DEREK (ed.). *The English Novelists: a survey of the novel by twenty contemporary novelists.* 1936.
James, Hardy, Conrad, etc.

WEYGAND, CORNELIUS. *A Century of the English Novel.* 1925.

WILSON, EDMUND. *Axel's Castle: a study in the imaginative literature of 1870–1930.* 1931.

WOOLF, VIRGINIA. *The Common Reader.* 1925.

YOUNG, G. M. *Victorian England: portrait of an age.* 1936.

CHAPTER I.—THOMAS HARDY

ABERCROMBIE, LASCELLES. *Thomas Hardy: a critical study.* 1912.

BEACH, J. W. *The Technique of Thomas Hardy.* 1922.

BRENNECKE, E. *Thomas Hardy's Universe.* 1924.

CATALOGNE, GÉRARD DE. *Le Message de Thomas Hardy.* Préface de François Mauriac. 1926.

CHEW, S. C. *Thomas Hardy, poet and novelist.* 1921.

CHILD, HAROLD. *Thomas Hardy (Writers of the Day).* 1916.

DUFFIN, H. C. *Thomas Hardy: a study of the Wessex novels.* 1916.

EXIDEUIL, PIERRE D'. *The Human Pair in the work of Thomas Hardy: an essay in the sexual problem as treated in the Wessex novels.* 1929.

GRIMSDITCH, HERBERT B. *Character and Environment in the Novels of Thomas Hardy.* 1925.

HARDY, FLORENCE EMILY. *The Early Life of Thomas Hardy, 1840–1891.* 1928.

The Later Years of Thomas Hardy, 1892–1928. 1930.

HEDGCOCK, F. A. *Thomas Hardy, penseur et artiste: étudié dans les romans du Wessex.* 1910.

JOHNSON, LIONEL. *The Art of Thomas Hardy.* 1923.

Post liminium: essays and critical papers, ed. Thomas Whittemore. 1911.
Notes on Walter Pater, Stevenson, Mr Hardy's later prose and verse, etc.

OLIVERO, FEDERICO. *An Introduction to Hardy.* 1930.

RIDDER-BARZIN, LOUISE DE. *Le Pessimisme de Thomas Hardy.* 1932.

SALT, H. S. *Richard Jefferies: a study.* 1894.

CHAPTERS III–IV.—MARK RUTHERFORD AND GEORGE GISSING

BOLL, THEOPHILUS E. M. *The Works of Edwin Pugh (1874–1930)*. 1934.

ENGLISH ASSOCIATION. *Essays and Studies*, V. 1914.
"The Novels of Mark Rutherford," by A. E. Taylor.

GAPP, SAMUEL VOGT. *George Gissing, classicist*. 1936.

GISSING, ALGERNON and ELLEN (ed.). *Letters of George Gissing to Members of his Family*. 1927.

ROBERTS, MORLEY. *The Private Life of Thomas Maitland*. 1923.

ROTTER, DR A. *Der Arbeiterroman in England seit 1880*. 1929.

SWINNERTON, FRANK. *George Gissing: a critical study*. 1912.

WEBER, ANTON. *George Gissing und die soziale Frage*. 1932.

CHAPTERS V–VII.—GEORGE MOORE, ÆSTHETES AND ECLECTICS, HENRY JAMES

BEACH, JAMES WARREN. *The Method of Henry James*. 1918.

BENSON, A. C. *Walter Pater (English Men of Letters)*. 1921.

BURDETT, OSBERT. *The Beardsley Period: an essay in perspective*. 1925.

DE LA MARE, WALTER (ed.). *The Eighteen-eighties: essays by Fellows of the Royal Society of Literature*. 1930.

FERGUSON, WALTER D. *The Influence of Flaubert on George Moore*. 1934.

GIDE, ANDRÉ. *Prétextes*. 1926.

HAMILTON, WALTER. *The Æsthetic Movement in England*. 1882.

HARRISON, FREDERIC. *John Ruskin (English Men of Letters)*. 1905.

HUNEKER, JAMES. *Unicorns.* n.d.
James, Mallock, George Moore, etc.

JACKSON, HOLBROOK. *The Eighteen-nineties: a review of art and ideas at the close of the nineteenth century.* 1913.

KENNEDY, J. M. *English Literature, 1880–1905.* 1917.

LE GALLIENNE, RICHARD. *The Romantic 90's.* 1926.

Retrospective Reviews: a literary log (1891–1895). 2 vols. 1896.

MAUROIS, ANDRÉ. *Études anglaises.* 1927.
Dickens, Walpole, Ruskin and Wilde, la jeune littérature.

MOORE, GEORGE. *Avowals.* 1919.

Confessions of a Young Man. 1916.

MORE, PAUL ELMER. *The Drift of Romanticism (Shelburne Essays, VIII.).* 1913.
Pater, Fiona Macleod, etc.

MORGAN, CHARLES. *Epitaph on George Moore.* 1935.

NOYES, ALFRED. *William Morris (English Men of Letters).* 1908.

POLAK, DR M. *The Historical, Philosophical, and Religious Aspects of "John Inglesant."* 1933.

PRAZ, MARIO. *The Romantic Agony*: tr. 1933.

ROSENBLATT, LOUISE. *L'Idée de l'art pour l'art dans la littérature anglaise pendant la période Victorienne.* 1931.

SYMONS, ARTHUR. *Studies in two Literatures.* 1897.

Aubrey Beardsley. 1898.

The Symbolist Movement in Literature. 1900.

WOLFE, HUMBERT. *George Moore (Modern Writers Series).* 1931.

CHAPTER VIII.—THE ROMANCERS

CORNFORD, L. COPE. *Robert Louis Stevenson* (*Modern English Writers*). 1899.

ELLIS, S. M. *Wilkie Collins, Le Fanu, and others.* 1931.
  Blackmore, Edward Bradley, Mrs Riddell, etc.

JAMES, HENRY. *Notes on Novelists, with some other notes.* 1914.

MORRIS, DAVID B. *Robert Louis Stevenson and the Scottish Highlanders.* 1929.

  By the Town Clerk of Stirling. Important on the genesis of *Kidnapped* and its historical basis, also on its indebtedness to Scott's *Rob Roy*.

OLIVERO, FEDERICO. *Edgar Allan Poe* (Edizione de l'Erma, Torino). 1934.

  Professor Olivero traces the influence of Poe on Oscar Wilde, Stevenson, Conan Doyle, Conrad, Chesterton, etc., as well as on De Quincey, Baudelaire, etc. This should be Englished, like the same author's *Introduction to Hardy*.

SWINNERTON, FRANK. *Robert Louis Stevenson: a critical study.* 1914.

INDEX

INDEX

A

B

347

C

D

This book may be kept

FOURTEEN DAYS

A fine will be charged for each day the book
is kept over time.

MAR 1 1 '0			
5/20			
MAR 8 7			